Bohdan Hrobon
Ethical Dimension of Cult in the Book of Isaiah

Beihefte zur Zeitschrift für die alttestamentliche Wissenschaft

Herausgegeben von
John Barton · Reinhard G. Kratz
Choon-Leong Seow · Markus Witte

Band 418

De Gruyter

Bohdan Hrobon

Ethical Dimension of Cult
in the Book of Isaiah

De Gruyter

ISBN 978-3-11-024748-0
e-ISBN 978-3-11-024749-7
ISSN 0934-2575

Library of Congress Cataloging-in-Publication Data

Hrobon, Bohdan.
    Ethical dimension of cult in the book of Isaiah / Bohdan Hrobon.
        p. cm. — (Beihefte zur Zeitschrift für die alttestamentliche Wissen-
schaft, ISSN 0934-2575 ; Bd. 418)
    Includes bibliographical references (p.   ) and index.
    ISBN 978-3-11-024748-0 (hardcover 23 × 15,5 : alk. paper)
    1. Bible. O.T. Isaiah — Theology.   2. Worship in the Bible.   3. Ethics
in the Bible.   I. Title.
    BS1515.6.W76H76   2010
    224'.106 — dc22

                                                                2010024280

Bibliographic information published by the Deutsche Nationalbibliothek

The Deutsche Nationalbibliothek lists this publication in the Deutsche
Nationalbibliografie; detailed bibliographic data are available in the Internet
at http://dnb.d-nb.de.

Printing: Hubert & Co. GmbH & Co. KG, Göttingen
∞ Printed on acid-free paper

Printed in Germany

www.degruyter.com

Table of Contents

Acknowledgements

I would like to thank a number of people without whose help and support this thesis would never have seen the light of day. First and foremost my gratitude goes to my supervisor Prof. Hugh G. M. Williamson, a scholar and a person par excellence, whose profound insight into the book of Isaiah and personal qualities have inspired and guided me all along. Dr. Paul Joyce, who acted as my interim supervisor during the last two terms of my second year, was a great encouragement to me. I have benefited also from Prof. John Barton, who was kind enough to read parts of my thesis and made many helpful suggestions. I am especially grateful to my good friends Dr. Lester Meyer and Dr. Tim Edwards for proofreading and making my arguments intelligible. For my three years of studies in Oxford, I am particularly indebted to three institutions. The Langham Partnership International, UK, and The Olker Foundation, USA, provided financial and personal assistance, and the Bible School in Martin, Slovakia, who provided release time. Many thanks go to the Bible School staff, especially Prof. Paul Berge, Dr. Adrian Kacian, and Dr. Michal Valčo, for working an extra load to cover for my absence. My wife, Bibiana, has been my loving companion the whole time – I would not have started, let alone finished this work without her. My gratitude to her goes beyond words. The sparkling presence of our recently-born son Martin has speeded up the completion of this thesis. I dedicate it to my late father, Pastor Ján Bohdan Hroboň, a true hero of the Christian faith under communist persecution, who nurtured my love of the Old Testament.

Abbreviations

AB	The Anchor Bible
ABD	D. N. Freedman (ed.), *The Anchor Bible Dictionary* (New York, 1992)
ANE	Ancient Near East
BDAG	F. W. Danker (ed.), *Greek-English Lexicon of the New Testament and Other Early Christian Literature* (The University of Chicago Press, 2000)
BDB	F. Brown, S. R. Driver, and C. A. Briggs, *Hebrew and English Lexicon of the Old Testament* (Hendrickson Pub., Peabody, MA, 1997)
BH	Biblical Hebrew
BHS	K. Elliger and W. Rudolph (ed.), *Biblia Hebraica Stuttgartensia* (4th ed., Stuttgart, 1983)
BKAT	Biblischer Kommentar: Altes Testament
BKR	Bible Kralická, 1613
BTB	*Biblical Theology Bulletin*
BTP	Polish Biblia Tysiaclecia, 1984
BWANT	Beiträge zur Wissenschaft vom Alten und Neuen Testament
BZAW	Beihefte zur *Zeitschrift für die alttestamentliche Wissenschaft*
CBQ	*Catholic Biblical Quarterly*
CEP	Český Ekumenický překlad, 1985
DBY	Darby Bible, 1884/1890
DCH	D. J. A. Clines (ed.), *The Dictionary of Classical Hebrew* (Sheffield, 1993-)
DI	Deutero-Isaiah
DSS	Dead Sea Scrolls
DtrH	Deuteronomistic History/historian
EIN	Einheitsübersetzung der Heiligen Schrift, 1980
ELB	Elberfelder Bibel revidierte Fassung, 1993
ELO	Darby Unrevidierte Elberfelder, 1905
Enc Jud	*Encyclopaedia Judaica* (16 vols; Jerusalem, 1972)

ESV	English Standard Version, 2001
FAT	Forschungen zum Alten Testament
FOTL	The Forms of the Old Testament Literature
Gibson	J. C. L. Gibson, *Davidson's Introductory Hebrew Grammar: Syntax* (4th ed., Edinburgh, 1994)
GK	*Gesenius' Hebrew Grammar*, edited and enlarged by E. Kautzsch, tr. by A. E. Cowley (2nd ed., Oxford/New York, 1910)
GNV	Geneva Bible, 1599
HALOT	W. Baumgartner, L. Koehler, *The Hebrew and Aramaic Lexicon of the Old Testament*, tr. by M. E. J. Richardson (Brill, Leiden: 1994-2000)
HCOT	Historical Commentary on the Old Testament
HUCA	*Hebrew Union College Annual*
IBHS	B. Waltke, M. O'Connor, *An Introduction to Biblical Hebrew Syntax* (Winona Lake, IN, 1990)
ICC	International Critical Commentary on the Holy Scriptures of the Old and New Testaments
JBL	*Journal of Biblical Literature*
JM	P. Joüon, T. Muraoka, *A Grammar of Biblical Hebrew* (Rome, 1991)
JPS	The Holy Scriptures, Jewish Publication Society,1917.
JSOT	*Journal for the Study of the Old Testament*
JSOTSup	*Journal for the Study of the Old Testament*, Supplement Series
JTS	*Journal of Theological Studies*
KJV	King James Version, 1611
LW	*Luther's works*, edited by H. J. Grimm, H. T. Lehmann, H. C. Oswald, and J. Pelikan, St. Louis: 1955.
LXX	Septuaginta
MT	Masoretic Text
NAB	New American Bible, 1991
NAS	New American Standard, 1977
NCBC	New Century Bible Commentary
NET	New English Translation, 2004
NICOT	New International Commentary on the Old Testament
NIDOTTE	W. A. VanGemeren (ed.), *New International Dictionary of Old Testament Theology & Exegesis* (5 vols; Carlisle, 1996)
NIV	New International Version, 1984
NJB	New Jerusalem Bible, 1985

NKJ	New King James Version, 1982
NLT	New Living Translation,1996
NRSV	New Revised Standard Version, 1998
OT	Old Testament
OTG	Old Testament Guides
OTL	Old Testament Library
OTS	*Oudtestamentische Studiën*
PI	Proto-Isaiah
RB	*Revue Biblique*
S	Peshitta
SBL	Society of Biblical Literature
SBLMS	Society of Biblical Literature Monograph Series
SBT	Studies in Biblical Theology
SJLA	*Studies in Judaism in Late Antiquity*
SSN	*Studia Semitica Neerlandica*
St	Stanza
T	Targum
TDOT	G. J. Botterweck and H. Ringgren (eds.), *Theological Dictionary of the Old Testament*, 15 vols., tr. J.T. Willis (Eerdmans, Grand Rapids, 1977-2007)
TI	Trito-Isaiah
TNK	Jewish Publication Society TANAKH, 1985 (English)
TWOT	R. L. Harris (et al., eds.), *Theological Wordbook of the Old Testament* (Moody Press of Chicago, IL, 1980)
UF	*Ugarit-Forschungen*
V	Vulgata
VT	*Vetus Testmentum*
VTSup	*Vetus Testmentum* – Supplement Series
WBC	Word Biblical Commentary
WEB	Noah Webster Bible, 1833
Williams	R. Williams, *Hebrew Syntax: An Outline* (2nd ed., Toronto, 1976)
WMANT	Wissenschaftliche Monographien zum Alten und Neuen Testament
ZAW	*Zeitschrift für die alttestamentliche Wissenschaft*

Introduction

The present thesis aims to contribute to the ongoing discussion of the prophetic understanding of the role of cult and ethics in the religion of ancient Israel. During the late 19th and first half of the 20th century, the religion of some of the so-called 'classical prophets' was often described as internal and spiritual in opposition to the external and formal religion of the priests.[1] The tendency in more recent OT scholarship is to mitigate this opposition in various ways.[2] The present thesis brings the prophets and the priests closer by proposing that their conception of cult is essentially the same, reflecting the same theology and co-creating one and the same religion.[3] Because a thorough assessment of this proposal is beyond the scope of this thesis, certain limitations are necessary. First, the discussion of the priestly and the prophetic view of cult (Part I) only focuses on some of its key concepts, namely sacrifice, purity and impurity, holiness, and the promised land. Second, the testing ground of this proposal is limited to the cult-critical passages in

---

1 As discussed below (1.3 and 1.4) in more detail. Many scholars still believe that 'the classical prophets interpreted the Torah in a radically new way,' Temba L. J. Mafico, "Ethics," ABD 2.652.

2 For a brief but apt description of the various ways to tone down the differences between what he understands as anti-cultic stance of the pre-exilic prophets and the pro-cultic stance of the post-exilic ones, see John Barton, "The Prophets and the Cult," in *Temple and Worship in Biblical Israel*, ed. John Day (Proceedings of the Oxford Old Testament Seminar; London: T & T Clark International, 2005).

3 *Contra*, e.g., Hendel who argues for the dichotomy between the two offices: 'The prophet and the priest occupied different social positions and were committed to different hermeneutical stances, hence they interpreted their world differently.' He believes that 'whereas the priests see a correspondence and mutuality between ritual and ethics, the classical prophets *contrast* the ethical with the ritual.' Therefore, 'the religious views of the prophets and priests are not merely opposed, but are in a sense incommensurate,' that is, their understanding of the order of things is incompatible. See Ronald S. Hendel, "Prophets, Priests, and the Efficacy of Ritual," in *Pomegranates and Golden Bells: Studies in Biblical, Jewish and Near Eastern Ritual, Law, and Literature in Honor of Jacob Milgrom*, ed. David P. Wright, David Noel Freedman, and Avi Hurvitz (Winona Lake, IN: Eisenbrauns, 1995) 191-194.

the book of Isaiah (Part II). These areas were chosen because of their relevance to what appears to be at the heart of the controversy between the prophets and the priests – the role of cult and ethics in the religion of Ancient Israel.

A methodological objection can be raised that superimposing modern categories of cult and ethics on the reading of the OT significantly contributed to the supposed differences between the priests and the prophets. Contemporary scholarship increasingly recognizes in OT books what Houston demonstrates in his study on Leviticus, namely that 'the distinction so characteristic of Christian interpretation, between ritual and moral, does not do justice to the character of this material.'[4] Even such a fundamental text as the so-called Ethical Decalogue in Exod 20:2ff illustrates that the distinction between cult and ethics was a foreign concept for ancient Israel where 'religion penetrated the entire social life of the nation.'[5] Green seems to be correct in saying

> the Old Testament knows nothing of religion without morality, nothing of faith which does not issue in right life and character. Neither does it [...] know anything of morality without religion, anything of conduct or character whose rightness or wrongness is independent of its relation to God. Hence, in the Old Testament the irreligious men are the immoral men, and the immoral men are the irreligious men.[6]

On the other hand, the use of the categories like ethics or cult seems to be necessary for the understanding of the OT by a contemporary western-world reader.[7] One solution is to demonstrate how these categories overlap, are interrelated, or even interdependent in the OT.

---

4   Walter J. Houston, "Toward an Integrated Reading of the Deitary Laws of Leviticus," in *The Book of Leviticus: Composition and Reception*, ed. Rolf Rendtorff, Robert A. Kugler, and Sarah Smith Bartel (VTSup 93; Leiden: Brill, 2003) 161.

5   Roland de Vaux, *Ancient Israel: Its Life and Institutions*, trans. John McHugh (London: Darton Longman and Todd, 1961) 271. Rowley maintains that the entire emphasis of the Ten Commandments 'is on standards of conduct in ordinary human relations, and not on ceremonial acts' and summarizes that 'the will of God is not defined primarily in terms of ritual acts, but in terms of behaviour,' Harold Henry Rowley, *Worship in Ancient Israel: Its Forms and Meaning* (London: S.P.C.K., 1967) 40-41.

6   William B. Green, "The Ethics of the Old Testament," *Princeton Theological Review* 27 (1929) 153-193: 156. Barton correctly lists religious obligations as one area of the OT ethics, claiming that 'in all ancient societies religious observance was a natural part of the social fabric, and no one could decide to ignore it,' John Barton and Julia Bowden, *The Original Story: God, Israel and the World* (London: Darton Longman and Todd, 2004) 77.

7   As stated by Barton, 'we cannot explain the presuppositions of another culture to ourselves without some translation into terms and categories which did not have

If cult is described as the vertical dimension of the Law and ethics its horizontal dimension, many scholars would agree with Jensen that 'the vertical and horizontal dimensions go together, equally expressions of God's will; and this in turn means that where the horizontal dimension (social justice, etc.) is lacking, the vertical dimension (worship, sacrifice) is impossible.'[8] However, the *nature* of the interrelatedness of cult and ethics in the OT is far from obvious. One of its most recent explorations comes from Janzen, who argues that in the Hebrew bible 'sacrifice, like other rituals, communicates social meaning to its participants, and like other rituals the meaning it expresses is a communication of the way one social group understands the world to be and, therefore, the moral actions that its members should adopt.'[9] Janzen specifies that, even though the OT writings of different social groups concerning sacrifices urge somewhat different social morality, they all agree on sacrifices communicating 'the absolute authority of YHWH and the necessity of adhering to the moral code that YHWH has revealed to Israel.'[10] There is no space here to evaluate Janzen's thesis fully, but one has to ask the question: If this were the case, why would the strongest promoters of social morality in the OT, viz. the Prophets, have so little to say in support of sacrifices and other rituals? Janzen justifies the absence of the Prophetic literature in his study by 'the actual paucity of references to sacrifice' in it,[11] but even the little that is there clearly reads against the grain of his main thesis. The cult-critical passages that discourage people from practising rituals would contradict Janzen's observation that in DtrH 'sacrifice becomes the most obvious way to gauge the nation's fidelity to its moral code,'[12] and would be contra-productive when it comes to ethical reform for which the individual prophets called.[13] The only way to explain this

---

exact linguistic equivalents in the culture in question,' John Barton, *Understanding Old Testament Ethics: Approaches and Explorations* (Louisville, KY; London: Westminster John Knox Press, 2003) 141.

8   Joseph Jensen, *Ethical Dimensions of the Prophets* (Collegeville, MN: Liturgical Press, 2006) 29.

9   David Janzen, *The Social Meanings of Sacrifice in the Hebrew Bible: A Study of Four Writings* (BZAW 344; Berlin: Walter de Gruyter, 2004) 4.

10   Janzen, *Social Meanings*, 8.

11   Janzen, *Social Meanings*, 7.

12   Janzen, *Social Meanings*, 137. Later on, he specifies that 'sacrifice does not replace moral rectitude in Dtr, it simply signals one's moral attitude,' Janzen, *Social Meanings*, 149.

13   Janzen agrees with Roy Rappaport that 'ritual does not only symbolically represent the social contract, it also contains acceptance of it in the very act of participation,' concluding that 'ritual demands a moral response from its participants, and it places

discrepancy is to suggest that these prophets failed to perceive the importance of rituals for the enhancement of social morality – an unlikely suggestion indeed. In any case, Janzen adopts a very different viewpoint of ritual in relation to ethics from the one presented in this thesis. For him, the purpose of cult is people-oriented – 'to ritualize as much behavior as possible' – so he views cult as 'ritualized morality',[14] while the present thesis understands the purpose of cult to be God-oriented (see below, 1.2) and analyses its ethical dimension. It can be said that it views the cult of ancient Israel as moralized rituality.[15]

As several quotations of and references to various OT scholars throughout the present thesis confirm, the idea that behind the ethical appeals of the prophets might have been the cultic concepts as defined in the Priestly literature is not a novelty. However, postulating these concepts as the main reason for what appears to be the criticism of cult in the book of Isaiah may be considered a fresh alternative to the interpretation of these (and similar) texts. The fact that the cultic concepts of the authors of these oracles are only assumed and not explicitly stated in the book makes the whole inquiry hypothetical. However, as Barton states, 'any message makes sense only against a background of unspoken assumptions, and it is these that this paper has attempted to draw out and make explicit.'[16] Since the understanding of cult and some of its concepts forms the basis of this inquiry, a more detailed discussion of these must pave the way for the exploration of cultic concepts behind selected Isaianic passages.

---

them fully into social roles which they must either fully accept or fully leave,' Janzen, *Social Meanings*, 20 and 21.

14   See Janzen, *Social Meanings*, 36-38.

15   Thus, e.g., Janzen's statement on p. 40 'It is ritualized morality that makes ritual work, and ritual that promotes ritualized morality,' can be adopted for the present thesis as 'It is moralized rituality that makes morality work, and morality that promotes moralized rituality.'

16   Barton, *OT Ethics*, 142.

PART I

Chapter 1: Conception of Cult in the Prophets

1.1. Introduction

De Vaux's definition of cult aptly describes its purpose; cult consists of 'all those acts by which communities or individuals give outward expression to their religious life, by which they seek and achieve contact with God.'[1] It is important to realize with Stern that this outward expression of the religious life of Israelites in what he labels the Assyrian period was very similar to the one of surrounding nations: 'Except for the differing images of their gods, the various nations used the same cult objects, the same types of incense burners, chalices, goblets and bronze and ivory sticks adorned with pomegranates etc.'[2] Cult consists of rituals. In its cultic sense, a ritual is 'a prescribed order of performing religious or other devotional service.'[3] Anthropologists agree that where there is a religion, there is a ritual: 'For it is a mistake to suppose that there can be religion which is all interior, with no rules, no liturgy, no external signs of inward states. As with society, so with religion, external form is the condition of its existence.'[4] In the religion of ancient Israel during the 1st and 2nd Temple periods, the main responsibility for performing and maintaining rituals was assigned to priests. Naturally, therefore, the description and prescription of cultic rituals such as purification and sacrifices dominate the so called priestly tradition (P and H). Ethics as commonly understood by the 21st century western world seems to play the role of Cinderella here.[5] On the other hand, there are several texts in the OT that appear to be

---

1   De Vaux, *Ancient Israel*, 271.

2   Ephraim Stern, "Religion in Palestine in the Assyrian and Persian Periods," in *The Crisis of Israelite Religion: Transformation of Religious Tradition in Exilic and Post-Exilic Times*, ed. Bob Becking and Marjo C. A. Korpel (OTS; Leiden: Brill, 1999) 246.

3   J. A. Simpson and E. S. C. Weiner, *The Oxford English Dictionary*, 2nd ed. (Oxford: Clarendon Press, 1989) 13.992.

4   Mary Douglas, *Purity and Danger: An Analysis of Concept of Pollution and Taboo* (Routledge classics; London: Routledge, 2002 (1966)) 77.

5   For the artificiality of applying cult and ethics as philosophical categories to the OT, see above.

critical of, even hostile to rituals.[6] Furthermore, the depreciation of ritual in these texts is juxtaposed with a commendation of some sort of ethical behaviour, creating an impression that the role of cult is taken over by ethics. The fact that most of these texts occur in the prophetic literature prompted many scholars to explain this discrepancy by comparing or contrasting the supposed ideologies of priestly and prophetic literature, or, more personally, the priest and the prophets.[7] Most of the studies on this subject fall into one of two groups – those that view the relationship between the two entities as antithetical and those that understand it as complementary.

The representatives of the first group often credit the prophets with antiritualism, promoting an internal religion as opposed to the external one of the priests. Since, as anthropologists claim, rituals and religion are inseparable, this antiritualistic attitude of the prophets would be rather immature and naïve. This, of course, is a real possibility, and various evolutionary models often use this naïveté to reconstruct the early stages of Israelite religion. The antithetical hypothesis must also deal with the problem of the origins of and the reasons for two opposing ideologies coexisting in one canon.[8] The relative dating of the priestly and prophetic materials becomes a prominent question that further subdivides this group. Those who put the prophetic material before P (most notably Wellhausen and his followers) often understand the priestly influence as overpowering the spontaneous interior religion of the prophets by the scrupulous exterior religion of the priests.[9] Priestly 'formalizing' of Israelite religion is seen as a step backward, creating a tension that was eventually resolved in Christianity.[10] Those who date P before the Prophets (most notably

---

6   See, e.g., 1 Sam 15:22; Amos 5:21-27; Mic 6:6-8; Hos 6:6, 8:13; Isa 1:11-15, 58:2-5, 66:2-4; Jer 7:21-23; Pss 40:6-8, 50:8-13, 51:18-19; Prov 21:3. For lack of a better term, these texts will be referred to as cult-critical throughout this study.

7   For a recent attempt to contrast priest with prophets, see, e.g., Hendel, "Prophets, Priests, and the Efficacy of Ritual."

8   For the plausibility that opposite views on ritual can coexist in the same religious culture, see Mary Douglas, *Natural Symbols: Explorations in Cosmology* (London: Barrie & Rockliff Cresset Press, 1970) *passim*.

9   See Julius Wellhausen, *Prolegomena zur Geschichte Israels*, 5 ed. (Berlin: G. Reimer, 1899) 101.

10   Douglas considers this development unlikely: 'The history of the Israelites is sometimes presented as a struggle between the prophets who demanded interior union with God and the people, continually liable to slide back into primitive magicality, to which they are particularly prone when in contact with other more primitive cultures. The paradox is that magicality seems finally to prevail with the compilation of the Priestly Code,' Douglas, *Purity and Danger*, 32.

Kaufmann and his followers) tend to understand the prophetic teaching as a progress toward the spiritualization of the Israelite religion, resulting in Judaism.

In spite of many valuable insights, a number of objections can be raised against both of the theories in this first group:

— The insufficiency of the textual evidence for the suggested developments forces the protagonists to look between the lines for the supposed contrasts and tensions, so some of the major arguments are from silence.[11]

— Some supportive arguments are circular, because both schools excessively rely on their own historical and sociological reconstructions of ancient Israel.[12]

— These studies interpret the criticism of rituals always in contrast to, not in connection with the juxtaposed endorsement of ethical behaviour.

— These studies tend to overlook the prophetic texts favourable toward rituals.

— The superimposed dichotomy between priestly and prophetic material results in a misguided search for two self-contained, even conflicting ideologies in one canon.[13]

— As the continuous coexistence of both theories paradoxically demonstrates, these evolutionistic or devolutionistic models do not do justice to both bodies of literature.[14] In the words of

---

11 The notorious one is the absence of references to priestly writings in the early prophets and vice versa.

12 'Just as Wellhausen had his reasons for supposing that Second Temple Judaism was in a state of moral decline, so too Milgrom and Knohl have their reasons for arguing that First Temple Israelite tradition exhibited a linear positive, ethical development over time,' Jonathan Klawans, *Purity, Sacrifice, and the Temple: Symbolism and Supersessionism in the Study of Ancient Judaism* (Oxford; New York: Oxford University Press, 2006) 51.

13 What Ben Zvi states about prophetic books even more applies to the cult-critical texts in them, namely that in order to be accepted as authoritative literature 'the world of these books could not stand in a flagrant contradiction with the world of knowledge and the theological or ideological viewpoints shared by authorship and primary readership and rereadership,' Ehud Ben Zvi, "The Prophetic Book: A Key Form of Prophetic Literature," in *The Changing Face of Form Criticism for the Twenty-First Century*, ed. Marvin A. Sweeney and Ehud Ben Zvi (Grand Rapids, MI; Cambridge, U.K.: W.B. Eerdmans, 2003) 289.

14 In this connection, Klawans rightly questions the assumptions that 'what is more ethical must be later, and what is earlier is deemed subject to due criticism,' Klawans, *Purity*, 51. Douglas sufficiently demonstrated that 'magical practice, in this

> Kraus, 'Hegel's philosophy of history with its three stages of
> development is a system into which the Old Testament texts
> cannot be pressed.'[15]

The second group consists of those who see the ideologies of P and of
the Prophets as complementary. The differences between the two
bodies of literature are not due to different ideologies, but to the
different realms in which they operate, the different purpose they
serve, and the different focus they have. The world of the priests is
defined and represented by the Temple and all that belongs to it. The
purpose of their writings is to maintain what the Temple symbolizes –
the presence of YHWH in the midst of his people. Naturally, their main
focus is on cult and rituals. Prophets, on the other hand, are thought to
operate outside the temple precincts, closer to the people and the real
world. Their concern, therefore, is society governed by YHWH and
functioning according to his principles, so ethics comes to the fore as a
matter of course. The negative treatment of cult and rituals in the
Prophets is not to be understood as their repudiation, but as a
rhetorical feature that forces the audience to focus on the importance of
their ethical behaviour.

Again, although fruitful and constructive, this approach is not
without shortcomings:

— Since the ritual as such is not seen as problematic, the
protagonists of the complementary hypothesis are forced to
look for the "true" object of the prophet's criticism through an

---

sense of automatically effective ritual, is not a sign of primitiveness, ... nor is a high
ethical content the prerogative of evolved religions,' Douglas, *Purity and Danger*, 23.

15 Hans-Joachim Kraus, *Worship in Israel: A Cultic History of the Old Testament*, trans.
Geoffrey Buswell (Oxford: Blackwell, 1966) 19. If only Judaism is taken into
consideration, Barton correctly states that rather than by Hegel or Darwin,
Wellhausen was influenced by Herder and German Romanticism with its belief that
'human awareness of the divine does not *improve* over time; what is earlier is usually
the best, and the later ages of a culture represent more a decline than a progress,'
John Barton, "Wellhausen's *Prolegomena to the History of Israel*: Influences and
Effects," in *Text & Experience: Towards a Cultural Exegesis of the Bible*, ed. Daniel L.
Smith-Christopher (Sheffield: Sheffield Academic Press, 1995) 327. Levenson also
argues that Wellhausen's model of Judaism cannot be classified as Hegelian or
evolutionary, because it works qualitatively in the opposite direction; it is
'degenerative', whereas Hegel's model was 'one of increasing manifestation of the
Spirit.' However, when Wellhausen's view of Christianity with its gospel as the
final, tension-resolving stage is brought into the picture, then the charge seems to be
justified. For further discussion, see Jon Douglas Levenson, *The Hebrew Bible, the Old
Testament, and Historical Criticism: Jews and Christians in Biblical Studies* (Louisville,
KY: Westminster/John Knox Press, 1993) 11-12.

oblique approach to the cult-critical texts. The frequent suggestions are a manipulative use of rituals, excessive reliance on their effect, performance of a ritual without corresponding interior disposition, use of ritual to cover immorality, etc. Besides the lack of textual support, the fact that some rituals atone for moral failures presents a paradox for these interpretations.[16]

— The cult-critical language in some statements is too radical and too straightforward not to be taken literally, and its mitigation by attributing it to rhetoric does not seem to do justice to the text.[17]

— The studies in this group allow for very little interaction between the worlds of the priests and the prophets. If the ideologies have developed out of the same religion and are supposed to be complementary, one would expect a significant interdependency between them.

In addition to the above objections, three methodological faults can be detected in both hypotheses. First, they often accumulate the evidence from texts that, although juxtaposing cult and ethics, apply to different situations or serve different purposes.[18] Second, these texts often mention sacrifices and, as Klawans argues, 'the hard-and-fast distinction between ritual and ethics has prevented scholars from appreciating the degree to which ritual and ethics are inherently

---

16 A good illustration of this paradox is the prescribed sin and guilt offerings for the so called 'inadvertent sins' in Lev 4-6. As Cothey observes, 'such sins are not confined to cases where the sin is a consequence merely of carelessness, accident or misfortune but can include actions that it would be impossible to commit while being wholly ignorant of the fact and without some sort of conscious intent, such as robbing or defrauding a neighbour (6.2),' Antony Cothey, "Ethics and Holiness in the Theology of Leviticus," *JSOT* 30 (2005) 131-151: 142.

17 If sacrifices as such were not the issue, one would expect a more mellow tone, such as in Ps 50:2 'Not for your sacrifices do I rebuke you ...' The questions like the following ones of Klawans often remain unanswered: If prophets speak of sacrifices hyperbolically (better justice than sacrifice), 'are we to understand that the priests and prophets had different priorities? If so, why, and what were they?' Klawans, *Purity*, 81.

18 One of the arguments and conclusions of the present thesis is that the efficacy of ritual and ethics depends on the situation into which the particular texts speak. Barton rightly accuses those who look for a unified 'prophetic message' across the Prophets of 'a Procrustean approach which forces either pre-exilic or post-exilic classical prophets to conform to the image of the other,' Barton, "Prophets," 116.

connected – and virtually inseparable – when it comes to sacrifice.'[19] Third, scholars often too hastily assume that a particular cultic or ethical term functions in a text as *pars pro toto*, using this text to support their theories about cult or ethics in general. The problem is not only in applying general categories to a prophetic oracle that addresses a specific situation,[20] but also in not dealing with a particular ritual or ethical conduct in its own right.

Obviously, the above objections are serious, and dealing with them would require a separate monograph. Nevertheless, since these theories have a significant bearing on the interpretation of some of the key texts in the present thesis (especially Isa 1:10-17), many of these objections need to be addressed later on in more detail.

1.2. Ritual according to Priestly Tradition

Ritual is used in OT scholarship as a general label for offering sacrifices, purificatory procedures, and related activities such as fasting or prayer. As already mentioned, this abstract category is foreign to ancient Hebrew thinking, so if it is to be used in the discussion of the OT texts it ought to be defined through what it represents in a particular body of literature. The goal of this section is to take a closer look at the purpose of ritual as understood by the priestly tradition. The discussion is limited to two ritual concepts that are believed to have important bearings on the understanding of the cult-critical texts in the Prophets – sacrifices and impurity/purity.

---

19 Klawans, *Purity*, 249. The same applies to purity and impurity; as Rodd correctly insists, 'by speaking of purity and ethical systems we are separating concepts which had not yet crystallized out in Israelite thought,' and that 'ethics within the Old Testament cannot be divorced from the question of purity,' Cyril S. Rodd, *Glimpses of a Strange Land: Studies in Old Testament Ethics* (Edinburgh: T&T Clark, 2001) 12 and 17.

20 This tendency to generalize is, fortunately, in decline. As Barton states, 'one of the great achievements of modern critical study of the prophets has been to stress that their message was always addressed to a concrete historical situation and that they did not enunciate theological systems or lay down general principles,' Barton, *OT Ethics*, 141.

1.2.1. Sacrifices

The system of sacrifices is very complex. Any in-depth study on this subject is bound to conclude that the sacrifices in ancient Israel serve more than one single purpose.[21] Hubert and Mauss are certainly correct that 'just like a magic ceremony or prayer, which can serve at the same time as an act of thanksgiving, a vow, and a propitiation, sacrifice can fulfil a great variety of concurrent functions.'[22] The texts about sacrifices in the priestly tradition (esp. Leviticus and Numbers) are much more concerned with the questions of 'what' and 'how' rather than 'why'. This may be because the meaning of a particular sacrifice was superfluous being well understood, perhaps even determined by the worshipper. Courtman's proposal points toward this direction: 'The meaning of any sacrificial act must be interpreted in the light of the motive with which it is offered rather than any significance artificially attributed to a particular kind of sacrifice.'[23] The study of sacrifices in ancient Israel is further complicated by the fact that they were a dynamic phenomenon, reflecting the theological and social development of their time. Is it therefore possible to talk about a meaning of sacrifices in general, or at least about a general meaning of a particular sacrifice? For instance, even though Milgrom does specify that עֹלָה and מִנְחָה are gifts to God to obtain his blessing or forgiveness, his rationale behind the sacrifices, based on P, is followed with the word of caution: '[T]he Lord is surely pleased with the offering of the penitent wrong-doer, but it is not a gift: it is his humble expiation. Thus, even if the idea of gift is the dominant motivation for Israelite sacrifice, it is not the only one.'[24] He concludes his comments on the theory of sacrifice with a quotation from anthropologist Bourdillon:

---

21 For a recent survey of 'universal theories of sacrifice' and their critiques, see Janzen, *Social Meanings*, 75-81.

22 Henri Hubert and Marcel Mauss, *Sacrifice: Its Nature and Function* (Chicago: University of Chicago Press, 1964) 97. According to them, the unity of sacrifice comes from the procedure that 'consists in establishing a means of communication between the sacred and the profane worlds through the mediation of a victim, that is, of a thing that in the course of the ceremony is destroyed.'

23 Nigel B. Courtman, "Sacrifice in the Psalms," in *Sacrifice in the Bible*, ed. Roger T. Beckwith and Martin J. Selman (Carlisle, UK; Grand Rapids, MI: Paternoster Press, Baker Book House, 1995) 52.

24 Jacob Milgrom, *Leviticus 1-16: A New Translation with Introduction and Commentary* (AB 3; New York, London: Doubleday, 1991) 442.

> Any general theory of sacrifice is bound to fail. The wide distribution of the
> institution of sacrifice among peoples of the world is not due to some
> fundamental trait which fulfils a fundamental human need. Sacrifice is a
> flexible symbol which can convey a rich variety of possible meanings.[25]

Being aware of these complexities, it is still not only legitimate, but also
beneficial to attempt to determine what sacrifices were *not* supposed to
mean for the people of ancient Israel, and what was the *primary*
purpose of a certain kind of sacrifice.

As far as the first question is concerned, the abundance of textual
evidence makes clear that in Israelite religion, sacrifices were not to be
a magic tool for manipulating God. This point is emphasized over and
over in the Prophets, Proverbs, and Psalms, and also illustrated by
many OT narratives. It was even incorporated into the sacrificial
system, where the sacrifice was offered *after* the associated event, e.g., a
person was to bring a particular sacrifice only after he or she was
healed. Thus, one can only speculate whence then the view of sacrifices
being magical and/or having power on their own came. Kraus
(following von Wilamowitz and others) believes that the basic pagan
motive for a sacrifice was to influence gods through its 'magical
efficacy', and, because of many similarities between the cultic tradition
of the Old Testament and of Canaanite religion,[26] this 'magical efficacy
of sacrifice cast its spell upon the Israelites time after time.'[27] As for the
idea of sacrifices having power on their own, Rowley suggests that
ancient concepts of unavoidable and involuntary sin, such as childbirth
or cleansing from leprosy, could lead to confusion of ritual and moral
sin, resulting in the use of sacrifice *ex opere operato* to expiate for both:

> Where "sin" was unwitting or unconscious or wholly ritual there could not
> be any true repentance, and the ritual cleansing could only be thought of as
> automatic. This could only tend to make men think of all sacrificial acts as
> automatic in their effects. This was the attitude which the great pre-exilic
> prophets condemned, and it was equally far from the mind of the framers
> of the Priestly law.[28]

---

25   M. F. C. Bourdillon and Meyer Fortes, eds., *Sacrifice* (London: Academic Press for
     the Royal Anthropological Institute of Great Britain and Ireland, 1980) 23.
26   For the biblical and inscriptional evidence of the similarities, see, e.g., de Vaux,
     Ancient Israel, 438-440.
27   Kraus, *Worship*, 22, 36, and 122-124.
28   Rowley, *Worship*, 131.

Also, the natural tendency of humans to cling more to the visible, physical aspect of religion than to its spiritual dimension could have enhanced the adoption of these ideas.[29]

The answer to the question about the main purpose for offering a certain kind of sacrifice is more complicated. In his short but seminal article, Marx persuasively argues that the primary purpose of the sacrificial cult 'is to establish a relationship with YHWH by means of an offering.'[30] He finds it significant that one of the most important sections on sacrifice, Lev 1-7, is preceded by the story of YHWH's entrance into the Tent of Meeting, Exod 40:34-38. 'This sequence suggests, as a matter of fact, a correlation between YHWH's presence and the sacrificial cult,' with the implication that 'only if sacrifices are brought to him will YHWH remain among his people and bless them.'[31] Different types of sacrifice, however, seem to serve this goal differently. Marx makes a purpose-based distinction between the sacrifices that are a pleasant fragrance for YHWH (רֵיחַ־נִיחֹחַ לַיהוָה) such as עֹלָה, מִנְחָה, and שֶׁלֶם, and those that serve to atone (כִּפֶּר), such as חַטָּאת and אָשָׁם. He observes that the presentation of the first set of sacrifices is characteristically described by the hiphil of קרב with YHWH as its explicit object, whereas 'there seems to be a reluctance to say that the sacrifices for atonement are brought to YHWH.'[32] Because of the above characteristics, Marx believes that only the first set of sacrifices establishes communication with YHWH. This does not mean that the sacrifices for atonement are unimportant, rather that their function is subsidiary – they ritually purify the person when he brings an offering

---

29 Cmp. John Oswalt, *The Book of Isaiah, Chapters 1-39* (NICOT; Grand Rapids, MI: Eerdmans, 1986) 96.

30 Alfred Marx, "The Theology of the Sacrifice according to Leviticus 1-7," in *The Book of Leviticus: Composition and Reception*, ed. Rolf Rendtorff, Robert A. Kugler, and Sarah Smith Bartel (VTSup 93; Leiden: Brill, 2003) 111.

31 Marx, "Leviticus," 105-106. According to Marx, the same correlation is demonstrated in Exod 29:38-46, 'where the daily sacrifices, vv. 38-42a, are at the same time Israel's answer to, and the condition for the presence of YHWH, vv. 42b-46.' The same theology is expressed negatively in 2 Chr 29:6-9. Janzen correctly states that 'the sacrifices in P [...] deal expressly with the difficulty of the placement of the holy within Israel.' He, however, understands the theological function of sacrifice in the opposite way to Marx, namely that 'sacrifice plays the necessary role of separating Israel and its impurity from the most holy presence of God,' Janzen, *Social Meanings*, 103 and 109-110.

32 Marx, "Leviticus," 111.

to YHWH. Thus 'the sacrifices for atonement are the necessary prerequisite for the offerings. They are not an end in themselves.'[33]

Marx's careful wording indicates that his arguments are by no means airtight. It can be countered that texts like Lev 4:31 or Num 15:24-25 blur the distinction between the two categories of sacrifice as defined above, for the sacrifices for atonement also function as רֵיחַ־נִיחֹחַ לַיהוָה. Also, the hiphil of קרב with YHWH as its explicit object can also be used for presenting חַטָּאת, as in Lev 4:3, Num 6:14, and Ezra 8:35. On a more general level, it can be argued that even such different purposes of sacrifice as expiation and communion do not suffice for clear-cut categorization. As Hubert and Mauss point out, 'we would perhaps seek in vain for examples of an expiatory sacrifice into which no element of communion is interpolated, or for examples of communion sacrifices which do not in some respect resemble expiatory ones.'[34] Nevertheless, Marx's proposal is well supported in the text of priestly tradition,[35] and it seems to reflect the role that this source assigns to sacrifices accurately.

Marx's conclusion was recently endorsed by Klawans who argues that just as the tabernacle or the sanctuary with its various elements serves to symbolize the notion of God's presence there, a sacrificial act, being an important part of the worship in the sanctuary, embodies the same metaphor.[36] One of his supportive arguments is that the concern with the attraction and maintenance of the divine presence accounts for other frequently promoted aspects of sacrifices, such as the bestowal of

---

33 Marx, "Leviticus," 111. According to Rodd, both חַטָּאת and אָשָׁם are concerned 'with the removal of uncleanness, resulting either from an impure condition or an ethical wrong, and so restoring relations with God and avoiding the destructiveness of divine holiness,' Rodd, *Glimpses*, 17. For more support, see the bibliography there.

34 Hubert and Mauss, *Sacrifice*, 17. Marx recognizes this double function when it comes to חַטָּאת – see Marx, "Leviticus," 117.

35 Besides the references listed in his study, see also the Passover and the Festival of Trumpets offerings in Num 28:19-24 and 29:2-6, where the offerings לְכַפֵּר and לְרֵיחַ נִיחֹחַ are clearly distinguished.

36 Klawans observes the paradox that many scholars speak about ritual system as symbolic expression since its very origin (mostly thanks to the influence of Douglas' *Purity and Danger*), but allow for metaphorical (versus literal) understanding of sacrifice only in a relatively late stage of religious development. According to him, 'such constructions of the remote past are ideologically biased and methodologically flawed.' He rightly argues that even such theories of sacrifice as a gift to the gods, as communion with the gods, or as food for the gods, are essentially metaphorical. See Klawans, *Purity*, 32 and 42. For additional support, see Joseph Blenkinsopp, "An Assessment of the Alleged Pre-Exilic Date of the Priestly Material in the Pentateuch," *ZAW* 108 (1996) 495-518, Hubert and Mauss, *Sacrifice*, 106-7, n. 9.

gifts, provision of food, communion, or "blood-ties".[37] While recognizing that 'a number of sacrificial rituals described in Leviticus in particular serve an expiatory role on some level (Lev. 1:4; Lev. 4; Lev. 16),' he maintains that the daily burnt offerings (as described in Exod 29:38-45 and Num. 28:3-8) are 'completely devoid of any concern with expiation.'[38]   On the basis of Exod 29:38-46, it is hard to avoid the conclusion that the primary purpose of these daily offerings, namely עֹלָה, מִנְחָה, and שֶׁלֶם, and of sacrificial cult in general was to establish a relationship with YHWH and maintain his presence. Atonement, facilitated especially by חַטָּאת and אָשָׁם, seems to serve this purpose only as a necessary prerequisite.

1.2.2. Impurity and Purity

The *Encyclopaedia Judaica* defines impurity as 'a concept that a person or object can be in a state which, by religious law, prevents the person or object from having any contact with the temple or its cult.'[39] However, a closer look at texts addressing impurity reveals that this definition is only partially correct when it comes to the OT. Adultery or murder are said to defile, yet a suspected adulteress or a murderer is, at least for the time being, granted access to the Temple. It may be objected that bodily impurity is essentially different from the contamination caused by sin; while the first is "real", the latter is metaphorical, borrowing the terminology of the first to describe the consequences of moral misbehaviour.   However, as Klawans objects, since both impurities have 'perceived effects that result from actual physical processes,' there is 'no reason why either type of impurity is any more, or less, real than the other.'[40]   The sources are different, but the effects of both contaminations on the divine sancta are essentially the same. Based on Milgrom's demonstration of the close analogy between the process of atonement for sin and the disposal of impurity, Schwartz concludes that 'because Israel's God is repelled not only by physical defilement ... but also by sin, the priestly legislators created an unparalleled system of thought based on the postulate that both sin and impurity invade and contaminate the divine abode and that unchecked they drive the

---

37   See Klawans, *Purity*, 69.

38   Klawans, *Purity*, 71.

39   *Enc Jud* 13.1405.

40   Jonathan Klawans, *Impurity and Sin in Ancient Judaism* (New York, Oxford: Oxford University Press, 2000) 33-34. Also, if the land of Israel is regarded as holy in a real sense, there is no reason to take its defilement metaphorically or figuratively.

divine Presence away.'[41] Looking at the OT concept of purity from the perspective of the divine presence, more precisely from the perspective of divine holiness (*sub specie sanctitatis Dei*), [42] maintains the focus on its very purpose.[43]

Even though various impurities have the same effect when perceived *sub specie sanctitatis Dei*, for the sake of other perspectives it is important to distinguish between what Klawans conveniently labels as 'ritual impurity' and 'moral impurity'.[44] The sources of ritual impurity include childbirth (Lev 12:1-8), scale disease (Lev 13:1-14:32), genital discharges (Lev 15:1-33), the carcasses of certain impure animals (Lev 11:1-47), human corpses (Num 19:10-22), and even certain purificatory procedures (e.g., Lev 16:28; Num 19:8).[45] The three main characteristics of this kind of contagion are that its sources are generally natural and more or less unavoidable, it is not sinful, and it can be reversed rather straightforwardly by performing various purificatory procedures.[46] Being an impurity, it cannot come into contact with what is sacred. Therefore, as Lev 15:31 implies, it is vital for Israelites to be aware of their ritual status at all times. The second kind of defilement, viz. moral impurity, does not automatically result from every immoral act, rather 'from committing certain acts so heinous that they are explicitly referred to in biblical sources as defiling,' such as certain sexual sins (e.g., Lev 18:24-30), idolatry (e.g., Lev 19:31; 20:1-3), or bloodshed (e.g., Num 35:33-34). These acts defile not only the sinner (Lev. 18:24), but also the land of Israel (Lev 18:25, Ezek 36:17), and the sanctuary of God (Lev 20:3; Ezek 5:11), and this defilement can eventually result in the

---

41   Baruch J. Schwartz, "The Bearing of Sin in the Priestly Literature," in *Pomegranates and Golden Bells: Studies in Biblical, Jewish and Near Eastern Ritual, Law, and Literature in Honor of Jacob Milgrom*, ed. David P. Wright, David Noel Freedman, and Avi Hurvitz (Winona Lake, IN: Eisenbrauns, 1995) 4-5.

42   This Latin expression is borrowed from Theodore C. Vriezen, "Essentials of the Theology of Isaiah," in *Israel's Prophetic Heritage: Essays in Honor of James Muilenburg*, ed. Bernhard W. Anderson and Walter J. Harrelson (London: SCM, 1962) 146.

43   The detailed studies of the cult-critical passages throughout the present thesis reveal that it is mainly this perspective from which their authors evaluate cultic practice. As Heschel argues, the OT prophets were in tune with God's perspective of the world because of their insight into the present pathos of God, see Abraham Joshua Heschel, *The Prophets* (New York: Harper & Row, 1962) esp. chapter 12.

44   For a survey of studies that categorize the impurity in the priestly tradition on the same basis but use different labels, see Klawans, *Impurity and Sin*, 3-20.

45   Klawans, *Impurity and Sin*, 23. Here he refers to Wright "Unclean and Clean," *ABD* 6.732.

46   Klawans, *Impurity and Sin*, 23.

expulsion of the people from the land of Israel (Lev 18:28; Ezek 36:19).[47] For the purposes of this study, the most important difference between ritual and moral impurity is that the latter is sinful and cannot be eliminated by purificatory procedures. Since no ritual can purify grave sinners or the land upon which the grave sins were committed, 'the defilement of sinners and the land by grave sins is, for all practical purposes, permanent.'[48] The reversal of this status is only possible for, and solely up to, God. As Milgrom simply states, 'the impure person needs purification and the sinner needs forgiveness.'[49] Without God's forgiveness, moral impurity brings permanent separation from God, death and exile.[50]

1.2.3. Connection between Sacrifices and Impurity

Hubert and Mauss draw attention to the preparatory rites required before sacrificing in various religions. According to them, the purpose of these rites is to become sacred, even god-like. 'A certain degree of relationship with the god is demanded first of all from those who wish to be admitted to the sacrifice. ... Moreover, temporary purity is required. The advent of the divinity is terrible for those that are impure.'[51] The religion of ancient Israel shares this fundamental concept with other religions. The best illustration is the sacrifice of well-being (זֶבַח הַשְּׁלָמִים); since its main purpose was communion with God, purity was compulsory for offering it in the sanctuary: 'But those who eat flesh from the LORD's sacrifice of well-being while in a state of uncleanness shall be cut off from their kin,' Lev 7:20. The reason is not difficult to deduce: impurity is offensive and repulsive to God's holiness; 'impurity and holiness are antonyms.'[52]

Following Klawans, two concerns central to the priestly traditions of the Pentateuch, namely imitating God and attracting and

---

47 Klawans, *Impurity and Sin*, 26. 'Moral impurity is best understood as a potent force unleashed by certain sinful human actions. The force unleashed defiles the sinner, the sanctuary, and the land, even though the sinner is not ritually impure and does not ritually defile. Yet ... the sinner *is* seen as morally impure,' Klawans, *Impurity and Sin*, 29.

48 Klawans, *Impurity and Sin*, 31.

49 Milgrom, *Leviticus 1-16*, 256.

50 Apparently, moral impurity as defined above blurs the modern distinction between the cult and ethics, for, even if the cause can be ethical, its effect is cultic.

51 Hubert and Mauss, *Sacrifice*, 22.

52 Milgrom, *Leviticus 1-16*, 46.

maintaining the presence of God within the community,[53] help to identify the interaction between purity and sacrifices. The *imitatio Dei* principle brings out the connection between sacrifices and ritual purity:

> By separating from sex and death – by following the ritual purity regulations – ancient Israelites (and especially ancient Israelite priests and Levites) separated themselves from what made them least God-like. In other words, the point of following these regulations is nothing other than the theological underpinning of the entire Holiness Code: *imitatio Dei* (Lev. 11:44-45, 19:2, 20:7, 26).[54]

The principle of attracting and maintaining the divine presence brings out the connection between sacrifices and moral purity. Contrary to the main purpose of עֹלָה, מִנְחָה, and שֶׁלֶם, moral impurity is repugnant to God and repels his presence, for sins such as idolatry, sexual transgressions, or murder defile the land in such an abhorrent way that it eventually becomes uninhabitable for the Holy One of Israel. Ezek 8-11 is the prime example of this principle; here the כְּבוֹד יְהוָה leaves the sanctuary and Jerusalem as a consequence of the people's תּוֹעֵבוֹת גְּדֹלוֹת. As Klawans puts it, 'abominable acts undo what properly performed sacrifice does.'[55] It needs to be emphasized again that, according to the priestly tradition, not *every* sacrifice and not *every* wrong action has this effect; it is only those sacrifices and offerings that are intended for attracting and maintaining the divine presence and those abominable acts that cause moral impurity. These are related in the opposite way than is commonly understood: 'It is not that the daily sacrifice undoes the damage done by grave transgression. Quite the contrary: grave transgression undoes what the daily sacrifice produces.'[56]

1.3. Ritual and Pre-Exilic Prophets

This section is limited to the pre-exilic prophets because their relationship to rituals is the most controversial one. Isa 1:10-17 is one of the texts that triggered this controversy, and special attention is paid to the issues relevant to this passage. Unlike the mostly synchronic discussion of cult above, the focus on a particular period of Israel's history requires us to discuss the date of the sources, especially of P and H. This question has been a matter of dispute over a century, and

---

53   Klawans, *Purity*, 48.
54   Klawans, *Purity*, 58.
55   Klawans, *Purity*, 71.
56   Klawans, *Purity*, 71.

even a brief attempt to address some of the issues relevant to the present thesis takes up a significant portion of this section. First, however, a few words about the limitations of this quest, using Isa 1:10-17 as an example.

It is fairly safe to assume that the reason for God's repudiation of the cultic practices listed in Isa 1:10-17 was the ethical misconduct of the people in Judah during the second half of the eighth century BCE. It is, however, much less clear why Isaiah in this passage used such strong language in relation to various rituals. Was it just a rhetorical device to enhance the importance of ethics?[57] Or was it that the people performed the rituals to cover up for their ethical wrongdoings? If so, was Isaiah reacting just to the cultic *practice* of the people, or was there something in the cult *per se*, especially in its theology, that encouraged such practice and gave rise to the prophet's criticism? Oswalt argues that one part of the problem was an erroneous *interpretation* of the role of cult by the people of ancient Israel:

> [T]he understanding was that a representative and the person or thing being represented could become identical if proper procedures were followed. Thus the sacrificial animal could become the sinner, and in the animal's death the sinner died. No repentance, no change of behavior was necessary. What was necessary was that the procedure be followed exactly.[58]

Oswalt further points out that the OT understanding markedly differs from the one above, where '[t]he ceremonial activities are but symbolic of free and responsible attitudinal changes on the part of both God and worshiper.'[59]   To support this argument, he lists Ps 51:18-19 and 66:8, Amos 5:22-24, Mic 6:6-8, and 1 Kgs 8:23-53. Rather than giving support, however, these passages provide an illustration of the problem: the prophetic passages seem to react against and therefore presuppose the existence of the first notion, viz. that the sacrifice would take effect *ex opere operato*, the selected Psalm passages appear to deny any role to the cult in their particular situation, and Solomon's prayer can be used in support of both Oswalt's quotes above. Furthermore, unlike P, none of these passages is cult-prescriptive, and reflect only certain aspects of the cult, not its ideology.   Finally, there is the issue of dating with relation to Isa 1:10-17, and even if the most conservative view is granted, it is still far from certain that the ideas in these (and similar)

---

57   De Vaux, among others, talks here about the rhetorical technique called 'dialectical negation', where 'Not this but that' is a way of saying 'Not so much this as that,' de Vaux, *Ancient Israel*, 454.

58   Oswalt, *Isaiah 1-39*, 96.

59   Oswalt, *Isaiah 1-39*, 97.

texts were incorporated into the eighth-century ideology of cult. The only general conclusion from the passages above, Isa 1:10-17 included, is that they reflect a certain *development* of the understanding of cult in Israel. The following quote from Rowley brings an appropriate caution into this discussion:

> The Old Testament covers a very long period, and neither the forms nor the spirit remained unchanged throughout the period. Nor can we assume a steady and unwavering progress from the lower to the higher in all the development. The mere routine performance of a ritual act may well be a very arid form of worship, as the Old Testament prophets realized, and it is not confined to a single age or to a single point in the development of religion.[60]

Even though, as the above quote indicates, determining the cultic background of Isa 1:10-17 seems almost impossible, it is worth the effort to look for at least some clues. Once these clues are determined, it would be natural to turn to the cultic material in the Priestly literature for their interpretation. OT scholars, however, radically differ over the question how much of P's description of the individual rituals and the stipulations connected with them can be projected into the text from as early as the second half of the 8th century BCE. Understandably, the answer is determined by one's adherence to the theories about the OT sources. The JEDP theory works with the assumption that P is the latest of the law-codes, dated around 500-450 BCE, and even its *Grundschrift* (P[G]) is not earlier than the late exilic period, so 'little or nothing of the law seems to have been known in the pre-exilic period.'[61] On the other end of the spectrum are scholars who maintain that, rather than with the postexilic theocracy, 'the reality reflected in the Priestly Code accords more with the ancient life of Israel, which was grounded on sacral dogma and prescriptions that continued to mould the life of the Israelites even after the establishment of the monarchy.'[62]

Before evaluating these opinions, two qualifications are necessary. First, the concern here is not the date of P, rather the antiquity of the ideas formulated in the individual units of P. As pointed out already by Driver,

---

60 Rowley, *Worship*, 3.
61 Ernest W. Nicholson, The Pentateuch in the Twentieth Century: The Legacy of Julius Wellhausen (Oxford: Clarendon, 1998) 3.
62 Moshe Weinfeld, The Place of the Law in the Religion of Ancient Israel (VTSup 100; Leiden: Brill, 2004) 83.

the date at which an event, or institution, is first mentioned in writing, must not, however, be confused with that at which it occurred, or originated: in the early stages of a nation's history the memory of the past is preserved habitually by tradition; and the Jews, long after they were possessed of a literature, were still apt to depend much upon tradition.[63]

Second, the purpose of the discussion below is not to evaluate the major source theories as such, but to see how they square with the picture of cult in Isa 1:10-17, and, by pointing out their possible shortcomings and advantages, to determine how much light P can throw on the discussion of sacrifices and offerings in the 8th century Israel.

1.4. Documentary Theory and Pre-Exilic Cult

The absence of what is known from the last four books of the Pentateuch as the Law in the prophetic literature prompted Wellhausen to accept Graf's hypothesis of dating the Law after the Prophets.[64] His arguments are well known and do not need to be repeated here. Also, there is neither need nor space to evaluate Wellhausen's theory in general.[65] However, two of his conclusions that still hold sway in OT scholarship are of special importance to the present thesis. First, Wellhausen argues that the Israelite cult of the First Temple was radically different from that of the Second Temple: 'früher war er naiv: auf die Menge und Güte der Gaben kam es vorzugsweise an; später wurde er legal: auf die scrupulose Ausführung des Gesetzes, d. i. des Ritus, wurde vor allem gesehen.'[66] Second, from his reading of pre-exilic prophetic texts, Wellhausen deduced that the pre-exilic prophets were unacquainted with the Mosaic Law as described in P. For them, Wellhausen concludes, the Torah of the Lord (mentioned explicitly in, e.g., Isa 1:10 or implicitly in, e.g., Mic 6:8) was not concerned with

---

63   S. R. Driver, *An Introduction to the Literature of the Old Testament* (International Theological Library; Edinburgh: Clark, 1891) 125.

64   Wellhausen, Prolegomena, 3-4. Wellhausen specifies that this hypothesis should be assigned to Graf's teacher Eduard Reuss, or to Leopold George and Wilhelm Vatke, or even back to Martin Lebrecht de Wette.

65   For a recent evaluation, see Nicholson, *Pentateuch*, passim.

66   Wellhausen, *Prolegomena*, 61. For a recent example of this categorization, see Jensen, who, when commenting on Haggai and Zechariah, observes that 'whereas the prophets of the monarchy were at pains to warn Israel against naïve trust in the cult and in the Temple – even in terms that seemed almost to condemn the cult itself – these two make the rebuilding of the Temple an important goal,' Jensen, *Ethical Dimensions*, 159.

rituals, only with social justice and mercy, and, by implication, they did not consider the cult to be divinely instituted. Obviously, these conclusions have a serious bearing on the interpretation of texts like Isa 1:10-17, so they need to be addressed at this point.

1.4.1. Fundamental Difference between First and Second Temple Cults?

According to Wellhausen, the radical change from the naïve First Temple cult to the legalistic Second Temple cult was generated by the birth of P during the late exilic and post-exilic periods. P not only introduced a scrupulousness to the old cultic system, but also new rituals and concepts, even a whole new understanding of cult and its role and place in Israelite religion. Wellhausen's proposal is attractive and makes good sense, explaining the gaps and omissions when comparing the Law and the Prophets, but it suffers from several methodological flaws and is driven by presuppositions that recent OT scholarship has shown to be erroneous.

When it comes to the methodology, Wellhausen's view of the pre-exilic cult incorporates texts that mention cultic practices, but are not meant to be cult-descriptive, let alone cult-prescriptive. The picture they offer is, of course, informative, but to compare it with the minutely-detailed description of the cult in P and to base conclusions on this comparison is methodologically unsound; it is not comparing like with like. To list one example related to the topic of this study, Wellhausen considers the ethical dimensions of passages like Amos 5:21-27 or Isa 1:10-17 to be characteristic of the pre-exilic understanding of the priestly Torah, but his picture of the Law in the post-exilic period consists solely of P, not allowing the ethics of texts like Isa 58, Zech 7-8, or Mal 2:13-16[67] to inform this picture.[68] Even the differences between the same kind of cultic texts in P and, e.g., J or D do not necessarily testify to different cultic stages in Israel's history, but, as recently

---

67 Jensen comments on Mal 2:13-16 that 'the fact that [the people's] behavior occasions the Lord's rejection of their sacrifices puts us in mind of similar passages from Amos and Isaiah that condemn in strongest terms sacrifices and other rites offered by those guilty of oppression (cf. Amos 5:21-24; Isa 1:10-16).' Jensen, *Ethical Dimensions*, 163.

68 Because of such a different concept of the Law, Wellhausen in his 2nd edition of *Prolegomena* even claimed that the pre-exilic prophets did not oppose, but defended the priestly Torah, which, however, had nothing to do with cultus, but only with justice and morality (see p. 58 there). This claim does not appear in the 5th edition, probably because it runs against another of Wellhausen's notions that the ethical motives manifest themselves in the prophets for the first time in history, see Wellhausen, *Prolegomena*, 49.

argued by Weinfeld, can result from a different agenda and sociological background of each source.[69] For instance, as suggested already by Driver, 'the plan of Dt. would not naturally include an enumeration of minute details' as in the case of P.[70] Furthermore, as de Vaux argues, 'Deuteronomy cannot be used to reconstitute the ritual followed in the Temple during the years after Josias' reform, because Deuteronomy contains no code of law about sacrifices.'[71] Taking shape in the social circle of priesthood, P is unique in its focus on the execution of the cult, and there is simply no pre-exilic material of the same nature to allow for a fair comparison of the Israelite cult in the two periods.[72] On a more general level, Wellhausen's methodology suffers from circularity: in the words of Levenson, he decomposed the Torah into its constituent documents, taking them out of their literary context, reconstructed history from those components, and let this history govern their reading. Thus 'the historical context replaces the literary context,' or, even more strongly put, 'biblical history replaces the Bible.'[73] The following example from Wellhausen's treatment of Isa 1:11-15 illustrates the point: Wellhausen's scheme of the history of sacrifice allows only for a rather primitive picture of ritual in 8th century Israel, reducing it to only two types of sacrifice, the holocaust (עוֹלָה) and the

---

69 See Weinfeld, *Law*, 29 and 77-94. He is mostly concerned with explaining the differences between P and D, concluding that 'the ideological realm of P reflects a religious-theocentric orientation, while the deuteronomic world has a religious-anthropocentric orientation,' Weinfeld, *Law*, 82.

70 Driver, *Introduction*, 138. He, however, considers the silence of D about P to be significant, supporting the dating of P after D, in the period of the Babylonian captivity. In general, Driver basically agrees with Wellhausen (as he explicitly states in the note on p. 141) that 'the pre-exilic period shows no indications of the legislation of P as being in operation,' Driver, *Introduction*, 136.

71 De Vaux, *Ancient Israel*, 425. He considers this point the fundamental weakness of Wellhausen's theory.

72 Ignoring this can result in wrong conclusions, as, for example, the comparison of the understanding of sacrifices in P and J in Wellhausen, *Prolegomena*, 54-55. Since, according to him, P puts 'ein ganz unverhältnismässiger Nachdruck' on how, when, where, and by whom the sacrifices are offered, and J is only concerned with to whom they are offered, Wellhausen suggests that J derives the legitimacy of the sacrifice from its addressee, whereas P derives it only from its form.

73 Levenson, *Hebrew Bible*, 15. As shown already in the closing years of the 19th century by *die religionsgeschichtliche Schule* and Hermann Gunkel in particular, it is possible to reconstruct the history of the religion without such circularity. For an excellent overview of the traditio-historical method, see Nicholson, *Pentateuch*, esp. 31-60. As Nicholson summed up the objection of this school to Wellhausen's method, 'it would not do simply to separate the sources from each other, arrange them chronologically and then solely on this basis attempt to depict the history and development of the religion,' Nicholson, *Pentateuch*, 32.

communion-sacrifice (זֶבַח שְׁלָמִים, or זֶבַח, or just שְׁלָמִים).[74] This picture, however, squares only partially with Isa 1:10-17, where the ritual system seems to be more colourful – besides עוֹלָה and זֶבַח sacrifices, it also mentions מִנְחָה and קְטֹרֶת. At this point, Wellhausen's circularity takes over: because מִנְחָה and קְטֹרֶת are defined as specific types of sacrifices or offerings only in P, and because P is post-exilic, מִנְחָה and קְטֹרֶת in pre-exilic texts must refer only to sacrifices in general, developing their specific meaning later in the cultic history. While this is a possibility, scholars like de Vaux have suggested that when מִנְחָה 'is mentioned alongside עוֹלָה in 1 S 2:29; 3:14; Is 19:21, alongside זֶבַח in Jr 14:12; Ps 20:4, and alongside שֶׁלֶם in Am 5:22, it must bear the more precise meaning of a vegetable offering,'[75] an argument that applies to the meaning of מִנְחָה in Isa 1:10-17 as well. As for קְטֹרֶת, Nielsen in his monograph on incense sufficiently demonstrated that the cultic use of incense was strong already in early monarchic times.[76] He agrees with de Vaux that since to offer incense was customary in other surrounding nations, especially in Egypt, 'it certainly existed in Israel from ancient times.'[77] Clearly the variety of the sacrifices in Isa 1:10-17 points to a much richer *Sitz im Kult* than the Documentary Theory allows.

When it comes to presuppositions, even though Wellhausen does not exclude the possibility of the existence of elaborate rituals in pre-exilic Israelite worship, he considers it much more likely that 'die ausschliessliche Legitimität einer so bestimmten Opferordnung, wie sie im Priesterkodex als die einzig mögliche in Israel gilt, eine Vorstellung ist, die sich nur in Folge der Centralisation des Kultus zu Jerusalem ausgebildet haben kann.'[78] There are several problems with this assumption: First, as far as the 'bestimmten Opferordnung' is considered, Weinfeld sufficiently demonstrated that 'in the Ancient Near Eastern documents from the second and first millennium BCE we encounter prescribed temple rites that are even more elaborate then those of the Priestly

---

74 There is sufficient evidence in ancient texts to confirm the practices of these rituals well before the eighth century. For עוֹלָה see, e.g., Judg 6:26-28 and 13:15-20, 1Sam 7:9, 10:8, and 13:9; for זֶבַח see, e.g., Josh 22:26f; 1 Sam 1:21, 2:13, 19:3, etc.

75 De Vaux, *Ancient Israel*, 430. See also Norman Henry Snaith, "Sacrifices in the Old Testament," *VT* 7 (1957) 308-317. While allowing for a general meaning of 'tribute, gift', Snaith maintains that מנחה can mean 'grain-offering' at all periods of Israel's history, see Snaith, "Sacrifices," 316.

76 Kjeld Nielsen, *Incense in Ancient Israel* (VTSup 38; Leiden: Brill, 1986) *passim*, esp. 107. On his treatment of קְטֹרֶת in Isa 1:13, see 4.4.3.

77 De Vaux, *Ancient Israel*, 431. For further support see Rowley, *Worship*, 84-86.

78 Wellhausen, *Prolegomena*, 56.

Code,'[79] so there is no reason to take the highly structured cultic system of P as an indication of P's late date. Second, the reason why Wellhausen takes the centralization of the cult in Jerusalem as a precondition for P is his conviction that 'die Centralisation ist mit Generalisurung und Fixirung gleichbedeutend; und das sind die äusseren Züge, wodurch sich das Festwesen des Priesterkodex von dem früheren unterscheidet.'[80] This relation is simply false, for, as Anderson documented, 'idiosyncratic and complex classification system is paradigmatic of *all* mature cultic centers in the ancient world,' so its absence in Israelite cult before the centralization is unlikely.[81] Finally, even if P's legislation presupposed the centralization of the cult, it does not follow that this centralization must have been a historical reality at the time of the text's composition. Liss's recent suggestion that the literary quality of P contains a significant element of fictionality that 'precludes one-dimensional literary-historical questions' is a real possibility.[82] In any case, while granting a development

---

79   Weinfeld, *Law*, 35. Blenkinsopp slightly misses the point when downplaying Weinfeld's argument based on ANE evidence, see Blenkinsopp, "Assessment," 505-506. He rightly states that not even Wellhausen went as far as implying that the rituals detailed in P originated at the time of its composition. However, Weinfeld primarily argued not for the pre-exilic origin of particular rituals, but for the pre-exilic origin of a highly developed cultic system in Israel – a possibility that Wellhausen rendered very unlikely. For more details, see the evaluation of Wellhausen in Douglas A. Knight, *Rediscovering the Traditions of Israel: The Development of the Traditio-Historical Research of the Old Testament, with Special Consideration of Scandinavian Contributions*, Rev. ed. (SBL Dissertation Series 9; Missoula, MT: Society of Biblical Literature: distributed by Scholars Press, 1975) 64-68. Blenkinsopp, nevertheless, rightly objects to Weinfeld's use of this evidence in support of pre-exilic dating of P, stating that 'the existence of a similar enactment or practice in another part of the Near East does not settle the date of the Israelite-Judean parallel,' Blenkinsopp, "Assessment," 517.

80   Wellhausen, *Prolegomena*, 101.

81   Gary A. Anderson, *Sacrifices and Offerings in Ancient Israel: Studies in their Social and Political Importance* (Harvard Semitic Monographs 41; Atlanta, GA: Scholars Press, 1987) 33, italics mine. It should also be noted at this point that H explicitly posits multiple sanctuaries, as argued in Jacob Milgrom, "Does H advocate the Centralization of Worship?," *JSOT* 88 (2000) 59-76. Milgrom also argues elsewhere that P allows for multiple sanctuaries as well, see Milgrom, *Leviticus 1-16*, 29-34.

82   Hanna Liss, "The Imaginary Sanctuary: The Priestly Code as an Example of Fictional Literature in the Hebrew Bible," in *Judah and the Judeans in the Persian Period*, ed. Oded Lipschitz and Manfred Oeming (Winona Lake, IN: Eisenbrauns, 2006). Scholars generally recognize some utopian features of P, especially in its account of the Tabernacle, and some, including Wellhausen, use these to illustrate the fictional character of P. Liss correctly observes that 'Wellhausen did not differentiate between "fictional" and "fictitious" literature. To him, the Priestly Code as fiction meant over all a splendid faking of the depiction of ancient Israelite cult and, as a corollary, a

in the meaning of various sacrifices, it is reasonable to conclude with de Vaux that 'the essential forms of the post-exilic cult are found also in the days before the Exile.'[83]

1.4.2. Pre-Exilic Prophets' Ignorance of Mosaic Law?

If, as Wellhausen suggests, the pre-exilic prophets did not consider the cult to be divinely instituted and were driven not by cultic but ethical concerns, the cult polemic found in that literature 'ist eine rein prophetische, d. h. individuelle, theopneuste in dem Sinn, dass sie von allen hergebrachten und vorgefassten Menschenmeinungen unabhängig ist,' and the whole historical movement of that period 'ist von Haus aus und wesentlich prophetisch, ... ; und sie kann nicht bloss, sondern sie muss aus sich heraus verstanden warden.'[84] In other words, P with its focus on rituals and dated around 500-450 BCE should not be used to throw any light on the understanding of the cult polemic in the pre-exilic prophets.

Again, objections can be raised against Wellhausen's methodology and some of his presuppositions. The main methodological problem with his argument above is that it is argued almost exclusively from silence, even though in some cases this silence may seem rather telling. His proof texts (Amos 2:4, 4:4-5, 5:21-27, Hos 4:6, 8:11-14, Isa 1:10-17, and Mic 6:6-8) do not necessarily support his thesis.[85] Even the ultimate example, Jer 7:21-23, does not have to be read in contradiction to P, as demonstrated by Milgrom.[86] In fact, as shown throughout the present thesis, some of these texts can be interpreted in the very opposite way, demonstrating the pre-exilic prophets' acquaintance with the main cultic concepts as outlined in P. Wellhausen's basic presupposition is apparent from his attempt to explain the different treatment of cult in the prophetic and priestly documents by assuming the interior religion of the prophets and the exterior religion of the priests. To support this assumption, he contrasts the spontaneity and indefiniteness in the pre-exilic literature with the statutory and sharply defined language of P

---

conscious veiling of the Priestly author(s) and his (their) historical setting, the Second Temple Period,' Liss, "Imaginary Sanctuary," 668.

83   De Vaux, *Ancient Israel*, 432.

84   Wellhausen, *Prolegomena*, 49-50.

85   For Wellhausen's reading of these passages, see Wellhausen, *Prolegomena*, 57-60.

86   See Jacob Milgrom, "Concerning Jeremiah's Repudiation of Sacrifice," *ZAW* 89 (1977) 273-275.

when it comes to sacrifices.[87] However, as Anderson points out, 'the problem with this analysis is that it takes the intellectual task of the priestly class – to classify and order a tremendously wide variety of agricultural and pastoral gifts and offerings – as indicative of a spiritual demeanor.'[88] *Contra* Wellhausen's legalistic (and von Rad's crudely materialistic) view of the cult, Anderson assigns the reason for idiosyncratic and complex classification system in P to the systematic thinking of P that 'reflects the attempt of each and every cultic center to provide order and meaning to the wide variety of gifts and offerings which it receives.'[89]

1.5. Knohl / Milgrom's Theory of P and H and Pre-Exilic Cult

OT scholars already in Wellhausen's time differentiated between P and what Klostermann later labelled *Heiligkeitsgesetz* - the Holiness Code (H).[90] According to Knohl, Wellhausen's ideas about the history of ritual worship of ancient Israel are to be blamed for the wide acceptance of the theory that 'there is a collection of laws antedating P that underlies the Holiness Code and that scribes of the P school edited this early collection at the time they included it in their writings.'[91] Knohl has introduced a radically different theory, namely that the school of H is later than P, and that H is P's redactor. In spite of some reservations and disagreements, [92] Milgrom emphatically accepts Knohl's thesis and elaborates on it:

---

87 See Wellhausen, *Prolegomena*, 101.

88 Anderson, *Sacrifices*, 33.

89 Anderson, *Sacrifices*, 33.

90 August Klostermann, *Der Pentateuch, Beiträge zu seinem Verständnis und seiner Enstehungsgeschichte* (Leipzig: 1893) 368-418. Even though H initially referred to Leviticus 17-26, scholars subsequently found its linguistic and stylistic features in other parts of P.

91 Israel Knohl, *The Sanctuary of Silence: The Priestly Torah and the Holiness School* (Philadelphia: Fortress Press, 1995) 2.

92 Both Knohl and Milgrom base their criteria for identifying H passages in the Pentateuch on the linguistic features of Leviticus 17-26, and end up with a more or less similar body of texts ascribed to H, as the comparison of Knohl's list of proposed H passages on pp. 104-106 with Milgrom's comments on these passages in his commentary on Leviticus reveals. Less agreement between the two scholars is found in their attempt to reconstruct characteristic features of the two documents (for some examples, see Appendix 1). For the purposes of the present thesis, it is important to note that the major difference between Knohl and Milgrom is in the understanding of the relationship between morality and cult in P. For more details on this issue, see

What can unquestionably be accepted from Knohl's study is that H arose from the socioeconomic crisis at the end of the eighth century. And as H also includes the redaction of P, this can only mean that H is the terminus ad quem of P and, hence, that P – not just its teachings but its very texts – was composed not later than the middle of the eighth century (ca. 750 B.C.E.).[93]

Needless to say, if Knohl/Milgrom's theory is correct, it would throw a lot of light on the cultic background of pre-exilic cult-critical passages like Isa 1:10-17. Even though an adequate testing of this theory is far beyond the scope of the present thesis, one hypothesis resulting from its potential implications should be examined: if, as widely accepted, Isaiah was connected with the Temple in Jerusalem, and if the time of the Isa 1:10-17 composition squares with the formation of H, then this passage, which deals with one of the main themes of the priestly schools – the relationship between cult and ethics – should in some way reflect the characteristic ideological, literary, and linguistic features of such a significant contemporary theological development. To be sure, Milgrom and Knohl already commented on the possible connection between H and the eighth-century prophets. Milgrom states that H endorses the prophetic program of social justice and located 'fifty-five individual ethical commandments in H, most of which are directed against social abuses.'[94]   Knohl even suggested 'a living, direct relationship between the prophet [Isaiah] and contemporary Priestly circles living in the area of Isaiah's preaching.' According to him, the most important link is the same concept of the relationship between holiness and morality: he maintains that one of the unique features of H is the infusion of holiness with morality, and that 'Isaiah is the only prophet who unequivocally expresses the moral dimension of holiness.'[95] However, Knohl (somewhat surprisingly) uses Isa 1:10-17 as an illustration of 'a fundamental disagreement between Isaiah and HS [Holiness School] on the relation of morality to the cult,' because he reads this passage as a claim that 'God desires not the offerings of Israel and their Sabbaths but the correction of social-moral injustice.'[96] Also

---

Knohl's response to Milgrom on pp. 225-230 and Milgrom's response to Knohl in: Jacob Milgrom, *Leviticus 23-27: A New Translation with Introduction and Commentary* (AB 3B; New York, London: Doubleday, 2001) 2440-2446.

93   Milgrom, *Leviticus 1-16*, 28.

94   Jacob Milgrom, *Leviticus 17-22: A New Translation with Introduction and Commentary* (AB 3A; New York: Doubleday, 2000) 1362. In Milgrom's opinion, 'there exists a striking parallel in the structure of the book of Isaiah' with the one of Leviticus (pp. 1364-1367).

95   Knohl, *Sanctuary*, 213.

96   Knohl, *Sanctuary*, 214.

Milgrom reads this passage as a condemnation of the 8th century Israelite cult.[97] Paradoxically, as Chapter 4 demonstrates, Isa 1:10-17 can be understood in such a way that what appears to Knohl and Milgrom as a disconnection between H and Isaiah over the issues of cult is, in fact, to be regarded as another argument in support of their theory: if Isa 1:10-17 is read *sub specie sanctitatis Dei*, its treatment of cult and ethics is fully compatible with that of H. In addition, as Appendix 1 shows, the testing on the literary and linguistic grounds (rhetorical analysis) speaks strikingly in favour of the links between Isa 1:10-17 and H.[98] Although Knohl/Milgrom's theory is still far from being generally accepted in OT studies, one consensus has already resulted from theirs and other predominantly Jewish scholars' work, namely that 'the Priestly material in the Pentateuch was not spun out of thin air in the exilic or post-exilic period, but embodies more ancient tradition, especially laws.'[99]

As the discussion so far has shown, there are no convincing arguments to eliminate the possibility that the cultic concepts of sacrifice and purity/impurity were understood in 8th century Israelite religion *essentially* as defined in P.[100] Generally speaking, one coherent cultic tradition within the OT should remain a real option. Wellhausen is certainly correct that the exile experience must have been instrumental in shaping Israel's cultic tradition, but it is very unlikely

---

97   Milgrom states: 'It is hardly to be expected that Isaiah and Micah, who focus on the grievous moral injustices in the land, would be concerned with cultic matters. On the contrary, even if worship were centralized in the Jerusalem Temple, they roundly condemned it (Isa 1:11-17; Mic 6:6-7),' Milgrom, *Leviticus 17-22*, 1512. Elsewhere, Milgrom considers the prophetic movement as one of the major influences or even the trigger of the shift from P to H, when stating: 'It would take the momentous events at the end of the eighth century, which led to an infusion of refugees from northern Israel and the prophetic rebuke concerning the social and economic injustices gripping the land, to provoke a major Priestly response which resulted in the creation of the radically news vistas and ideology of H,' Milgrom, *Leviticus 1-16*, 34. Also Knohl arrives at the same conclusion on p. 216. They both, however, understand the 8th century prophetic view of cult to be incompatible with the ideology of H.

98   The reason for placing this rhetorical analysis in an appendix is that, according to some scholars, it is methodologically rather dubious, as shown, e.g., in 6.6.4.

99   Nicholson, *Pentateuch*, 220.

100 If P, as the consensus now stands, was composed after the time of Isaiah of Jerusalem, it might have only systematized the already existing cultic concepts in question. Blenkinsopp's word of caution should be kept in mind when it comes to P's individual textual units: 'In principle, any of these could be of considerable antiquity, but each must be considered on its own merits,' Blenkinsopp, "Assessment," 517.

that such a process would ignore, let alone contradict, the message of the pre-exilic and exilic prophets who predicted this exile, struggled to interpret it, and were venerated by it. It seems that it was not the development from naivety to legalism that caused the cult in P to look at odds with some other OT material, rather the fact that the Hebrew Bible is, as Levenson puts it, a 'most unsystematic book.'[101]

1.6. Implications

The above observations throw some light on those cult-critical texts in the Prophets that mention sacrifices and offerings. It is remarkable that these texts use עֹלָה, מִנְחָה, and שֶׁלֶם,[102] but never חַטָּאת and אָשָׁם.[103] Of course, this absence does not have to be intentional; the expiatory offerings might have been a later development. It can also be argued that even if the prophets did know about sin and guilt offerings, they were not keen on the technicalities of the ritual,[104] so they just used more common and general terms for ritual practices. Whatever the reason, this absence speaks against a proposal that the prophets criticized sacrifices because the people performed them with the intention of covering up for their ethical trespasses. The exclusive use of עֹלָה, מִנְחָה, and שֶׁלֶם seems to suggests that the primary interest of the ritual performance in these texts was to attract and maintain God's presence.[105] The conclusion about sacrifices that Klawans based on priestly tradition seems to be valid for the Prophets as well: 'Ancient Israelites conceived of sacrifice not primarily as a solution to the problem of transgression but rather as a productive expression of their religious ideals and hopes: the imitation of the divinity, in order to maintain the divine presence among them.'[106]

Furthermore, the above observations help to recognize concerns about purity of cult in the Prophets. Although ritual impurity in these

---

101 Levenson, *Hebrew Bible*, 18.

102 שֶׁלֶם is mentioned in these texts only once, Amos 5:22.

103 The possible exception may be Mic 6:7, where the prophet speaks of sacrificing 'the fruit of his body for the sin of his soul.' Outside of the Prophets, the only exception is Ps 40:6, stating that YHWH does not require חַטָּאת (here in a unique form – חַטָּאָה).

104 Except, maybe, Ezek 40-48.

105 Barton similarly observes: 'the pre-exilic prophets who are opposed to sacrifice seem to me to be overwhelmingly concerned with the kind of sacrifice which accompanies feasting [...] offered with rejoicing and thanksgiving in mind,' Barton, "Prophets," 119.

106 Klawans, *Purity*, 73.

texts is not nearly as prominent as in the priestly tradition, moral impurity is very high on the prophets' agenda. First, several texts confirm that the prophets, just like the priests, recognized the impurity caused by grave sins like murder, adultery, or idolatry. Hos 6:9-10 is a good example: 'As robbers lie in wait for someone, so the priests are banded together; they murder on the road to Shechem, they commit a monstrous crime. In the house of Israel I have seen a horrible thing; Ephraim's whoredom is there, Israel is defiled (נִטְמָא).'[107] As a result, 'their deeds do not permit them to return to their God,' Hos 5:4a. Also Ezekiel makes an explicit connection between idolatry and defilement: 'Will you defile yourselves after the manner of your ancestors and go astray after their detestable things? When you offer your gifts and make your children pass through the fire, you defile yourselves with all your idols to this day' (Ezek 20:30b-31a, see also 22:1-4). Jer 7:9-11 is probably the best illustration how moral impurity upsets the cult:

> Will you steal, murder, commit adultery, swear falsely, make offerings to Baal, and go after other gods that you have not known, and then come and stand before me in this house, which is called by my name, and say, "We are safe!" -- only to go on doing all these abominations? Has this house, which is called by my name, become a den of robbers in your sight? You know, I too am watching, says the LORD.

This text lists all the characteristic sources of moral impurity.[108] Even though it does not mention impurity or defilement explicitly,[109] it is obvious that the listed sins are irreconcilable with what the Temple represents.[110]

---

107 Significantly, this account immediately follows v. 6 – 'For I desire steadfast love and not sacrifice, the knowledge of God rather than burnt offerings.'

108 It may seem that stealing and swearing falsely do not belong to this list. However, as observed by Douglas from Lev 5:20-26, an issue between fellow men (like stealing and others listed in vv. 21-22aA) becomes a cultic issue by swearing falsely about it (vv. 22aB- 23aA). 'The Levitical text uses the oath to raise a civil crime to the level of sacrilege,' Mary Douglas, *Leviticus as Literature* (Oxford: Oxford University Press, 2000) 131. This mechanism is more explicit in Lev 19:11-12 – stealing often leads to swearing falsely by God's name, thus profaning it. (For the legitimacy of using these two texts in parallel as the illustration of the same principle, see Jacob Milgrom, *Studies in Cultic Theology and Terminology*, ed. Jacob Neusner (SJLA 36; Leiden: Brill, 1983) 47-51.) Douglas adds that this is 'a standard technique for appealing to a higher court. So far from being concerned exclusively with the cult it reflects a care to protect the system of justice, like our penalties for perjury,' Douglas, *Leviticus*, 131.

109 Elsewhere, Jeremiah explicitly states that idolatry defiles the people (2:23), the land (3:9, 13:27), and the sanctuary (7:30, 32:34).

110 As in the case of Hos 6 above, this ritual impurity account in Jeremiah comes after the repudiation of sacrifices in 6:20 and the call to social justice in 7:5-6. Klawans points in the right direction when insisting that 'for Jeremiah, the rejection of

The prophets took moral impurity very seriously, for, as it appears, they also believed that no ritual could purify the person or the object defiled by it. Once its level reached the point when YHWH became weary of relenting (Jer 15:6), the doom was inevitable: the people would be "purified" only by capital punishment, and the land by purging out its inhabitants. The inevitability of the capital punishment and the exile as predicted by, e.g., Amos 7:11b ('Jeroboam shall die by the sword, and Israel must go into exile away from his land') finds its explanation in, e.g., Num 35:33 ('You shall not pollute the land in which you live; for blood pollutes the land, and no expiation can be made for the land, for the blood that is shed in it, except by the blood of the one who shed it'), and Lev 18, where the people are warned not to defile themselves with the abominations of the nations that were before them, lest the land vomits them out *for defiling it* (vv. 24-30).

The priests as well as the prophets knew that the best cure for the illness called moral impurity was prevention. The following quote from Marx aptly describes the mechanism that was their ongoing concern: 'Each Israelite is called to draw near to YHWH with his offering, and to enjoy YHWH's presence. And YHWH's presence has repercussions for each Israelite who must behave in perfect accordance with YHWH's commandments, and is in this way ultimately responsible for YHWH's presence or absence among His people.'[111] As the story about the death of Aaron's sons in Lev 10 graphically illustrates, it was vital for the people to follow the commandments when they וַיַּקְרִבוּ לִפְנֵי יְהוָה (v. 1). Because it was a matter of life and death to distinguish בֵּין הַקֹּדֶשׁ וּבֵין הַחֹל וּבֵין הַטָּמֵא וּבֵין הַטָּהוֹר (v. 10), priests are to teach the people כָּל־הַחֻקִּים אֲשֶׁר דִּבֶּר יְהוָה (vv. 10-11). Interestingly, the same words occur in Ezek 22:26, where the priests' neglect of this very task (along with disregard of the Sabbaths) is listed as one of the reasons why YHWH consumed the people with the fire of his wrath (v. 31, notice the similarity with Lev 10:2), a reference to the exile. In addition, the rest of Ezek 22 is probably the most complete description of Israel's moral impurity.

It should be clear by now how the concept of moral impurity is operative in some of the texts with strong cult-critical language such as Isa 1:11-15 or Amos 5:21-23. When the person, the sanctuary, and the land are defiled by the sin for which no ritual can atone, to perform the rituals that are designed to attract and maintain God's presence is to

---

sacrifice (6:20) must be closely related to his warning that the temple would be destroyed (7:1-15),' Klawans, *Purity*, 91.

111 Marx, "Leviticus," 119.

bring impurity into the presence of holiness. No matter how well intended and performed, these rituals become counterproductive, repulsing God's presence.

1.7. Conclusion

This chapter is too short to do justice to such complex and controversial issues, so the following conclusions are only preliminary and must be further shaped by a careful exegesis of the OT texts that address these issues.

It seems likely that the priestly concept of sacrifice and purity is compatible with how these rituals were understood by the prophets. For the priests as well as the prophets, the main purpose of cult was the same – attracting and maintaining the presence of God within the community.[112] The reason why the priests were more occupied with ritual impurity and the prophets with moral impurity may be found in their different standpoints – the priests guarded the presence of God from the inside of the Temple, the prophets from the outside. It seems plausible that, far from being antiritualistic, the prophets took very seriously the purpose of rituals and therefore also the defilement caused by grave sins (moral impurity).[113] What often appears to be the prophets' zeal for ethics may, in fact, be their zeal for God's presence in the midst of his people.[114] Certainly, ethical misbehaviour is taken very seriously; however, the reason may not be because of how such

---

112 As Kaiser stated: 'In Israel, we should not suppose that the work of the priests and the prophets was completely distinct. With different degrees of exclusiveness, the work of both theses groups was connected with the temple, as the place of the presence of God, who approached the community for sacrifices of intercession and thanksgiving,' Otto Kaiser, *Isaiah 1-12: A Commentary*, trans. John Bowden, 2nd ed. (OTL; London: SCM, 1983) 25. Douglas goes even further, stating that 'one serious look at Leviticus shows that there is no line-up of priest and prophet, and no conflict between internal versus external religion, or justice versus ritual,' Mary Douglas, "Holy Joy: Rereading Leviticus: The Anthropologist and the Believer," *Conservative Judaism* 46, no. 3 (1994) 3-14: 10.

113 This understanding is more explicit after the exile. Referring to Isa 24:5, 27:9, Dan 11:31, 12:10a, Zech 3, 5, and 13:1-2, Gammie showed how the apocalyptic writers held 'a profound conviction that human acts of defiance against the divine sovereign can pollute land as well as persons,' John G. Gammie, *Holiness in Israel* (Overtures to Biblical Theology; Minneapolis: Fortress Press, 1989) 183-184.

114 Oswalt seems to be correct when claiming that the presence of God 'is ultimately what biblical religion is all about,' John Oswalt, *The Book of Isaiah, Chapters 40-66* (NICOT; Grand Rapids, MI; Cambridge: Eerdmans, 1998) 505.

misbehaviour affects one's neighbour or the society, but how the defilement caused by it affects the presence of God. If granted, then the value of ethics for the prophets was determined by cult, not vice versa as is often assumed. In such case, one can think of moral (im)purity as the ethical dimension of cult.

Chapter 2: Conception of Holiness in the Book of Isaiah

2.1. Introduction

Holiness is one of the essential attributes of God, intrinsically connected with his presence. Its manifestation is akin to, if not synonymous with, כְּבוֹד־יְהוָה, with the distinction that 'while "holiness" marks out [God's] inaccessible exaltation and power, which are restrictive on human activities, His "glory" exhibits Him in His earthly and visible self-manifestation.'[1] For this reason the concept of holiness plays an important part in the religion of ancient Israel.[2]

Holiness in the OT is attributed not only to God, but also to people, things, places, or festivals. However, as Jones points out, 'it was only in virtue of its relation to God as his property that anything became holy.'[3] According to him, this derivative holiness results from the Hebrew conception of property: 'the Hebrews thought of a man's property as being in some sense an extension of his personality,' and applied this view to God's property as well – 'what belongs to God participates in his wholeness which is a personal wholeness.'[4] Even though at this point Jones falls into an etymological trap of connecting the Hebrew

---

1   Owen C. Whitehouse, "Holiness: Semitic," in *Encyclopædia of Religion and Ethics*, ed. James Hastings, John A. Selbie, and Louis H. Gray (Edinburgh: T & T Clark, 1913) 758. Jacob states that God's glory is a 'visible extension for the purpose of manifesting holiness to men,' Edmond Jacob, *Theology of the Old Testament* (London: Hodder & Stoughton, 1958) 79. This connection is best illustrated in the book of Ezekiel. As Gammie argues, 'the vision that is the basis of the inspiration for Ezekiel's priestly prophecy (chapters 1-3), his vision of the return of God to Jerusalem (expanded by his school in chapters 40-48), and his vision of the initial departure of the divine glory from Jerusalem (chapters 8-11) are visions of holiness,' Gammie, *Holiness*, 49.

2   Ringgren even claims that 'the notion of holiness holds a central position in Israelitic religion,' Helmer Ringgren, *The Prophetical Conception of Holiness* (Uppsala Universitets Årsskrift 12; Uppsala: A.-B. Lindquist, 1948) 3.

3   O. R. Jones, *The Concept of Holiness* (London: Allen and Unwin, 1961) 107.

4   Jones, *Concept of Holiness*, 92 and 94.

term for 'holy' with the English term 'wholeness',[5] his main idea stands: the land, the temple, etc. are not holy by themselves, but because they belong to holy God. Jones' erroneous notion of 'what belongs to God participates in his wholeness' may imply that for God to disown his land or his people means to become incomplete. However, as Milgrom states, these things are termed holy 'by virtue of divine dispensation' and therefore 'this designation is always subject to recall.'[6]

This chapter focuses predominantly on *God's* holiness: first on its connection with purity, then on its essence (cultic and/or ethical), and finally on its use in the book of Isaiah.

2.2. Holiness and Purity

The close relationship between holiness and purity in the OT is unanimously acknowledged. Gammie has persuasively demonstrated that 'holiness summoned Israel to cleanness' throughout the entire Hebrew Scriptures.[7] The reason behind this call for purity is in the ambivalence of holiness – it could cause destruction as well as blessing, as illustrated in, e.g., 2 Sam 6: Uzzah died because he touched what was holy, namely the ark of God (vv. 6-8), and the household of Obed-edom was blessed because of the presence of this very ark (v. 11). Ringgren reads Isa 10:17a as another illustration of this ambivalence: 'The light of Israel will become a fire, and his Holy One a flame.'[8] He rightly concludes that the intention behind the purification of the Israelites, especially before partaking in a cult ceremony, 'was evidently partly to remove that which is incompatible with holiness, partly, so to speak, to put oneself in the state of holiness that is required by the holy act.'[9] It comes, therefore, as no surprise that the term קדשׁ is often related to טהר and כבס, 'since being "consecrated" or "sanctified" does presuppose a condition of cultic acceptability and purity.'[10]

---

5   On the fallacy of this very connection, see James Barr, *The Semantics of Biblical Language* (London: Oxford University Press, 1961) 111-114.

6   Milgrom, *Leviticus 1-16*, 730. These characteristics of derived holiness will become important especially when analysing Isa 43:22-28.

7   Gammie, *Holiness*, 195. He adds: 'A unity of the Old Testament can be discerned in this unified response to holiness on the part of Israel: holiness requires purity.'

8   Ringgren, *Prophetical Conception of Holiness*, 30.

9   Ringgren, *Prophetical Conception of Holiness*, 10.

10   Kornfeld, "קדשׁ," *TDOT* 12.527.

A closer look at the relationship between holiness and purity in the OT reveals that most of its illustrations are concerned with *ritual* impurities. Holiness seems to be connected with ethics only implicitly, confining the few instances to only certain parts of the OT. This disproportion led Gammie to argue that the holiness of God required different kinds of cleanness for the priests than for the prophets – for the former a cleanness of ritual purity, right sacrifices, and separation, for the latter a cleanness of social justice and equity in human relations. He believes that 'in contradiction to the priests of Israel, the prophets clearly taught that the holiness of God required the cleanness of social justice.'[11] Paradoxically, Gammie's own study shows that this differentiation is untenable. Based on Gen 17:1, he claims that 'vocation to moral living was an integral part of the priestly theology of separation,' and concludes his section on the priestly understanding of holiness by asserting that, even though personal uncleanness and defilement of the sanctuary had to be dealt with via ritual, 'both were deeply rooted in a world view that unflinchingly affirmed that the holiness of God requires a highly ordered and just conduct with one's fellow human beings as well as a scrupulous maintenance of personal purity.' Furthermore, he starts the section on the prophetic understanding of holiness by stating that 'the prophets of Israel were heirs of the priesthood and cultus – and not least in their conception of holiness,' endorsing Ringgren's statement that 'the prophets obviously accepted the cultic notion of holiness, as it is preserved to us in the ritual laws of the Pentateuch.'[12] It becomes obvious from Gammie's study that to determine whether the nature of the relationship between holiness and purity is cultic, ethical, or both depends on how one defines the nature of the two concepts. The concept of purity and impurity has already been discussed in the previous chapter (1.2.2), so the subject of the present discussion is the nature of holiness.

2.3. Holiness as a Cultic Notion

Almost a century ago, Whitehouse stated:

---

11 Gammie, *Holiness*, 100.

12 Gammie, *Holiness*, 25, 44, and 71 respectively, see also 191. These and similar statements do not presuppose a particular view of dating the sources (such as P to predate the Prophets), only the antiquity of the priestly tradition as described in, e.g., Milgrom, *Cultic Theology and Terminology*, ix-xiii.

> The conception of holiness when traced to its historic origins among Semitic peoples is stripped of all the ethical qualities with which our Christian modern consciousness has invested it. The ethical elements which have become absorbed into its content entered at a much later stage in the evolution of ideas which became attached to the term.[13]

This idea is developed in Rudolf Otto's influential monograph on holiness,[14] providing a suitable ideological framework for the study of this concept in the OT, and is especially helpful for understanding the relation of holiness to cult and ethics. Like Whitehouse, Otto persuasively argues that the ethical element 'was not original and never constituted the whole meaning of the word.' According to him, the ethical meaning only subsequently shaped and infiltrated the terms like קָדוֹשׁ, ἅγιος, or *sanctus*, whose original and unique substance was non-ethical (ethically neutral) and non-rational, a feeling-based response to the presence of a divinity, the 'extra Something' in the meaning of 'holy' that Otto calls 'numinous'.[15] Correspondingly, when a human being is encountered by the numinous reality (as, e.g., in Isa 6), the feeling-response does not result from a sense of *moral* unworthiness (caused by the transgression of the moral law), but 'it is the feeling of absolute profaneness.' Only when this feeling of 'numinous unworthiness' is transferred to moral delinquency does mere 'unlawfulness' become 'sin', 'impiety', or 'sacrilege'. This dual essence of sin corresponds to the two kinds of self-depreciation contained in the religious feeling that arises from moral transgression: we not only 'esteem ourselves *guilty* of a bad action and the action itself as morally evil,' but we are also 'defiled in our own eyes.'[16] Consequently, the need for atonement results from the feeling of profaneness, i.e., from 'the feeling that the "profane" creature cannot forthwith approach the

---

13   Whitehouse, "Holiness," 751.

14   Rudolf Otto, *The Idea of the Holy: An Inquiry into the Non-rational Factor in the Idea of the Divine and Its Relation to the Rational*, trans. John W. Harvey, 2nd ed. (London: Oxford University Press, 1950).

15   See Otto, *Idea*, 5-7. The 'moralization' and 'rationalization' of the term 'holy' is to be distinguished from the transmutation of the actual feeling (as often assumed by evolutionism), e.g., from a feeling of numinous tremor or uniform custom to a feeling of moral obligation. Otto rightly objects that, since these feelings are qualitatively different, the transmutation *par la durée* is very unlikely. See Otto, *Idea*, 42-43 and 18.

16   Otto, *Idea*, 50-55. Based on this postulate, Otto further argues that 'the meaning of "sin" is not understood by the "natural", nor even by the merely moral man; and the theory of certain dogmatists, that the demand of morality as such urged man on to an inner collapse and then obliged him to look round for some deliverance, is palpably incorrect.'

numen, but has need of a covering or shield against the ὀργὴ [anger] of the numen.' As Otto further elaborates, 'such a "covering" is then a "consecration", i.e. a procedure that renders the approacher himself "numinous", frees him from his "profane" being, and fits him for intercourse with the numen.'[17]

Because of its close connection with cult, Ringgren agrees with Otto that holiness is a cultic notion. 'This is easily understood if we remember that cult is the normal way of getting into contact with the divinity.'[18] Study of the root קדשׁ only confirms the ideas above. After surveying its use in various Semitic languages, Kornfeld concludes that, even though the original meaning of the root itself can no longer be determined, every context of the קדשׁ derivatives suggests a religious-cultic implication. 'The focus is never on ethical or moral issues, but rather on an act of consecration, surrender, or dedication to a deity.'[19]

Based on this brief survey, it is safe to conclude that the idea of holiness as essentially a cultic notion is well established in the OT, especially in the Priestly literature.[20] Now the question is whether this idea is consistent throughout the OT, or whether it has been somehow modified in different bodies of OT literature. More specifically, did the prophets work with the same (cultic) idea of holiness as the priests, or did they (through their teaching) supplement this concept with an ethical notion?

2.4. Holiness as an Ethical Notion?

Contrary to the expectation that 'the vivid interest in ethical matters that is characteristic of the prophets should manifest itself in a more ethical conception of holiness,' Ringgren observes that 'the ethical aspect of holiness plays a very subordinate part in prophetic preaching.'[21] His explanation is twofold. First, he points out that 'such a sharp distinction between cult and ethics as we are wont to draw' simply did not exist in the times of the OT prophets. Second, since God

---

17 Otto, *Idea*, 54.

18 Ringgren, *Prophetical Conception of Holiness*, 8.

19 W. Kornfeld, "קדשׁ," *TDOT* 12.526. Mowinckel even claims that 'the word "holy" practically never has any ethical reference in the Old Testament,' Sigmund Mowinckel, *He That Cometh* (Oxford: Blackwell, 1956) 381n.

20 For specification of holiness in P and D, see Weinfeld, *Law*, 88-94.

21 Ringgren, *Prophetical Conception of Holiness*, 22-23.

is the source of holiness, 'the development of an ethical conception of holiness is intimately bound up with the transformation of the idea of God as being more decidedly ethical and moral.' He credits prophets with enhancing this new development alongside the old cultic aspect of holiness (Otto's *tremendum*).[22]

While Ringgren's first argument is very likely correct (see Introduction), the second one finds little support in the OT. God is pictured as decidedly ethical and moral already in the earliest texts (e.g., Exod 20:22-23:33), acting as a protector of the weak ones of the society (slaves, widows, orphans, resident aliens, victims of crime or misfortune, etc.) and as a righteous, incorruptible judge who makes sure justice is not perverted.[23] In fact, the very first OT use of the word pair מִשְׁפָּט and צְדָקָה (as well as the first mention of מִשְׁפָּט and the second of צְדָקָה in the OT) in Gen 18:19 characterizes YHWH's ways as ethical.[24] In the same passage, Abraham expects of God, the Judge of all the earth, to act justly as a matter of course (v. 25). Expressions such as אֱלֹהֵי מִשְׁפָּט יְהוָה used by Isaiah in 30:18 hardly contributed anything new to the already established idea of YHWH as being decidedly righteous and just, even ethical according to the standards of ancient Israel.[25] Ringgren's and similar theories about ethicizing of the

---

22 Ringgren, *Prophetical Conception of Holiness*, 22 and 24. This idea was formulated already by Whitehouse. While maintaining that the prophets 'did not in any degree diminish, but rather exalted' those aspects of holiness that mark out 'Jahweh's unapproachable and terrible power and His manifested grandeur,' he believes that 'the stress which Amos and Isaiah placed on the righteousness of Jahweh and His ethical requirements ... shifted the centre of gravity in religion from ceremonial to conduct,' which, in turn, resulted in ethicizing of the conception of the divine holiness. He recognizes that the ethical elements must have belonged to Israel's religion before the time of the Prophets ('since all religion involves social relations and a social order'), but insists that 'the prophetic teaching gave them a new and primary importance, and they came to displace the externalities of ceremonial religion.' However, Whitehouse has to admit that what he calls 'the old and primitive non-ethical ideas of holiness' 'still held sway and persisted in post-Exilic Judaism.' See Whitehouse, "Holiness," 758-759.

23 In the case of premeditated murder, justice even takes precedence over the sanctity of God's altar when the killer is taken from it for execution (21:14).

24 As vv. 24-25 confirm, the dialog of Abraham with YHWH can be called ethical discourse even by modern standards, because 'it shows that there exists a rule of justice outside of the will of God and allowing him to be called to account,' Ze'ev W. Falk, "Law and Ethics in the Hebrew Bible," in *Justice and Righteousness: Biblical Themes and Their Influence*, ed. Yair Hoffman and Henning Reventlow (JSOTSup 137; Sheffield: JSOT Press, 1992) 87.

25 For an attempt to evaluate divine justice in the book of Isaiah by contemporary criteria, see Andrew Davies, *Double Standards in Isaiah: Re-Evaluating Prophetic Ethics and Divine Justice* (Biblical Interpretation Series 46; Leiden: Brill, 2000). He comes to a

conception of the divine holiness seem to be anachronistic and presuppose the artificial theological abyss between the priests and the prophets as discussed in the previous chapter (1.4).

The incorporation of the ethical notion into the concept of holiness did not result from the prophetic transformation of the idea of God, but more likely from the prophetic rejuvenation of the idea of the proper human response to the holiness of God. The following proposal of Raphael aptly captures this process:

> Yet gradually, as the original numinous experience is accommodated to everyday conditions of life and the teaching of religion, the sense of the numinous is 'translated' into the sense of the holy and one's proper duties towards it. Some of these duties will be ritual, others ethical, so that holiness and morality may come to overlap in the finite world. But this does not entail that the beginning and end of morality cannot, ultimately, be absorbed into the holy as its source and judge.[26]

The ethical response to holiness is not limited to the Prophetic literature. Ringgren observes that in Deuteronomy (and DtrH), the meaning of קדש 'fluctuates between ethical obedience, abstinence from what is impure, and worship of the one God.'[27] This range of meaning is most famously present in Lev 19. Although it appears to be an ad hoc mixture of ethical and ritual laws, Rodd believes that 'the present completed text marks the intention of the final redactor.'[28] This intention, according to Rodd, is expressed in the initial call to holiness:

> Essential to understanding the chapter is the call to be holy because God is holy and to do nothing to impair the holiness of this land and his people. It is less a matter of keeping God's laws simply because he commanded them and will punish those who break them, than that both actions which break ethical precepts and those which infringe cultic and ritual purity equally affect Israel's holiness.[29]

Reading Lev 19 from the perspective of securing holiness in Israel and, ultimately, the presence of the Holy One in her midst redefines the role of ethics and cult as commonly understood: not that ethical concepts substantiate cult, but cultic concepts substantiate ethics. Probably the most graphic illustration of this principle are the condemnations of sexual offences listed in Lev 18 and 20: they are substantiated not by

---

very different conclusion. However, the objection can be raised that judging the ethics of an ancient Near East text by the 20th century western standards is methodologically dubious.

26 Melissa Raphael, *Rudolf Otto and the Concept of Holiness* (Oxford: Clarendon Press, 1997) 130.

27 Ringgren, "קדש," *TDOT* 12.531.

28 Rodd, *Glimpses*, 5, n1.

29 Rodd, *Glimpses*, 7. As argued below, this line of thinking is consonant with PI.

the harm that they may cause to one's neighbour, but by concerns for purity, whether of the land (18:25, 27-28) or of the people (18:20, 24; 20:22-26), and for holiness (20:26).[30] A more ambivalent example is the dietary laws (as found in Lev 11 and elsewhere). Milgrom's attempt at an ethical interpretation is especially instructive. He rightly insists that since God alone is the source of holiness, for people to be holy means the life of godliness - *imitatio Dei*. Then, however, referring to texts like Lev 19, Ps 24:3-4, Isa 5:16 and Isa 6, he states:

> The emulation of God's holiness demands following the *ethics* associated with his nature. But because the demand for holiness occurs with greater frequency and emphasis in the food prohibitions than in any other commandment, we can only conclude that they are Torah's personal recommendation as the best way of achieving this higher ethical life.[31]

Not only is Milgrom's argument based on texts whose use in support of an ethical notion of holiness is questionable,[32] but, as Houston pointed out, it suffers from a failure of logic when the cultic element - the impurity of the unclean animals - is taken into consideration, for the supposed ethics would demand reverence for something that defiles.[33] Instead, Houston suggests a connection between God's holiness and human behaviour that does more justice to texts like Lev 11: 'If the

---

30   Notice the frequent occurrence of the phrase אֲנִי יְהוָה at the end of the prohibitions there. An interesting attempt to explain the ritual character of these prohibitions comes from André. Based on the fact that both chapters combine the prohibitions of sexual uncleanness with prohibitions of idolatry (18:21; 20:2-5), he suggests that 'the laws concerning sexual uncleanness might be based on a refusal to divinize any aspect of sexuality,' G. André "טָמֵא," *TDOT* 5.331. Milgrom believes that in contrast to P, H's doctrine of pollution is nonritualistic. His arguments are that the uses of טָמֵא in passages like 18:20 [mistakenly quoted as 21], 24 and 19:31 are metaphoric and that 'the polluted land cannot be expiated by ritual, and, hence, the expulsion of its inhabitants is inevitable (18:24-29; 20:22 [mistakenly quoted as 2]),' Milgrom, *Leviticus 1-16*, 49. For the repudiation of the metaphorical use of טָמֵא, see 1.2.2 above. While the second statement is by itself correct, its use as an argument for nonritualistic doctrine of pollution is twisted. Milgrom elsewhere (p. 710) assigns Num 35:33, from which the idea of no expiation for the land comes, to P, so it cannot be used to characterize the doctrine of H. If Num 35:33 is assigned to H, Knohl correctly states that 'just as the priests atone for the impurity of the Temple through the sprinkling of blood, so too may the land be atoned for from the impurity imparted to it by the murder victim's blood,' Knohl, *Sanctuary*, 179. Knohl argues that H attempted to do just the opposite of nonritualization – 'to integrate the laws of morality and social justice into the religious-cultic corpus,' Knohl, *Sanctuary*, 178. This way of arguing is harmonious with the search for the ethical dimension of cult or moralized rituality as described in the Introduction.

31   Milgrom, *Leviticus 1-16*, 731, italics mine.

32   The Isaianic passages are discussed below.

33   For the details, see Houston, "Deitary Laws of Leviticus," 149-150.

attainment of holiness which is the goal of the law in Leviticus 11 is held to involve *imitatio Dei*, it would seem to make more sense to argue that Israel is commanded to avoid what is unworthy of the presence of God.'[34] This in daily life means refraining from *every* kind of impurity, regardless of its source. The only moral in a text like Lev 11 is of principle: 'It is important for our present purpose to understand that this *religious* idea, as we would understand it, is also an *ethical* idea. Loyality to one's superior is a key moral duty in most ancient societies.'[35] However, *sub specie sanctitatis Dei*, the reason for sexual, dietary or any other prohibitions in Leviticus is cultic, namely preservation of holiness via purity. This perspective of the divine holiness rearranges the relations between the discussed concepts as follows: 'It might seem to us that impurity was treated as a 'sin', but the reverse is probably the case: to break ethical norms is a form of impurity and impairs the holiness of Israel before the holy God.'[36]

Chapters 4-6 demonstrate how the cult-critical passages in the book of Isaiah are to be read *sub specie sanctitatis Dei*. First, however, it needs to be determined how the above described concept of holiness squares with its use throughout this book.

2.5. Holiness in the Book of Isaiah

Commentators often suggest that God's holiness is an important concept in the book of Isaiah,[37] bringing to attention the frequent occurrence of the otherwise rare divine epithet קְדוֹשׁ יִשְׂרָאֵל throughout the book and the significance of ch. 6 with the famous *trisagion*.[38]

---

34   Houston, "Deitary Laws of Leviticus," 150. Wright's response to Milgrom is basically the same: '[The] negative characterization of nonpermitted animals seems to me not to support a desire to inculcate a reverence for animal life. A different motivating ideology lies at the base of the food prohibitions in Leviticus 11: a desire that the people remain holy,' David P. Wright, "Observations on the Ethical Foundations of the Biblical Dietary Laws: A Response to Jacob Milgrom," in *Religion and Law: Biblical-Judaic and Islamic Perspectives*, ed. Edwin Brown Firmage, Bernard G. Weiss, and John W. Welch (Winona Lake: Eisenbrauns, 1990) 197.

35   Houston, "Deitary Laws of Leviticus," 157.

36   Rodd, *Glimpses*, 8. He correctly concludes on the same page: 'Securing holiness in Israel requires both obedience to the ethical norms and upholding ritual purity.'

37   E.g., Gammie states that 'the holiness of God plays a significant role in the theologies of Isaiah of Jerusalem and his successors,' Gammie, *Holiness*, 72.

38   In one of his articles, Roberts attempts to demonstrate that 'if there is any one concept central to the whole Book of Isaiah, it is the vision of Yahweh as the Holy

Williamson puts this by and large correct assumption into a more
nuanced perspective. First, based on the numerous indications that the
only two occurrences of קְדוֹשׁ יִשְׂרָאֵל in Isa 56-66 (60:9 and 14) may be
attributed to DI's direct influence (citation or allusion) and on their
secondary role in this text, he states that this divine title 'was not of
great significance for Trito-Isaiah,' and 'it cannot be held to be in any
way central to his thought.'[39] Second, by reducing the fourteen
occurrences of קְדוֹשׁ יִשְׂרָאֵל and its variants in the text of PI to those five
that can be unquestionably assigned to the 8th century prophet (5:19;
30:11, 12, 15; 31:1) and by considering the probable date of these
utterances in the prophet's career, Williamson demonstrates that 'Isaiah
himself made only occasional use of this divine title, and that mainly, if
not entirely, in the final stages of his long ministry.'[40] Therefore,
Williamson concludes, it was Isaiah's later editors, DI in particular,
who picked up the title קְדוֹשׁ יִשְׂרָאֵל and made it characteristic of the
book, thus echoing the *trisagion* in what they considered to be the most
influential experience of the 8th century prophet – his vision in ch. 6.

2.5.1. Holiness in PI

With the number of uses of the title קְדוֹשׁ יִשְׂרָאֵל that can be assigned to
Isaiah of Jerusalem significantly reduced, can the concept of holiness
still be considered central to his theology? In other words, has the
vision in Isa 6 as profound an influence on the 8th century prophet as
the editors of his material thought? Vriezen's answer is affirmative; he
believes that Isaiah's encounter with the glory and holiness of God
'remained in his mind during his whole life and dominated his
existence completely,' including his thoughts and words.[41] Similarly,
Roberts claims that the message of this prophet 'can be unfolded as a
transformation of inherited traditions in the light of that central
vision.'[42] While tracing down the impact of Isa 6 throughout the whole
of PI's corpus is beyond the scope of the present study,[43] it can, at this

One of Israel,' J. J. M. Roberts, "Isaiah in Old Testament Theology," *Intrepretation* 36
(1982) 130-143.

39   H. G. M. Williamson, "Isaiah and the Holy One of Israel," in *Biblical Hebrew, Biblical
Texts: Essays in Memory of Michael P. Weitzman*, ed. Ada Rapoport-Albert and Gillian
Greenberg (JSOTSup 333; Sheffield: Sheffield Academic Press, 2001) 26.

40   Williamson, "Isaiah and Holy One of Israel," 31.

41   Vriezen, "Theology of Isaiah," 131.

42   Roberts, "Isaiah in Old Testament Theology," 131.

43   For a rudimentary attempt, see the above articles and Gammie, *Holiness*, 71-96.

point, be examined in the passages that explicitly mention YHWH's holiness and/or its revelation – YHWH's glory and majesty[44] – and likely express the 8th century prophet's opinion. Arguably, such passages are Isa 2:19; 8:13; 10:16-17; 29:23; 30:12, 15; and 31:1. If these texts are influenced by Isa 6, they should reflect some of the following features: The major characteristic of YHWH's holiness in Isa 6 is what Otto calls *tremendum*, profoundly illustrated by seraphs covering their faces from the fearsome glory of YHWH and by Isaiah's immediate reaction אוֹי לִי. Another important characteristic is that the revelation of YHWH's holiness not only exposes but is also hostile toward every impurity, as Isaiah realized to his horror. The only solution to how to be in the presence of the Holy One and stay alive is purification. Here the sovereign YHWH determines the time and the means of purification – the immediate cultic fire (for Isaiah), or the upcoming fire of judgment (for the people). Overall, holiness in Isa 6 is exclusively a cultic notion.[45]

Interestingly, these and only these characteristics and elements can be found in the above listed passages. The *tremendum* aspect of YHWH's holiness is described in 2:19, where the people 'enter the caves of the rocks and the holes of the ground, from the terror of the LORD, and from the glory of his majesty (מֵהֲדַר גְּאוֹנוֹ), when he rises to terrify (לַעֲרֹץ) the earth,' in 8:13, where the people are told to regard YHWH as holy and let him be their fear and dread (וְהוּא מוֹרַאֲכֶם וְהוּא מַעֲרִצְכֶם), and in 29:23, where the people 'will sanctify the Holy One of Jacob, and will stand in awe (יַעֲרִיצוּ) of the God of Israel.' All PI's usages of קְדוֹשׁ יִשְׂרָאֵל (5:19; 30:11, 12, 15; 31:1) are connected with judgment, and Isa 10:16-17 speaks of the fire of judgment being kindled under YHWH's glory (תַּחַת כְּבֹדוֹ) and, in fact, of Israel's Holy One becoming this devouring fire.

A closer look at the passages in Isa 1-39 that mention YHWH's holiness or his glory but are generally assigned to the editor(s) is also instructive. Here the picture changes significantly: not only there is no *tremendum* and connection to judgment, but people will 'lean on the Lord, the Holy One of Israel, in truth' (10:21), they are to 'sing for joy'

---

44 Just as in Ezekiel, 'the unity of God's holiness and God's majesty has been apprehended as a fact by Isaiah,' Vriezen, "Theology of Isaiah," 132.

45 Since the cleansing of the uncleanness in Isa 6 consists in a removal of עָוֹן and an expiation (כפר) of חַטָּאת, Ringgren believes that 'here the reader seems to be closer than elsewhere in the OT to an ethical determination of holiness,' Ringgren, "קדשׁ," *TDOT* 12.536. Gammie, however, rightly insists that Isaiah's vision 'is neither anticultic nor acultic. For whether or not the prophet was actually situated in the temple when he had it, temple, incense, altar, (incense) smoke, fire on the altar, and the notion of sin purged are hardly cultically neutral,' Gammie, *Holiness*, 81.

for great in their midst is the Holy One of Israel (12:6), 'their eyes will look to the Holy One of Israel' (17:7), 'the neediest people shall exult in the Holy One of Israel,' (29:19), and even natural elements shall see כְּבוֹד־יְהוָה (35:2).[46] In Otto's terms, this picture is dominated by the element of fascination.[47]   When the context is not positive, Otto's *majestas* of YHWH's holiness takes over to emphasize the absurdity of human behaviour:[48] Israel despised the Holy One of Israel (1:4) and his word (5:24), the people rebelled 'against the eyes of his glory' (3:8),[49] and Sennacherib of Assyria mocked and reviled him (37:23). The only editorial use of holiness in PI that shares one of the features with ch. 6 is 35:8, but the holiness here is only derivative, namely דֶּרֶךְ הַקֹּדֶשׁ, on which an unclean person (טָמֵא) is not allowed to travel. Furthermore, the idea of holiness excluding uncleanness is too general to argue for Isa 6 influence. Even though derivative holiness is not the focus of this study, it should be noted that none of its uses in Isa 1-39 can be safely assigned to the 8th century prophet.[50] It can be concluded that Isaiah ben Amoz reserved the attribute קְדֹשׁ for YHWH only.

---

46   For 35:2 as well as the rest of the chapter being a later addition, see mainly Odil Hannes Steck, *Bereitete Heimkehr: Jesaja 35 als redaktionelle Brücke zwischen dem Ersten und dem Zweiten Jesaja* (Stuttgarter Bibelstudien 121; Stuttgart: Verlag Katholisches Bibelwerk, 1985). Williamson generally endorses Steck's conclusion, stating that Isa 35 'represents a relatively late stage in the composition of the book as a whole, and in particular that it is later than, rather than simultaneous with, the composition of Deutero-Isaiah,' H. G. M. Williamson, *The Book Called Isaiah: Deutero-Isaiah's Role in Composition and Redaction* (Oxford: Clarendon Press, 1994) 215.

47   See Otto, *Idea*, 31-40.

48   The element of 'overpoweringness', see Otto, *Idea*, 19-23.

49   For this translation as well as the very likely editorial origin of this verse, see H. G. M. Williamson, *A Critical and Exegetical Commentary on Isaiah 1-27*, vol. 1 (ICC; London, New York: T & T Clark, 2006) 235-236 and 251-253. One of the minor reasons for assigning this verse to a later redactor is, according to Williamson, 'the use of כבוד in a manner which reflects later developments within the book of Isaiah as a whole.'

50   Holiness is attributed to people twice: the holy remnant in 4:3 and the holy seed in 6:13. Holy mountain occurs in 11:9 and 27:13. While the latter text belongs to a distinct unit (Isa 24-27) that has been generally recognized as late, the date of 11:9 is debated. For a detail survey, see Hans Wildberger, *Jesaja* (BKAT 10; Neukirchen-Vluyn: Neukirchener Verlag des Erziehungsvereins, 1965) 442-446. Wildberger himself argues for Isaianic authorship of 11:1-9. Sweeney, on the other hand, assigns this text to the so called Josianic redaction, see Marvin A. Sweeney, *Isaiah 1-39: With an Introduction to Prophetic Literature* (FOTL 16; Grand Rapids, MI: Eerdmans, 1996) 203-210. If Wildberger is followed, a case can be made for the influence of Isa 6 on 11:9 – in both cases, YHWH's revealed holiness (his glory) extends beyond the Temple, filling the whole earth. Finally, the holy festival in 30:29 also likely belongs to Josianic edition, as argued by Sweeney, *Isaiah 1-39*, 356.

These observations confirm Gammie's conclusions with regard to PI's doctrine of holiness, namely that 'reverence and a sense of the need for cleanness are the most immediate and lasting products of the prophet's encounter with holiness,' and that 'throughout his career the prophet clung to the notion that sin defiles but holiness requires cleanness. He is at pains to reveal how cleanness may most appropriately be attained.'[51] The above study and the previous chapter on cult lead to the conclusion that Isaiah ben Amoz perceived YHWH's holiness as a cultic notion, and assessed the role of cult and ethics from this perspective.[52] In Vriezen's words, 'just as Isaiah's own life is exposed to the eyes of the Holy One, so he sees his people in their world *sub specie sanctitatis Dei.*'[53]

2.5.2. Holiness in DI

DI's use of YHWH's holiness is so different from PI that one wonders whether they speak of the same thing.[54] Ringgren believes that they do, insisting that DI does not introduce a new type of holiness, but his use of certain motifs (esp. of the great annual festival) resulted in a particular idea of God that 'coloured' his otherwise traditional conception of holiness.[55] This traditional conception might resemble the one of Isaiah ben Amoz,[56] but is much closer to the one presented in priestly literature. Gammie's observations point this way: in comparison with PI, he notices that 'with Isaiah of Babylon there is an increased use of priestly genre, notably the priestly oracle of salvation (Isa. 41:8-16; 43:1-7; 44:1-5; etc.) and the grounds for uncleanness are

---

51 Gammie, *Holiness*, 80 and 83.
52 Chapter 4 demonstrates how this conclusion applies to Isa 1:10-17.
53 Vriezen, "Theology of Isaiah," 146.
54 Thus, e.g., Hänel believes that DI works with a special concept of holiness, which he calls 'Jenseitsheiligkeit', Johannes Hänel, *Die Religion der Heiligkeit* (Gütersloh: C. Bertelsmann, 1931) 94.
55 Ringgren, *Prophetical Conception of Holiness*, 27-28.
56 Gammie claims that DI 'clearly both drew upon the theology of holiness of Isaiah of Jerusalem and creatively developed it.' He believes that besides the frequent use of the designation קדוש for deity, holiness in DI plays the same role in Israel's salvation history as in PI: 'judgment was purgative (cf. Isa. 48:10; 1:25), the city Jerusalem is holy (cf. Isa. 48:2; 52:1; 11:9), cleanness is enjoined (cf. Isa. 52:11-12; 1:16-17), and a restoration of cleanness is envisioned for the city (Isa. 52:1) just as Isaiah of Jerusalem had envisioned a restoration of faithfulness and righteousness (Isa. 1:26),' Gammie, *Holiness*, 97. However, as argued throughout the present thesis, Gammie's PI references are either editorial (1:26 and 11:9) or misinterpreted (1:25 and 1:16-17).

more priestly in orientation (Isa. 52:1),' and also that DI shares with the priestly tradition the idea of the relationship between holiness and creation (40:25-26, 41:20, 43:15, 45:11).[57] If the concept of holiness in PI was essentially cultic (as argued above), it is even more so in DI.

In contrast to PI, all the references to YHWH's holiness in DI occur in markedly positive contexts: YHWH as maker and creator (40:25; 41:20; 43:15; 45:11; 54:5), YHWH as saviour and redeemer (41:14; 43:3, 14; 47:4; 48:17; 49:7; 52:10; 54:5), and YHWH as the one in whom the people can rejoice and glory (41:16) and the one who has glorified them (55:5, פֵּאֲרָךְ). Not only is there no *tremendum* aspect and connection with judgment on Israel, but the people are repeatedly told not to fear because of the presence of קְדוֹשׁ יִשְׂרָאֵל (41:10-14; 43:1-5; see also 44:1-8; and 54:4-5). One feature that DI shares with Isaiah ben Amoz is that they both reserve the attribute קדשׁ exclusively for YHWH. The only exception is 52:1, where envisioned Jerusalem is called עִיר הַקֹּדֶשׁ.[58] Finally, DI's use of YHWH's כָּבוֹד is in accord with his use of holiness: YHWH does not give it to another (42:8 and 48:11), and when all people shall see it together, it will be a jubilant moment for the people of God (40:1-5), for those whom he created for his glory (43:7)

These observations raise a legitimate question about the reason behind such contrasting uses of YHWH's holiness in PI and DI. One way to look for the answer is to state the obvious – unlike Isaiah ben Amoz, DI did not have the same kind of encounter with YHWH's holiness as described in ch. 6. This is not to say that DI did not have any "first hand" exposure to YHWH's holiness, but that, if there were such (unrecorded ones), they took place under very different circumstances, namely that by his time the main cause for *tremendum* – impurity of the people and of the land – has already been dealt with via judgment. Williamson is therefore very likely correct that DI's use of קְדוֹשׁ יִשְׂרָאֵל is contrasting to PI's deliberately, being 'part of the way in which he emphasized God's new work of salvation in reversal of the older message of judgment.'[59]

---

57 Gammie, *Holiness*, 97-98. See also Joachim Begrich, "Das priestliche Heilsorakel," *ZAW* 52 (1934) 81-92.
58 The remaining uses of קדשׁ in 43:28 and 48:2 do not reflect DI's concept of holiness, but function as a rhetorical feature to emphasize the irony in the text. For 43:28, see 5.4.5.
59 Williamson, "Isaiah and Holy One of Israel," 38.

2.5.3. Holiness in TI

The picture of YHWH's holiness radically changes again in TI. The first striking difference in comparison with PI and DI is that there are only two texts where קָדֹשׁ is directly attributed to YHWH – 60:9 and 14, and, as has already been mentioned, even these uses are very likely due to the direct influence of DI. The closest to the notion of divine holiness that TI comes is 57:15, describing YHWH as the high and lofty one who inhabits eternity and whose name is holy, but this passage seems to depend heavily on Isa 6:1, the only other place in the OT that uses the identical phrase רָם וְנִשָּׂא.[60] God's holy spirit in 63:10 and 11 (רוּחַ קָדְשׁוֹ, used otherwise only in Ps 51:11) represents a category on its own. Otherwise, קָדֹשׁ in TI is used only for derivative holiness, attributed most frequently to places like God's holy mountain (56:7; 57:13; 65:11, 25; 66:20), a holy place of God's dwelling (57:15), the holy courts of the sanctuary (62:9), the holy temple (64:10), and holy cities (64:9), or to the Sabbath day (58:13), or to the people (62:12; 63:18).[61]

Just like קָדֹשׁ, YHWH's כָּבוֹד in TI is now much more "down to earth" and closely connected with God's people: it has risen upon them (60:1), will appear over them (60:2), ready to be their rear guard (58:8). The *tremendum* is now reserved for the nations, who will fear (ירא) YHWH's glory (59:19); it will be declared among them (66:19), and they will eventually see it (66:18).

Again, one can only speculate about the reason why TI's use of holiness is so markedly different from the previous parts of the book. The tentative suggestion is the same as in the case of DI – because of the transformed milieu. Purified people are back in a purified land, so YHWH's holiness and glory not only can be present, but also enjoyed, and even transferred to what has been purified. The primary conditions for eschatology have been met, and the possibility of its full realization presents a great excitement as well as a great concern for TI – purity must be preserved. This concern is reflected in the frequent use of derivative holiness in Isa 56-66.

---

60 There are other OT passages that come very close to expressing this idea. For the references and the detailed discussion of the possible influence of Isa 6:1 on the other Isaianic passages, see Williamson, *Book Called Isaiah*, 38-41. TI's addition to PI's picture, namely that YHWH not only dwells in the high and holy place but also with those who are contrite and humble in spirit, coincides with PI's idea of God being the only one exalted and humans being humble. As Barton remarks on this verse, 'Isaiah of Jerusalem would surely have applauded,' Barton, *OT Ethics*, 152.

61 As the context makes apparent, the uses of קָדֹשׁ for individuals in 65:5 and 66:17 do not represent TI's concept of holiness.

2.6. Conclusion

This discussion can be conveniently summarized by endorsing the statement from Ringgren that 'there is no essential difference between the prophets and, for instance, the books of law, as to the conception of holiness. The prophets obviously accepted the cultic notion of holiness, as it is preserved to us in the ritual laws of the Pentateuch.'[62] As the above survey has just shown, this statement holds true also for the book of Isaiah: even though each part of the book is concerned with a different aspect of holiness, this concept constantly emerges as a cultic notion, never contradicting, not even going beyond its priestly definition throughout the entire book. The emphasis on the different aspects of holiness in each part is intelligible against their different milieux.

---

62 Ringgren, *Prophetical Conception of Holiness*, 18. He additionally supports this conclusion by referring to Isa 30:29, 56:6 and 64:10, et al. He concludes his study with the statement that 'the notion of holiness seems to have been surprisingly constant' throughout the OT, adding that 'the ethical import of holiness is not fully developed until in the New Testament,' Ringgren, *Prophetical Conception of Holiness*, 30.

Chapter 3: Conception of the Land in the Book of Isaiah

3.1. Introduction

Von Rad in his influential essay on the ideology of the land in the Hexateuch distinguishes between what he calls historical and cultic conceptions of the land.[1] The historical conception consists of the events that led to and justified Israel's ownership of the land – from God's promise of the land of Canaan to Abraham to its conquest by Joshua. The cultic conception is based on the belief that YHWH is the true owner of the land, and it is in the light of this belief that the proscriptions of any kind of cultic defilement of the land, the regulations of the Sabbatical year or the Jubilee year, and the laws concerning firstlings, tenths, or gleanings are to be understood and interpreted. Since the defilement of the land plays an important part in the present thesis, the cultic conception of the land is the focus of this chapter. The purpose is to investigate a possibility that the Prophets in general and the book of Isaiah in particular reflect this conception. Before that, however, a brief outline of the cultic conception of the land in the Law is needed, for it is here where its major characteristics are most clearly defined.

3.2. Cultic Conception of the Land in the Law

The clearest expression of the cultic conception of the land is found in Leviticus and Numbers.[2] Here YHWH claims: 'The land is mine,' Lev

---

1   Gerhard von Rad, "The Promised Land and Yahweh's Land in the Hexateuch," in *The Problem of the Hexateuch and Other Essays* (Edinburgh; London: Oliver & Boyd, 1966).

2   Deuteronomy also warns against the human conduct that pollutes the land. Deut 21:23 says 'You must not defile (לֹא תְטַמֵּא) the land that the LORD your God is giving you as an inheritance (נַחֲלָה).' 24:4 is very similar; while its last part is identical with 21:23 (a phrase exclusive to Deuteronomy, occurring there eight times), the command reads 'you shall not bring guilt (לֹא תַחֲטִיא).' (LXX renders both commands as οὐ μιανεῖτε – 'you shall not defile'.) While it may seem that these verses add two new sources of the land's pollution, namely leaving a corpse on a tree over night and

25:23. He gave it to Israel 'for a possession' (לַאֲחֻזָּה), Lev 14:34, but he remains its ultimate owner. Being God's property, the land is considered holy.[3] Moreover, the land is the place where the holy God has chosen to dwell among his people, Lev 26:11-12 and Num 35:34.[4] For these reasons, its inhabitants must avoid those acts that have the capacity to affect the land's purity.[5] Failing to do so results in the kind of impurity for which no ritual can atone,[6] and when the defilement reaches the level that God's holiness can no longer tolerate, God forsakes his people and his land, withdrawing his protection and care.[7] As Zimmerli puts it, 'in the cultic defilement of God's land, Israel encroaches on God's own possession and compels him to pass judgement on people and land.'[8] Lev 18:24 -25 mentions a precedent for this 'mechanism': the nations that YHWH cast out before Israel practised the sort of things that defiled them *as well as* the land, so YHWH's punishment was that the land 'vomited out its inhabitants.' As Martens correctly observes at this point, these nations were removed from the

---

remarrying a wife who was married to another man, it is more likely that these cases are just derivatives of already mentioned sources, namely murder and adultery. For relating the corpse on a tree to a murder-like source of pollution, see S. R. Driver, *A Critical and Exegetical Commentary on Deuteronomy*, 3rd ed. (ICC; Edinburgh: T. & T. Clark, 1902) 284f. For relating the remarriage to adultery-like source of pollution, see W. D. Davies, *The Gospel and the Land: Early Christianity and Jewish Territorial Doctrine* (Berkeley; London: University of California Press, 1974) 32-34.

3   For a good discussion of the derivative holiness of the land, see Davies, *Gospel and Land*, 29-35. See also the chapter on Holiness, esp. 2.1. This derivativeness might account for the fact that the expression 'holy land' occurs only once in the Hebrew Bible, namely אַדְמַת הַקֹּדֶשׁ in Zech 2:12.

4   Wright observes that the Leviticus passage expresses YHWH's dwelling in the same manner as Gen 3:8 – the hithpael form of הלך ("stroll"), see C. J. H. Wright, "אֶרֶץ," *NIDOTTE* 1:519.

5   'You shall not defile the land in which you live, in which I also dwell; for I the LORD dwell among the Israelites,' Num 35:34.

6   The so called moral impurity (discussed in 1.2.2), caused, e.g., by murder: 'You shall not pollute the land in which you live; for blood pollutes the land, and no expiation can be made for the land, for the blood that is shed in it, except by the blood of the one who shed it,' Num 35:33.

7   Lipiński correctly points out that 'the notion of such a departure by a national god was by no means unique to the religious mentality of Israel. The Moabite Mesha Inscription (9th century) furnishes an excellent extrabiblical parallel: Mesha considers that Omri's conquest of Moab was caused ultimately by the national god, "for Chemosh was angry with his land,"' Lipiński, "נָחַל; נַחֲלָה," *TDOT* 9.332.

8   Walther Zimmerli, "The 'Land' in the Pre-Exilic and early Post-Exilic Prophets," in *Understanding the Word: Essays in Honor of Bernhard W. Anderson*, ed. James T. Butler, Edgar W. Conrad, and Ben C. Ollenburger (JSOTSup 37; Sheffield: JSOT Press, 1985) 254.

land because of things like sexual perversion or human sacrifice even though they did not possess a revealed Torah. This means that the land is rendered impure not because of its relation to Israel, but 'because of the close relationship of the land to Yahweh.'[9] In the case of Israel, however, there is one major difference: according to Lev 26:14-45, YHWH's judgment is not ultimate and the Israelites can eventually return to the land. As far as the land is concerned, the people's absence (the exile) has a purging effect – the land denuded of its people will get her rest and regain its holiness.[10] Von Waldow rightly concludes that 'in this context, the expulsion of Israel seems to be a cultic necessity.'[11]

3.3. Examples of Cultic Conception of the Land in the Prophets

Since the key texts for defining this conception come from H,[12] it may be argued that it is relatively late. However, von Rad (following Alt) believes that 'the fundamental notion expressed in Lev. xxv.23 is very ancient, and had cultic significance in ancient Israel.'[13] Certainly the idea of a god possessing a particular land and dwelling there had been known to Canaanite religion long before Yahwism.[14] It does not necessarily follow, however, that the Israelite tribes who had invaded Palestine adopted this idea by replacing Baal with YHWH.[15] Von Rad maintains that some of the very oldest commandments in the OT already imply YHWH's ownership of the land, and that the notion itself is an original part of Israelite religion.[16] He does not give any specific examples, but one of the OT earliest texts can be used in support: Ex 15:17 speaks of the mountain and the place that presumably refers to

---

9   E. A. Martens, *God's design: A Focus on Old Testament Theology*, 2nd ed. (Grand Rapids, MI, Leicester: Baker Book House, Apollos, 1994) 109.

10   On this idea, see especially Robert P. Carroll, "The Myth of the Empty Land," *Semeia* 59 (1992) 79-93. He, however, believes that 'a land empty over a lengthy period of time is simply a construct derived from the ideology of pollution-purity values in the second temple community.'

11   Hans Eberhard von Waldow, "Israel and Her Land: Some Theological Considerations," in *A Light unto My Path: Old Testament Studies in Honor of Jacob M. Myers*, ed. Carey A. Moore (Gettysburg Theological Studies 4; Philadelphia: Temple University Press, 1974) 506.

12   For assigning Num 35:33-34 to H see footnote 30.

13   Von Rad, "Promised Land," 85, see also 88-89.

14   As sufficiently demonstrated by R. E. Clements, *God and Temple* (Oxford: Blackwell, 1965).

15   Contra von Waldow, "Israel and Her Land," esp. 494.

16   See von Rad, "Promised Land," 88.

Canaan as YHWH's own נַחֲלָה.[17] Also the idea of certain practices of
people defiling the land and its consequences (as described, e.g., in the
above mentioned Lev 18), seems to be very ancient.[18] In any case, it is
very probable that the cultic conception of the land was hardly a
novelty in, let alone an invention of, the 8th century Israelite prophets.
What still remains to be seen is whether the prophets adhered to this
conception, and what role it played in their message. Before turning to
Isaiah, brief examples from some other prophets serve to prepare the
ground.

3.3.1. Hosea

The cultic conception of the land in Hosea has been most advanced by
Braaten, who demonstrated the importance of the story of God's
relationship with the land in this prophetic book.[19] His claim that אֶרֶץ
in Hos 1-2 does not connote God's people but the land *per se* and his
identification of the bride in 2:4-13 and 18-23 as the land further
amplify the presence of this conception in Hosea:

— The land belongs to YHWH (אֶרֶץ יְהוָה, in 9:3) and it is his
  house(hold) (בֵּית יְהוָה in 8:1, same idea in 9:15).

---

17 See, e.g., the note on this verse in NET or E. Lipiński, "נַחֲלָה ;נָחַל," *TDOT* 9.333.
    Lipiński persuasively argues that נַחֲלָה refers to a possession acquired by inheritance,
    not by some other transaction (for which the noun אֲחֻזָּה is reserved). This notion
    presents no problem when the text speaks of the land as Israel's or Jacob's נַחֲלָה, for,
    as Lipiński points out, Israel is often pictured as YHWH's son who received this
    glorious inheritance from his (heavenly) father. It is rather dubious when the land or
    the people are designated as YHWH's נַחֲלָה. Lipiński, among others, believes that this
    idea 'is of mythological origin and goes back to the notion of the division of the
    nations or their lands among the sons of the gods,' as reflected in Deut 32:8-9 and Ps
    82:6. This hypothesis is attractive, but, as Lipiński himself recognizes, far from
    trouble-free. Goldingay, following Habel, prefers the translation 'entitlement',
    claiming that the traditional 'inheritance' for נַחֲלָה 'is misleading; the word does not
    intrinsically refer to land as passed down within families, but to land as the rightful
    possession of those who live on it,' John Goldingay, *Old Testament Theology, vol. 1:
    Israel's Gospel* (Downers Grove, IL: InterVarsity Press, 2003) 516-517. When it comes
    to the Prophets, Lipiński's suggestion to read the references to YHWH's נַחֲלָה
    figuratively is to be preferred: 'The use of this figurative expression does not
    emphasize the transfer or inheritance of property, but rather the constant, enduring
    nature of its possession,' Lipiński, "נַחֲלָה ;נָחַל," *TDOT* 9.331.
18 See, e.g., von Waldow, "Israel and Her Land," 503.
19 Laurie J. Braaten, "Earth Community in Hosea 2," in *The Earth Story in the Psalms and
    the Prophets*, ed. Norman C. Habel (Earth Bible 4; Sheffield: Sheffield Academic,
    2001).

— The people commit idolatry along with whoredom (2:8, 4:12-14, 5:3-7, 9:1, 11:2, 13:1-2) and bloodshed (1:4, 4:2, 6:8, 12:14), thus defiling not only themselves (5:3, 6:10, 9:4) but also the land, turning YHWH's bride into a whore (1:2, 2:4-7).[20]

— YHWH, therefore, decides to bring judgment upon the land and the people – the land will be completely stripped of all its attractiveness (2:11-15) and of her inhabitants, who will be taken to exile (8:8-10, 9:3-6 and 15).

— This judgment, however, has a purging effect, making the reconciliation between YHWH, the land and the people possible (2:17-25).

Even though some of Braaten's interpretation of Hosea's imagery can be questioned,[21] there can hardly be any doubt that the cultic conception of the land as presented in the Law is operative in the book of Hosea.

3.3.2. Jeremiah

When it comes to the Prophets, the cultic conception of the land is at its best in the book of Jeremiah. 2:7 describes the situation from YHWH's point of view: 'I brought you into a plentiful land to eat its fruits and its good things. But when you entered you defiled (וַתְּטַמְּאוּ) my land, and made my heritage (נַחֲלָתִי) an abomination (תוֹעֵבָה).'[22] As Habel comments on this verse, 'it is not the violation of God's covenant law code that is emphasized, but the defilement of God's precious personal

---

20 The same idea is expressed in Ps 106:38-39.

21 Braaten's identification of the wife in the marriage metaphor of Hos 2 with the land runs against the consensus view that the wife there represents the people of Israel. For a recent list of scholars who hold this consensus and its sharp repudiation, see Brad E. Kelle, *Hosea 2: Metaphor and Rhetoric in Historical Perspective* (Academia Biblica 20; Leiden, Boston: Brill, 2005) 82-83. Kelle, however, disagrees also with Braaten and others who interpret the wife as the land, but his arguments at this point are dubious. In any case, his suggestion to identify the wife of Hos 2 with Samaria, the capital of the Northern Kingdom in the time of Hosea, does not seriously affect the point above for two reasons: first, a city or a mountain in Israelite religion can epitomize a whole land (as argued below, 3.4), and, second, there is enough evidence besides ch. 2 to support the cultic conception of the land in the book of Hosea.

22 Similarly 12:10-11.

property.'[23] 16:18 speaks about the severe consequences of this defilement and specifies its source: 'I will doubly repay their iniquity and their sin, because they have polluted (חִלְּלוּ) my land with the carcasses of their detestable idols, and have filled my inheritance (נַחֲלָתִי) with their abominations (תוֹעֲבוֹתֵיהֶם).'[24] 3:1 seems to suggest that this defilement has reached its limit, and Israel has passed the point of no return: 'If a man divorces his wife and she goes from him and becomes another man's wife, will he return to her? Would not such a land be greatly polluted? You have played the whore with many lovers; and would you return to me? says the LORD.'[25]

Jeremiah refers not only to the land, but also to the people of Judah as YHWH's נַחֲלָה, thus creating an ambiguity similar to Hosea's imagery of YHWH's bride. Zimmerli believes that this ambiguity is intentional; commenting on 12:7-11, he claims that 'it is in the use of this designation to refer almost indistinguishably to the land and to the people that the close connection between this, God's land, and the people called by God is recognized.'[26] Indeed, Jeremiah is very concerned not only about the land's purity, but also about the purity of the people. Ch. 2 identifies some of the sources of their impurity. The question in v. 2 'How can you say, "I am not defiled, I have not gone after the Baals?"' implies that the idea of defilement by illegitimate cultic practices was known to the people, and most of the chapter

---

23   Norman C. Habel, *The Land is Mine: Six Biblical Land Ideologies* (Overtures to Biblical Theology; Minneapolis: Fortress Press, 1995) 80. The focus of 4:19-20 on the land indicates that Jeremiah's concern was essentially the same. Habel concludes that 'this portrait of the overwhelming pain of God's prophet is not focused on the fate of the foolish people who have provoked this disaster, but on the precious land of YHWH that suffers such ugly devastation,' Habel, *The Land is Mine*, 87.

24   Besides idolatry, Jeremiah intensifies the picture of the land's pollution by mentioning the carcasses (נְבֵלָה), of which Lev 21:23 specifically says that they pollute the land. Notice also the use of מלא with תוֹעֵבוֹת.

25   A majority of contemporary scholars reads the expression וְשׁוֹב אֵלַי at the end of this verse as a question that renders the possibility of Israel's return to YHWH impossible because of her defilement. The simple infinitive absolute here allows for other readings, including the imperative 'Yet return to me!' (see, e.g., KJV or NAB). Thompson, however, is likely correct that this reading 'is out of harmony with the whole tenor of the passage,' J. A. Thompson, *The Book of Jeremiah* (NICOT; Grand Rapids: Eerdmans, 1980) 192. In any case, this verse shows that the cultic conception of the land in Jeremiah is in accord with the Law, namely Deut 24:1-4.

26   Zimmerli, "The Land," 253-254. Similarly, Habel believes that 'the repeated use of the term נַחֲלָה in this passage ... seems to be deliberately ambiguous and further underscore the symbiotic dimension of the land-god-people relationship,' Habel, *The Land is Mine*, 85.

describes the explicit or implicit idolatry.[27] Furthermore, vv. 33b-34 identify the people's ethical misconduct as another source of their pollution. Even though the ambiguities of this text allow for various readings,[28] its point is to add to idolatry another evil that defiles Judah, namely murder. Holladay suggests that the text 'on your skirts is found the lifeblood of the innocent poor' in v. 34 recalls v. 22 where the people were trying as it were to wash off the stain of their guilt with lye and soap.[29] However, blood pollution is deadly serious, and YHWH informs them in this verse that this washing is in vain – 'your guilt is still before me.'[30] As a result, YHWH has abandoned and even hates his נַחֲלָה, giving it into the hands of the enemies (12:7-8). According to Jeremiah, YHWH appointed the Babylonians (21:4-10; 25:8-14; 29:4-7) to purge and clear his נַחֲלָה – to cut off (הִשְׁבִּית) the people from the land and take them to exile (36:29). The Chronicler interprets Jeremiah's prediction of seventy years of exile (29:10 and 25:11) as the time the land needed 'to make up for its sabbaths' (2 Chr 36:21). The people in exile will also be transformed; they will know YHWH, because he will write his law on their hearts (Jer 31:33).[31] They are the good figs (24:5) with which the purified land will be replanted (v. 6, cf. 31:27-28 and 32:41) and of which YHWH says 'they shall be my people and I will be

---

27 The implicit idolatry was, e.g., Judah's political alliances with Egypt or Assyria, for, according to 2:13-19, they effectively meant forsaking YHWH. As Habel rightly comments, 2:13-19 reflects 'the belief that becoming involved in seeking aid from foreign powers was tantamount to idolatry, whether or not the recognition of specific deities was part of the deal,' Habel, *The Land is Mine*, 84. This notion is characteristic of (and the reason for?) PI's political discourses.

28 Holladay's reading of 2:33-34 requires at least three revocalizations and two emendations, supported mostly by LXX only, see William Lee Holladay, *Jeremiah 1: A Commentary on the Book of the Prophet Jeremiah, Chapters 1-25* (Hermeneia; Philadelphia: Fortress Press, 1986) 56, 109-110. Nevertheless, it remains very attractive, and, if correct, it brings out the full force of the text's ethical focus. Even if MT is retained, social justice can still be considered as the main theme of this text, as recently demonstrated by Jack R. Lundbom, *Jeremiah 1-20: A New Translation with Introduction and Commentary* (AB 21A; New York, London: Doubleday, 1999) 293-297.

29 Holladay, *Jeremiah 1*, 110.

30 In 4:14, the people, symbolized by Jerusalem, are asked the very thing of which they are, according to 2:22, incapable (the only uses of כבס in Jeremiah). The reason for this contrasting use of images may be the speakers; v. 2:22 is נְאֻם אֲדֹנָי יְהוִה, whereas 4:14 is 'the mediating word from Jrm: now the prophet acts to intercede with the people,' Holladay, *Jeremiah 1*, 157. As Thompson comments on this verse, 'even though judgment was at the doors, it would seem that Jeremiah never thought an appeal to repent was too late,' Thompson, *Jeremiah*, 225.

31 From this follows that 'YHWH's action is not based on their intrinsic goodness, their remarkable change of heart, or their potential as the "educated" of the community, but on YHWH's grace,' Habel, *The Land is Mine*, 95.

their God,' (v. 7). A holy God can enter again into a relationship with his purified נַחֲלָה, establishing a new covenant with her (31:31-34). 'The new order will be possible in the redeemed land because all the people will have the knowledge of God in their hearts.'[32]

3.3.3. Ezekiel

As expected of a prophet with a priestly background, cultic pollution is of much concern to Ezekiel: he frequently mentions the defilement of the people, whether as individuals (4:13f; 18:6ff; 22:10-11) or as a whole (14:11; 20:7, 18, 26, 30-31, 43; 23:7, 13, 17, 30; 33:26; 37:23; 44:25), of the sanctuary (5:11; 9:7; 23:38-39; 24:21; 25:3; 44:7), and of the city (22:3-5). Pollution in Ezekiel expands to various things (7:20ff; 28:7; 22:26), to sabbaths (20:13, 16, 21, 24; 22:8; 23:38), and even to YHWH himself (13:19; 22:26), who, in response, also acts as the agent of pollution (7:20; 20:26; 24:21). In the light of this evidence, the lack of references to the defilement of the land is striking. To be sure, Ezekiel frequently mentions the land;[33] not only in connection with the envisioned glorious future,[34] but also remembering it as 'the most glorious (צְבִי) of all lands' that YHWH has chosen for his people (20:6). Defilement is a central theme of this chapter, but the idea of the land's pollution seems to be replaced by the references to the defilement of the sabbaths and of YHWH's holy name.[35] Correspondingly, YHWH does not act for the sake of his נַחֲלָה (as in Jeremiah), but for the sake of his own name (e.g., 36:22 and 32, cf. Isa 43:25). An explanation lies readily to hand: because Ezekiel talks to the people who are in the land of Babylon, the pressing issue is the purity of YHWH's name and his sabbaths rather than the purity of the land.

Nevertheless, Ezekiel's retrospective in 36:17-18 clearly shows that he also adheres to the cultic conception of the land:

---

32   Habel, *The Land is Mine*, 93.

33   Besides the usual expressions, he also uses אַדְמַת יִשְׂרָאֵל – a designation unique to this book.

34   E.g., Ezek 17:22-23; 36:24-38. As Davies observes, 'the ingathering of all scattered Israelites in the land is a constant theme of Ezekiel,' Davies, *Gospel and Land*, 45.

35   The expressoin שֵׁם קָדְשִׁי can also be considered characteristic of Ezekiel; it occurs in this book 8 times (20:39; 36:20ff; 39:7, 25; 43:7f) and only 4 times elsewhere (Lev 20:3; 22:2, 32; Amos 2:7). Except Ezek 39:25 where God is said to be jealous for his holy name, this expression is always connected with the idea of profaning (חלל) or defiling (טמא) it. In contrast, Jeremiah explicitly mentions profaning God's name only once – 34:16.

> Mortal, when the house of Israel lived on their own soil, they defiled it with their ways and their deeds; their conduct in my sight was like the uncleanness of a woman in her menstrual period. So I poured out my wrath upon them for the blood that they had shed upon the land, and for the idols with which they had defiled it.

And to those remaining in the land, for whom the ownership of the land is still high on the agenda, Ezekiel addresses the rebuke that reflects the same conception:

> Therefore say to them, Thus says the Lord GOD: You eat flesh with the blood, and lift up your eyes to your idols, and shed blood; shall you then possess the land? You depend on your swords, you commit abominations, and each of you defiles his neighbor's wife; shall you then possess the land? (33:25-26)

As Zimmerli comments on this passage, 'in the concrete unfolding of the commandment we recognize the priest, who has the ritual prescriptions for purity before him.'[36]

The conclusion based on this short survey is that the cultic conception of the land as defined in the Law is very much present and operative in the message of Hosea, Jeremiah, and Ezekiel. It is, therefore, legitimate to anticipate it in the book of Isaiah.

3.4. Land in the Book of Isaiah

Starting from what appears to be the latest unit, the clearest expression of the cultic conception of the land in the book of Isaiah is found in the so-called 'Isaiah Apocalypse', chs. 24-27. 24:5 spells out the reason for the impending judgment: 'The earth lies polluted under its inhabitants; for they have transgressed laws, violated the statutes, broken the everlasting covenant.' The use of the rare verb חָנֵף ('to be polluted') here is significant: the only time this verb is used in the Law is in one of the key texts for the cultic conception of the land – its pollution in Num 35:33 – and, except Dan 11:32, it retains this sense throughout the OT (Jer 3:1, 2, 9; 23:11;[37] Mic 4:11; Ps 106:38). As the uses of this root show, חָנֵף comprises a cultic ingredient intolerable to the presence of the holy

---

36 Zimmerli, "The Land," 257-258.

37 חָנֵף in Jer 23:11 refers to prophets and priests, but its translation in NRSV as 'ungodly' is unjustified, probably an (anachronistic) import of this meaning by the translators from the book of Job. Here it should be also rendered as 'polluted', keeping in mind v. 15, where the same root is used in a noun form (חֲנֻפָּה) in connection with the land.

God.[38] Also the use of the phrase בְּרִית עוֹלָם in this verse is noteworthy. It is not vital for the purpose of this discussion to determine to which of the OT covenants this phrase here refers.[39] As argued already by Sweeney, the author of Isa 24-27 tends to use traditional concepts in a new way, namely 'one that looks toward the universal or cosmic significance of God's punishment of the earth and his restoration of Israel in Zion.'[40] This means that, even though the overall context favours the identification of בְּרִית עוֹלָם in v. 5 with the Noachic covenant,[41] the author very likely used also some of the characteristics of the Mosaic covenant[42] (or the Davidic covenant) and universalized them.[43] Even Hibbard, who most recently argued that this phrase here is 'primarily related to the covenant with Noah,' allows for the possibility that 'the author has also been influenced by covenantal language and ideology drawn from elsewhere in the Hebrew Bible.'[44] To look for these concepts requires reading that goes beneath the surface (in this case universalistic) reading of the text. This reading uncovers the cultic conception of the land as defined in P governing Isa 24:5-6:[45] 'The land (הָאָרֶץ) lies polluted (חָנְפָה) under its inhabitants; for they have transgressed laws, violated the statutes, broken (הֵפֵרוּ) the

---

38   For more details, see K. Seybold, "חָנֵף," *TDOT* 5.36-44.

39   While the expression בְּרִית עוֹלָם describes the Noachic covenant in Gen 9:16, elsewhere it refers to the covenants with Abraham (Ps 105:9-10 // 1 Chr 16:16-17) or David (2 Sam 23:5), or to the new covenant that God promises to make with his people (Isa 55:3; Jer 32:40 and 50:5; Ezek 16:60 and 37:26), so to which covenant Isa 24:5 alludes has to be decided on other grounds.

40   Marvin A. Sweeney, "Textual Citations in Isaiah 24-27: Toward an Understanding of the Redactional Function of Chapters 24-27 in the Book of Isaiah," *JBL* 107 (1988) 39-52: 51.

41   See, e.g., Joseph Blenkinsopp, "Cityscape to Landscape: The 'Back to Nature' Theme in Isaiah 1-35," in *'Every City Shall be Forsaken': Urbanism and Prophecy in Ancient Israel and the Near East*, ed. Robert D. Haak and Lester L. Grabbe (JSOTSup 330; Sheffield: Sheffield Academic Press, 2001) 43.

42   For the identification of בְּרִית עוֹלָם in Isa 24:5 with the Mosaic covenant, see, e.g., Dan G. Johnson, *From Chaos to Restoration: An Integrative Reading of Isaiah 24-27* (JSOTSup 61; Sheffield: JSOT Press, 1988) 27-29.

43   The most elaborate argument of this sort comes from Donald C. Polaski, *Authorizing an End: The Isaiah Apocalypse and Intertextuality*, vol. 50 (Biblical Interpretation Series; Leiden: Brill, 2001).

44   James Todd Hibbard, *Intertextuality in Isaiah 24-27: The Reuse and Evocation of Earlier Texts and Traditions* (FAT 16; Tübingen: Mohr Siebeck, 2006) 68.

45   For P pre-dating and being in some form available to the author of Isa 24-27, see Hibbard, *Intertextuality*, 56-64.

ancient covenant (בְּרִית עוֹלָם).[46] Therefore a curse (אָלָה) devours the land (אֶרֶץ)...' At this level of reading, it should be observed that it is the Mosaic covenant breaking of which is explicitly warded off by curses (אָלוֹת הַבְּרִית, Deut 29:20). Accordingly, the term אֶרֶץ should not be rendered at this level as 'the earth' in the sense of 'the world', but as 'the land' in the sense of *orbis Israeliticus*, for it is only from this sphere that the above-mentioned concepts derive their validity. Johnson seems to be on the right track here when concluding that the religious context of this text suggests 'tradition similar to that of Jer. 3.2, 9 and Ps. 106.38 where idolatry and religious harlotry are the cause of the pollution of the land.'[47] Apparently, this tradition is governed by the cultic conception of the land.[48]

Further reading of Isa 24-27 only confirms this impression. The land suffers because 'its sin lies heavy upon it' (24:20). When the judgment comes, 'the land will disclose the blood shed on it, and will no longer cover its slain' (26:21). The purging effect of the judgment that is implicit here is explicit in 27:8-9:

> By expulsion, by exile you struggled against them; ... Therefore by this the guilt of Jacob will be expiated, and this will be the full fruit of the removal of his sin: when he makes all the stones of the altars like chalkstones crushed to pieces, no sacred poles or incense altars will remain standing.

There are several obscurities in this passage, as its different renderings in various OT translations make clear. Nevertheless, it is safe to conclude that these verses convey the idea that YHWH's judgment purifies the people and the land in a cultic sense.[49] Finally, the grand

---

46 For translating בְּרִית עוֹלָם here as 'the ancient covenant', see Jon Douglas Levenson, *Creation and the Persistence of Evil: The Jewish Drama of Divine Omnipotence* (San Francisco, London: Harper & Row, 1988) 27. Cmp. חָרְבוֹת עוֹלָם ('the ancient ruins') in Isa 58:12, 6.5.10.

47 Johnson, *Chaos*, 29.

48 Hayes lists 24:4-5 as one of the examples that the author (according to him Isaiah of the 8th century) was familiar with priestly theology, namely 'impurity/defilement and purity/cleanliness,' John Haralson Hayes and Stuart A. Irvine, *Isaiah, the Eighth Century Prophet: His Times & His Preaching* (Nashville: Abingdon Press, 1987) 57.

49 A few observations in support of this conclusion should suffice: Sweeney believes that the introductory לָכֵן of v. 9 presents the outcome of the situation in v. 8, so 'the purpose of the exile as expiation of sin is stated explicitly in v. 9a,' Sweeney, *Isaiah 1-39*, 348. The note on this verse in NET suggests that כֻּפַּר in the first line should be understood in a sarcastic sense – 'Jacob's sin is "atoned for" and removed through severe judgment.' As correctly pointed out, 'this interpretation is more consistent with the tone of judgment in vv. 8 and 10-11.' The emendation proposed in BHS, namely that כָּל־פְּרִי may be a corruption of לְכַפֵּר, which in turn might be a gloss on the following הָסֵר, could be used as another support for this reading, but, in spite of its attractiveness (mainly due to its suitability for the present thesis), this reading

finale of the Isaiah Apocalypse fully endorses the cultic conception of
the land in this section of the book of Isaiah: the exiles will return to
their homeland and 'worship the LORD on the holy mountain at
Jerusalem' (27:13).

The reference to the holy mountain brings up another point
important for the quest for the cultic conception of the land in the rest
of the book of Isaiah. Even though the land plays a very important role
throughout the book, the cultic concepts relate predominantly to mount
Zion, the city of Jerusalem. This fact, however, does not frustrate the
quest, because, as Clements sufficiently demonstrated, the idea that a
mountain as a dwelling-place of a god epitomized a whole land or even
the whole world or cosmos was a common idea not only in Israelite
religion, but also in the religions of the Ancient Near East.[50] Clements
also points out that this idea must have been very ancient in Israel, for
it is found in texts like the Song of Miriam (Exod 15:13-18) or Ps 78:51-
55. Moreover, mount Zion was not only symbolic of YHWH's land, but
was also 'the means through which [YHWH's] blessing flowed out to
it.'[51] Of course, this blessing resulted from YHWH's presence on this
mount, symbolized by the temple. If the concept of YHWH's presence
and of the holiness that derives from it applied to the land, it applied
even more so to mount Zion and Jerusalem.

If Zion/Jerusalem passages are not included, the examples of the
cultic conception of the land in PI are present only implicitly in
passages like 1:5-9 where the condition of the land is understood as the
consequence of sin,[52] or where the vision of the future of the new

---

must be resisted, because it breaks up a strong parallelism between 9a and 9b
(indicated by the two deictics בְּזֹאת and וְזֶה and a semantic link between עֲוֹן־יַעֲקֹב and
חַטָּאתוֹ). A recent suggestion of Leene seems to do more justice to the syntax of the
text, it does not require any emendations, and it still retains the idea of the expiatory
effect of the judgment, carried out solely by YHWH: he simply assigns the actant of v.
9b to YHWH, so it is he who 'makes all the stones of the altars like chalkstones ...' For
details, see Hendrik Leene, "Isaiah 27:7-9 as a Bridge between Vineyard and City," in
Studies in Isaiah 24-27, ed. Hendrik Jan Bosman and Harm van Grol (OTS 43; Leiden:
Brill, 2000).

50   See Clements, *God and Temple*, passim. In addition, see a more recent survey of this
idea with the same conclusion by Martti Nissinen, "City as Lofty as Heaven: Arbela
and other Cities in Neo-Assyrian Prophecy," in *'Every City Shall be Forsaken':*
Urbanism and Prophecy in Ancient Israel and the Near East, ed. Robert D. Haak and
Lester L. Grabbe (JSOTSup 330; Sheffield: Sheffield Academic Press, 2001). For the
OT references to this idea, see D. P. Wright, "Holiness," *ABD* 3.243.

51   Clements, *God and Temple*, 51-55 and 85.

52   It may be of significance that the phrase אַרְצְכֶם שְׁמָמָה in v. 7 can elsewhere be found
only in the key passage on the cultic conception of the land – Lev 26:14-45 (v. 33).
The expression שְׁמָמָה along with the whole concept appears most frequently in

kingdom in 9:6 implies the restored land.[53] The cultic conception of the land can also be assumed in Isa 5, where the crime of the rich landowners in Isa 5 who 'accumulate house to house and add field to field' (v. 8) was, according to Premnath, 'a violation of the sacred ordinance, the principle of distribution of land under Yahweh's ultimate ownership.'[54] However, once mount Zion/Jerusalem is substituted for the land, its cultic conception in PI is much more obvious. Isaiah ben Amoz clearly believes that that is where YHWH lives (e.g., 8:18, 18:7, or 31:9). To his horror, this city, once full of justice and righteousness, has become a whore (1:21), and the whole land is 'filled with idols' (2:6b-8a). This impurity (1:22) is irreconcilable with YHWH's presence (3:8), and in the light of such a pollution, YHWH's presence in this city takes on different significance – his fire is in Zion, his furnace in Jerusalem (31:9), and the judgment becomes inevitable (8:5-8, 10:11, 31:4). As a result, Jerusalem will be purified (1:25), suitable to become בֵּית אֱלֹהֵי יַעֲקֹב, הַר־יְהוָה, הַר בֵּית־יְהוָה, or (2:2-3). As correctly noted by Zimmerli, '[Isaiah's] conception of the land is shaped by his familiarity with Zion as the site of God's presence.'[55]

It was very likely the redactor(s) of PI who adjoined the landscape to Isaiah's cityscape. At this level, the cultic conception of the land is very clear: YHWH's ownership of the land is expressed by אַדְמַת יְהוָה in 14:2,[56] and he refers to the land of Judah as אַרְצִי (parallel to הָרַי) in 14:25. The question "Who among us can coexist (יָגוּר) with destructive fire? Who among us can coexist with unquenchable fire?" (33:14, NET) indicates that a cleansing in the form of judgment is necessary.[57] 'Once

---

Jeremiah (4:27, 6:8, 9:10, 10:22, 12:10-11, 34:22, reversed in 32:43) and Ezekiel (6:14, 12:20, 14:15-16, 15:8, 33:28-29, reversed in 36:34), but also in Isa 1:7, 6:11-12, 64:9, and reversed in 49:8,19 and 62:4.

53   The significance of these passages for Isaiah's theology of the land is pointed out by Davies, *Gospel and Land*, 42-43.

54   D. N. Premnath, "Latifundialization and Isaiah 5.8-10," *JSOT* 40 (1988) 49-60: 56.

55   Zimmerli, "The Land," 249. In addition, according to Clements, 'this particular prominence of Jerusalem and its temple in Isaiah's prophecies can be traced back to his call vision, which took place in the temple,' Clements, *God and Temple*, 80.

56   For attributing this verse to a redactor (probably DI), see Williamson, *Book Called Isaiah*, 162-167.

57   Interestingly, this question is asked by so called חֲנֵפִים – the adjectival form of the verb characteristically used for land pollution (as discussed above). The book of Job offers a perspective from which a חָנֵף 'stands outside the sacred precincts', K. Seybold, "חָנֵף," *TDOT* 5.43. In Isa 33, the solution to the dilemma is ethical (v. 15), just like 1:16-17, but, as the subsequent events show, this solution is only theoretical. For attributing these verses to a redactor (probably DI), see Williamson, *Book Called Isaiah*, 221-239.

the Lord has washed away the filth of the daughters of Zion and
cleansed the bloodstains of Jerusalem from its midst by a spirit of
judgment and by a spirit of burning' (4:4), complete restoration can
take place (4:2-6).[58] YHWH's presence will be continuously manifested at
mount Zion (4:5, 12:6), Jerusalem will be called the city of
righteousness, the faithful city (1:26), and the land 'will be full of the
knowledge of the LORD' (11:9). Clearly the redactor(s) make the cultic
conception of the land in PI more explicit.[59] To evaluate the theological
adequacy of these additions, however, would be rather presumptuous,
for, as von Rad cautions us, 'how may we determine the rightness or
wrongness of such subsequent actualizations of old Isaianic
prophecy?'[60]

In DI, YHWH is presented as 'the God of the whole earth' (אֱלֹהֵי
כָל־הָאָרֶץ, 54:5), but, since his universal ownership and lordship will be
demonstrated mainly in bringing his people from Babylon back to their
homeland, the main focus is again on Zion/Jerusalem. YHWH has
afflicted Zion with 'devastation and destruction, famine and sword'
(51:19). Zion's desperate situation is best captured in her saying:
"YHWH has forsaken me, my Lord has forgotten me" (49:14). YHWH,
however, affirms his affection toward her, promising her a glorious
future (49:15-26). He will return to her (40:9, 52:8), take her back as his
wife (54:5-8), rebuild and revive her (44:26, 45:13), so she will become
'like Eden', 'like the garden of YHWH' (51:3). In 52:1, YHWH promises to
protect her purity – 'the uncircumcised and the unclean shall enter you
no more.' DI describes the situation of the people analogously: because
of their sins and transgressions, YHWH claims "I was angry with my
people, I profaned (חִלַּלְתִּי) my heritage (נַחֲלָתִי)" (47:6, similarly in 42:24
and 43:22-28). In the exile, he refined them (צרף, 48:10, as in 1:25),
blotting out their transgressions and not remembering their sins
(43:25).[61] These purified people are then called in 49:8 'to establish the

---

58 Also v. 4 is listed by Hayes as an example of author's familiarity with the priestly
theology of purity/impurity, see Hayes and Irvine, *Isaiah*, 57. For attributing this
passage to a post-exilic redactor, see Williamson, *Isaiah 1-27*, 305-306.
59 As Williamson suggests in his comment on 4:4-5a, this may reflect the emphasis of
the Ezra/Nehemiah reforms on purity, adding that this observation does not exclude
an even later dating, Williamson, *Isaiah 1-27*, 306. While this is certainly a good
possibility, the instances above show that the purity of the people, the land, or the
city was on the prophetic agenda even before the exile, so the reference to it should
not be included among the arguments for the late dating of a particular text.
60 Gerhard von Rad, *Old Testament Theology*, trans. David Muir Gibson Stalker (New
York: Harper & Row, 1965) 2.168.
61 In both texts, YHWH emphatically claims to do this 'for his own sake' (לְמַעֲנִי, 48:11
and 43:25).

land, to apportion the desolate heritages (לְהַנְחִיל נְחָלוֹת שֹׁמֵמוֹת).' Even
though still in ruins, Jerusalem has been redeemed (52:9). People are to
depart from unclean Babylon and return there, and, since they are to be
closely accompanied by YHWH, their purity is required (52:11-12). Ch.
54 describes the glorious symbiosis of Jerusalem, Israelites, and YHWH.
The Holy One of Israel can again dwell in Jerusalem in the midst of his
people because all the impurity has been removed.

One more interesting expression of the cultic conception in DI
should be mentioned. In 40:2, it is said of Jerusalem that נִרְצָה עֲוֹנָהּ. OT
exegetes struggle with the meaning of this phrase.[62] They often note
that the combination of רצה with עָוֹן occurs only here and in Lev 26:41
and 43,[63] which, as pointed out above, is a key passage for
understanding the exile as the purification of the land and the people:
the land תִּרְצֶה for its sabbaths while it is made desolate (בְּהֳשַׁמָּה)[64] and
without the people who יִרְצוּ אֶת־עֲוֹנָם. While the rendering of רצה in
this text is also far from unanimous,[65] it certainly functions as a cultic
term. There is, therefore, no reason to obliterate this cultic sense in Isa
40:2 by renderings like 'her penalty is paid' (NRS) or 'her punishment
is completed' (NET), and the translation 'her guilt has been atoned for'
(NJB) is preferable. Geller is very likely correct that, since the niphal of

---

62 Compare, e.g., 'her penalty is paid' (NRSV) with 'her iniquity has been removed'
    (NAS) or 'her punishment is completed' (NET) or 'her guilt has been atoned for'
    (NJB).

63 On the basis of this unique combination of vocabulary, some scholars even argue for
    a direct influence between Isa 40:2 and Lev 26:41. Thus, e.g., Levine believes that
    Leviticus has borrowed this combination from DI, see Baruch A. Levine, *Leviticus*
    (Philadelphia: Jewish Publication Society, 1989) 279. Milgrom, on the other hand,
    claims that Isaiah of the exile was the actual borrower from Leviticus, see Milgrom,
    Leviticus 23-27, 2333 and 2363. This issue has no bearing on the present argument, so
    it does not need to be resolved here.

64 As the comparison with v. 34 clarifies, the preposition בְּ in this expression is
    temporal (so correctly NAS or NET), not of means or instrument as understood by
    NRSV.

65 The rendering of NRSV as 'to enjoy' in case of the land and 'to make amends' in case
    of the people presupposes a play upon the root רצה in this verse, cf. Peter R.
    Ackroyd, *Exile and Restoration: A Study of Hebrew Thought of the Sixth Century B.C.*
    (OTL; London: SCM, 1968) 241-242. While the possibility of a word play here is
    certainly possible, the idea that the land would 'enjoy' its sabbaths בְּהֳשַׁמָּה is
    paradoxical and rather forced. Hossfeld seems to be closer to the mark with
    suggesting the term 'accept' for רצה of the land, meaning that 'the land must accept
    involuntary sabbath years on account of the many sabbath years incurred as a debt
    during the period before the exile,' F.L. Hossfeld "רצה," *TDOT* 13.625. In this study,
    Hossfeld also sufficiently demonstrated that there is no reason to postulate רצה II
    ('to pay, redeem' or 'to restore') as listed in Gesenius-B or *HALOT* to account for the
    unclear meaning of this root in Lev 26:34, 41, 43 and Isa 40:2.

רצה is 'an overtly cultic term,' its use in Isa 40:2 'implies that the exile was a time of purification.'[66] In connection with this, the question what does Jerusalem in this text represent needs to be briefly addressed. While the previously common opinion that Jerusalem here is a metaphor for the exiled people has been sufficiently repudiated,[67] a number of commentators still think that Jerusalem in 40:2 does not stand for the real city, but, by metonymy, for the people mentioned in the previous line – the Israelites in general.[68] The argument, of course, is the parallelism between vv. 1 and 2a, but it does not necessarily follow that 'my people' and 'Jerusalem' are synonymous.[69] For instance, Isa 52:9 and 65:19 also parallel Jerusalem with the people without equating the two. Moreover, there is little support for this metonymy in the rest of DI; in fact, the other passages that mention Jerusalem (40:9, 41:27, 44:26-28, 51:17, 52:1-2 and 9) suggest that it stands for the city itself. It seems, therefore, safe to conclude that, just as the land in Lev 26 is a real geographical entity, Jerusalem in Isa 40 is a real city.[70]

---

66   Stephen A. Geller, "A Poetic Analysis of Isaiah 40:1-2," *The Harvard Theological Review* 77, no. 3/4 (1984) 413-420.

67   See most recently John Goldingay and David F. Payne, *A Critical and Exegetical Commentary on Isaiah 40-55*, 2 vols. (ICC; London; New York: T&T Clark, 2006) 1.67-69.

68   See again Goldingay and Payne, *Isaiah 40-55*, 1.67. However, Goldingay's contextual arguments for the defense of this view are rather feeble: the picture of Jerusalem receiving good news in vv. 9-11 is a sign of personification rather than metonymy (just as in v. 2), and, out of the references that he lists in support for the identification of Zion with 'my people', only 51:16 is acceptable, whereas the use of 10:24 is incorrect (the people here are not identified with Zion, but specified as יֹשֵׁב צִיּוֹן) and 52:9 and 65:19 actually point the opposite direction, that is to the real city. Furthermore, Goldingay on the next page approves of the Targum's assumption that the real city is spoken of here.

69   As recognized also by Goldingay and Payne, *Isaiah 40-55*, 1.67. Furthermore, Snaith points out that the parallelism that this pair of 3:2 couplets creates is incomplete and thereby weaker than often assumed, for, unlike in the longer   lines, there is no semantic parallelism in the shorter lines, see Harry Meyer Orlinsky and Norman Henry Snaith, *Studies on the Second Part of the Book of Isaiah* (VTSup 14; Leiden: Brill, 1967) 177.

70   Thus, e.g., Klaus Baltzer, *Deutero-Isaiah: A Commentary on Isaiah 40-55* (Hermeneia; Minneapolis, MN: Fortress Press, 2001) 51. The most radical defence of this conclusion comes from Snaith in Orlinsky and Snaith, *Studies,* 177-179. He follows a possible lead from Vulgate in making the people the subject and Jerusalem the object of the comforting, so it is 'my people' who bring comfort to the ruined city upon their return from the exile, and, further on, it is Jerusalem who had sinned and received the punishment. Snaith's reading of Isa 40:1-2 did not receive much acceptance, but, as shown above, one does not have to adopt his understanding of Jerome's translation to uphold the naturalistic meaning of Jerusalem. In fact, Elliger

Finally, TI upholds the ultimate vision of DI when it comes to Jerusalem and the land: "You shall no more be termed Forsaken, and your land shall no more be termed Desolate; but you shall be called My Delight Is in Her, and your land Married; for the LORD delights in you, and your land shall be married" (62:4). Ch. 60 describes how Jerusalem will be rebuilt, revived, and glorified before all the nations. It will rightly be called עִיר יְהוָה and צִיּוֹן קְדוֹשׁ יִשְׂרָאֵל (v. 14), for the most glorious thing about it will be YHWH's continuous presence there – he will be its everlasting light and its glory (vv. 19-20). True to form, Mount Zion will be holy, and TI's primary concern in this regard is the right of citizenship – to denote the sort of people entitled to live in this holy place with the One 'whose name is Holy' (57:15). Everyone that would cause the impurity of this place is excluded: those who profane (חלל) the sabbath (56:2-8 and 58:13-14, both by implication),[71] those who practise idolatry (57:3-13, 65:11b, 66:3 and 17), those who are violent (65:25 by implication and 66:3),[72] those who rebel against YHWH (66:24), and, by definition, those who forsake YHWH and who forget his holy mountain (65:11).[73] On the other hand, the ones who will possess the land and inherit YHWH's holy mountain are his chosen ones, his servants (65:9), those who take refuge in him (57:13), those who are contrite and humble in spirit (57:15),[74] those who keep sabbath from

---

endorses Snaith's exegesis of 40:1a, and he still lists this passage along with 52:9b for support that Jerusalem here means 'die Bevölkerung', Karl Elliger, *Deuterojesaja* (BKAT 11; Neukirchen-Vluyn: Neukirchener-Verlag, 1978) 1 and 13.

71 For more details on these passages, see 6.8.2.

72 For more details on 66:3 see 6.8.4.

73 As Koole correctly points out, the name 'holy mountain' has an antithetical value here, being 'the opposite of any idolatrous practice,' Jan Leunis Koole, *Isaiah III/3,* trans. Anthony P. Runia, vol. 3 (HCOT; Leuven: Peeters, 2001) 523.

74 The understanding of 57:15 here follows Koole, *Isaiah III/3,* 96-100. He persuasively argues that v. aB ('I dwell in the high and holy place') is 'suggestive of Yahweh's kingship in Zion,' so just as in the previous pericope that ends with the holy mountain, 'the question remains of the approachability of this God; there is the distance of insignificant man to the high God, and of the sinner to the Holy One.' Considering the structure of v. b, he also argues for connecting 'the crushed of heart with God's holiness and the humility of spirit with his exaltedness,' and, referring to some uses of the verb דכא, he interprets דַּכָּא and שְׁפַל־רוּחַ in terms of penance and humility. Finally, referring to Lev 16:16, he maintains that שֹׁכֵן in v. aB can be construed with אֶת־ as preposition in v. bA, so the meaning of these lines is that 'Yahweh lives in the high and the holy, but with the crushed and humble in spirit … [H]is dwelling-place is among people and this vicinity of God puts a great strain on his approachability, but it may also lead to full fellowship. As long as the stumbling-block of sin and unbelief has not been cleared away, the proximity of the Exalted and Holy One destroys, but when it is removed, the high God accepts humble man and lives in all his holiness with the broken-hearted.'

profaning it (56:2-8 and 58:13-14), in one word צַדִּיקִים (60:21). 'They shall be called, "The Holy People, The Redeemed of the LORD"' (62:12), and will worship YHWH on his holy mountain, bringing acceptable sacrifices and offerings 'in ritually pure containers' (בִּכְלִי טָהוֹר as rendered by NET) into the house of YHWH (56:7 and 66:20).

TI's interest in keeping sabbaths from being profaned deserves a comment here. As already mentioned, the regulations of the Sabbatical year and the Jubilee year are a characteristic component of the cultic conception of the land, seeing the land as 'sabbath bound'.[75] Even though it seems that שַׁבָּת or שַׁבָּתוֹת in TI refers principally to the Sabbath day, the Sabbatical year and the Jubilee year should not be excluded. When the people are cautioned to keep YHWH's שַׁבְּתוֹת in Lev 26:2, the context makes clear that the Sabbatical year and the Jubilee year are a part, if not the essential part of what could be understood as a sabbath concept.[76] Furthermore, just as in Lev 26, the blessings that result from observing the sabbath regulations are explicitly connected with the land in TI: YHWH will bring the adherers to his holy mountain (56:7), make them 'ride upon the heights of the land' and feed them with Jacob's נַחֲלָה (58:14).[77]

3.5. Conclusion

Based on the above observations, it can be concluded that cultic conception of the land as defined in the Law is present in the book of Isaiah. The degree of this presence varies from part to part, and it seems to intensify in the later layers of the book, but its characteristics can be found throughout the whole book. The application is that Isaianic texts concerning the land, Jerusalem, and Zion are best understood *sub specie sanctitatis Dei*. From the human perspective, the practical implications are as follows: If the land belongs to YHWH and Israelites are only sojourners and tenants (גֵּרִים וְתוֹשָׁבִים) who reside there with him (Lev 25:23), the question of coexistence, as posed by חַטָּאִים and חֲנֵפִים in Isa 33:14, becomes of prime importance: "Who

---

75 The expression comes from Habel, *The Land is Mine,* passim. For more details, see his discussion there, especially pp. 101-114.

76 For the detailed discussion of this concept, see 6.3.2. NRSV is slightly misleading at this point, when it translates שַׁבְּתוֹת as 'sabbath years' in connection with the land (Lev 26:34 and 43), but as 'sabbaths' otherwise (Lev 26:2, 35 and elsewhere).

77 For more details on these verses, see 6.5.12.

among us can coexist (יָגוּר) with the devouring fire?" The answer is to avoid every kind of behaviour that defies YHWH's presence, for he is a God with whom no evil can coexist (לֹא יְגֻרְךָ רָע, Ps 5:5).

Conclusion of Part I

Throughout the chapters of Part I, it has been suggested that in the Priestly literature cultic concepts such as purity/impurity, holiness, or the land substantiate ethics. It seems that if the focal point of cult is YHWH's presence (with which holiness is intrinsically connected), the reason for an ethical appeal in conjunction with ritual practice is the capacity of certain immoral behaviour to effect the purity of the people, the land, the city or the sanctuary. The laws that regulate such behaviour are therefore cultic in nature, so one can think of them as the promulgation of the ethical dimension of cult.

Now the question is whether ethics and cult are related this way also in the book of Isaiah. The fact that the discussion of the cultic concepts in all the chapters of Part I has not revealed any essential differences between the Priestly literature and the book of Isaiah suggests an affirmative answer: the conceptions of sacrifices, (im)purity, holiness, and the land in the book of Isaiah are governed by theology compatible with P. The main reason for ethical appeals in the book appears to the fact that certain unethical behaviour seriously affects YHWH's presence. It seems well justified in the following three chapters to adhere to Rowley's counsel: 'It should never be forgotten that the prophetic demand was religious, and that it sprang from the conception of God.'[1]

---

1   Harold Henry Rowley, *The Faith of Israel: Aspects of Old Testament Thought* (London: SCM, 1956) 128.

PART II

Chapter 4: Cult and Ethics
in Isaiah 1:10-17

4.1. Introduction

In spite of or because of the variety of its interpretations, Isa 1:10-17 is probably the most frequently quoted text to illustrate the view of the pre-exilic prophets on cult and ethics.[1] Kaiser's comment is hardly an exaggeration: 'The present text, a prophetic instruction on sacrifice or a sacrifice Torah, is one of the most significant texts in the book of Isaiah from a historical point of view, though at the same time it is one over which there is the most dispute.'[2] The dispute to which Kaiser refers is caused not only by the presuppositions the interpreters hold regarding the role of cult and ethics in the ideology of the Prophets, but also by the number of text-critical issues present in this passage. Probably the best instance of the latter is the treatment of what appears to be the crux of the passage – the last phrase of v. 13, particularly the term אָוֶן in MT, rendered by LXX as νηστεία (presumably reading צוֹם in its *Vorlage*). [3] As argued below, Wildberger correctly supposes that 'die Zusammestellung von אָוֶן und עצרה für die Deutung des Abschnittes entscheidend ist.'[4] He also suggests that, in this case the text-critical decision should be based on the overall assessment of Isaiah's mind-set about the cult.[5] Even though the coherence of Isaiah's message is no

---

1   Gray calls it 'one of the most notable statements of the common standpoint of the prophets,' George Buchanan Gray, *A Critical and Exegetical Commentary on the Book of Isaiah I-XXVII* (ICC; Edinburgh: T&T Clark, 1912) 16.

2   Kaiser, *Isaiah 1-12*, 24.

3   For various translations, compare, e.g., NRSV ("solemn assemblies with iniquity") with NEB ("sacred seasons and ceremonies"); for commentaries, compare, e.g., Gray with Delitzsch.

4   Wildberger, *Jesaja*, 43. Similarly, Williamson points out that the possible emendation of אָוֶן to צוֹם has 'a significant bearing' on the interpretation of Isa 1:10-17, H. G. M. Williamson, "Biblical Criticism and Hermeneutics in Isaiah 1:10-17," in *Vergegenwärtigung des Alten Testaments: Beiträge zur Biblischen Hermeneutik; Festschrift für Rudolf Smend zum 70. Geburtstag*, ed. Christoph Bultmann, et al. (Göttingen: Vandenhoeck & Ruprecht, 2002) 82.

5   Wildberger, *Jesaja*, 34.

doubt a strong support of a particular solution to a textual problem, there is a potential danger in projecting the results of so called higher criticism into the text-critical issues. The preference here is, whenever possible, to work the argument from the bottom up: from lexical, syntax, form, and structure studies, to immediate and wider context studies. However, some of these exegetical steps inevitably presuppose a particular historical background, so this needs to be addressed first.

4.2. Historical Background of Isa 1:10-17

Isa 1:10-17 enjoys relatively homogeneous treatment when it comes to date and authorship. Even though there are exceptions (most notably and notoriously Kaiser), the following quote from Williamson about Isa 1 can be safely applied to this passage:

> [I]t is still the opinion of the overwhelming majority of commentators that the bulk of this chapter … stems from the prophet Isaiah himself, even though the oracles may have been subsequently gathered from elsewhere in his work and given their present position as the result of a redactor's desire to provide a suitable introduction to the book as a whole.[6]

If Isaiah of Jerusalem is the author of this passage, it is legitimate to search for some clues that would place Isa 1:10-17 into a particular period of his long ministry.[7] Many scholars connect it with one of the two major crises in Judah during the second half of the 8th century – the Syro-Ephraimitic war during the reign of Ahaz, or Sennacherib's invasion during the reign of Hezekiah. Their major argument comes from the description in the previous unit (vv. 7-8) that would fit the aftermath of both events very well – the whole land laid desolate apart from Jerusalem.[8] If, however, the oracles in this chapter were collected

---

6   Williamson, *Book Called Isaiah*, 80.

7   The exact time-span of Isaiah's ministry is disputed. Many scholars take Isa 6 as Isaiah's initial call, taking 'the year that king Uzziah died' (v. 1) as the start of his ministry. This year, however, is also disputed; it could be '742 according to the Bright – Albright chronology, but as early as 747 or as late as 735 according to others,' Joseph Jensen, *Isaiah 1-39* (Old Testament Message, vol. 8; Wilmington: Michael Glazier, 1984) 29. Furthermore, as Williamson points out, Isaiah's vision in ch. 6 does not necessarily describe his initial call, so one must not exclude the possibility that his ministry started already during Uzziah's lifetime, see Williamson, *Isaiah 1-27*, 20-21. As far as the end of Isaiah's ministry is concerned, scholars generally agree that his latest prophecies come from 701 or shortly thereafter.

8   Thus, e.g., Blenkinsopp sees the thematic connection with the preceding stanza, dated by most commentators (including himself) right after Sennacherib's campaign during the reign of Hezekiah in 701, in that 'the ritual appeasement of the deity

from various parts of the Isaianic corpus to serve as an introduction to the book, the chronological sequence between them cannot be presupposed.[9] Vargon correctly states that the historical background of this prophecy 'must be deduced from the prophecy itself.'[10] The problem is that the clues that Isa 1:10-17 offers in this regard are too general: all that is required for the functioning of religious life seems to be in place, cultic activities are regular and probably intensified, and social justice is being perverted.

Nevertheless, a number of scholars place Isa 1:10-17 into the time of Hezekiah on the basis of these clues. Thus Vargon, among others, believes that the economic situation significantly improved for Judah in 720-705 as a result of economic hegemony of the Assyrians and Hezekiah's loyalty to this empire. This provided suitable conditions not only for opulent cult practices, but also for a social crisis as a result of escalating social injustice.[11] To these and similar arguments, several objections need to be raised. First, as Houston sufficiently demonstrated, the conditions for a social crisis in 8th century Judah and Israel certainly recurred on more than one later occasion, and that 'there is no archaeological evidence for any elements of the rural population living in abject poverty, and particularly no evidence for any dramatic change in the conditions of life during the eighth century or at any other period prior to the final downfall of the respective kingdoms.'[12] Second, even if there was an economic boom in

---

would tend to be intensified in times of crisis, which remains true even if some of the religious observances mentioned here are more or less routine,' Joseph Blenkinsopp, *Isaiah 1-39: A New Translation with Introduction and Commentary* (AB 19; New York: Doubleday, 2000) 184.

9   For the most recent arguments in support of this increasingly more accepted idea of the Isa 1 composition and function, see Williamson, *Isaiah 1-27*, passim.

10   Shmuel Vargon, "The Historical Background and Significance of Isa 1, 10-17," in *Studies in Historical Geography and Biblical Historiography: Presented to Zecharia Kallai*, ed. Gershon Galil and Moshe Weinfeld (VTSup 81; Leiden: Brill, 2000) 187.

11   Vargon, "Historical Background," 188f. For a similar opinion, see, e.g., Sweeney, *Isaiah 1-39*, 80. Dating Isa 1:10-17 sometime between 715-701, he attributes the prophet's denunciation of the cultic activity to 'the relationship between Hezekiah's religious reforms and his policy of preparing for armed revolt against the Assyrians.' Williamson rightly objects that this 'seems to read more into the text than is there,' Williamson, *Isaiah 1-27*, 85.

12   Walter J. Houston, "Was there a Social Crisis in the Eighth Century?," in *In Search of Pre-Exilic Israel: Proceedings of the Oxford Old Testament Seminar*, ed. John Day (JSOTSup 406; London: T & T Clark International, 2004) 146-147 and 136. For the archaeological support of this conclusion, see John S. Holladay, "The Kingdoms of Israel and Judah: Political and Economic Centralization in the Iron IIA-B (ca. 1000-

Hezekiah's time, it is not a necessary precondition for the cultic activities described in Isa 1:10-17. A rich cultic life does not presuppose exceptional economic growth of a particular group, nor the general well-being of society.[13] Third, nothing in Isa 1:10-17 indicates that the cultic practices there took extraordinary proportions.[14] In short, there are other periods during Isaiah's ministry besides Hezekiah's era that provide equally suitable conditions for the cultic and social activities described in Isa 1:10-17.

Another argument for Hezekiah's date is unique to Vargon: he observes several linguistic parallels between Isa 1:10-17 and the text in Chronicles that describes the reign of Hezekiah (2 Chr 29-31), and believes that they 'indicate a link between the two, providing grounds to suppose that the compiler of Chronicles derived his description from a source from the reign of Hezekiah.' As a result, he establishes the date of the Isaianic oracle in the days of Hezekiah.[15] The circularity of this argument is rather obvious. Furthermore, Vargon's use of the book of Chronicles as 'the biblical historiographical literature' is highly questionable. Instead of resembling Isa 1:10-15, the picture of numerous sacrifices in 2 Chr 29 (esp. vv. 31-35) finds a much closer parallel in 1 Kgs 8:62-66, the sacrifices during the dedication of the Temple by Solomon. As Williamson sufficiently demonstrated, 'the Chronicler has gone out of his way to present Hezekiah as a second Solomon,'[16] and the description of cultic activities seems to be driven by this concern, rather than by historical reality. If there was some historicity in the Chronicler's description of Hezekiah's reform,[17] it would point in the opposite direction for which Vargon argues: its emphasis is on real

---

750 BCE)," in *The Archaeology of Society in the Holy Land*, ed. Thomas Evan Levy (London: Leicester University Press, 1995).

13   As Blenkinsopp in the footnote 8 above suggests, increased cultic activity may reflect the time of crisis.

14   The expressions רֹב־זִבְחֵיכֶם and רְמֹס חֲצֵרָי (vv. 11-12) do not necessarily imply masses going to the Temple offering a multitude of sacrifices comparable to 2 Chr 29-30, *contra* Vargon, "Historical Background," 187-188.

15   Vargon, "Historical Background," 188.

16   H. G. M. Williamson, *1 and 2 Chronicles* (NCBC; Grand Rapids, London: Eerdmans, Marshall Morgan & Scott, 1982) 350-351.

17   Scholars disagree how much of what is unique to 2 Chr 29-31 comes from possible alternative accounts and how much is the Chronicler's own composition. Lowery persuasively argues that the unusual elements and irregularities, especially in the account of the all-Israel Passover, indicate historical reality at the core of these chapters, Richard H. Lowery, *The Reforming Kings: Cult and Society in First Temple Judah* (JSOTSup120; Sheffield: JSOT Press, 1991) 161-167. Williamson decides to leave this question open, see Williamson, *Chronicles*, 351.

purity and sanctification,[18] coming, as said of the Levites in 29:34, from יִשְׁרֵי לֵבָב, even to the extent that those people 'who set their hearts to seek God' but 'had not cleansed themselves' were pardoned by YHWH and could eat the Passover meal (30:17-20), with the result that, unlike in Isa 1:15, 'their voice was heard; their prayer came to his holy dwelling in heaven' (30:27). Isaiah would hardly object to cultic practices carried out with such attitude. When comparing Isa 1:10-17 with 2 Chr 29-31 and its *Vorlage* in 2 Kgs 18, one could even argue that Isaiah's admonitions served as one of the bases for Hezekiah's reform.[19] A king acting against the usual cultic practices as described in 2 Kgs 18:4, even to the point of breaking the bronze serpent that Moses had made, can hardly be accused of putting a main emphasis only on cult.[20] This picture of Hezekiah's era does not provide a suitable historical background for Isa 1:10-17.

In contrast to Hezekiah, Ahaz is portrayed in 2 Kgs 16 as being preoccupied with cult. It is said from the start that he 'made his son pass through fire,' and 'sacrificed and made offerings on the high places, on the hills, and under every green tree' (vv. 3-4). He was so inspired by a great altar he saw in a Damascus temple that his orders to install its copy in Jerusalem were carried out even before his return, and, after he saw the result, he offered numerous sacrifices on it (vv. 10-13). He commanded that all the required sacrifices and offerings will take place on this new altar, while keeping the old one for his private cultic use (vv. 14-15). Admittedly, every part of this story raises more questions than answers about Ahaz and his cultic activities,[21] especially the unparalleled episode about the new altar. Cogan argues that Ahaz's innovations were neither idolatrous nor syncretistic for the following reasons: Assyrians did not impose the worship of their gods on vassal states, the description of rituals in vv. 13-15 shows that the new altar in the Jerusalem temple was used for the same legitimate practices of YHWH cult as the old one, and Uriah, priest of YHWH and otherwise known as Isaiah's supporter (Isa 8:2), expressed no objections to this

---

18 Notice the frequency and prominence of the root קדשׁ throughout the story.

19 Compare, e.g., 2 Chr 29:5-6 with Isa 1:16.

20 *Contra* Vargon, "Historical Background," 193. The high places, altars, etc. in this passage are understood to serve primarily for illegitimate worship of YHWH (as explicitly stated in v. 22), not of the other gods. Certainly, as Lowery argues, the worship there was highly syncretic, but 'whatever non-Yahwistic cult services were offered in addition, the Judean high place remained a Yahweh sanctuary,' Lowery, *Reforming Kings*, 79.

21 For a brief but accurate summary of the major research on this chapter in the 20th century, see Lowery, *Reforming Kings*, 134-140.

innovation.[22] Cogan's theory needs to be modified. First, as Lowery correctly points out, since kings were believed to be the chosen sons of YHWH, they could not only change cult policies, but also appoint and depose priests, so the absence of Uriah's objections to Ahaz's innovations can be explained by fear.[23] Second, and more importantly, Spieckermann has demonstrated that the Assyrians were far from relaxed about the religion of their subjects, and imposed harsh religious-political measures against rebellious vassals. He adds, however, that since Judah, with the brief exception of Hezekiah, was a very faithful vassal, these harsh measures were not necessary.[24] Spieckermann sees Ahaz's cultic innovations as a clever compromise: the new, impressive Damascene altar served for sacrifices and offerings to YHWH, while, at the same time, the king reserved 'the bronze altar' for the rituals required of him as a king of a vassal country.[25] In spite of the differences, the above scholars agree that these cultic innovations described in 2 Kgs 16 were voluntarily adopted by the leaders of Judah,[26] and not only did not eliminate, but probably even enhanced the Yahwistic official cult.[27] Ahaz appears to be the one in charge of cultic matters, taking initiative, giving orders and performing the rituals. Although these activities are not unusual for a king of the First Temple period, Lowery correctly maintains that, in the book of Kings, Ahaz's personal involvement and participation in the cultic matters is

---

22 See Mordechai Cogan, *Imperialism and Religion: Assyria, Judah, and Israel in the Eighth and Seventh Centuries B.C.E* (SBLMS 19; Missoula, MT: Scholars Press, 1974). He further elaborates on this view in Mordechai Cogan and Hayim Tadmor, *II Kings: A New Translation with Introduction and Commentary* (AB 11; New York: Doubleday, 1988) 184-194. Here he suggests that the construction of the new altar was motivated 'by a spirit of assimilation to the current international fashions,' and that Ahaz's innovations are criticized in the book of Kings because they 'upset the order of things in the Temple as established by Solomon,' Cogan and Tadmor, *II Kings*, 193.

23 Lowery, *Reforming Kings*, 124.

24 Hermann Spieckermann, *Juda unter Assur in der Sargonidenzeit* (Forschungen zur Religion und Literatur des Alten und Neuen Testaments 129; Göttingen: Vandenhoeck & Ruprecht, 1982) 371.

25 Spieckermann, *Assur*, 367-369. According to Jones, this double altar solution held through until Josiah's reform, Gwilym H. Jones, *1 and 2 Kings* (NCBC; Grand Rapids, MI, London: Eerdmans, Marshall Morgan & Scott, 1984) 369.

26 As observed by Lowery, *Reforming Kings*, 139.

27 An attractive supportive argument comes from Jones, who suggests that if the sacrifices in v. 13 would be offered to an alien god, 'the deuteronomistic compiler would not have missed the opportunity to castigate Ahaz,' Jones, *1 and 2 Kings*, 539. For more support of the idea that the new altar served the Yahwistic official cult, see J. W. McKay, *Religion in Judah under the Assyrians 732-609 BC* (SBT 26; London: SCM, 1973) 5-12.

unprecedented.[28] At the same time, he calls himself the servant and the son of Tiglath-pileser, turning to him for help and bribing him with the silver and the gold from YHWH's temple (vv. 7-8).[29] According to Isaiah,[30] such activities equal rebellion against YHWH, breaking 'the central element in the treaty relationship, the lord's claim to an exclusive fidelity from the vassal which forbade all serious dealing with outsiders.'[31] When this treacherous behaviour is combined with Ahaz's zeal for cult, one gets the very profile of a leader that Isa 1:10-17 criticizes: a person capable of cultic conduct and ethical misconduct at the same time.

Dating Isa 1:10-17 back to the time of Ahaz can be further supported by arguments from Wildberger and Williamson, who look for similarities and differences between this passage and the other prophetic treatments of the same topic. Wildberger argues that 'da amoseische und hoseanische Gedanken anklingen, mag der Abschnitt aus Jesajas Frühzeit stammen.'[32] Williamson refers to Isa 29:1-2, 29:13-14, and 22:12-14 where the prophet deals with the same topic of cultic observance with a noticeable shift in his thinking, leaving no room for the averting of the coming judgment via repentance. Since these passages refer to the periods shortly before and after Sennacherib's invasion, Williamson prefers to place Isa 1:10-17 with its message of possibility for reform in the early years of Isaiah's ministry. He even implies its *terminus a quo*, when suggesting that the attitude in Isa 1:10-17 reflects Isaiah's personal experience of 'forgiveness and cleansing in a cultic setting (6:5-7).'[33] The following discussion endorses this proposal.

4.3. Literary Genre of Isa 1:10-17

Discussing the essentials of form criticism, Campbell aptly cautions that 'the decision about the literary type (genre) is not an understanding imposed on the text; it is a decision that emerges out of

---

28 See Lowery, *Reforming Kings*, 67-69.

29 In the light of the context, NRSV's rendering of שֶׁחַד in v. 6 as 'gift' seems rather weak.

30 See especially ch. 30, where God's people are called rebellious and faithless sons (vv. 1 and 9), because they 'take refuge in the protection of Pharaoh' (v. 2).

31 Dennis J. McCarthy, "Notes on the Love of God in Deuteronomy and the Father-Son Relationship between Yahweh and Israel," *CBQ* 27 (1965) 144-147.

32 Wildberger, *Jesaja*, 37.

33 Williamson, *Isaiah 1-27*, 85.

the understanding of the text.'[34] The placement of this section here, before textual analysis, does not mean ignoring Campbell's admonition. Quite the reverse; the purpose of this discussion is to eliminate some rather common presuppositions about the genre of Isa 1:10-17 in order to approach the text without an unnecessary bias. This order is followed also in the next two exegeses (Chapters 5 and 6) for the same reason.

Isa 1:10-17 is often listed as the prime example of the so-called 'prophetic Torah' genre for two main reasons: first, v. 10b designates the rest of the passage as תּוֹרַת אֱלֹהֵינוּ;[35] second, there are cultic issues raised in vv. 11-15, and these are addressed in what is considered a prophetic-like manner, namely emphasizing ethics over cult.[36] The first reason is seriously undermined by Williamson and others who take v. 10 as a redactional introduction. If correct, the expression תּוֹרַת אֱלֹהֵינוּ is not the author's label for the passage, but the redactor's understanding of it.[37] For those who assign the authorship of this expression to Isaiah, an even more complicated question arises, namely what was the meaning of the term תּוֹרָה for the 8th century prophet. Jensen, who devoted a whole monograph to this question, concludes that תּוֹרָה in Isa 1:10 is best understood as 'instruction' in a broad sense, similar to its use in the wisdom tradition, rather than as 'law' in the legal tradition.[38] Both of these theses weaken the links between the genre of this passage and the 'priestly Torah' genre. Regardless of v. 10, the second reason mentioned above can still suffice to view Isa 1:10-17 as imitation of 'priestly Torah', viz. 'prophetic Torah'.[39] However, a closer look at the form-critical studies of this passage reveals that this label is not only

---

34   Antony F. Campbell, "Form Criticism's Future," in *The Changing Face of Form Criticism for the Twenty-First Century*, ed. Marvin A. Sweeney and Ehud Ben Zvi (Grand Rapids, MI; Cambridge, U.K.: W.B. Eerdmans, 2003) 24.

35   Cf. Joseph Jensen, *The Use of tôrâ by Isaiah: His Debate with the Wisdom Tradition* (CBQ monograph series 3; Washington, D.C.: Catholic Biblical Association of America, 1973) 25.

36   See, e.g., Marvin A. Sweeney, *Isaiah 1-4 and the Post-Exilic Understanding of the Isaianic Tradition* (BZAW 171; Berlin; New York: De Gruyter, 1988) 111. Wildberger gives even more prominence to the influence of the supposed priestly genre by labeling the genre of this passage 'priesterliche Thora', only because, according to him, 'der Abschnitt beansprucht, תורה zu sein, und die einzelnen Termini doch stark in der Sprache des Kultes verwurzelt sind,' Wildberger, *Jesaja*, 36.

37   See Williamson, *Isaiah 1-27*, 81-85.

38   See Jensen, *Use of tôrâ*, esp. 65-84. For further bibliography on this issue, see Williamson, *Isaiah 1-27*, 86.

39   Just like, e.g., Amos 5:21-27 or Micah 6:6-8, which do not mention תּוֹרָה, but which are often labeled as 'prophetic Torah'.

unproductive,[40] but even counterproductive, especially when understood in either of the following two ways.

The first way is to believe that the imitation here is for the purpose of creating defamiliarization. As Ben Zvi explains, defamiliarization of genres is a rhetorical device frequently used in the prophetic books, when the literary texts 'run counter to the expectations and associations created by even well-known literary genres.'[41] The problem is obvious: even if the genre of priestly Torah were properly reconstructed (which it is not, as will be argued below), to reconstruct the expectations and associations evoked by it in the mind of an ancient Israelite is beyond the bounds of credibility. As Jensen sufficiently demonstrated, there is no solid ground for assuming that, e.g., when an 8th century Jerusalemite heard a prophet using the expression תּוֹרַת אֱלֹהֵינוּ, he expected a list of cultic prescriptions to follow.[42] And even if this were the case, would he be unfamiliar with incorporating ideas such as God's refusing sacrifices offered by a murderer or ceasing to do evil and learning to do good into such a list? Although the answer is most likely 'no', these and similar reactions would have to be expected if the defamiliarization via imitation of 'priestly Torah' in Isa 1:10-17 were to have some force.

A second counterproductive way to apply the label 'prophetic Torah' to Isa 1:10-17 is to understand the imitation of 'priestly Torah' here as caricature, sarcasm, or irony. Thus, e.g., Sweeney maintains that Isaiah 'employs the term in a satirical manner to demonstrate his point that "the Torah of YHWH" in this instance does not pertain to correct sacrificial procedure, but to the underlying purpose that the sacrifice serves.'[43] Even though sarcasm concerning cultic practice is not unknown to the OT prophets (e.g., Amos 4:4), it is anything but evident in Isa 1:10-17, except perhaps in the questionable v. 10. One cannot resist an impression that this negative connotation implied by some scholars through the tag 'prophetic Torah' is fuelled by their

---

40   In the words of Childs, the scholarly debate concerning the genre of this passage 'has become quite sterile without much exegetical illumination,' Brevard S. Childs, *Isaiah* (OTL; Louisville, KY; London: Westminster John Knox Press, 2001) 19.

41   Ben Zvi, "Prophetic Book," 291.

42   *Contra* Oswalt, *et al.* In the words of Jensen: 'Certainly it was not the ritual prescriptions of the various collections in P that Isaiah had in mind when he spoke of Yahweh's *tôrâ*,' Jensen, *Use of tôrâ*, 65.

43   Marvin A. Sweeney, *Form and Intertextuality in Prophetic and Apocalyptic Literature* (FAT 45; Tübingen: Mohr Siebeck, 2005) 21-22. Similarly, Blenkinsopp suggests that what is going on in this passage is 'perhaps sarcastic imitation of the priestly Torah,' Blenkinsopp, *Isaiah 1-39*, 184. Oswalt is inclined to believe that the use of the term תּוֹרָה in v. 10 is 'probably ironic,' Oswalt, *Isaiah 1-39*, 96.

presuppositions such as antagonism between the prophets and the priests in ancient Israel or aversion of the prophets to rituals.[44]

The biggest problem with defining 'prophetic Torah' as an imitation of 'priestly Torah' is, however, that there is no clear idea of what it is supposed to imitate – the original 'priestly Torah' genre. The following remark by Gunkel about one form of priestly Torah raises the suspicion of a methodological flaw, namely that the original is defined predominantly by its imitation: 'This form was once much more common than the postexilic priestly legal ruling still allows one to recognize as is shown by the imitations which are found precisely in this form of priestly torah among the prophets.'[45] This suspicion is only confirmed by Begrich's proposal about how the original form of priestly Torah is to be determined: 'Die Form wird uns erfaßbar durch einige prophetische Nachahmungen priesterlicher Tora, ferner durch einige Beispiele der hexateuchischen Tradition.' When it comes to practising this method, Begrich believes that 'der prophetische Ein-schlag, die Umkehrung des priesterlichen Urteiles und die Einführung der spezifisch prophetischen Forderungen, leicht erkennbar ist, und das Priesterliche durch den Vergleich mit den hexateuchischen Beispie-len leicht gesichert werden kann.'[46] 'Leicht' it may sound, but, as Jensen correctly points out, this method suffers from circularity: 'the clearest evidence for the form of priestly *tôrâ* is found in prophetic imitations of the form; but how can we recognize them as imitations of priestly *tôrâ* unless we have already clearly established the elements of the latter?'[47]

---

44   Thus, e.g., Gunkel believes that the prophets 'gladly made use' of different forms of priestly Torah 'in opposition to the dominant cultic religion,' Hermann Gunkel and Joachim Begrich, *Introduction to Psalms: The Genres of the Religious Lyric of Israel* (Mercer Library of Biblical Studies; Macon, GA: Mercer University Press, 1998) 250. Gunkel develops this line of thought even further when discussing the cult-critical passages in Psalms. He considers texts like Ps 50 to be an imitation of prophetic Torah, preserving the prophetic emphasis on ethics over cult, but obliterating its antiritualistic radicalism, thus appropriating these texts for cultic use. According to Gunkel, this (by now) imitation of imitation, shows, that 'the prophets certainly succeeded in breaking the overvaluation of the sacrifice in cultic religion … [but] they were unable to get the entire content of their torah accepted,' Gunkel and Begrich, *Introduction to Psalms,* 281. This use of form-criticism seems to be speculative and counterproductive.

45   Gunkel and Begrich, *Introduction to Psalms,* 250.

46   Joachim Begrich, "Die priesterliche Tora," in *Werden und Wesen des Alten Testaments : Vorträge gehalten auf der Internationalen Tagung Alttestamentlicher Forscher zu Göttingen vom 4.-10. September 1935,* ed. Johannes Hempel, Friedrich Stummer, and Paul Volz (BZAW 66; Berlin: A. Töpelmann, 1936) 73.

47   Jensen, *Use of tôrâ,* 13. See also pp. 12-14 of this monograph for Jensen's sharp critique of Begrich's thesis.

When it comes to the 8th century prophets, the original genre of priestly Torah that they are supposed to imitate can only be presupposed, not demonstrated.

If Isa 1:10-17 is stripped of all the above mentioned presuppositions and implied concepts, the only thing left to induce the tag 'priestly Torah' or 'prophetic Torah' is the cultic and ethical terminology. To establish the genre of the text on this, however, would be a case where, in Williamson's words, 'terminological parallels are confused with form-critical analysis.'[48] Taking the above discussion into consideration, the study of Isa 1:10-17 may actually benefit from dropping the labels 'priestly Torah' and 'prophetic Torah' altogether.[49] One should at least pay close attention to the introductory quote from Campbell that cautions us not to put a genre tag on a particular passage before a thorough examination of the text has been undertaken.[50]

4.4. Structural Analysis and Text-Critical Issues of Isa 1:10-17

There is a consensus among OT scholars with regard to the unity of Isa 1:10-17 in its final form. It is determined by the two introductory imperative calls in vv. 10 and 18. MT marks off its beginning and its end by a marginal ס, and there is obvious spacing (*vacat*) before v. 10 and after v. 17 in 1QIsa[a]. The analysis below also confirms its unity. Far from obvious, however, are the relationships of the various building blocks within this passage. The purpose of this section is to identify the structure of the text with regard to its syntax,[51] focusing on its smallest units such as words and colons, and the relationship between them within the stanzas. Some text-critical issues of Isa 1:10-17 are also addressed here. The following section deals with the relationships between the stanzas and the overall structure of the passage. In order to eliminate the danger of preoccupation with an intuitively accepted interpretation during this process, close attention is paid to the following two features of Khan's methodology:

---

48   Williamson, *Isaiah 1-27*, 84.
49   These, however, are die-hard labels, as some of the latest studies on the form of Isa 1:10-17 show; see, e.g., Sweeney, *Isaiah 1-39*, 28-29, 66 and 80.
50   Unlike many commentaries that implicitly encourage their readers to do otherwise by putting the discussion of the genre *before* analysing the text.
51   For various proposals, see, e.g., K. Fullerton, "The Rhythmical Analysis of Is. 1:10-20," *JBL* 38 (1919) 53-63, Susan Niditch, "The Composition of Isaiah 1," *Biblica* 61 (1980) 509-529, Ambrogio Spreafico, "Nahum i 10 and Isaiah i 12-13: Double-Duty Modifier," *VT* 48 (1998) 104-110, Sweeney, *Isaiah 1-39*, 78-79.

(a) that a clear dichotomy is drawn between the structure of a syntactic construction on the one hand and its function on the other, and (b) that structure is the starting point of the analysis, i.e. my aim is to seek the function which is performed by a given structure rather than the structure which performs a given function.[52]

It has been a long recognized fact that the human mind is fond of structures, patterns, and rhythms; it not only recognizes and appreciates them when they are present, but it also tends to create them when they are not. When it comes to analysing a Hebrew text, especially poetry and its rhythm (*metre*), this human predisposition is a good servant, but an evil master. Kugel talks about the damage of 'metrical hypothesis' and calls for more caution in applying it (if at all) to the text: 'The whole idea that parts of the Bible are written in meter, and the hundreds of trial scansions and textual emendations it has emerged, is a concomitant of this notion'.[53] Watson speaks of metre in Hebrew poetry more optimistically, and, while affirming its existence, he warns against its rigid use: 'Confusion arises because scholars fail to distinguish between metre as actually present in verse, and *regular* metre. There is metre, yes, but not regular metre, since metrical patterns are never maintained for more than a few verses at a stretch, if even that.'[54] There seems to be sufficient ground (especially in the light of Kugel's study) to doubt the contribution of counting stresses or syllables of the MT to determining the structure of the text.[55] In the following analysis, metre is taken into consideration only when it is compelling, but never used as an argument for determining the structure, let alone emendation of the text.

Following Watson's terminology, the smallest unit taken into consideration when dividing the poetic text of Isa 1:10-17 is hemistich, followed by colon, strophe, and finally stanza.[56] Working with these

---

52 Geoffrey Khan, *Studies in Semitic Syntax* (London Oriental Series 38; Oxford: Oxford University Press, 1988) xxvii. On the same page, Khan insists that 'one must start with a single structure (or a group of closely related structures) and seek its several, and often diverse, functions or else start with a single delimited function and seek its various exponent structures.' While these two approaches may be mutually exclusive at the outset, it is possible to make the first the departure point and follow with the second, as is the procedure in this section.

53 James L. Kugel, *The Idea of Biblical Poetry: Parallelism and Its History* (New Haven; London: Yale University Press, 1981) 71.

54 Wilfred G. E. Watson, *Classical Hebrew Poetry: A Guide to Its Techniques* (JSOTSup 26; Sheffield: JSOT Press, 1984) 92.

55 For such an attempt with questionable results, see Niditch, "The Composition." Struggling for balance in the text, she emends with LXX whenever it fits the purpose.

56 For the definitions of these terms, see Watson, *Hebrew Poetry*, 11-13.

units is not problem-free; even though there are certain rules for their identification, they do not yield 'clear cut' results, and allow for a considerable amount of subjectivity. Nevertheless, as the chart below illustrates, such division provides the necessary building blocks of which the landscape of the passage is constructed, and, consequently, brings to light its characteristic elements as well as the relations between them (the dynamic of the text). For describing the connection between hemistiches or colons at the morphological level (grammatical parallelism), the conventions of Collins are used,[57] where NP$_1$ represents subject, NP$_2$ object, V verb, and M modifiers of the verb (such as adverbs, prepositional phrases, locatives, etc.). When the link is only the one of meaning (semantic parallelism), the colons are designated by capital letters. On both levels, the corresponding part has the same label with an apostrophe. Watson's terminology and define-tions are followed also in determining the particular poetic devices in the text. The middle part of the chart consists of the MT as it appears in BHS (without accents), with extra spacing and extra 'new-lines' to point out the divisions and relations of the units within the text.

---

57 Terence Collins, *Line-forms in Hebrew Poetry: A Grammatical Approach to the Stylistic Study of the Hebrew Prophets* (Studia Pohl. Series Maior 7; Rome: Biblical Institute Press, 1978).

Strophe and Poetic Device	MT of Isaiah 1:10-17 (BHS)	St
Bicolon with grammatical and semantic paral.: V NP2 NP1 // V' NP2' NP1', using traditional word-pairs.	שִׁמְעוּ דְבַר־יְהוָה קְצִינֵי סְדֹם הַאֲזִינוּ תּוֹרַת אֱלֹהֵינוּ עַם עֲמֹרָה	I
Introductory monocolon, opens the stanza with rhetorical question.	לָמָּה־לִּי רֹב־זִבְחֵיכֶם יֹאמַר יְהוָה	
Bicolon with grammatical and semantic chiastic paral.: V NP2 // NP2' V', with (overlapping) ellipsis of V and V', merismus made of NP2 + NP2', and ballast variant in NP2'.	שָׂבַעְתִּי עֹלוֹת אֵילִים וְחֵלֶב מְרִיאִים וְדַם פָּרִים וּכְבָשִׂים וְעַתּוּדִים לֹא חָפָצְתִּי	II
Introductory monocolon, opens the stanza with rhetorical question.	כִּי תָבֹאוּ לֵרָאוֹת פָּנָי מִי בִקֵּשׁ זֹאת מִיֶּדְכֶם	
Pivot-patterned bicolon with silent stress and double-duty modifier.	רְמֹס חֲצֵרָי לֹא תוֹסִיפוּ הָבִיא מִנְחַת־שָׁוְא	III
Pivot-patterned bicolon with double-duty modifier, balanced according to the isocolic principle.	קְטֹרֶת תּוֹעֵבָה הִיא לִי חֹדֶשׁ וְשַׁבָּת קְרֹא מִקְרָא	
Climatic monocolon.	לֹא־אוּכַל אָוֶן וַעֲצָרָה	
Tricolon with parallel pattern A/A'/A'', where the object of A becomes the subject in A' (antecedent of Wyh') and the implicit second object in A''. The link is the one of meaning.	חָדְשֵׁיכֶם וּמוֹעֲדֵיכֶם שָׂנְאָה נַפְשִׁי הָיוּ עָלַי לָטֹרַח נִלְאֵיתִי נְשֹׂא	IV
Tetracolon with alternating paral.: A B // A' B', crescendo through כִּי גַם.	וּבְפָרִשְׂכֶם כַּפֵּיכֶם אַעְלִים עֵינַי מִכֶּם גַּם כִּי־תַרְבּוּ תְפִלָּה אֵינֶנִּי שֹׁמֵעַ	
Closing monocolon, a dramatic gap for reflection.	יְדֵיכֶם דָּמִים מָלֵאוּ	
Introductory tricolon with parallel pattern V/V'/ V'' NP2 NP1, where the last cola is an exposition of the synonymous word-pair V – V'.	רַחֲצוּ הִזַּכּוּ הָסִירוּ רֹעַ מַעַלְלֵיכֶם מִנֶּגֶד עֵינָי	V
Bicolon with grammatical and semantic paral.: V NP2 // V' NP2', where NP2 - NP2' is an antonymic word-pair.	חִדְלוּ הָרֵעַ לִמְדוּ הֵיטֵב	
Bicolon with grammatical and semantic paral.: V NP2 // V' NP2'.	דִּרְשׁוּ מִשְׁפָּט אַשְּׁרוּ חָמוֹץ	
Bicolon with grammatical and semantic paral.: V NP2 // V' NP2', where NP2 - NP2' is a correlative word-pair.	שִׁפְטוּ יָתוֹם רִיבוּ אַלְמָנָה	

While the dissection into stanzas (right column) coincides with the one indicated by the MT (viz. *Soph Pasuq*), there are deviations from the MT text division with regard to some strophes that require explanation. Such discussion will, in turn, clarify the delimitation of the stanzas.

4.4.1. Stanza I (v. 10)

This one-strophe introductory stanza is a textbook example of parallelism called 'proper congruence'. It consists of fixed word-pairs: hear // listen; the word of the Lord // the Torah of our God; rulers // people; Sodom // Gomorrah. Such pairs are predictable, and Kugel rightly believes that for this reason they were not the centre of the listeners' attention. 'The use of pairs does not mean the *clauses* are equivalent, and what is interesting in these lines are the subtle variations'.[58] Furthermore, if Kugel's idea of the basic functions of parallelism – 'A is so, and *what's more*, B' – is granted, then parts of v. 10 could read: the word of the Lord, and what's more, the Torah of our God; the rulers, and, what's more, all the people. By equating the rulers and (by implication) the people of Israel with the citizens of Sodom and Gomorrah, this introductory verse indicates the main issue of the passage – the people's behaviour. This equation also sets up the overall harsh tone of the passage.

4.4.2. Stanza II (v. 11)

The combination of עֹלָה and זֶבַח in this verse deserves closer attention. Milgrom insists that in non-Priestly sources this combination appears 'only as voluntary offerings of the individual and never as the required staple of the public cult.'[59] Furthermore, he believes that by the eighth century the expiatory character of עֹלָה had passed on to the חַטָּאת and אָשָׁם sacrifices, and עֹלָה retained solely its joyous nature.[60] It is, therefore, possible that the prophet purposefully singled out sacrifices that were non-obligatory and non-expiatory (as already discussed in 1.6). However, it may be objected that such a technical understanding

---

58 Kugel, *Idea*, 31.
59 Milgrom, *Leviticus 1-16*, 483.
60 See Milgrom, *Leviticus 1-16*, 177. Milgrom further observes that while P prescribes חַטָּאת and אָשָׁם as mandatory expiation sacrifices, the combination of עֹלָה and זֶבַח is found only in the context of individual, voluntary sacrifices.

is out of place, for the Isaianic passage is a genre rather different from P or other sources of the Pentateuch, and, just as the list of sacrificial animals, the sacrifices mentioned in v. 11 represent sacrifices in general, that is, they function as *pars pro toto*.

The division of this stanza proposed above seems to support this objection, suggesting the reading of v. 11 in the following way: the rhetorical question in the first colon introduces the main point, and the rest of the verse is the expansion of the main point via a tour.[61] The function of this tour, however, is more significant than just to lengthen the poem; it has a function of merismus, expressing completeness. It is well possible that the five sacrificial elements in the chiastically structured bicolon are random on purpose (the list does not follow any order known from the similar lists of sacrificial animals in the OT) – to communicate the all-encompassing character of רֹב־זִבְחֵיכֶם. This unorthodox register, along with the fact that assorted sacrificial elements are listed instead of the variety of sacrifices, can indicate that the sacrificial system as such is not the point here. Two more interesting rhetorical features are worth mentioning. First, the ellipses[62] of the initial and final verbs in the second strophe seem to be overlapping, because the overreaching force of each one impacts all the elements in between. The second feature, related to ellipsis, is the writer's regard for the isocolic principle in the second couplet. The expression וּכְבָשִׂים can be seen as a 'ballast variant,' eliminating thus the metrical reason for its omission.[63]

4.4.3. Stanza III (vv. 12-13)

Before analysing the structure of this stanza, several of its expressions and text-critical issues related to them require closer examination.

---

61 A tour is 'a series of one or more verses where the poet lists pairs of from three to ten words all meaning roughly the same thing, or having something to do with the same subject, or being in some way related.' This definition is adopted by Watson from William R. Watters, *Formula Criticism and the Poetry of the Old Testament* (BZAW 138; Berlin: De Gruyter, 1976) 152.

62 'Ellipsis is the omission of a particle, word or group of words within a poetic or grammatical unit, where its presence is expected' Watson, *Hebrew Poetry*, 303-304.

63 *Contra* Niditch, "The Composition," 524. Rather than concern for metre, the notoriously 'light' handling of lists by the Septuagint translators would more likely account for the absence of the Greek counterpart of this expression in LXX, as argued by Williamson, *Isaiah 1-27*, 75.

a) לֵרָאוֹת פָּנַי — Williamson persuasively argues that the MT's vocalization of לֵרָאוֹת as a niphal with syncopated ה ('to appear in my presence') is the result of a reverential correction that goes back to the compiler of Isa 1. He inclines to believe that in the pre-exilic times lay worshipers were allowed access even to the part of the sanctuary where the ark was stationed 'to see God's face', hence the supposed original qal form לִרְאוֹת.[64] If correct, this expression originally referred to the moment of the ultimate exposure of humans to God's holiness, the intensity of which is captured in Isa 6. As this chapter describes, in such a moment, there is no place for uncleanness; in fact, it can spell disaster for a human being.

b) רְמֹס חֲצֵרָי — According to de Vaux, the concept of the holy place in the Semitic religion was not limited to an altar, a sanctuary or a temple, but included also a space around them, a space clearly marked 'to make a separation between the holy and the profane' (Ezek 42:20).[65] The term חָצֵר with YHWH as the subject most likely referes to such a space. As Hamp describes, these enclosed precincts 'possessed a numinous aura,' and, besides separating the sacred from the profane, they 'placed those who entered them under the spell of the sacred.'[66] Passages like Exod 20:25-26 make clear that such a place can be profaned by people's inappropriate conduct. This conduct is in Isa 1:12 described by the verb רמס, a term that occurs almost exclusively in the context of violation and destruction. The structural analysis of vv. 12-13 below reveals the close connection of the phrase רְמֹס חֲצֵרָי with its immediate context. This connection suggests that the violation here is not just an annoying sound of the multitude of worshipers, but refers to something more serious, something that makes the worshiper's מִנְחָה worthless (שָׁוְא): just like the people of Israel profane the name of YHWH in Ezek 20:39 by bringing their מִנְחָה and serving idols at the same time, the worshipers in Isa 1:10-17 profane YHWH's court by exposing its (derived) holiness to אָוֶן.

c) אָוֶן — In his study of אָוֶן, Bernhardt points out this term's wide range of meaning, stating that 'אָוֶן is not connected with a special category of wicked activity, but … denotes a fundamental religio-ethical condition which collectively influences man.'[67] Based on a number of OT texts, it can be concluded that אָוֶן refers to such mental state, mindset, or (in Hebrew terms) inclination of one's heart that

---

64   See Williamson, *Isaiah 1-27*, 75 and 90-91. See also bibliography there.

65   De Vaux, *Ancient Israel*, 274-276.

66   V. Hamp, "חָצֵר," *TDOT* 5.135.

67   K. Bernhardt, "אָוֶן," *TDOT* 1.143.

potentially results in corrupted religious or ethical behaviour.[68] Just as in the case of its most used English equivalent 'iniquity', the meaning of אָוֶן can be narrowed down only by its context. The fact that is not found in the so called legal texts[69] may explain why, in the words of Livingston, 'little attention to 'āwen as a contributor to an understanding of sin' is paid by biblical theologians.[70] Despite solid textual evidence (see below), it is apparent that the 'religio' aspect of אָוֶן is often ignored, especially when interpreted in the prophetic literature.

Bernhardt states that because those 8th century prophetic texts that use אָוֶן 'encompass the most important areas of prophetic criticism: social injustice, cultic wrongs, corrupt politics,' this term clearly 'denotes a deed or an attitude which in the view of the prophets is opposed to the will of God.'[71] While very likely correct, this characterization is too general to enrich the interpretation of a particular prophetic passage. In Isa 1:10-17, אָוֶן is buried in the midst of cultic terms, and such a specific immediate context calls for a more narrow, most naturally cultic definition of this term. Such a definition is at hand – as proposed by BDB, אָוֶן can be rendered as 'idolatry' in a number of prophetic texts.[72] Most of these come from the 8th century prophet Hosea: אָוֶן of Gilead in 12:12 parallels the illegitimate cultic practices in Gilgal,[73] and the expression בָּמוֹת אָוֶן in 10:8 uses אָוֶן 'to inveigh against Canaanite cultic practices which had been adopted in Israel.'[74] Furthermore, the immediate context of the expression בֵּית אָוֶן in 4:15, 5:8, and 10:5 is idolatry, and, provided this expression serves in

---

68   See, e.g., Job 15:35; Ps 36:5, 41:7, 66:18; Prov 6:18; Isa 32:6, 55:7, 59:7; Ezek 11:2; Mic 2:1.

69   As observed by Bernhardt, "אָוֶן," TDOT 1.141. He adds that אָוֶן can be found 'exclusively in prophetic, cultic, and sapiental texts.'

70   G. H. Livingston, "אות," TWOT 1.23-24. He continues by saying that, 'since the word stresses the planning and expression of deception and points to the painful aftermath of sin, it should be noted more.'

71   Bernhardt, "אָוֶן," TDOT 1.143.

72   BDB, p. 19. As the comparison below of Isa 1:13 with BDB's possible instances for rendering אָוֶן as idolatry reveals, the absence of this verse among these examples is rather surprising.

73   NET also understands אָוֶן here this way, as explained in the footnote to this verse: 'the second-half of the verse refers to cultic sins, suggesting that Hosea is denouncing Gilead for its idolatry. Cf. NLT 'Gilead is filled with sinners who worship idols.'

74   Bernhardt, "אָוֶן," TDOT 1.143. Even if this expression reads בָּמוֹת בֵּית אָוֶן as in some Hebrew manuscripts, the negative cultic connotation of the term remains (see the discussion above).

Hosea as a polemical or even derogatory reference to בֵּית־אֵל, the choice of אָוֶן for אֵל speaks strongly for the negative cultic aspect of אָוֶן.[75]

Another apt candidate for אָוֶן referring to 'idolatry' is 1 Sam 15:22-23. This short passage is, at the same time, a close theological parallel to Isa 1:10-17, so it deserves a more detailed examination. It presents a climax of what is known as the story about the rejection of king Saul in 1 Sam 15. As a token of his victory over the Amalekites, king Saul spares their king Agag and 'the best of the sheep and of the cattle and of the fatlings, and the lambs, and all that was valuable' (v. 9). When confronted by the prophet Samuel over this booty, he defends the breach of חֵרֶם command by designating the spared animals for sacrifices to YHWH (vv. 15 and 21). To this, Samuel replies:

> Has the LORD as great delight in burnt offerings and sacrifices,
>> as in obeying the voice of the LORD?
> Surely, to obey is better than sacrifice,
>> and to heed than the fat of rams.
> For rebellion is the sin of divination,
>> and insubordination is אָוֶן וּתְרָפִים
> Because you have rejected the word of the LORD,
>> He has also rejected you from being king.

Because of its prophetic features, namely poetic form and cult-critical content, some scholars consider this passage to be a part of the prophetic rewriting of an earlier story.[76] Long, however, persuasively defends the originality of vv. 22-23 to their present context in ch. 15 by showing how these verses function in and are connected with the story.[77] Furthermore, he repudiates the objection that so called anti-cult polemic originated with the 8th century prophets, referring to the already mentioned article by Weinfeld, who demonstrated that such cult-critical ideas were around hundreds of years before the prophets,

---

75 As also implied in Amos 5:4-6, where the אָוֶן character of the Bethel cult in v. 5 is contrasted with the command to seek the Lord and live (vv. 4b and 6a).

76 Thus, e.g., Klein is inclined to believe that, because Samuel's response in vv. 22-23 is 'couched in Hebrew poetry,' it might have been 'once preserved independently of the narrative,' Ralph W. Klein, *1 Samuel* (WBC 10; Waco, TX: Word Books, 1983) 152. For the most recent and detailed proposal of the prophetic rewriting in 1 Sam 15, see Antony F. Campbell, *1 Samuel* (FOTL 7; Grand Rapids, MI; Cambridge: W.B. Eerdmans, 2003) 157-159. Campbell, however, does not consider vv. 22 and 23a to be a part of this prophetic editing, and even this editorial work, according to him, took place rather early, before the Deuteronomic History and the Prophetic Record.

77 V. Philips Long, *The Reign and Rejection of King Saul: A Case for Literary and Theological Coherence* (Atlanta, GA: Scholars Press, 1989) 150-155.

as documented in Egyptian literature.[78] In support of their authenticity, two simple observations may be added to Long's arguments: first, if these verses are, as many recognize, the climax of the story, an elevated form of language is to be expected; second, when Samuel's prophetic role is taken into consideration, the prophetic forms and ideas in the story appear genuine.

A more complicated issue is to determine the sense of the clause אָוֶן וּתְרָפִים הַפְצַר in v. 23a. The biggest help with the *hapax legomenon* הַפְצַר and with the unique combination אָוֶן וּתְרָפִים comes from the parallel with the preceding clause חַטַּאת־קֶסֶם מֶרִי. Thus, while the meaning of הַפְצַר still remains an educated guess (usually translated as 'presumption' or the like), it clearly refers to something in Saul's unacceptable behaviour. Similarly, because the terms קֶסֶם and תְרָפִים clearly refer to illegitimate cultic practices, the meaning of אָוֶן should be sought within this area as well. Budde leaves no room for doubt, claiming that 'אָוֶן kann hier nur heissen *Götzendienst,* was sich freilich in so selbständigem Gebrauch nicht belegen lässt, auch durch Num 23 21 nicht.'[79] Many scholars, however, prefer to delete the ו before תְרָפִים, arguing that such a construction makes for a better parallel, referring to the rendering of this expression in LXX[B] for support.[80] Some of those who opt for retaining MT propose to read אָוֶן וּתְרָפִים as a hendiadys, suggesting 'evil teraphim' or 'worthless teraphim' for translation.[81] However, such a combination of two different meanings cannot be regarded as hendiadys. If two terms are to function this way, they must both refer to one common thing, in this case to idol worship. The solution is to recognize that 1 Sam 15:23 is another instance of אָוֶן referring to idolatry, and conclude with Long that

---

78 Moshe Weinfeld, "Ancient Near Eastern Patterns in Prophetic Literature," *VT* 27 (1977) 178-195: esp. 189f.

79 Karl Budde, *Die Bücher Samuel,* vol. 8 (Kurzer Hand-Commentar zum Alten Testament; Tübingen: J.C.B. Mohr, 1902) 111.

80 Thus, e.g., McCarter translates this phrase as 'presumption [is] the wickedness of idolatry,' P. Kyle McCarter, *I Samuel: A New Translation* (Garden City, N.Y.: Doubleday, 1980) 259.

81 So Klein, translating v. 23Ab as 'presumption [is] like the vanity of teraphim,' Klein, *1 Samuel,* 145 and 153.

Saul's disobedience (v. 22), likened in v. 23 to rebellion and presumption
(?), involves "a kind of rejection of Yahweh" which places it on a level with
idolatry and divination (and other forms of apostasy). Thus, so long as the
basic problem of disobedience remains unresolved, any attempt on Saul's
part to make amends by ritual means is useless at best and at worst
idolatrous.[82]

Considering the use of אָוֶן in the passages above, especially in 1 Sam
15:23, and the fact that אָוֶן in Isa 1:13 is surrounded by cultic terms, it is
reasonable to conclude that אָוֶן in Isa 1:13 refers to idolatry or/and some
other form of cultic apostasy, present in the minds or/and in the actual
cultic practices of the Israelites. One can only speculate about the
connection between 1Sam 15:22-23 and Isa 1:10-17, but reading the
latter with the knowledge of the former makes one appreciate the
ingenuity of choosing the term אָוֶן in Isa 1:13 to make the point.

Now the question is: why would LXX render אָוֶן as νηστείαν (fasting),
likely reading צוֹם instead? Even though any answer to this question is
speculative, there are several good reasons that speak for maintaining
אָוֶן in Isa 1:13. The presupposition in the following list is that the LXX
of Isaiah is essentially the work of a single translator.[83]

— The possibility of mechanical error can be safely excluded for at
least three reasons: the interchange of these two words is not
hinted at in any available Hebrew manuscript, the LXX
translator of Isaiah was apparently familiar with אָוֶן and its
nuances,[84] and it is unlikely that ו would be mistaken for ם.

---

82 Long, *Reign and Rejection*, 155. Gordon arrives at the same conclusion, stating that
Saul's sin 'is classed with *divination* and *idolatry* ... because it is no less an affront to
the unique authority of Yahweh,' R. P. Gordon, *1 & 2 Samuel: A Commentary* (Exeter:
Paternoster, 1986) 145. This understanding supports Quinn-Miscall's suggestion that
'much of 1 Samuel is the paraenesis or sermon' on Deut 16-18, here esp. 18:9-14,
where is said that the nations have been driven out of the land by Yʜᴡʜ because of
their diviners and soothsayers, but also the previous verses which talk about
sacrifices, obedience and respect of the priests, careful observance of their
instructions, and about how a king should behave (17:10-18:13), see Peter D. Quinn-
Miscall, *1 Samuel: A Literary Reading* (Indiana Studies in Biblical Literature;
Bloomington, IN: Indiana University Press, 1986) 108-109. Reading 1 Sam 15 with
this background in mind makes one conclude that, in words of Green, Saul 'has
omitted the task of reading his scroll of *torah*,' Barbara Green, *How Are the Mighty
Fallen?: A Dialogical Study of King Saul in 1 Samuel* (JSOTSup 365; London: Sheffield
Academic Press, 2003) 233.
83 For support, see, e.g., H. G. M. Williamson, "Isaiah 1.11 and the Septuagint of Isaiah,"
in *Understanding Poets and Prophets: Essays in Honour of George Wishart Anderson*, ed.
A. Graeme Auld (JSOTSup 152; Sheffield: JSOT Press, 1993) 401.
84 Even though the LXX translator is rather interpretative in his rendering of אָוֶן as
πονηρία in 10:1; κακία in 29:20; μάταιος in 31:2, 32:6 and 41:29 (same root); ἄνομος in

— According to Preuss, 'The distribution of occurrences [of צוֹם]
shows that only a few unequivocal or possible texts date to the
pre-exilic period ... Except for Jer 14, the pre-exilic prophets do
not mention fasting; nor do even the older law collections.'[85] He
further explains that although fasting was a familiar custom
before the exile, it became organized and more frequent during
the postexilic period. It is therefore likely that the LXX
translator would be inclined to supply this word in the list of
festivals in v. 13-14.

— If the LXX translator understands אָוֶן as just a next item of the
list in vv. 13-14, his emendation is somehow understandable,
for צוֹם would fit into this list much better than אָוֶן.[86] However,
this impression changes when the whole structure of 1:10-17 is
considered (see below, 4.5.1 and 4.5.2).

— It is plausible that the LXX translator was influenced by Isa
58:5-6, where צוֹם is a key word (occurring three times) in a
very similar context.[87] In addition, Williamson suggests a
possible influence from the expression in Joel 1:14 and 2:15
where צוֹם and עֲצָרָה are connected.[88]

— One more possible influence, also suggested by Williamson,
comes from LXX's understanding of מִקְרָא קְרֹא in the previous
line. For reasons that are not entirely clear, the translator
renders it as ἡμέραν μεγάλην, possibly referring to the Day of
Atonement.[89] This allusion 'may have naturally led the
translator to the thought of fasting.'[90]

55:7 and 59:4, 6; γογγυσμός in 58:9; ἄφρων in 59:7; βλάσφημος in 66:3 (a special nuance
of אָוֶן?), he consistently understands the term as negative in its core, unlike the word
νηστείαν.

85   H. Preuss, "צוֹם," *TDOT* 12.298.

86   For LXX translator's rather lax treatment of lists in Isaiah, see Williamson, "Isaiah
1.11." To this, one example of free rendering of אָוֶן in LXX may be added: in Isa 59:4
and 6, the Greek word is ἄνομος, whereas in the next verse 7 it is βλάσφημος.

87   The influence from the later Isa 58-59 on the earlier Isa 1 can also be found in 1QIsa[a]:
as Williamson in one of his reviews argues, the expression אצבעותיכם בעאון in 1QIsa[a]
version of Isa 1:15 'has clearly been added secondarily under the influence of 59:3,'
H. G. M. Williamson, "Review: Paulson Pulikottil, *Transmission of Biblical Texts in
Qumran: The Case of the Large Isaiah Scroll 1QIsa[a],*" *JTS* 54 (2003) 641-646.

88   קָדְשׁוּ־צוֹם קִרְאוּ עֲצָרָה, see Williamson, "Biblical Criticism," 87-88.

89   See Isac Leo Seeligmann, *The Septuagint Version of Isaiah: A Discussion of Its Problems*
(Leiden: E. J. Brill, 1948) 102-103.

90   Williamson, *Isaiah 1-27*, 78. He also adds that the argument of harder reading in this
case is rather subjective and two-edged.

Although there is still some room for doubt, the cumulative force of these arguments in addition to the fitting meaning outlined above allows us to conclude that אָוֶן in Isa 1:13 should be retained.

d) עֲצָרָה — Although some commentators limit the meaning of עֲצָרָה to particular religious occasions,[91] most scholars agree with Kutsch's general rendering of this term *das Feiern, Feiertag*, the time of solemn or festive assembly, during which people were to refrain from work and to celebrate. [92] This general meaning in pre-exilic times is more apparent in Amos 5:21, where עֲצָרָה is parallel with חַג in a context very similar to Isa 1:10-17. Furthermore, Williamson believes that, instead of referring to a single occasion, עֲצָרָה in Isa 1:13 refers to a single aspect of several different occasions, presumably 'the idea of assembly for a variety of religious purposes.'[93] For every participant, this aspect implies, in words of Seebass, 'Zurücklassung der Ungeeigneten' to maintain the state of ritual cleanness in order to participate in cult. [94] Seebass therefore rightly objects to Kutsch that עֲצָרָה involves more than just refraining from work. The structural analysis below shows that, understood this way, עֲצָרָה is a very fitting term in what seems to be a summarizing statement of its immediate context.

As indicated above, the structure of this stanza significantly contributes to the understanding of its meaning. The present analysis is very much indebted to the work of Williamson on these two verses in his recent commentary.[95] He discusses the ambiguous division in MT where the expression רְמֹס חֲצֵרָי at the end of verse 12 seems to 'hang in the air' and accounts for a variety of translations.[96] Williamson eventually follows the proposal of Spreafico in taking the negative imperative לֹא תוֹסִיפוּ at the beginning of verse 13 as a 'double-duty modifier',[97] governing both the preceding and the following expres-

---

91 Thus, e.g., Gray suggests that עֲצָרָה meant 'a time during which men are under taboo,' Gray, *Isaiah 1-27*, 22.

92 Ernst Kutsch, "Die Wurzel עצר im Hebräischen," *VT* 2 (1952) 57-69: 69.

93 See Williamson, *Isaiah 1-27*, 95.

94 Horst Seebass, "Tradition und Interpretation bei Jehu ben Chanani und Ahia von Silo," *VT* 25 (1975) 175-190: 182. 1Sam 21:2-7 can serve as an example of abandoning all that is unfitting for participating in a ritual (here the abstinence of sexual intercourse with women before eating the holy bread, notice the use of עצר in v. 6).

95 See Williamson, *Isaiah 1-27*, 76-77.

96 Compare, e.g., NAS, NIV, KJV, and ESV "When you come to appear before me, who has required of you this trampling of my courts?" with, e.g., NRSV, TNK, and NAB "When you come to appear before me, who asked this from your hand? Trample my courts no more."

97 Spreafico, "Nahum i 10 and Isaiah i 12-13," 108.

sions. Watson calls such formation 'pivot-patterned bicolon with silent
(final) stress', where the final stress is a result of the absence of the
second verbal phrase (expected due to a balance in a couplet).[98]
Applied to vv. 12-13, Williamson's division is 'a string of equal-length
half lines':

כי תבאו לראות פני

מי בקש זאת מידכם

רמס חצרי לא תוסיפו

הביא מנחת שוא (silent stress)

קטרת תועבה היא לי

חדש ושבת קרא מקרא

לא אוכל און ועצרה

Moving from focusing on *metre* (stress-pattern) to a more distant
perspective reveals two ellipses – one in the bicolon with silent stress
(discussed above), and one immediately following it. In case of the
second 'pivot-patterned bicolon', תּוֹעֵבָה הִיא לִי serves a 'double-duty'
as well, and the list of festivals in its second colon makes up for the lack
of verb and object, functioning as 'ballast variant' to the first cola (the
isocolic principle).

Williamson in his discussion of חֹדֶשׁ וְשַׁבָּת calls attention to another
syntactical feature called *casus pendens*.[99] He treats חֹדֶשׁ וְשַׁבָּת as a casus
pendens, resumed by אָוֶן וַעֲצָרָה. The study of עֲצָרָה above confirms
that this term is appropriate for resumption of חֹדֶשׁ וְשַׁבָּת, functioning
as a resumptive synonymous noun. A resumptive element can have a
form of 'different lexical item from extraposed element, yet nonetheless
construed as coreferential with it.'[100] Furthermore, it can be argued that
עֲצָרָה functions on a larger (macrosyntactic) scale as a resumptive
synonymous noun for what Waltke would call a family of nominative
absolute constructions, for the following reasons:

— 'A verbal clause may form a unit which can be considered and
   treated as a substantive.'[101] Thus כִּי תָבֹאוּ לֵרָאוֹת פָּנַי can be
   taken as a substantival clause, functioning as the object of the

---

98 Watson, *Hebrew Poetry*, 215.

99 For definition and examples see 'Extraposition' in Gibson §149-151, or Khan, *Semitic
    Syntax*, 67-104. See also discussion of 'Nominative Absolute' in *IBHS* 4.7.

100 Khan, *Semitic Syntax*, 74. One of the Khan's illustrations of such case is actually Isa
    1:13b.

101 JM §157a.

following verb בקשׁ resumed by the pronoun זאֹת.[102] Thus the
first line of v. 12 can be treated as an objective (accusative)
causus pendens.[103]

— As suggested by Nielsen, the pronoun ayhi in this verse does
not need to refer back to קְטֹרֶת (מִנְחָה being in a construct state),
but it can refer to קְטֹרֶת and thus to a different type of offering,
viz. that of incense.[104] In this case, ayhi functions as the
resumptive pronoun for קְטֹרֶת as another objective casus
pendens.

— The expressions רָמֹס חֲצֵרַי, הָבִיא מִנְחַת־שָׁוְא and קְרֹא מִקְרָא can
be treated in one group with חֹדֶשׁ וְשַׁבָּת which has already been
discussed – they all appear disconnected (especially in MT
division) and can all function as objective causus pendens
resumed by the synonymous noun עֲצָרָה. Even כִּי תָבֹאוּ לֵרָאוֹת
פָּנַי and קְטֹרֶת may be included in this group as causus pendens
'once-removed'.

Admittedly, this overarching, long-range function of עֲצָרָה as a
resumptive synonymous noun may seem exaggerated, but it is
plausible to suggest that such a connection would operate especially in
the oral presentation of these verses. It may be suggested that this
syntactical correlation in vv. 12-13 is an example of the macrosyntactic
role of extraposition for the sake of highlighting the climax of a
speech.[105]

The discussion above clarifies (and justifies) the proposed division
of this stanza: just as in the previous case, the rhetorical question in the
first monocolon introduces the main point, extended in the following
two bicolons (possibly another 'tour'), and concluded by the climactic
monocolon. The discussion of the meaning of this monocolon, namely

---

102 Such a syntactical construction might seem to frustrate the understanding of the
sentence; however, the opposite is the case; as Waltke rightly suggests when
discussing a similar construction, 'it allows a grammatically complex part of the
clause to stand on its own, thus increasing clarity,' *IBHS* 4.7c. In the subsequent
illustration (#6 – Gen 30:30), he translates כִּי as 'with respect to'. In our case, כִּי
could also have *recitative* function, introducing direct speech; see Williams §451. For
more examples, see JM §157c.

103 See JM §156c.

104 For details, see Nielsen, *Incense*, 53-54 and 79-80. Initially, when discussing קְטֹרֶת in
Isa 1:13, he claims that it refers to offerings in general, or to their odour or smoke,
because it is parallel to מִנְחָה and therefore has hardly anything to do with the מִנְחָה of
Lev 2, viz. a grain offering. This, as argued in 1.4.1, does not necessarily have to be
the case.

105 For discussion and examples of this phenomenon, see Gibson §151b.

the combination of עֲצָרָה with אָוֶן, is reserved for the section on functional analysis below.

4.4.4. Stanza IV (vv. 14-15)

The division of this stanza is straightforward and follows the MT disjunctive accents. Strictly speaking, the parallelism in v. 14 is only partial: the object of the first colon, חָדְשֵׁיכֶם וּמוֹעֲדֵיכֶם, becomes the subject of the second, and an implied object in the third. There is, however, a clear link of meaning between the parts (semantic parallelism). Furthermore, the absence of an object in the third cola ties it with the previous two, so one can legitimately talk about a tricolon. The role of this arrangement is obvious: to confirm and reconfirm the shocking statement that YHWH hates חָדְשֵׁיכֶם וּמוֹעֲדֵיכֶם.

The following tetracolon consists of two concessive clauses. This nuance of causal construct is in the first clause rendered by וּ (introducing the circumstantial clause וּבְפָרְשְׂכֶם כַּפֵּיכֶם),[106] whereas in the second by stronger כִּי גַם.[107] The parallelism between the two clauses (A B // A' B') is a good illustration of Kugel's idea mentioned above: A B is so, and *what's more*, A' B'. As in the previous verse, this structure accentuates the shocking nature of both statements. Even though the symbolic significance of spreading out one's hands (towards heaven or the Temple) remains unknown,[108] it seems to be characteristic of a petition, as Solomon's prayer of dedication in 1Kgs 8:22-54 demonstrates. The statement in Isa 1:15a seems to run against Solomon's appeal: instead of having his eyes open day and night toward the Temple (1Kgs 8:29) and hearing כָּל־תְּפִלָּה כָל־תְּחִנָּה אֲשֶׁר תִּהְיֶה לְכָל־הָאָדָם לְכֹל עַמְּךָ יִשְׂרָאֵל (v. 38a) when that person פָּרַשׂ כַּפָּיו toward the Temple (v. 38c), YHWH in Isa 1:15 hides his eyes from petitioners and refuses to listen to any of their prayers.[109] Solomon, however, conditions the outcome of the petition upon the petitioner's behaviour and heart when asking YHWH וְנָתַתָּ לָאִישׁ כְּכָל־דְּרָכָיו אֲשֶׁר

---

106 See JM §171f, and Williams §528.

107 See JM §171a and c, and Williams §530.

108 See David J. A. Clines, *Job 1-20* (WBC 17; Dallas, TX: Word Books, 1989) 267-268.

109 The following quote from de Vaux helps to realize that God's turning away his eyes and refusal to listen goes against the basic notion of cult: 'Cult is the outward homage paid to a god. Since the god is thought of as receiving this homage and listening to the prayer of his suppliant in the place where this worship is offered, the god is considered to be present there in some way or other, at least while the act of worship is being performed,' de Vaux, *Ancient Israel*, 274.

תֵּדַע אֶת־לְבָבוֹ (v. 39, cmp. v. 32). As the closing monocolon of Isa 1:14-15 reveals, YHWH's response is fully in accord with this principle, since the hands that these people spread out to him are full of blood.[110]   As observed by many commentators, the plural דָּמִים is usually connected with murder, rendering thus the sense of bloodguilt.[111]   In the connection with social justice, it should be noted that bloodguilt can be acquired even through "legal" means, as suggested by the expression לִשְׁפָּךְ דָּם נָקִי in 59:7a, which Park interprets as 'eine unberechtigte Todesstrafe aufgrund eines Unrechtsurteils im Torgericht.'[112] Wildberger broadens the meaning of דָּמִים in 1:15 even further, by maintaining that it does not have to be limited to its literal sense, but, according to priestly understanding, can mark 'jede Schuld, bei der die göttliche Ordnung, die gottgesetzten Tabus mißachtet worden sind.' He continues that 'mit דמים ist die Schuld nach ihrer hintergründigen, rational nicht zu bewältigenden, durch das Gegengewicht guter Werke nicht aufzuhebenden Art charakterisiert.'[113] In short, v. 15c makes clear that the reason for YHWH's repudiation of cult is moral impurity, specifically bloodguilt.[114]

4.4.5. Stanza V (vv. 16-17)

This stanza consists of a list of imperatives. While the ones in v. 17 apparently belong to the ethical sphere, the character of the first two in v. 16, רַחֲצוּ הִזַּכּוּ, is a matter of debate.   Even though the term רחץ occurs predominantly in cultic contexts, most commentators diminish

---

110 YHWH's response can also be based on v. 13c, for, as the author of Ps 66 recognizes, if he had cherished אָוֶן in his heart, YHWH would not have listened to his prayer (v. 18).

111 See, e.g., Williamson, *Isaiah 1-27*, 98.

112 Kyung-Chul Park, *Die Gerechtigkeit Israels und das Heil der Völker: Kultus, Tempel, Eschatologie und Gerechtigkeit in der Endgestalt des Jesajabuches (Jes 56, 1-8; 58, 1-14; 65, 17-66, 24)* (Beiträge zur Erforschung des Alten Testaments und des Anitken Judentums, Band 52; Frankfurt: Peter Lang, 2003) 264.

113 Wildberger, *Jesaja*, 159. Wildberger here comments on דמים in 4:2-6, a passage for which he presumes 'priesterlichen Verständnis'. As argued throughout the present thesis, the priestly background, or at least some of its agendas can be presumed for 1:10-17 as well.

114 Commenting on this verse, Kaiser correctly points to Ps 24, according to which only those who have 'clean hands' can 'stand in [YHWH's] holy place' (vv. 3-4), and notes that a person with 'hands full of blood' deserves death not only because of committing murder, but also 'because it has made the temple precinct unclean by entering the inner courtyard,' Kaiser, *Isaiah 1-12*, 34.

or even rule out its cultic reference here. The following quote from
Jensen represents the usual line of argument: '[I]t would seem poor
psychology to insist on the uselessness of cultic observances and then
to call for reform in terms that suggest a merely ritual purification; an *a
priori* judgment would suggest that Isaiah would not be likely to
deliberately choose such terminology.'[115] Jensen is very likely correct
that the prophet does not have a merely ritual ablution in mind.[116]
However, as shown throughout this chapter, the point of vv. 11-15 is
not the uselessness of cultic observances, rather their observance in a
state of impurity, and, since there is no difference between ritual and
moral impurity *sub specie sanctitatis Dei*, a call for ritual purification
would certainly not be out of place here. In fact, *sub specie sanctitatis Dei*,
the cultic regulation רַחֲצוּ is the vital first step when approaching the
Holy One.[117] In addition, Isaiah personally experienced the vitality of
ritual cleansing as a prerequisite in the presence of the Holy One in 6:5,
so there is no reason to assume that he would be indifferent to it.[118]

The real problem is, however, that the impurity of which the
community is guilty, specifically idolatry and murder, cannot be
removed by cultic ablutions. This may be the reason why רחץ in this
passage is not followed by the usual טהר, but by זכה (or, possibly, זכך),
a term that 'pre-eminently carries the meaning of moral and inner
purification.'[119] Also the last part of v. 16 confirms that what the
prophet considers to be the main problem of the community is moral
impurity – רֹעַ מַעַלְלֵיכֶם. Even when the focus of the individual
commands is now and throughout the whole v. 17 on ethics, the main
concern of the prophet remains cultic, as the first command in the list

---

115 Jensen, *Use of tôrâ*, 78.

116 *Contra*, e.g., Brueggemann, who believes that these commands mean that 'Israel
must engage in ritual purification because it has been defiled and made
unacceptable to the holy God,' Walter Brueggemann, *Isaiah*, 2 vols. (Westminster
Bible Companion; Louisville, KY: Westminster John Knox Press, 1998) 1.18.

117 As apparent from passages like Exod 29:4, 40:12; Lev 8:6, 16:4 and 24. Noth
comments on the first of these passages that 'bodily purity obtained through
washing with water … is at the same time a part of cultic purity and stands in a
mysterious relationship with it,' Martin Noth, *Exodus: A Commentary*, trans. John
Stephen Bowden (OTL; London: SCM, 1962) 230. This comment calls for more
caution to read רחץ figuratively.

118 As correctly argued by Brueggemann, *Isaiah*, 1.18.

119 Blenkinsopp, *Isaiah 1-39*, 185. Gray even goes as far as claiming that 'זכה is never
used of ceremonial cleanness, but of ethical purity,' Gray, *Isaiah 1-27*, 23. However, a
closer look at the use of this root reveals that it is more accurate to speak about 'a
certain semantic duality', encompassing both ritual and ethical purity, the latter one
being predominant, as maintained by Negoiță and Ringgren, "זכה," *TDOT* 4.62-64.

(רָחֲצוּ) indicates.[120] There certainly is a movement in vv. 16-17, but not 'from figurative language to the most literal,'[121] but rather from cult in general to its ethical dimension, narrowing down the divine perspective (*sub specie sanctitatis Dei*) to human perspective (ethics, social justice).

The structure of this stanza brings out this movement. It is governed by the same principle as Stanza II: the opening line introduces the main point, and the following lines are its expansion via a tour, of which the primary role is merismus. The following comment from Watson is helpful to recognize the three-strophic-units structure of v. 16: 'Although tricola of this type, which do not exhibit consecutive parallelism, might justifiably be classed as 'bicolon + monocolon', they are considered as strophic units because there is usually a link bonding the three lines. In nearly all cases, the link is one of meaning or content.'[122] The link becomes apparent when each consequent colon is viewed as a commentary on the previous command, narrowing down the idea of purification to the removal of evil deeds. This idea is then illustrated in the next three bicolons, which (as with every good merismus) create the impression of an open ending. Such ending, in turn, calls the listener (or the reader) to active involvement – to fill in his/her own items to complete the concept under discussion, in this case the one of ethics.

4.5. Functional Analysis of Isa 1:10-17

Following Watson's method of analysis of Hebrew poetry, after delimitation (determining the beginning and end of the poem), segmentation (dividing the poem into stanzas, strophes, colons, bicolons, etc.), inner-strophic analysis and isolation of poetic devices, comes another important stage – synthesis, or functional analysis (depending on the point of view). Its purpose is to determine how various poetic devices interact within the poem and how the individual stanzas relate to each other.[123] Before analysing the proposed structures

---

120 *Contra* the usual viewpoint that vv. 16-17 emphasize moral considerations over ceremonial procedure, maintained by, e.g., Sweeney, *Isaiah 1-4*, 111.

121 *Contra* Franz Delitzsch, *Biblical Commentary on the Prophecies of Isaiah* (Clark's Foreign Theol. Libr. 4th ser. vol. 14, 15; Edinb.: 1867) 1.95.

122 Watson, *Hebrew Poetry*, 180.

123 See Watson, *Hebrew Poetry*, 18-20.

of the text, the question of handling what seem to be later additions needs to be addressed.

Carroll in his article 'Prophecy and Society' argues that the prophetic text available to a modern reader underwent irreversible transformations, hence there is no validity in a search for the 'original' words of a prophet, and reconstructing the setting of the text from the text itself is simply an erroneous procedure. Since prophecy was by and large an oral phenomenon, the first transformation, according to Carroll, was from the spoken word to the written word. 'Such a shift from orality to literacy has removed prophecy from its original social setting to a decontextualised, timeless setting and any search for the *Sitz im Leben* of specific prophecies is irrelevant.'[124] The second type of transformation is generally known as the editing process. Carroll comments on it with regards to the prophetic material:

> The selection of material, its written forms edited in places to extend its meaning and reference, the juxtaposing of discrete and disparate pieces, and the provision of introductory colophons for each book all contributed to the further removal of prophecy from its original setting in the life of ancient Israel. These editorial transformations of material already transformed by writing must be regarded as the original creations of the prophetic traditions and it is now simply not possible to get back behind such editing to whatever may have constituted the 'original' prophecies![125]

In addition, it is a growing consensus among contemporary scholars that not only the prophets, but also the writers and the editors of the prophetic books were artists who skilfully shaped the inherited material to give it the present shape.[126] It is, therefore, justifiable to consider the text in its final (written) form also at this level of analysis.

However, even a word-by-word recorded speech appears differently to a listener than to a reader. An audience is more likely to enjoy various sound-plays, dynamics of speech, and non-verbal elements of rhetoric denied to a reader; on the other hand, even a skilful listener is not able to appreciate all the corresponding elements of a complex structure apparent to a competent reader. Therefore, while adhering to Carroll's view above, it can be a fruitful endeavour to venture one step back from the structure apparent to a reader to what

---

124 R. Carroll, "Prophecy and Society," in *The World of Ancient Israel: Sociological, Anthropological and Political Perspectives*, ed. R. E. Clements (Cambridge: Cambridge University Press, 1989) 207-208.

125 Carroll, "Prophecy and Society," 208.

126 'The discovery some modern scholars have yet to appropriate fully is that the composers responsible for the present text were knowledgeable, skilful, and presumably aesthetically aware,' Campbell, "Form Criticism's Future," 23.

could be called *audible structure* – a structure recognizable to an audience. The major difference between this endeavour and an attempt to recover the 'original' prophetic oracle is that it works with the final form of the text, focusing on its main characteristics and overlooking the detailed elaborations that might have resulted from writing or editing the (presupposed) speech.[127] This procedure is similar to a surface reading and can be likened to producing a sketch of a finished painting. Of course, this procedure is highly hypothetical, and the primary value still lies in analysing the structure of the text in its fullness, here called *readable structure*.

The chart below attempts to capture the discussion above: on the left is the proposal of the audible structure, and on the right that of the readable structure. In the middle, there is the full MT text, but this time with extra spacing and 'new-lines' that bring out the vertical parallelism of the text. This parallelism captures the main tension of the passage, namely the action of the people and the reaction of YHWH (notice the respective headings over the MT section after v. 10).

---

127 The assumption here is, as generally agreed, that the written prophetic message is very likely more elaborated, refined and stylized than its presumed oral counterpart.

Audible Struct.	MT of Isaiah 1:10-17		Readable Struct.
INTRODUCT. of the conflict	שִׁמְעוּ דְבַר־יְהוָה קְצִינֵי סְדֹם / הַאֲזִינוּ תּוֹרַת אֱלֹהֵינוּ עַם עֲמֹרָה		CALL TO INSTRUCTION
	Action of People	React. of יהוה	
	רֹב־זִבְחֵיכֶם יֹאמַר יְהוָה / עֹלוֹת אֵילִים / וְחֵלֶב מְרִיאִים / וְדַם פָּרִים / וּכְבָשִׂים / וְעַתּוּדִים	לָמָּה־לִּי / שָׂבַעְתִּי	SACRIFICES 1 (A)
ILLUSTRAT. 1 of the conflict		לֹא חָפָצְתִּי	
	כִּי תָבֹאוּ לֵרָאוֹת פָּנָי / זֹאת מִיֶּדְכֶם / רְמֹס חֲצֵרָי / הָבִיא מִנְחַת־שָׁוְא / קְטֹרֶת	מִי־בִקֵּשׁ / לֹא תוֹסִיפוּ / תּוֹעֵבָה הִיא לִי	OFFERINGS 1 (B)
	חֹדֶשׁ / וְשַׁבָּת / קְרֹא מִקְרָא		FESTIVALS 1 (C)
REASON 1	אָוֶן וַעֲצָרָה	לֹא־אוּכַל	CLASH (X)
	חָדְשֵׁיכֶם / וּמוֹעֲדֵיכֶם / הָיוּ	שָׂנְאָה נַפְשִׁי / עָלַי לָטֹרַח / נִלְאֵיתִי נְשֹׂא	FESTIVALS 2 (C′)
ILLUSTRAT. 2 of the conflict	וּבְפָרִשְׂכֶם כַּפֵּיכֶם מִכֶּם / גַּם כִּי־תַרְבּוּ תְפִלָּה	אַעְלִים עֵינַי / אֵינֶנִּי שֹׁמֵעַ	OFFERINGS 2 (B′)
REASON 2	יְדֵיכֶם דָּמִים מָלֵאוּ		
SOLUTION to the conflict	רַחֲצוּ הִזַּכּוּ / הָסִירוּ רֹעַ מַעַלְלֵיכֶם / חִדְלוּ הָרֵעַ / לִמְדוּ הֵיטֵב / דִּרְשׁוּ מִשְׁפָּט / אַשְּׁרוּ חָמוֹץ / שִׁפְטוּ יָתוֹם / רִיבוּ אַלְמָנָה	מִנֶּגֶד עֵינָי	SACRIFICES 2 (A′)

4.5.1. Audible Structure (Surface Reading)

As apparent on the left side of the chart, the proposed audible structure is linear. The following discussion elucidates how this straightforward-ness of the structure helps to drive home the main point of the oracle.

4.5.1.1. Introduction of the Conflict (v. 10)

As most recently argued by Williamson, there are some serious indications that this verse is a redactional introduction.[128] Whether an original word of the prophet or a later addition, it is a very suitable opening for what follows. A call like this would undoubtedly get attention in ancient Israel; not because of its exhortation to listen, but because of its labelling the Israelites 'leaders of Sodom' and 'people of Gomorrah'. Also, it creates a strong tension by juxtaposing these two labels with the expressions דְּבַר־יְהוָה and תּוֹרַת אֱלֹהֵינוּ. One can only speculate what associations this combination would evoke in the mind of an ancient Israelite. Even though the people of that time were hardly familiar with the story of Sodom and Gomorrah as it is described and available to us in Genesis 18-19, Ezek 16:46-58 testifies to the general consciousness about the cities' ethical misconduct during what was then the past 'days of Israel's pride' (16:56).[129] Blenkinsopp believes that 'by the time of writing, the Cities of the Plain had come to exemplify egregious social disorder and injustice ... as well as annihilating divine judgment, which such conduct warranted.'[130] If correct, v. 10 indicates both the nature of the problem (ethical misconduct) and its seriousness (the imminent threat of divine judgment). Williamson even claims that the latter 'has the effect of making of the following verses a most urgent call to repentance.'[131] Thus the conflict as described in vv. 11-15 and its solution as described in vv. 16-17 could be derived already from the affiliations evoked by v. 10.

---

128 See Williamson, *Isaiah 1-27*, 81-88. See, however, the introduction to this section.

129 For the plausibility of such awareness, see Gray, *Isaiah 1-27*, 17-19.

130 Blenkinsopp, *Isaiah 1-39*, 184. He continues that 'for emphasis on homosexual conduct we have to wait until the Hellenistic period.'

131 Williamson, *Isaiah 1-27*, 87.

4.5.1.2. Illustration I of the Conflict (vv. 11 – 13b)

The elaborate list of sacrifices, offerings, and festivals, along with YHWH's reaction to them would very likely produce a simple but intense reaction from the audience: Why? Why would YHWH have no use for, be fed up with, take no delight in, and even forbid the things that are an outward expression of people's faith and devotion? Jensen observes a certain progress (crescendo) in the list of the people's actions and YHWH's reaction to them – a rhetorical device for building the tension.[132] It is important to point out that this section generates questions only, and therefore cannot be used for deducing a solution (such as: get rid of the cult!). Even the main question that this illustration produces is a rather general one: Why is YHWH so upset with sacrifices, offerings and festivals?

4.5.1.3. Reason I for the Conflict (v. 13c)

This phrase provides a general answer to the above question: "Because I cannot endure sacred gathering accompanied with cultic apostasy."[133] At this point, the choice of the terms עֲצָרָה and אָוֶן can be truly appreciated. However, this answer is as general as the question that has caused it. To Isaiah's audience, this may still sound only like a dramatized theological lecture, for it is predominately about God and his (dis)likes. Moreover, it offers only a reason for the conflict, not a solution.

4.5.1.4. Illustration II of the Conflict (vv. 14 – 15b)

The purpose of the second illustration is to generate an important shift from general and public to specific and personal. It is indicated by the increased occurrence of personal suffixes, more intimate kind of offerings (petitions and prayers), and an intensified anthropomorphic description of God along with his reaction directed not just to the things but to the people ('...my soul hates; they have become a burden to me, I am weary of bearing [them]; ... I will hide my eyes from you; I

---

132 See Jensen, *Isaiah 1-39*, 45.

133 The conjunction ו functions here as of accompaniment (see Williams §436). For this understanding, see rendering of Isa 1:13c in, e.g., NJB, NRSV, or TNK. The word-order of the translation has been changed accordingly.

will not listen'). It still does not produce any solution, but the question now becomes specific and personal: Why is YHWH so upset with *our* acts of worship?

4.5.1.5. Reason II for the Conflict (v. 15c)

Also the answer is specific: "Because your hands are full of blood." An impure people cannot have fellowship with a holy God. Only now, when the people get their theology and their self-image right, are they ready to hear the solution.

4.5.1.6. Solution to the Conflict (vv. 16-17)

It is unlikely that the audience would link the individual commands of vv.16-17 in such a sophisticated manner as suggested by Sweeney:

> [W]ashing (v. 16aα1) leads to purification (v. 16aα2) which, of course, means the removal of evil (v. 16aβ) and this allows one to stop doing evil (v. 16b). Once one ceases doing evil, he may begin to learn good (v. 17aα). This naturally leads to the general goals of seeking justice (v. 17aβ) and correcting oppression (v. 17aγ) as well as the more specific goals of judging the orphan (v. 17bα) and pleading for the widow (v. 17 bβ).[134]

The audience, however, would probably capture the movement mentioned above (4.4.5) – from cultic and general to ethical and specific. The people would certainly grasp at least the main idea: If you are to have fellowship with YHWH, stop doing evil like the people of Sodom, and start doing good like the people of God.

4.5.2. Readable Structure (Close Reading)

As noted earlier, the written text is likely to have a more elaborate structure than its spoken counterpart. Also a reader is more likely to amuse himself with looking for such a structure. Because of the natural inclination of a writer to create a stylish structure of the text and, on the other side, of the temptation of a reader to impose a certain structure on the text, the label 'chiastic' is used here only for the lack of a better term. The purpose is not to uncover, e.g., a chiastic structure of Isa 1:10-17, but to demonstrate that this passage is well balanced around

---

134 Sweeney, *Isaiah 1-4*, 110-111.

what appears to be its main theological point – v. 13c. The structure under discussion is outlined on the right side of the chart above, and what follows is the description how the individual parts function in this structure.

4.5.2.1. Call to Instruction (v. 10)

From the structural point of view, this verse connects vv. 11-17 with the previous vv. 2-9 by picking up some of its terminology from v. 2a and v. 9.[135] From the semantic point of view, v. 10 implicitly summarizes the passage (as argued in 4.5.1.1), but does not explicitly contribute to its message. At this point, its function as redactional introduction can be truly appreciated and also gives reason for moving v. 10 outside of the unit's readable structure.[136]

4.5.2.2. Sacrifices I and Sacrifices II (A - A', vv. 11 and 16-17)[137]

As already mentioned, both sections (v. 11 and vv. 16-17) are built by the same technique, viz. the main idea in the opening monocolon is expanded via tour in the following bicolons. This parallel greatly contributes to the overall balance of the passage. Both lists (the one related to sacrifices in v. 11, and the other related to social justice in vv. 16-17) cover a variety of examples in order to denote generalization.[138] As for the first, Miller observes that 'when זֶבַח is joined with עֹלָה, the combination may refer to offerings and sacrifices in general or identify two of the primary forms of sacrifice.'[139] As for the second, its general character is explicit in the expression חִדְלוּ הָרֵעַ לִמְדוּ הֵיטֵב, but it is also

---

135   For details, see Williamson, *Isaiah 1-27*, 82.

136   Additional reasons are 'the inclusion of a separate speech formula in v. 11 as well, perhaps, as […] the shift from the first to second person plural address,' Williamson, *Isaiah 1-27*, 82.

137   The designation of social justice in vv. 16-17 as sacrifices cannot be justified from this passage alone. However, it is implicit in the parallel passage Mic 6:6-8 and, as the later development showed, it became explicit in Judaism: 'The one who keeps the law makes many offerings; one who heeds the commandments makes an offering of well-being. The one who returns a kindness offers choice flour, and one who gives alms sacrifices a thank offering. To keep from wickedness is pleasing to the Lord, and to forsake unrighteousness is an atonement,' Sir 35:1-5.

138   For the discussion of merismus in these passages, see 4.4.2 and 4.4.5.

139   Patrick D. Miller, *The Religion of Ancient Israel* (Louisville, KY: Westminster John Knox Press, 2000) 112.

implicit in listing 'orphans' together with 'widows', representing thus the weak ones of the society in general.

4.5.2.3. Offerings I and Offerings II (B - B', vv. 12-13a and 15)

V. 15 (B') complements vv. 12-13a (B) in several ways:

— People are coming to see God's face (12a), but God is hiding his eyes from them (15aβ).

— God's refusal to receive anything from peoples' hands (12b, מִיֶּדְכֶם) is justified in 15c – 'Your hands (יְדֵיכֶם) are full of blood.'

— Increasing (hiphil of יסף, 13aα[1]) of cultic activities (trampling the temple courts in 12c, and bringing offerings in 13aβ) is ineffective, because, in spite of the increase (hiphil of רבה, 15bα[1]), God will not listen (15bβ).

— 'In the Old Testament, liturgical prayer was not an institution independent of other cultic acts, as it has come to be in synagogue services.'[140] The close connection between תְּפִלָּה (15bα[2]) on one side and מִנְחָה and קְטֹרֶת (13aα[3] and 13aβ[1]) on the other is well established.[141] Ps 141:2 is especially instructive here: 'Let my prayer (תְּפִלָּתִי) be counted as incense (קְטֹרֶת) before you, and the lifting up of my hands (מַשְׂאַת כַּפַּי) as an evening sacrifice (מִנְחַת־עָרֶב).' Reciprocally, when people do not listen to God's instructions, not only their מִנְחָה and קְטֹרֶת are תּוֹעֵבָה (13bβ[2]), but so is their תְּפִלָּה (see Prov 28:9).

4.5.2.4. Festivals I and Festivals II (C - C', vv. 13b and 14)

The most obvious connection between v. 13b and v. 14 is the use of the same word חֹדֶשׁ. Even though its second occurrence is supported by every available ancient textual witness, many commentators suggest its emendation or omission simply on aesthetic grounds. However, the repetition of חֹדֶשׁ can be regarded as a poetical device, and 'since *repetition* is an acknowledged factor in Hebrew poetry, there is no need to alter the second occurrence of the same word to a synonym, or delete

---

140 De Vaux, *Ancient Israel*, 457.

141 See H. Fabry, "מִנְחָה," *TDOT* 8.407-21, esp. 415-18.

it.'[142] Even if the (most reasonable) emendation of חָרְשֵׁיכֶם to חַגֵּיכֶם in
v. 14 is granted,[143] the complementary relationship between vv. 13b and
14, consisting of listing the festivals and YHWH's reaction to them, is
preserved.

4.5.2.5. Clash (X, v. 13c)

The phrase לֹא־אוּכַל אָוֶן וַעֲצָרָה is the encapsulation of the conflict as
described in the passage; therefore it is appropriately placed at the
centre of the structure.[144]

Both of the above proposed structures facilitate that kind of
listening to or reading of Isa 1:10-17 in which the phrase לֹא־אוּכַל אָוֶן
וַעֲצָרָה plays the pivotal role. Positioned in the centre, it brings out an
important theological message through which the whole passage ought
to be interpreted: impurity and holiness do not mix!

4.6. Translation of Isa 1:10-17

The translations of Isa 1:10-17 as well as of 43:22-28 and 58 in the
following chapters are based on NRSV. They endeavor to incorporate
all the observations in the particular chapter regarding the text. This, of
course, is possible only to a certain extent if the proposed translation is
to follow the Hebrew text reasonably closely.

[10] Hear the word of the LORD, you rulers of Sodom!
Listen to the Torah of our God, you people of Gomorrah!

[11] What to me is the multitude of your sacrifices? says the LORD;
I have had enough of burnt offerings of rams
          and the fat of fed beasts;
I do not delight in the blood of bulls,
          or of lambs,
          or of goats.

---

142 Watson, *Hebrew Poetry*, 42.
143 Most recently advocated by Williamson, *Isaiah 1-27*, 79.
144 For those who value counting accents and syllables it may be of interest that the key
     phrase in v. 13 is located in the very centre of the whole passage (if one can be
     determined).

[12] When you come to see my face – who asked this of you?
        (No more) trampling of my courts,
        [13] no more bringing of worthless offering(s),
        incense is an abomination to me,
        (just as) New moon
        and Sabbath
        and calling of convocation …
I cannot endure sacred gathering(s) accompanied with cultic
apostasy!

[14] Your new moons and your appointed festivals my soul hates;
        they have become a burden to me,
        I am weary of bearing them.
[15] When you stretch out your hands, I will hide my eyes from you;
even though you make many prayers, I will not listen,
(because) your hands are full of blood.

[16] Cleanse yourselves,
purify yourselves,
remove the evil of your doings from before my eyes:
cease to do evil,
[17] learn to do good;
seek justice,
rescue the oppressed,
defend the orphan,
plead for the widow.

4.7. Conclusion

The study of the historical background and the form of Isa 1:10-17
helped to set aside at least a couple of rather common anti-ritualistic
presupposition with regard to this passage. First, the few clues from the
text about the overall situation do not support the theory that Isaiah
spoke during a time of crisis to which the people of Judah reacted by
increased cultic activity, trusting in the saving power of rituals. If, as
argued, this oracle originated in the days of Ahaz, it is likely that cult
had a prominent place, but the problem of that time was more likely its
purity – the cult of YHWH was practised by a spiritually and politically

adulterous leadership. Second, the study of the form did not result in
any specific label for Isa 1:10-17, but seriously undermined the tag
'Prophetic Torah' frequently attached to this passage, giving thus one
less reason for its anti-ritualistic reading.

A closer look at the text yielded the following picture: The people
of Israel are gathering for a religious occasion (עֲצָרָה) to have fellowship
with YHWH via cultic means designed for this very purpose. They are
coming to see his face (לְרִאוֹת פָּנָי), which is the moment of the ultimate
exposure of humans to YHWH's holiness. In this moment, the people's
impurity caused by idolatry (אָוֶן) and murder (יְדֵיכֶם דָּמִים מָלֵאוּ) turns
their sacrifices, offerings, and prayers into an abomination (תּוֹעֵבָה),
accomplishing the very opposite of the ritual's purpose – YHWH hides
his face away from the people (אַעְלִים עֵינַי מִכֶּם). Isaiah, being aware of
the disastrous effect of such cultic practice, calls for the people's purity
(רַחֲצוּ הִזַּכּוּ). He is also aware of the fact that the kind of impurity of
which the people are guilty (moral impurity) cannot be removed by
any ritual, and calls for the abolishment of its source, namely the
unethical conduct of the people.

This picture makes clear that Isaiah's ultimate concern is cultic – the
fellowship with YHWH materialized in the cult, and the presence of his
holiness in the people's midst.[145] Jensen correctly states that 'Isaiah
clearly knew of demands for moral behavior that he believed the
people should be familiar with and he castigated them for non-
observance,'[146] but the problem it is not so much, as Park believes, 'das
Doppelleben des Volkes,'[147] rather 'das Doppelleben des Kultes', a
cultic practice that mixes impurity with holiness. This concern is
expressed most clearly in what, also from structural point of view,
appears to be the key phrase: לֹא־אוּכַל אָוֶן וַעֲצָרָה.[148] The ethical appeal

---

145 The so called entrance liturgies (as, e.g., Ps 15) provide a good parallel: even though
     the exhortations are ethical, the concern is cultic – to worship YHWH in his Temple.

146 Jensen, *Use of tôrâ*, 66.

147 Park, *Gerechtigkeit Israels,* 263. Park elsewhere (p. 251) recognizes, that 'der Kult nicht
     in Verbindung mit sozialer Ungerechtigkeit durchgeführt werden soll,' but does not
     attribute Isaiah's reaction to this mixture to his cultic concepts.

148 A similar way of reading Isa 1:10-17 is based on the phrase 'your hands are full of
     blood' in v. 15, which implies, in words of Barton, 'the (surely widely shared) belief
     that those who offer sacrifice must be in a state of purity, and moral transgression –
     especially such sins as murder or theft – pollute the would-be worshipper just as
     much as offences against purity regulations do, and make his sacrifices
     unacceptable,' Barton, "Prophets," 114. This reading is represented by, e.g., Melugin:
     'The words, "wash yourselves, make yourselves clean," fit well in a text which
     speaks of a cultic meal. The people have profaned that meal and the prayers made
     by their uplifted hands because their hands are defiled with blood (v. 15). They must

of vv. 16-17 is a result of the movement from cult in general to its ethical dimension, narrowing down the divine perspective (*sub specie sanctitatis Dei*) to human perspective (ethics, social justice).

Obviously, this picture of Isa 1:10-17 makes coherent sense only with the cultic concepts discussed in Part I. It can be, therefore, suggested that Isaiah's conception of the role of sacrifices and other rituals, of the sources and effects of impurity, and of holiness in the background of this passage could have been essentially the same as defined in the Priestly literature. His passionate reproach and ethical appeal would then be the logical outcome of these conceptions.

---

therefore wash and become clean. And, in becoming clean, they would come to behave properly in the legal sphere – by "judging" the orphan and "pleading" for the widow,' Roy F. Melugin, "Figurative Speech and the Reading of Isaiah 1 as Scripture," in *New Visions of Isaiah*, ed. Roy F. Melugin and Marvin A. Sweeney (JSOTSup 214; Sheffield: Sheffield Academic Press, 1996) 290.

Chapter 5: Cult and Ethics
in Isaiah 43:22-28

5.1. Introduction

Isa 43:22-28 appears to be one of the most favourite OT passages of Martin Luther. He quite often referred to its parts throughout his works, and expressed his excitement over them in words like 'A golden text!' (on v. 24) or 'This is by far the most beautiful text' (on v. 25).[1] On the other hand, contemporary OT scholars refer to this passage only seldom. This popularity drop of Isa 43:22-28 nowadays seems to be the consequence of at least three exegetical issues. First, there has been a consensus for almost 70 years that this passage is cast in the form of *Gerichtsrede*, the consensus that, as argued below, has damaging effects on its interpretation. Second, modern exegetes tend to ignore or overlook the fact that the terms describing the sacrifices and rituals in Isa 43:22-24 imply a demanding and opulent cultic practice, a nuance that, as shown below, plays an important role in the understanding of the whole passage. The third factor that also has a rather significant impact on the interpretation of Isa 43:22-28 is the suggested semantic intersection of חלל, חֶרֶם, and גִּדּוּף of v. 28 in the area of cult. This chapter focuses mainly on these three issues, because they, in return, illuminate the understanding of the role of cult and ethics in DI.

5.2. Historical Background of Isa 43:22-28

Most scholars date Isa 43:22-28 (along with chs. 40-48) to the exilic period, shortly before the fall of Babylon.[2] The second half of the passage supports this dating by making an impression that, even though Jacob/Israel still suffers the consequences of her sinful past (vv.

---

1   *LW* 17.100.
2   So recently Goldingay and Payne, *Isaiah 40-55*, passim, e.g., 1.29.

27-28),[3] Yнwн's forgiveness is already operational (v. 25).[4] The mentioning of sacrifices (or rather of their absence) in the first half of the passage can indicate any period of Israel's history, depending on how the text is understood. If Yнwн is accusing the Israelites of neglecting his cult, the text most likely refers to the First Temple or the Second Temple period; such accusation would be unjustified during the exile when cultic practices were severely limited by the absence of the Temple. It can still be argued that this passage originated in the exilic period, accusing the present audience of their forefathers' reluctance in cultic matters.[5] Thus Blenkinsopp comments on this passage that 'the entire drift of the accusation, especially the reference to the ancestors, points to religious practice in the pre-destruction period along the lines of a well-established prophetic critique of the sacrificial system …, with special reference to the last decades of Judah's independent existence.'[6] This line of thought, however, is misleading for two reasons: first, the reference to the ancestors in v. 27 concerns חטא and פשע, not the cultic practice, and, second, the issue in pre-exilic prophetic critique of the sacrificial system was certainly not its negligence (in contrast to this passage). As the study of literary genre below shows, the main source of the misconceptions about Isa 43:22-28 is to read it as an accusation. Once its descriptive character is recognized, this passage perfectly fits the situation in exile, the time when Yнwн's cult was drastically reduced by the circumstances.

As for the location of the intended audience of Isa 43:22-28, the usual choice is between Babylon and Jerusalem. Thus, e.g., Williamson believes that DI in this oracle describes the exiles in Babylon, and that the terms Israel and Jacob in vv. 22 and 28 'are interchangeable terms

---

3   Reading the form וַאֲחַלֵּל in v. 28 as simple ו plus yiqtol, just as the parallel expression וָאֶתְּנָה, and, instead of referring to the future, denoting the unfinished aspect of a past action. The verbs of this verse 'might be heard as suggesting a vivid account of a divine abandonment of Israel, in process,' Goldingay and Payne, *Isaiah 40-55*, 1.317. For more details, see below.

4   The use of a noun clause, participle and yiqtol verb in v. 25 very likely refers to the present and/or the near future.

5   In this regard, Goldingay correctly maintains that the exilic and pre-exilic generations should not be strictly differentiated, because 'all belong to one people, and the present generation is implicated in the sins of the past (and vice versa),' Goldingay and Payne, *Isaiah 40-55*, 1.309.

6   Joseph Blenkinsopp, *Isaiah 40-55: A New Translation with Introduction and Commentary* (AB 19A; New York; London: Doubleday, 2002) 231. Similarly, Jan Leunis Koole, *Isaiah III/1*, trans. Anthony P. Runia (HCOT; Kampen: Kok Pharos, 1997) 344, Claus Westermann, *Isaiah 40-66: A Commentary* (OTL; Philadelphia, PA: The Westminster Press, 1969) 131.

for this prophet and that both refer to the community in exile in Babylon.'[7] This location, however, presents a problem for those who read vv. 22-24 as an accusation and, at the same time, believe that exile did not allow for the cultic practices mentioned in these verses. Logically, they either opt for Jerusalem of exilic days, where sacrificial worship probably continued in some limited form and so the supposed rebuke would make sense,[8] or deduce that the prophet connects the community in Babylon with their pre-exilic predecessors in Palestine.[9] The assumed non-existence of YHWH's cult in Babylon prompted others to reconsider the literary genre of theses verses, especially of v. 23; rather than a reproach, vv. 22-24 simply describe the present state of cultic practices, viz. their absence.[10] As the following exegesis shows, this reading of the text is closer to the mark with one correction: 'we cannot exclude the possibility that, like the Jewish settlers at Elephantine, the Jewish ethnic minority in Babylon built a sanctuary, of however modest proportions […] since it is difficult to imagine a clergy-training center in Babylonia at that time, unattached to a temple of some kind.'[11] The possibility of some cultic activities in Babylon, however, does not undermine this reading, for Isa 43:22-28 neither mentions nor implies the *total* absence of YHWH's cult.

As the above discussion demonstrates, the description of cultic practice in vv. 22-24 does not help to identify more closely the location or the audience of Isa 43:22-28, because it can reflect the situation in Babylon as well as in Jerusalem. The use of the word pair Jacob/Israel probably refers to the community in Babylon, but the mentioning of אָבִיךָ הָרִאשׁוֹן and מְלִיצֶיךָ in v. 27 suggests that the author has the whole nation in mind. It is, therefore, unwarranted to make any conclusions regarding this passage based on a hard and fast distinction between the two communities and the two geographical locations. It is more

---

7   H. G. M. Williamson, "The Concept of Israel in Transition," in *The World of Ancient Israel: Sociological, Anthropological and Political Perspectives*, ed. R. E. Clements (Cambridge: Cambridge University Press, 1989) 145.

8   So, e.g., James D. Smart, *History and Theology in Second Isaiah: A Commentary on Isaiah 35, 40-66* (London: Epworth, 1967) 108. However, Goldingay argues that Jerusalem's cultic activities during the exile actually speak against this theory, for, according to Jer 41:5 it was precisely the offerings mentioned in Isa 43:23b (מִנְחָה and לְבוֹנָה) that people did bring, Goldingay and Payne, *Isaiah 40-55*, 1.310.

9   As discussed in the previous paragraph.

10   For a list of the proponents, see Koole, *Isaiah III/1*, 343-344. Koole does not support this reading of the text, mainly because he views vv. 22-24 'as God's refutation of Israel's complaint regarding his alleged justice.' This, again, is the problem of literary genre, as argued in the next section.

11   Blenkinsopp, *Isaiah 40-55*, 231.

reasonable to include Isa 43:22-28 among those DI poems which some scholars (most recently Goldingay) proposed to read as addressing Judeans both in Babylon and in Palestine, 'both lamenting Jerusalem-Zion and battling Israel-Jacob.'[12]

5.3. Literary Genre of Isa 43:22-28

Watts emphatically claims that Isa 43:22-28 'is cast in the form of a judgment as virtually everyone, from Begrich to Merendino [...] has recognized.'[13] This trial genre, or *Gerichtsrede*, often shapes the message of the prophets. Sweeney lists some of its characteristic elements: a call to attention, an appeal for a legal proceeding, an accusation, and an announcement of judgement or some form of instruction in proper behaviour.[14] Begrich's idea was developed by its most influential proponent – Westermann. His classification of Isa 43:22-28 as *Gerichtsrede*, 'in which Yahweh opposes his chosen people Israel,'[15] has been followed by many[16] and exercised a considerable influence over the interpretation of the passage. It resulted in various attempts to reconstruct the supposed accusation that the people made against God: 'You delivered Jacob to utter destruction and Israel to shame. ... How could you do this, when we faithfully served you by bringing our sacrifices?'[17] or 'Why, Yahweh, are we now suffering when we have called upon you?'[18] Analogically, the accusatory tone has been implied in YHWH's speech, resulting in statements like:

---

12   Goldingay and Payne, *Isaiah 40-55*, 1.33. See there for additional arguments and bibliography.

13   John D. W. Watts, *Isaiah 34-66* (WBC 25; Waco, TX: Word Books, 1987) 143. For Begrich, see Joachim Begrich, *Studien zu Deuterojesaja* (BWANT 4e; Stuttgart: Kohlhammer, 1938) 31. He maintains that 'die Voraussetzung des Textes ist, daß Israel auf Grund bestimmter Leistungen Jahwe für verpflichtet erklärt, ihm zu helfen,' p. 25. For Merendino, see Rosario Pius Merendino, *Der Erste und der Letzte: Eine Untersuchung von Jes 40-48* (VTSup 31; Leiden: Brill, 1981) 356.

14   Sweeney, *Isaiah 1-39*, 541-542.

15   Westermann, *Isaiah 40-66*, 130.

16   Most notably by Schoors in his study of DI forms, see A. Schoors, *I am God your Saviour: A Form-Critical Study of the Main Genres in Is. xl-lv* (VTSup 24; Leiden: Brill, 1973) 190. He lists Isa 43:22-28 as an example of the trial speech 'that comes closest to the basic structure described by Westermann in his *Grundformen prophetischer Rede*.'

17   Westermann, *Isaiah 40-66*, 130. Similarly Oswalt, *Isaiah 40-66*, 157.

18   'The presumption is that we (Jacob/Israel) are innocent and you (YHWH) are guilty,' Michael Rosenbaum, *Word-Order Variation in Isaiah 40-55: A Functional Perspective* (SSN 35; Assen: Van Gorcum, 1997) 82.

The meaning behind God's accusation that Israel has withheld offering is clearly this: Israel's niggardliness is a sign of the deadness of its heart in what should be the most precious of all relationships; Israel is incapable of extending even the simple gesture of gratitude symbolized by food.[19]

Or even more peculiar:

> In our text [vv. 22-24] ... Yahweh rebukes Israel for not bringing offering and sacrifices. It is as though, in a situation of dispute with Babylonian gods, Yahweh wants and must have visible, dramatic, generous acknowledgments of allegiance from Israel.[20]

These quotations illustrate that, even though the reconstruction of a trial can be of some value when dealing with the last stanza of the passage (vv. 26-28), it has had a damaging effect when applied to its first part (vv. 22-24). As Booij has put it, 'the opinion that in Is 43 Israel *is* reproved on account of its sacrifices, to the effect that it is blamed of cultic neglect, is probably the most serious misunderstanding of this text.'[21] Even the passage itself proves the above interpretations wrong, for in v. 23b YHWH asserts: 'I have not burdened you with offerings, or wearied you with frankincense.' It goes against the grain of the prophetic theology that YHWH would accuse his people of not practising rituals to the point that they would weary themselves by them for him (v. 22), of not buying him the expensive קָנֶה (v. 24aA), and of not soaking him in the fat of their sacrifices (v. 24aB).[22] As already discussed above, such an accusation is even more inconceivable if this passage is addressed to the people in exile, where offering sacrifices to YHWH was very limited. Moreover, charging people with niggardliness, or even with reluctance in the cultic sphere when v. 24b claims that אַךְ הֶעֱבַדְתַּנִי בְּחַטֹּאותֶיךָ הוֹגַעְתַּנִי בַּעֲוֹנֹתֶיךָ misses the mark regardless of geographical or political context. Such behavior would make *any* sacrifices invalid, and the more lavish ones would appear even more preposterous, as Jeremiah expresses in 6:20 'Of what use to me is frankincense (לְבוֹנָה) that comes from Sheba, or sweet cane (קָנֶה הַטּוֹב) from a distant land? Your burnt offerings are not acceptable, nor are your sacrifices pleasing to me.' It is very unlikely that the prophetic literature of exile would promote the idea that YHWH desires to be glorified (כבד) by sacrifices of animals (זֶבַח), as v. 23a may seem to imply. In fact, unlike in typical *Gerichtsreden*, a formal accusation is

---

19   Paul D. Hanson, *Isaiah 40-66* (Interpretation; Louisville, KY: John Knox Press, 1995) 77.

20   Brueggemann, *Isaiah,* 2.61.

21   T. Booij, "Negation in Isaiah 43:22-24," *ZAW* 92 (1982) 390-400.

22   For this rendering, see the discussion of these verses in 5.4.1 and 5.5.1.

hardly to be found anywhere in Isa 43:22-28.[23] Since v. 24b lies outside
of the trial speech proper, and v. 27 is hardly an accusation of the
people present at the trial, it is safe to conclude that there is no formal
accusation in Isa 43:22-28. Furthermore, the absence of an appeal to do
what is right (an element present in pre-exilic cult-critical passages) is a
strong indication that Isa 43:22-28 serves a different purpose. Finally, if
this passage was a *Gerichtsrede*, one would at least expect a verdict
relevant to the action of the accused party (punishment or reward). As
the study of the structure below shows, reading v. 28 as a verdict is not
the most satisfactory approach. True, there are some expressions in the
passage that belong to the trial speech genre; most notably in v. 26,
which can be regarded as an appeal for a legal proceeding. However,
one trial speech element is not sufficient to qualify Isa 43:22-28 as a
Gerichtsrede.

If labelling the form of this passage is necessary, it would be more
justifiable to speak about a disputation, more specifically '[a]
theological dispute concerning the basis for Israel's future
deliverance.'[24] According to von Waldow, a disputation always consists
of two parts: *Disputationsbasis*, 'the starting point, which the adversary
is supposed to have already agreed to,' and *Schlussfolgerung* 'which is
drawn from it.'[25] Further analysis will show that vv. 22-24 and 26-28
function as *Disputationsbasis*, and v. 25 as *Schlussfolgerung*, and that this
passage has the same function as the other disputations in DI – 'the
defence of his salvific message.'[26]

At this point, it is sufficient to realize that the difference between
labelling Isa 43:22-24 and 27-28 not as *Gerichtsrede* but as *Disputations-*

---

23   Even Westermann admits that the trial speech proper begins only in v. 26. In his
     Basic Forms of Prophetic Speech he claims that two accusations can be found in Isa
     43:22-28, one that the people in exile make against God, opposed by one that God
     raises against the people, so 'the content completely justifies this usage of the term
     "accusation" in both of these originally quite different places,' Claus Westermann,
     Basic Forms of Prophetic Speech (London: Lutterworth Press, 1967) 69. However, in his
     commentary on DI he seems to change his mind on the form of vv. 22-24, labelling
     them as a disputation; see Westermann, *Isaiah 40-66*, 131.

24   Roy F. Melugin, *The Formation of Isaiah 40-55* (BZAW 141; Berlin: De Gruyter, 1976)
     49. Isa 43:22-28 may be considered as another illustration of what Melugin elsewhere
     calls 'an imitation of disputation speech with an arbitrary fusion of disputation and
     cultic styles,' Roy F. Melugin, "Deutero-Isaiah and Form Criticism," *VT* 21 (1971) 326-
     337. Melugin, however, somewhat surprisingly still adheres to Begrich's designation
     of Isa 43:22-28 as a trial speech, see Melugin, *Formation*, 48-50 and 115-118.

25   Schoor's summary of Hans Eberhard von Waldow, *Der traditionsgeschichtliche
     Hintergrund der prophetischen Gerichtsreden* (BZAW 85; Berlin: A. Töpelmann, 1963)
     28-36.

26   Schoors, *I am God*, 295.

basis is that one reads these verses not as accusatory, but as descriptive. The following two quotes summarize the important consequence of this conclusion: first, 'the passage ... cannot be a complaint on Yahweh's part that the Israelites had not brought him sacrifices,'[27] and, second, 'the nation, which Jehovah was now redeeming out of pure unmingled grace, had not been burdened with costly tasks of this description.'[28]

5.4. Structural Analysis and Text-Critical Issues of Isa 43:22-28

This section focuses only on those problematic syntactical and structural issues that decisively contribute to the understanding of the text: correlation of cola 22aA and 22aB, structure of strophe 25 and 26, dynamics in strophe 27, and authenticity of colon 28aA. As far as the methodology is concerned, the following discussion uses the same approach and principles as the structure and syntax study of Isa 1:10-17 in the previous chapter. Again, the analysis is based on MT (BHS) excluding accents, but with additional spacing and new-lines to bring out the divisions in the text.

---

27   Christopher R. North, *The Second Isaiah: Introduction, Translation and Commentary to Chapters XL-LV* (Oxford: Clarendon Press, 1964) 127.

28   Delitzsch, *Prophecies of Isaiah*, 2.199.

Strophe and Poetic Device	MT of Isaiah 43:22-28	Colon	St
Opening bicolon with grammatical and semantic paral.: NP₂ V NP₁ // V′ NP₂′ NP₁′	וְלֹא־אֹתִי קָרָאתָ יַעֲקֹב כִּי־יָגַעְתָּ בִּי יִשְׂרָאֵל	22aA 22aB	
Bicolon with grammatical and semantic chiastic paral.: V NP₂ // NP₂′ V′	לֹא־הֵבֵיאתָ לִּי שֵׂה עֹלֹתֶיךָ וּזְבָחֶיךָ לֹא כִבַּדְתָּנִי	23aA 23aB	
Bicolon with grammatical and semantic paral.: V NP₂ // V′ NP₂′	לֹא הֶעֱבַדְתִּיךָ בְּמִנְחָה וְלֹא הוֹגַעְתִּיךָ בִּלְבוֹנָה	23bA 23bB	I
Bicolon with grammatical and semantic chiastic paral.: V NP₂ // NP₂′ V′	לֹא־קָנִיתָ לִּי בַכֶּסֶף קָנֶה וְחֵלֶב זְבָחֶיךָ לֹא הִרְוִיתָנִי	24aA 24aB	
Closing bicolon with grammatical and semantic paral.: V NP₂ // V′ NP₂′	אַךְ הֶעֱבַדְתַּנִי בְּחַטֹּאותֶיךָ הוֹגַעְתַּנִי בַּעֲוֹנֹתֶיךָ	24bA 24bB	
Introductory monocolon	אָנֹכִי אָנֹכִי הוּא	25aA	
Pivot-patterned bicolon with partial grammatical and semantic chiastic paral.	מֹחֶה פְשָׁעֶיךָ לְמַעֲנִי וְחַטֹּאתֶיךָ לֹא אֶזְכֹּר	25aB 25aC	II
Opening tricolon with climatic paral.: V // V′ NP₁ // V″ NP₁ NP₂	הַזְכִּירֵנִי נִשָּׁפְטָה יָחַד סַפֵּר אַתָּה לְמַעַן תִּצְדָּק	26aA 26aB 26aC	
Bicolon with grammatical and semantic paral.: NP₁ V // NP₁′ V′	אָבִיךָ הָרִאשׁוֹן חָטָא וּמְלִיצֶיךָ פָּשְׁעוּ בִי	27aA 27aB	III
Closing tricolon with grammatical and semantic paral.: V NP₂ // V M NP₂ // NP₂′ M′, with ellipsis (verb gapping) and chiasm in 28aB-C.	וַאֲחַלֵּל שָׂרֵי קֹדֶשׁ וְאֶתְּנָה לַחֵרֶם יַעֲקֹב וְיִשְׂרָאֵל לְגִדּוּפִים	28aA 28aB 28aC	

In the chart above, the delimitation of cola follows MT for the most part, as indicated there by major division markers. Korpel and de Moor's work provides the supporting evidence for the MT's division from other main Hebrew manuscripts and ancient versions of the text, differing only in cola division of v. 25.[29] The division into stanzas is

---

29　See Marjo C. A. Korpel and Johannes C. de Moor, *The Structure of Classical Hebrew Poetry: Isaiah 40-55* (OTS 41; Leiden: Brill, 1998) 176-179.

inevitably more subjective; since it reflects the function performed by a given structure, it will be discussed only after the structural analysis. Most of the following discussion is devoted to the places where the text division in the chart differs from MT. However, none of these delimitations can be argued without paying careful attention to the relations within each individual colon – the syntax.

5.4.1. Correlation of Cola 22aA and 22aB

When it comes to the analysis of vv. 22-24, even a brief survey of commentaries confirms Booij's statement that the opinions about their meaning widely differ and 'some interpreters seem to be rather at a loss.'[30] The great variety of interpretations of these verses results primarily from different understandings of three correlations: how and if at all v. 22 relates to the preceding verses, how v. 22 relates to vv. 23-24, and how 22aB relates to 22aA.[31] This section discusses the last correlation.

The argument boils down to the authenticity and the function of the conjunction כִּי in this sentence. Its authenticity has been questioned because the usual causal function of כִּי (for, because) does not appear to fit the context. The emendation to וְלֹא has often been suggested, rendering 22aB as 'you did not weary yourself for me, Israel.' This suggestion is attractive due to seven other occurrences of the negative particle לֹא in vv. 22-24a, and encouraged by LXX (οὐδὲ κοπιᾶσαί σε ἐποίησα Ισραηλ) and V (nec aborasti in me Israhel). It has not only been advocated by a number of scholars, e.g. Westermann, Schoors, and Elliger,[32] but also made its way into many OT translations.[33] Westermann only refers to LXX and V without further explanation,[34] and Schoors merely indicates his reason, viz. parallelism.[35] Elliger recognizes the fact that the other leading ancient texts and versions (1QIsaª, S, and T) support MT, but resolves the dilemma by suggesting that 'es scheint zwei Traditionen gegeben zu haben,' and follows the

---

30 Booij, "Negation," 391.
31 For an extensive (but incomplete) list of various interpretations see John Goldingay, "Isaiah 43, 22-28," ZAW 110 (1998) 173-191: 178-179.
32 For a more extensive list of scholars, see Elliger, Deuterojesaja, 361.
33 For English, see, e.g., JPS or NIV, for German, see EIN, and also the main contemporary Russian, Ukrainian, Bulgarian, Czech, or Slovak translations.
34 Westermann, Isaiah 40-66, 130.
35 Schoors, I am God, 190.

long list of scholars who 'וְלֹא statt כִּי als das Ursprüngliche angesehen.'[36]

The following reasons, however, speak for the retention of MT:

— LXX and V are well counterbalanced by the S, T, and especially by 1QIsaᵃ and a small fragment 4QIsaᵍ.[37] Furthermore, there is no textual evidence for interchanging וְלֹא with כִּי in any available Hebrew manuscript.

— LXX and V do not necessarily follow the same *Vorlage*. Even though all the above proponents of emendation refer to both versions, they, in fact, follow only V (as do all the OT translations mentioned in the above footnote), because they do not change the subject in the first part of the verse from Jacob to YHWH as does LXX: οὐ νῦν ἐκάλεσά σε Ιακωβ. As Oswalt points out, 'LXX makes God the subject of both clauses, while Vulg. has the same syntax as MT. Thus they are not a unified witness against the MT.'[38]

— There are good reasons other than a Hebrew *Vorlage* for the variations in V and LXX. As Goldingay argues, 'Vg *nec laborasti in me* … may simply assume that the negative in v. 22a carries over to v. 22b.'[39] One can also see why LXX would prefer οὐδὲ (instead of ὅτι, δὲ, or some other conjunction), viz. grammatical parallelism with its rendering of v. 22a.

— Reading כִּי with MT is *lectio difficilior*.

— As the following discussion demonstrates, כִּי in v. 22 makes good sense.

If MT is granted, an even more complicated question follows: What is the function of כִּי in 22aB? Since כִּי is one of the most frequent words in BH, answers vary considerably. Here are some of the main views along with some of their proponents and corresponding OT translations:

— Causal כִּי ('because', 'for') is the most frequent function of this conjunction. In v. 22, it makes 22aB the reason for Israel's failure to call upon YHWH ('you did not call upon me, O Jacob, for you grew weary of me, O Israel'), and it is preferred by,

---

36   Elliger, *Deuterojesaja*, 361.
37   Other DSS do not contain this verse.
38   Oswalt, *Isaiah 40-66*, 156.
39   Goldingay, "Isaiah 43," 177.

e.g., Goldingay[40] and Watts.[41] As for the OT translations, see DBY, NAB, or Polish BTP.

— Adversative כִּי ('but', 'rather') usually comes after a negative clause, so there is a sufficient precedent for taking it this way in v. 22. It brings out the contrast between the sought-after and the real behaviour of Jacob-Israel, viz. between calling upon YHWH and being tired of him ('you did not call upon me, O Jacob; but you have been weary of me, O Israel'). This approach is taken by, e.g., Schoors,[42] Brueggemann,[43] and Aejmelaeus.[44] As for the OT translations, see NRSV, NAS, ESV, GNV, KJV, or Czech BKR.

— Asseverative כִּי can function as an emphatic particle ('truly', 'indeed', 'really'),[45] making 22aB a full clause. This function is preferred by Merendino[46] and Baltzer, who suggests that כִּי begins 'an interrogative sentence, which might be rendered: "Is it really the case that ...?"'[47] As for the OT translations, see NJB.

— Concessive כִּי ('though', 'even though') makes 22aB a circumstantial clause, and maintains the focus on the speaker (YHWH). To bring out the contrast with the circumstance, Vriezen suggests a special sub-category, viz. *emphatisch-konzessiv* כִּי, where 'der ursprüngliche Charakter des Wortes als deiktische Interjektion' is preserved. כִּי is then translated 'wie sehr auch' ('however much'), rendering Isa 43:22 as follows: 'Nicht Mich hast du angerufen, Jakob, wie sehr du dir auch um Mich Mühe gegeben hast.'[48]

— כִּי is often ignored in rendering of BH, e.g., Blenkinsopp.[49] As for the OT translations, see NLT.

---

40   Goldingay, "Isaiah 43," 173 and 177.

41   Watts, *Isaiah*, 136.

42   Schoors, *I am God*, 80.

43   Brueggemann, *Isaiah*, 2.60.

44   Anneli Aejmelaeus, "Function and Interpretation of כִּי in Biblical Hebrew," *JBL* 105 (1986) 193-209: 206.

45   See Williams §449.

46   Merendino, *Der Erste*, 347-348.

47   Baltzer, *Deutero-Isaiah*, 177.

48   Theodore C. Vriezen, "Einige Notizen zur Übersetzung des Bindewortes kī," in *Von Ugarit nach Qumran: Beiträge zur alttestamentlichen und altorientalischen Forschung*, ed. Johannes Hempel and Leonhard Rost (BZAW 77; Berlin: A. Töpelmann, 1958) 270-271.

49   Blenkinsopp, *Isaiah 40-55*, 228.

 — Resultative, or consecutive כִּי ('that', 'so that', 'to the point that') 'introduces the clause which explains and fulfils the idea of the principal sentence.'[50] Proposed already in the translation of Isa 43:22 by Delitzsch,[51] it has been followed by Booij,[52] Oswalt,[53] Koole,[54] and Korpel and de Moor.[55] As for the OT translations, see TNK, German ELO, or ELB.

Even though the last approach in the list above seems to have undergone a revival in recent scholarship, little has been said in its support. Aejmelaeus even claims that, with some exceptions in Job, 'it is doubtful whether כִּ should ever be interpreted as consecutive in the OT.'[56] She is, however, an isolated voice. Follingstad's survey of ancient and modern views on כִּי shows that its consecutive function was already recognized by early Jewish sages, e.g., Rabbi Lakish, and grammarians, e.g., Judah Ibn Balaam, and even today there is 'substantial agreement that כִּי plays a role in … consecutive/result clause types.'[57]

Excursus: The Case for Consecutive כִּי

In BH, there are several examples of כִּי introducing a consecutive or, as some grammars call it, resultative clause (*Folgesatz*) in general.[58] As the BDB examples illustrate, consecutive כִּי occurs most frequently 'after a question implying surprise or deprecation,'[59] e.g., מִי אָנֹכִי כִּי אֵלֵךְ אֶל־פַּרְעֹה (Exod 3:11). It is to this group that Aejmelaeus objects, saying that 'such questions are actually more or less equal to why-questions; that is, they demand the reason for an exceptional event or state of things,' and prefers 'to regard these cases as a special group within the

---

50 *HALOT* #4219.

51 'And thou hast not called upon me, O Jacob, that thou shouldst have wearied thyself for me, O Israel!' Delitzsch, *Prophecies of Isaiah*, 2.198.

52 Booij, "Negation," 391.

53 Oswalt, *Isaiah 40-66*, 156.

54 Koole, *Isaiah III/1*, 340-342.

55 Korpel and de Moor, *Structure*, 163.

56 Aejmelaeus, "Function," 202.

57 Carl Martin Follingstad, *Deictic Viewpoint in Biblical Hebrew Text: A Syntagmatic and Paradigmatic Analysis of the Particle* כ *(kī)* (Dallas, TX: SIL International, 2001) 37.

58 For the consecutive function of כִּ, see, e.g., GK §166b, *IBHS* 38.3b, Gibson §129, JM §169e, and Williams §450. For more examples of this function, see BDB 472b. f., *HALOT* #4219 II.B.9, and DCH 4.386.

59 BDB 472b. f.

causal function of כִּי.' She admits that 'a few cases in Job seem to come closer to the consecutive interpretation,' e.g. Job 38:19-20,[60] explaining them away by a suggestion that 'this was a peculiarity of the language used in Job.'[61] However, the difference between the function of כִּי in Job 38:19-20 and the examples of consecutive כִּי following an interrogative clause listed in BDB or DCH is not evident.

More importantly, Aejmelaeus turns a blind eye to the second group of examples with consecutive כִּי listed in BDB, viz. when following a negative clause. In a footnote, she dismissed the ones listed by Schoors in his article on כִּי, viz. Gen 40:15, Job 41:2, and Ps 44:19-20,[62] with a remark that 'none of them – if not the case in Job – is convincing.'[63] Noticeably, it is Gen 40:15 לֹא־עָשִׂיתִי מְאוּמָה כִּי־שָׂמוּ אֹתִי בַּבּוֹר that became a textbook example of consecutive כִּי after a negative clause.[64] Consecutive כִּי in Gen 40:15 and Ps 44:19-20 is also confirmed by *HALOT* #4219. Schoors' list is included in BDB, where further examples can be found: Hos 1:6, Ruth 1:12, and, most importantly, Isa 43:22. [65] DCH does not have Ps 44:19-20 and Ruth 1:12 among its consecutive כִּי examples, but contains all the others, Isa 43:22 included. DCH further proposes that כִּי functions consecutively or resultatively also after a positive clause in Num 11:19, 1 Sam 28:22, Jer 48:9, 2 Chr 4:18, and perhaps Jer 51:62.[66] This is satisfactory evidence for consecutive כִּי outside an interrogative sentence, and a sufficient reason to explore the possibility of its presence in Isa 43:22.

---

60   אֵי־זֶה הַדֶּרֶךְ יִשְׁכָּן־אוֹר וְחֹשֶׁךְ אֵי־זֶה מְקֹמוֹ: כִּי תִקָּחֶנּוּ אֶל־גְּבוּלוֹ וְכִי־תָבִין נְתִיבוֹת בֵּיתוֹ:

61   Aejmelaeus, "Function," 201-202.

62   A. Schoors, "The Particle כִּי," in *Remembering All the Way: A Collection of Old Testament Studies Published on the Occasion of the Fortieth Anniversary of the Oudtestamentisch Werkgezelschap in Nederland*, ed. A. S. van der Woude (OTS 21; Leiden: Brill, 1981) 264.

63   Aejmelaeus, "Function," n30. Further on, when she questions the concessive function of כִּי, Aejmelaeus does address Isa 43:22aB, insisting that it 'either must be interpreted as an adversative clause …, or it must be supplied with a negation,' n. 40.

64   See, e.g., *IBHS* 38.3b, Gibson §129, and, with some hesitation, also JM §169e.

65   BDB 472b. f. Strictly speaking, כִּי in Ruth 1:12 does not come after a negative, but it fits this category semantically: I am too old to have an husband כִּי אָמַרְתִּי *that* I should have said, etc.

66   DCH 4:386. In addition, consecutive כִּי following a negative non-interrogative clause is defensible also in Isa 57:16 ('nor will I always be angry כִּי רוּחַ מִלְּפָנַי יַעֲטוֹף – *to the point that* the spirit would grow faint before me …') and Hos 7:14 ('They do not cry to me from the heart כִּי יְיֵלִילוּ עַל מִשְׁכְּבוֹתָם – *to the point that* they would howl upon their beds …'). This rendering of Hos 7:14 is plausible only if ילל is understood as 'an inarticulate, shattering scream such as is found in primitive funerary laments and in the face of sudden catastrophe,' A. Baumann, "ילל," *TDOT* 6.82.

Even a quick look at the various OT translations of the examples above shows that none of them would go undisputed, and the other functions of כִּי in each example are possible. To establish consecutive כִּי as the most plausible would require each text to undergo a scrutiny similar to the present one on Isa 43:22. That is, however, beyond the scope of the present thesis. In general, one cannot but agree with Aejmelaeus that 'the interpretation of the various functions of a multipurpose particle in a language no longer spoken can never reach more than a fair approximation of what was once in the minds of the speakers and writers of that language.'[67] Nevertheless, some approximations are fairer than others, and it should come down to which function of a multipurpose particle makes the most sense not only in a given sentence, but also in its context.

Before moving on to next verses, one more syntactical feature of v. 22 requires clarification: when qal of יגע is connected with an object by בְּ, the preposition 'indicates the object *for* which (land, Josh. 24:13; wine, Isa. 62:8; fire, Hab. 2:13; nought, Jer. 51:58) or *with* which (sorceries, Isa. 47:12) one labours.'[68] As in Ps 69:4, it is natural that קרא would be the source of יגע, viz. the object *with* which one labours.[69] Logically, if כִּי in v. 22 is understood as consecutive, the source of יגע becomes קרא, whereas the speaker (Yahweh) is the object *for* which the audience (Jacob/Israel) labours; therefore the translation '… that you would have wearied yourself *for* me.'[70]

5.4.2. Structure of Verse 25

The structure of this short stanza is rather complicated. Elliger lists the various attempts of those who wish to obtain a metrical balance in v. 25 via emendations: thus, e.g., Duhm suggests crossing out the whole

---

67   Aejmelaeus, "Function," 209.

68   Hasel, "יָגַע," *TDOT* 5.389. After defining these two groups, it is rather surprising that Hasel ambiguously translates יגע + בְּ in Isa 43:22aB 'to be weary *of* Yahweh' (italics mine), especially when two paragraphs before he states: 'the basic verbal meaning of the root יגע may properly be defined as "be/become weary" in the objective sense of bodily fatigue, i.e., "be/become weak, weary, exhausted," rather than in the subjective psychological sense of "be/become weary of something."'

69   יָגַעְתִּי בְקָרְאִי נִחַר גְּרוֹנִי כָּלוּ עֵינַי מְיַחֵל לֵאלֹהָי; similarly Ps 6:7 and Jer 45:3, where the speaker is יגע with his אֲנָחָה (groaning, moaning).

70   For the same rendering, see Korpel and de Moor, *Structure*, 163. According to Follingstad, such a shift in viewpoint from the speaker space to the propositional content of utterance is a characteristic function of consecutive כִּי; see Follingstad, *Deictic Viewpoint*, 281-286.

second part (v. 25aB), Köhler wants to leave out וְחַטֹּאתֶיךָ and read only לְמַעַן, Steinmann, on the other hand, proposes to omit פְּשָׁעֶיךָ לְמַעֲנִי, and Zeigler, Penna, and Fohrer delete לְמַעֲנִי. Many scholars prefer to read לְמַעֲנִי with the second part of the verse, either dropping the copula with the next word (Westermann and Schoors) or, based on Brockelmann's *Hebräische Syntax* §123f (*waw* apodosis), maintain the copula (Koole and Elliger himself).[71] Some try to lengthen the second line by adding עוֹד with 1QIsaª.[72] While all these changes are possible, Elliger correctly disregards those proposals that destroy the parallelism in v. 25 (Duhm, Köhler, Steimann). To delete לְמַעֲנִי only because it is not rendered in LXX is unpersuasive in the light of other textual witnesses, and Rosenbaum's attempt to justify the omission of לְמַעֲנִי by vertical dittography from v. 26b below is desperate.[73] To add עוֹד on the basis of 1QIsaª (not in 1QIsaᵇ) and one medieval manuscript is more attractive,[74] but it only improves the metre of the colon, not its understanding. In addition, to both of these emendations applies the argument that 'it is wrong to emend the verse because of rhythm.'[75]

An interesting solution has been proposed in recent scholarship by Blenkinsopp, Goldingay, Watts, and Korpel and de Moor – to treat v. 25 as a tricolon:

25aA אָנֹכִי אָנֹכִי הוּא

25aB מֹחֶה פְשָׁעֶיךָ לְמַעֲנִי

25aC וְחַטֹּאתֶיךָ לֹא אֶזְכֹּר׃

Surprisingly, only Korpel and de Moor attempted to justify the break between הוּא and מֹחֶה, referring to Deut 32:39 and nearby Isa 43:11.[76] However, the syntax in both references differs from v. 25, for the separation of the almost identical phrases comes before וְאֵין, not before

---

71   For more discussion and refutation of some of the proposals as well as for bibliography, see Elliger, *Deuterojesaja*, 361-362.

72   Thus, e.g., TNK, NAB, NIV, NLT, or North, *Second Isaiah*, 127.

73   See Rosenbaum, *Word-Order*, 81.

74   The combination of זכר with עוֹד is fairly common, see, e.g., Isa 54:4. For the possibility of this addition in Isa 43:25, see Dominique Barthélemy, *Critique textuelle de l'Ancien Testament, 2: Isaïe, Jérémie, Lamentations, Rapport final du Comité pour l'analyse textuelle de l'Ancien Testament hébreu* (Orbis biblicus et orientalis 50/2; Fribourg, Göttingen: Editions universitaires, Vandenhoeck & Ruprecht, 1986) 319-320.

75   Schoors, *I am God*, 193.

76   See Korpel and de Moor, *Structure*, 177-178.

a participle.[77] In fact, there is apparently no example in BH where a pronoun followed by a participle would be separated from each other when referring to the same subject. It is safe to conclude that the suggested separation between הוא and מֹחֶה in v. 25 is unjustifiable on syntactical grounds. There is, however, a semantic factor that prompted the above scholars to read v. 25 as a tricolon: הוא can function as a pronominal predicate.[78] Following Driver's suggestion to regard הוא in Isa 43:25 'as anticipating the predicate'[79] renders the translation 'I, I am He' or even 'I, I am the One', which resembles a self-predication or a self-introductory formula. This might seem a bit of a stretch if the verse is read on its own. However, when the whole ch. 43 is considered, starting with the glorious אֲנִי יְהוָה אֱלֹהֶיךָ קְדוֹשׁ יִשְׂרָאֵל מוֹשִׁיעֶךָ in v. 3, picked up by אֲנִי הוּא in v. 10, reinforced by אָנֹכִי אָנֹכִי יְהוָה in v. 11, and again אֲנִי הוּא in v. 13, and אֲנִי יְהוָה קְדוֹשְׁכֶם in v. 15, it is sound to expect the expression in 25aA to play the role of self-introductory formula as well. It is reasonable to believe that this role, so prominent in ch. 43, took precedence over the rhythm in v. 25, creating thus an irregularity in what otherwise would be a well balanced, pivot-patterned bicolon with silent stress,

אָנֹכִי מֹחֶה פְשָׁעֶיךָ לְמַעֲנִי

וְחַטֹּאתֶיךָ לֹא אֶזְכֹּר (silent stress)

where לְמַעֲנִי, being the centre of chiasm, performs double-duty,[80] and וְ functions resumptively.[81] Oswalt also recognized this unusual mix: 'The usage of the pronoun הוא shows that the formula of self-predication is in mind because it is unnecessary in a normal participial phrase.'[82]

---

77 Deut 32:39 – רְאוּ עַתָּה כִּי אֲנִי אֲנִי הוּא וְאֵין אֱלֹהִים עִמָּדִי
    Isa 43:11 – אָנֹכִי אָנֹכִי יְהוָה וְאֵין מִבַּלְעָדַי מוֹשִׁיעַ

78 Instead of just strengthening the pronoun, as suggested by GK §141h and JM §154j.

79 S. R. Driver, *A Treatise on the Use of the Tenses in Hebrew and Some Other Syntactical Questions*, 2d ed. (Clarendon Press Series; Oxford: Clarendon Press, 1881) §200.

80 Goldingay recognizes this role of לְמַעֲנִי, maintaining that it 'stands at the centre of the chiasm formed by the second two cola in v. 25, and no doubt applies to both these cola,' Goldingay and Payne, *Isaiah 40-55*, 1.312.

81 For this function of וְ see Williams §440. Syntactically, this solution is very close to the one proposed by Elliger.

82 Oswalt, *Isaiah 40-66*, 160. Ackroyd believes that the use of this phrase 'strongly suggests an attempt at theological explanation of the divine name as being equivalent to the personal pronoun, so that just as Exod. 3:14 provides us with the interpretation אֶהְיֶה (I am), Second Isaiah appears to understand the divine name Yahweh as meaning "He", i.e., "The one" or "He who is",' Ackroyd, *Exile and Restoration*, 133.

Understood this way, the following conclusions can be made about the structure and syntax of v. 25:

— לְמַעֲנִי, being the centre of a chiastically structured bicolon and performing double duty, plays a prominent role in this verse.

— Recognizing the formula of self-predication in v. 25aA suggests dividing v. 25 into (climactic) monocolon (v. 25aA) and bicolon (v. 25aB and C). Whereas translating it into English as a tricolon renders the meaning of the Hebrew very well, there is no need to force the rules of BH syntax to break MT into a tricolon.

— There is no persuasive ground for emending MT of v. 25.

The proposed reading makes v. 25 the climax of the passage, indicated by the emphatic אָנֹכִי אָנֹכִי הוּא as in anacrusis.[83] It also connects this verse and thereby the whole passage well with the rest of the chapter.

5.4.3. Structure of Verse 26

To label v. 26 as a tricolon presupposes two things: the imperatives in each part are syntactically parallel, and there is a single structure that binds all the parts together.[84] As far as the first imperative הַזְכִּירֵנִי is concerned, Childs argues that 'the form is the appellation of the accused who demands a trial' and should be translated as 'accuse me'.[85] Adhering to Begrich's forensic reading of v. 26, he believes that 'the usual translation "put me in remembrance" completely misses the parallelism.' Childs undoubtedly means the parallelism only with נִשָּׁפְטָה, an expression denoting a forensic setting, for שׁפט usually is a technical term in judicature. However, the last part of the three-step parallelism, the imperative סַפֵּר, meaning in piel 'to count off, check, recount' or in the larger sense 'relate, tell'[86] is not a juridical term. It may be argued that its character of advocacy can be derived from the connection with צדק, but it can equally be argued that the niphal of שׁפט conveys a rather general meaning 'to dispute' or, even more broadly,

---

83 As suggested by H.G.M. Williamson in personal conversation.

84 The structure of this verse is the same as of Isa 1:16. For supporting arguments to read it as a tricolon, see the discussion of Isa 1:16 in 4.4.5.

85 Brevard S. Childs, *Memory and Tradition in Israel* (SBT 37; London: SCM Press, 1962) 15.

86 See J. Conrad, "סָפַר," *TDOT* 10.311.

'to quarrel (with one another)'[87] to find out who is right. The latter
argument supports the assertion above concerning the literary genre of
Isa 43:22-28, reading the whole verse as a non-forensic disputation:
'Remind me. Let us dispute with one another. You recount so that you
may be proved right.'[88]

There is a noteworthy dynamic in this verse. The first stipulation
turns the focus from YHWH to the matter of dispute.[89] The objects of the
second stipulation are the involved parties, emphasized by יַחַד. The
emphatic position of אַתָּה in the third stipulation completes the shift of
focus from YHWH to Jacob/Israel. In addition, the last phrase of v. 26
discloses the reason for all three stipulations: לְמַעַן תִּצְדָּק. This dynamic
and the parallelism justify the classification of v. 26 as a tricolon with
climatic parallelism. More specifically, in the terms of Greenstein, this
climatic parallelism is a case of suspended analysis.[90]

5.4.4. Progress in Verse 27

Dynamics of progress seem to work also in the relation between 27aA
and 27aB. Even though the precise identification of אָבִיךָ הָרִאשׁוֹן and
מְלִיצֶיךָ is not certain,[91] one can safely assume a progress in time

---

87   As argued by H. Niehr, "שָׁפַט," TDOT 15.421. Niehr believes that the setting of Isa
     43:26 is forensic, but allows also for a civic use of this form, as in 2 Chr 22:8. The
     reciprocity of the niphal in this verse is confirmed by the following יַחַד.

88   As Jensen points out, 'it is human nature to want to be right with God, and
     participation in religious rites is one way of persuading ourselves that we are right
     with God,' Jensen, *Ethical Dimensions*, 85.

89   As Goldingay specifies with regard to הַזְכִּירֵנִי, 'rather than a person as object, this is a
     technical term for bringing a matter to the attention of a court,' Goldingay, "Isaiah
     43," 187. Contrast *TDOT* 4.75 by H. Eising.

90   For more discussion of this phenomena, see Edward L. Greenstein, "One More Step
     on the Staircase," *UF* 9 (1977) 77-86: esp. 80.

91   In early OT scholarship, the usual candidates for 'the first ancestor' were Adam or
     Abraham, and for 'the interpreters' Moses and Aaron. Elliger argues in detail that
     אָבִיךָ הָרִאשׁוֹן refers to Jacob and מְלִיצֶיךָ to *Wortführer*, or *Sprecher*, or 'ist vielleicht
     eine Sammelbezeichnung für die Regierung,' namely 'die Könige und ihre Beamten.'
     With regard to 27aB, he claims that 'Gedacht ist parallel zu dem seine Sippe
     anführenden Erzvater Jakob anscheinend in der Königzeit an die Spitzen des
     inzwischen zum Volk herangewachsenen Israel,' Elliger, *Deuterojesaja*, 383. Another
     interesting explanation comes from Calvin, who argues that the word אָבִיךָ does not
     include 'one or a few of their [Israelites'] ancestors, but many. It is an interchange of
     the singular and plural number, which is very frequently employed by Hebrew
     writers,' John Calvin, *Commentary on the Book of the Prophet Isaiah*, trans. William

between the two, viz. from the early beginnings to the more recent past. Furthermore, Elliger calls attention to another possible progress in this verse, viz. *Steigerung* from חטא in 27aA to פשע in 27aB. His paraphrastic rendering of v. 27 neatly captures both developments: 'Schon Jakob "verfehlte sich"; aber was deine Wortführer sich geleistet haben, war mehr: sie "rebellierten", sie "brachen mit mir".'[92]

The adjective רִאשׁוֹן very likely refers to the same time in Israel's history as רִאשֹׁנוֹת in v. 18 – the former things that are to be forgotten, הָרִאשֹׁנוֹת that have come to pass (42:9). Unlike רִאשֹׁנוֹת of YHWH that are to be remembered (46:9), 65:2-7 mentions the former actions (פְּעֻלָּתָם רִאשֹׁנָה, v.7) of Israel's ancestors (אֲבוֹתֵיכֶם, v. 7), such as idolatry (vv. 2-7), that provoked YHWH (v. 3) and resulted in exile. In the announced new era, the former troubles (הַצָּרוֹת הָרִאשֹׁנוֹת) are forgotten and hidden from God's sight (v. 16); because YHWH is creating new heavens and a new earth, הָרִאשֹׁנוֹת will not be remembered, nor come to mind (v. 17). Therefore, Isa 43:27 is not an accusation, but a piece of evidence that has become irrelevant because the case has already been resolved and closed (via serving the exile sentence and the upcoming deliverance). Lest the people would like to reopen the case לְמַעַן תִּצְדָּק (v. 26), the prophet reminds them, in Luther's words: "[Y]ou cannot be justified, because you are the son of Adam, who sinned first. Therefore you also are a sinner, because you are the son of a sinner.'[93]

5.4.5. Colon 28aA – A Later Addition?

Almost every aspect of the first line of v. 28 has been questioned: Is it a part of the *Urtext*, or a later addition? Who is the subject – YHWH or, as LXX suggest, οἱ ἄρχοντες? Who or what is the object designated by שָׂרֵי קֹדֶשׁ? What is the tense of וָאֲחַלֵּל? What is the syntactical function of the initial *waw*? The last two questions cannot be answered without considering the wider context, so the discussion of them needs to be postponed to the section on synthesis below. This section deals with the first three problems.

Westermann, Merendino, and Elliger consider v. 28aA a later addition. Westermann keeps the initial וָאֲחַלֵּל, but deletes שָׂרֵי קֹדֶשׁ

Pringle, vol. 3 (Calvin's Commentaries; Grand Rapids, MI: Baker Book House, 1998) 351.

92   Elliger, *Deuterojesaja*, 382.

93   *LW* 25.302.

וְאֶתְנָה without any justification.[94] Merendino believes that the cult polemic in vv. 23-24 neither suits DI style and message nor reflects the situation in exile; therefore it must be 'als ein nachträgliches Interpretament von V. 22 anzusehen.' And since the expression שָׂרֵי קֹדֶשׁ 'nimmt der Text wieder auf den Kult, [m]an kann in V. 28a die Hand des Interpolators von VV. 23-24 erblicken.'[95] Elliger also argues that 28aA has been added later to pick up the cult theme from the first part of the passage: '[28a ist] ein Zusatz, der von jemandem stammt, der eine Bemerkung über das Schicksal der Vertreter des Kultus vermißte, nachdem dieser im ersten Teil der Rede so breiten Raum eingenommen hat.'[96]

The overall discussion here should sufficiently repudiate the above arguments. One cannot help but think that Elliger's picture of the editor of this verse is not a Jewish scribe, but a western systematic theologian. Moreover, reading vv. 23-24 the way that is suggested in this study does not generate any need to comment on 'das Schicksal der Vertreter des Kultus.' The argument that v. 28aA is redundant because it breaks the bicolon pattern in the passage and has no corresponding part in the parallel Jacob/Israel v. 22 is aptly rejected by Koole: 'Views on what is superfluous in (poetic) literature may differ, a longer verse at the end of a pericope is not unusual, ... , and just as 'your father' (v. 27a) is elaborated in the names Jacob-Israel (v. 27b), so there may be a closer connection between v. 27b and v. 28a.'[97] In fact, the translator of LXX uses this chiastic correspondence when struggling with the rendering of מְלִיצֶיךָ in v. 27b and שָׂרֵי קֹדֶשׁ in v. 28, giving the term οἱ ἄρχοντες for both expressions.

The last objection of Elliger against the authenticity of v. 28aA is 'die Zweiteiligkeit der gesamten Rede ... wobei der Kult das Material für den ersten Teil, genaugenommen nur für dessen ersten Abschnitt, liefert, was gegen die Metabasis eis allo genos in 28a spricht.'[98] However, as the division into stanzas in the chart above and their functional analysis below show, the passage can be divided and read in a way that the theme of cult is an integral part of the overall picture of Israel's impotence with regard to its salvation. Furthermore, as the following word study of the key terms in v. 28 demonstrates, the cultic

---

94   Westermann, *Isaiah 40-66*, 130.
95   Merendino, *Der Erste*, 350 and 353.
96   Elliger, *Deuterojesaja*, 362-363.
97   Koole, *Isaiah III/1*, 352.
98   Elliger, *Deuterojesaja*, 367.

aspect is present in all three cola, presenting one theme – the impure status of Jacob/Israel:

a) חלל — Dommershausen leaves little room for doubt that חלל in this verse refers to desecration as opposed to its other, non-religious meanings: 'In the OT, חלל in the piel ... always means "profane, desecrate."' Specifically about Isa 43:28 (along with Lam 2:2), he says that 'in neither passage should חלל be read as "slain" or "pierced."'[99] Also the LXX's rendering and the connection of חלל with the unusual construction שָׂרֵי קֹדֶשׁ support the *res exsecranda* function of this verb.[100] In the words of Goldingay, YHWH by this expression declares that Israel '*has* been radically profaned.'[101] And, as Goldingay elsewhere points out, '"profaneness" is the antonym of "holiness".'[102]

b) חֵרֶם — The occurrence of חֵרֶם in the expression וְאֶתְּנָה לַחֵרֶם (v. 27) is rather unexpected. If extermination or desolation was in view, לַחֶרֶב ('to the sword') would be more suitable, as predicted in Mic 6:14 and Jer 15:9 against Israel and in Jer 25:31 against הָרְשָׁעִים, in all instances with the verb נתן and YHWH as the subject. An even better candidate would be חָרְבָּה ('desolation') – a term that is predominantly used by Ezekiel (14 times), Jeremiah (10 times), and DI (5 times), and almost exclusively connected with Judah/Israel and the Babylonian exile, even outside prophetic literature.[103] Furthermore, חָרְבָּה often takes the preposition לְ as well as the verb נָתַן.[104] חֵרֶם, on the other hand, never occurs with נָתַן except in Isa 43:28, and the only other place where it is combined with לְ in the OT is Josh 6:18 and 7:12 (although without the article). The Joshua passage is very instructive for understanding one nuance of חֵרֶם. Jericho and all that was in it was

---

99 Dommershausen, "חלל," *TDOT* 4.410 and 414. For the opposite view, see Schoors, *I am God*, 196.

100 According to Ringgren, חלל in this verse 'fits well contextually in the sense of robbing the holy of their holiness,' "קדש," *TDOT* 12.537. Elsewhere he explains that 'to profane someone, or something, is to act in such a manner as to cause its holiness to be lost,' and his examples (Amos 2:7; Zeph 3:4; Isa 56:6; Ezek 22:26; 28:18; Mal 2:11) include ritual as well as ethical transgressions, Ringgren, *Prophetical Conception of Holiness*, 17. For further support, see also Goldingay and Payne, *Isaiah 40-55*, 1.316.

101 Goldingay and Payne, *Isaiah 40-55*, 1.316.

102 John Goldingay, *The Message of Isaiah 40-55: A Literary-Theological Commentary* (London: T & T Clark, 2005) 226.

103 It occurs 30 times with Jacob/Israel, 4 times with Edom, twice with Egypt, once with Tyre, and three other uses. Notice especially Lev 26:31-33, where חָרְבָּה 'sandwiches' the description of exile as a punishment for Israel's disobedience, allusion to which would be expected in Isa 43:22-28 if the physical punishment were in view.

104 Another alternative would be לְטֶבַח ('to slaughter') as in Isa 34:2 (against the nations, with נתן), Isa 53:7 (about the suffering Servant), etc.

proclaimed חֵרֶם לַיהוָה (Josh 6:17). In spite of the explicit prohibition,
Achan took מִן־הַחֵרֶם (7:1). Consequently, as cautioned in 6:18, the
Israelites הָיוּ לְחֵרֶם (7:12a). This expression does not refer to their
(future) physical destruction,[105] but to their present cultic state: Israel
became *pollutus est anathemate* (V).[106] YHWH could not be with such
polluted people (7:12b), for, again, impurity and holiness do not mix.[107]
In the following verse, YHWH provides instructions about how to revert
this impure status of the Israelites: purify/sanctify yourselves (הִתְקַדְּשׁוּ)
and take away הַחֵרֶם from your midst (מִקִּרְבְּכֶם). Only then, YHWH can
again be קָדוֹשׁ בְּקִרְבְּךָ (Hos 11:9, similarly Isa 12:6), enabling the
Israelites to be victorious over their enemies. Clearly, לְחֵרֶם in this story
refers to the impurity of the people, and there is no obvious reason to
understand it differently in Isa 43:28.[108] Further support comes from the
facts that Israel has never been an object of annihilation, and that the
parallel חֹלֵל in the preceding colon and גִּדּוּף in the following colon
also refer to the cultic status of the people.[109] Grammatically speaking,
חֵרֶם in v. 28 is a concrete noun, expressing a quality or a substance, as
opposed to a noun expressing an action.[110] The preposition לְ is that of
product – 'when an action results in a state or condition.'[111] The phrase
נתן לַחֵרֶם may therefore be translated 'to turn into an accursed thing',

---

105 As translations like 'they have been made liable to destruction' (NIV or NRSV)
     suggest, and as commonly understood in Isa 43:27.

106 LXX also renders חֵרֶם here as ἀνάθεμα ('an accursed thing'). Similarly KJV, NAU or
     JPS.

107 Kornfeld points out that the verb חרם constitutes 'the contrasting sphere to *qdš* in the
     sense of consecrating something to Yahweh for destruction,' "קדש," *TDOT* 12.527.

108 Baltzer makes the connection between Isa 43:28 and Lev 27:28, claiming that 'what
     has been consecrated to Yahweh through the curse is excluded from "redemption"
     (גאל),' Baltzer, *Deutero-Isaiah*, 183, n244. He apparently fails to distinguish between
     res exsecranda and *res sacrosancta* aspects of חֵרֶם. In spite of his detailed analysis of
     חֵרֶם, Koole also diverts for a moment to *res sacrosancta* when stating: 'Because Israel
     had not brought true sacrifices to God, vv. 22ff., she had to be "sacrificed" herself,'
     Koole, *Isaiah III/1*, 353. However, his final translation – 'to give up to the curse' –
     concurs with the one proposed in this study.

109 Already Calvin used the parallel of חֵרֶם with גִּדּוּף to argue for rendering חֵרֶם as 'a
     curse' rather than 'destruction', see Calvin, *Isaiah*, 353.

110 For a detailed discussion of both nuances, see Lohfink, "חָרַם," *TDOT* 5.185-186.
     Lohfink is inconsistent when it comes to the function of חֵרֶם in Isa 43:28: on p. 184 he
     claims that it designates a kind of countersphere to the sacred because it is parallel to
     חֹלֵל, presumably as a concrete noun, then on p. 185-86 he treats it as an action noun
     because of its parallelism with גִּדּוּפִים, and finally on p. 198 he suggests that, through
     the influence of Deuteronomistic usage, the root חרם in Isa 43:28 simply means 'to
     kill, destroy'.

111 Williams §278.

or even 'to turn into an impurity' to eliminate the undertone of physical destruction and to emphasize its connection with the immediate context – Israel's present status as anathema to YHWH's holiness.

c) גִּדּוּף — The noun גִּדּוּף is found only four times in the OT (once in a feminine form גְּדוּפָה). It can be reasoned that, if reviling or a taunt was the point,[112] one would expect a more apt and far more frequent term חֶרְפָּה, because it is often connected with the Babylonian exile (either in the prophecies concerning it or their fulfillments)[113] and it often takes the preposition לְ as well as the verb נָתַן. The fact that it is twice parallel to גִּדּוּף (Isa 51:7 and Zeph 2:8) does not mean that the two words are synonyms.[114] Studying the total of seven occurrences of the verb גדף,[115] Wallis rightly concludes that the figurative meaning 'to revile, blaspheme' is predominant in BH.[116] However, he fails to discuss the noun form as such. Also, his differentiation between secular and religious usage of this root is questionable, for such a distinction is very likely foreign to Hebrew thinking. Moreover, translating all the occurrences of the root גדף with the religious term 'to blaspheme' makes good sense in every case. It is helpful to realize here that in order to blaspheme, words are not necessary.[117] Num 15:30-31 and Ezek 20:27-28 instruct that to blaspheme against YHWH means to intentionally and flauntingly violate his commandment, and sacrifice to idols.[118] Isa 43:28 conveys that, guilty of these moral impurities, Israel has been 'turned into a blasphemy'. This rendering of לְגִדּוּפִים preserves both the syntactical and grammatical parallelism with the previous colon: גִּדּוּף is a concrete noun, expressing a quality or a substance, and the preposition לְ is that of product. Designating Israel as גִּדּוּף here

---

112 As suggested by many translations, e.g., NRSV, NAU, or TNK.

113 For the prophecies, see Hos 12:15; Mic 6:16; Jer 24:9; 29:18; 42:18; 44:8, 12; Ezek 5:14, 15; for the fulfilment see Jer 51:51; Lam 5:1; Ezek 16:57; 22:4; 36:15, 30; Ps 44:14; 79:4; 89:42; 109:25; Dan 9:16.

114 In both cases, גִּדּוּף is second, so if Kugel's idea of parallelism in biblical poetry is applied, גִּדּוּף would mean something more than חֶרְפָּה. However, it would not be sound to derive a conclusion from only two examples.

115 Four out of these seven occurrences refer to the words of *Rabshakeh* against YHWH in the story of Sennacherib's invasion against Judah.

116 See G. Wallis, "גָּדַף," *TDOT* 2.416-418.

117 According to Blank, the fear that a blasphemous word would return upon the head of the blasphemer probably discouraged verbal blasphemy, see S. H. Blank, "The Curse, Blasphemy, the Spell and the Oath," *HUCA* 23 (1950/51) 73-95: esp. 83-85.

118 Wallis states that Num 15:30 concerns indirect blasphemy 'by the sin of omission, of withholding a sacrifice,' Wallis, "גָּדַף," 418. However, for Num 15:30-31 as a reference to *intentional* sinning, see the treatment of this passage in Milgrom, *Leviticus 1-16*, .

means that she became the very opposite of what YHWH has formed her to be – a light to the nations (42:6), the people who declare his praise (43:21).[119]

This word-study of חלל, חֵרֶם, and גִּדּוּף shows that there is a semantic intersection of these terms in the area of cult. The structure of v. 28 supports this conclusion: the verse is built as a closing tricolon with grammatical and semantic parallelism, reinforced by ellipsis with verb gapping in the last part. It is, therefore, legitimate to pursue the idea that the point of v. 28 is to remind Israel of her present cultic status, namely impurity.

One more issue in v. 28 deserves a comment: the LXX rendering of v. 28aA, καὶ ἐμίαναν οἱ ἄρχοντες τὰ ἅγιά μου, has raised questions about the subject of this cola. The best explanation is that the LXX translator shied away from making YHWH an agent of μιαίνω or βεβηλόω, and has changed the subject intentionally for reverential reasons. LXX's rendering of Isa 47:6 supports this hypothesis.[120] The picture of YHWH as an agent of חלל in v. 28 can be seen as another illustration of poetic justice: Israel through her action profaned YHWH's holy name (Amos 2:7; Mal 1:11-12; Jer 41:16; Ezek 13:19; 20:39; 36:20, 21, 22, 23; 43:8), his holy things (Zeph 3:4; Ezek 22:26), the covenant of the ancestors (Mal 2:11), YHWH's sanctuary (Mal 2:11; Ezek 23:39; 44:7), his land (Jer 16:18), his sabbaths (Ezek 20:13, 16, 21, 24; 22:8; 23:38), even to the point that YHWH himself claims to be profaned in her midst (Ezek 22:26). It should, therefore, not come as a surprise that in response, YHWH profaned his servant's crown or dignity (Ps 89:40),[121] his inheritance (Isa 47:6), Judah's מַמְלָכָה וְשָׂרֶיהָ (Lam 2:2), and שָׂרֵי קֹדֶשׁ (Isa 43:28).[122]

---

119 Goldingay also recognizes that for Israel to become the object of גִּדּוּף 'constitutes a denial of central elements in what Yhwh has affirmed concerning its destiny,' Goldingay, *Message of Isaiah*, 226.

120 Outside of Isaiah, βεβηλόω for חלל with YHWH as a subject does occur in LXX, the closest parallel to Isa 43:28 being Lam 2:2.

121 LXX renders נִזְרוֹ as τὸ ἁγίασμα αὐτοῦ, 'his sanctuary'.

122 It is much less certain (and not likely to be resolved without future evidence) to whom or to what the expression שָׂרֵי קֹדֶשׁ refers. Many commentators turn to its only other occurrence in the OT, viz. 1 Chr 24:5, where it refers to priests. However, North is most likely right that, 'this usage is late, after the functions of the kings had passed to the priesthood.' He concludes that שָׂרֵי קֹדֶשׁ in DI 'is almost certainly to the "sacral" kings,' North, *Second Isaiah*, 131. The facts that DI uses the noun שַׂר and שָׂרָה in parallel with מֶלֶךְ (49:7 and 23 respectively), and the already mentioned similarity of Isa 43:28aA with Lam 2:2 support this conclusion. For Elliger, however, the collocation in 1 Chr 24:5 is yet another indication that Isa 43:28aA is a late addition. This view allows him to bring out evidence from other late passages, e. g. Ezra, and

5.5. Functional Analysis of Isa 43:22-28

This section deals with the relations between strophes as well as stanzas. It addresses only those links that are disputed or neglected in the commentaries, namely the internal correlation of vv. 22-24, the internal correlation of vv. 26-28, and the relation of v. 25 to the rest of the passage.

5.5.1. Stanza I: Correlation of 22 and 23-24

Delimitation of this stanza is straightforward thanks to its orderly structure, confirmed by major division markers in the textual tradition.[123] Several links bind this structure together:

— Thematic unity, the form of which was discussed above. Its content is to be determined in the discussion below.
— Series of seven negatives [ו]לֹא in vv. 22-24a, contrasted by אַךְ in the closing bicolon 24b.
— Chiastic structure: 22a-24b, 23a-24a, with the centre in 23b. As recognized by Goldingay, this chiasm is created by repetition of some key terms (יגע in 22a, 23b, and 24a; זבח in 23a and 24a), by the same theme in 23a and 24a, and by the importance of 23b as the central element.[124]
— Alternation of lineally and chiastically parallel bicola (22a, 23b, 24b, and 23a, 24a respectively), as noted by Koole.[125]

Watts, along with Rosenbaum, Schoors, North,[126] and a number of other scholars, links v. 22 and vv. 23-24 closely together by making v. 22aA crucial for the interpretation of the rest of the stanza. Watts claims that 'the emphatic opening וְלֹא אֹתִי [...] sets the tone for all three verses by claiming that Israel's worship was not directed to Yahweh. The underlying issue, then, is not cultic laxity but once again idolatry.'[127] There are at least three problems with this interpretation:

---

conclude that 'jedenfalls meint שָׂרֵי קֹדֶשׁ eher Priester als Könige,' Elliger, *Deuterojesaja*, 387. See there for further discussion.

123 For details, see Korpel and de Moor, *Structure*, 176-177.
124 See Goldingay, "Isaiah 43," 175.
125 See Koole, *Isaiah III/1*, 340.
126 See North, *Second Isaiah*, 128, Rosenbaum, *Word-Order*, 81, Schoors, *I am God*, 191.
127 Watts, *Isaiah*, 144. Similarly, e.g., North, *Second Isaiah*, 128. His reference to the 'strange [god]' of v. 12 in support of implicit idolatry in v. 22 is highly questionable.

— The supposition that 'when Yahweh says this [v. 22aA], it means that other gods have indeed been invoked'[128] is simply reading too much into the text. Booij rightly points out that if a contrast between YHWH and other gods was the intention of the passage, 'it would be strange ... that the contrast is not made explicit.'[129]

— If the underlying issue was idolatry, then v. 23b would be semantically out of place: why would YHWH accuse Israel of sacrificing to other gods and, at the same time, maintain that he did not demand sacrifices for himself? However, v. 23b has strong formal links with the rest of the stanza, and to exclude it on purely semantic grounds would be unsound.

— The tone, of which Watts and others speak in v. 22aA, would be in dissonance with the rest of the stanza, because of the different focus of vv. 22-24; it would be rather odd to criticize the direction of Israel's worship via criticising the worship itself.[130] In other words, the focus of vv. 23-24 is on *how* YHWH is being treated by Israel, not *to whom* Israel offers her worship.[131]

Similar objections can be raised to the interpretation of v. 22 as indicating that Israel did not *really* called on YHWH, only formally.[132] Again, nothing in the following verses suggests that the formality or superficiality of Israel's worship is the problem.[133]

Goldingay recognizes that 'the emphasis on *me* in v. 22 does not explicitly continue in vv. 23-24, and there is neither ground nor need to

---

128   Baltzer, *Deutero-Isaiah*, 177.

129   Booij, "Negation," 394. Similarly Blenkinsopp states that 'here there is no suggestion that sacrifice has been offered to any deity other than Yahveh,' Blenkinsopp, *Isaiah 40-55*, 231.

130   'The word-order in v. 23aα.24aα and the verbal suffix-construction in 23aβ.24aβ strongly suggest that here the negations somehow concern the cultic acts in themselves,' Booij, "Negation," 394.

131   Goldingay correctly states that already the second colon of v. 22 'hints that what offends Yhwh about the people's calling lies in a different direction from that of calling on/serving of other gods,' Goldingay, *Message of Isaiah*, 219.

132   Thus, e.g., Koole, *Isaiah III/1*, 341. Koole believes that, as in 48:1, something like בֶּאֱמֶת should qualify קְרָא of v. 22a. Contra Koole, it is argued below that no (implied) qualification is necessary, as v. 22b offers not qualification but quantification of קְרָא.

133   Commentators who opt for this reading compensate for this drawback by supplying a hypothetical dispute between YHWH and Israel to which Isa 43:22-28 is a reaction: Israel accuses YHWH of her distress in spite of faithfully bringing sacrifices to him, to which YHWH contests that Israel did not *really* serve him. For a classic example, see Westermann, *Isaiah 40-66*, 130-131.

assume that it does so implicitly.' He explains this ambiguity by suggesting that 'the focus turns to the nature of their [Jacob's/Israel's] action rather than the direction of it.'[134] However, there is neither ground nor need to assume the turn of focus in vv. 23-24. The ground is too small to accommodate such a turn (it would appear abrupt) and too syntactically frail to be justified, because its only indicator is the unusual word-order in 22aA, for which there can be another reason (see below). The need also disappears if the tone is set by the entire v. 22 with its consecutive כִּי, for the focus stays the same throughout vv. 22-24, viz. the inadequacy of Israel's cultic activity. A short word-study of some of the terms used confirms that the quantity rather than quality or direction of Israel's cult is the focus of vv. 23-24:

a) עבד — North points out that, with one exception, wherever the hiphil of עבד is found in BH, it always has the sense of 'reduce to slavery.'[135] This coerciveness is reflected in many translations: 'I did not make you serve,'[136] 'I did not burden you,'[137] or, even stronger, 'I did not make you slave' and 'I did not enslave you.'[138]

b) יגע — The root יגע is used nine times in DI, which is more than in any other OT book. BDB distinguishes between יגע meaning *to toil, to labour*, and *to grow weary* or *to be weary*.[139] Whether this double meaning is justified or not,[140] the demanding nature of this verb is evident. As for יגע in vv. 23bB and 24bB, they are two out of the total of four hiphil form occurrences in BH,[141] which makes it impossible to substantiate its range of meaning with an acceptable degree of certainty. In all four cases, יגע is connected with an object by בְּ, and Hasel seems to be right that the preposition here 'designates the means by which someone is made weary.'[142] It can be argued, therefore, that the hiphil form turns the demanding nature of יגע into coerciveness. יגע is in vv. 23b and 24b

---

134 Goldingay, "Isaiah 43," 178.

135 North, *Second Isaiah,* 129. Similarly, Koole states that 'עבד hi. is said in Ex. 1:13; 6:5 of the Pharaoh with his subjugation of the Israelites and in 2 Chron. 2:12 of Solomon and the labour which he enforced,' Koole, *Isaiah III/1,* 343. (He erroneously quotes 2 Chron. 2:12 instead of 17.). For further support, see also H. Ringgren, "עָבַד," *TDOT* 10.382.

136 So, e.g., Koole, Goldingay, or Schoors.

137 So, e.g., Blenkinsopp, Watts, or Elliger (*beschwer*).

138 North and Oswalt respectively.

139 BDB 388.

140 Hasel may be correct that 'it is unnecessary to postulate two relatively independent semantic fields, "be/become weary" and "toil," which rarely touch or overlap in Hebrew,' G. F. Hasel, "יָגַע," *TDOT* 5.387.

141 The other two are in Mal 2:17.

142 Hasel, "יָגַע," 389.

parallel to עבד, and to keep Kugel's 'A is so, and *what's more*, B' asks for a term stronger than 'to enslave'; therefore the choice here is 'to tyrannize'.

c) רוה — In v. 24, it is sometimes translated as 'to satisfy',[143] 'to refresh',[144] 'to please',[145] or even 'to let slurp'.[146] These renderings do not do justice to the vigour of רוה; as Rüterswörden correctly maintains, the parallel use of the verbs שבע and מלא 'shows that the root implies copious and occasionally excessive drinking.'[147] Moreover, every context of רוה in the OT stipulates emphasis on abundance or excess of some kind.[148] It is, therefore, suitable that 'the LXX usually translates *rāwâ* with a verbal form of *methýskein* (act.: "make drunk"; pass.: "become drunk, intoxicated").'[149] Since YHWH is the subject of this verb in Isa 43:24, it comes as no surprise that the versions render 24aB rather differently for reverential reasons.[150] The translations 'filled me up,'[151] 'drenched me,'[152] 'sated me,'[153] 'soaked me with/in,'[154] 'mich gefättigt,'[155] 'lavished on me,'[156] or even 'made mee drunke'[157] are to be preferred, for they capture the lavishness evoked by רוה.

d) קָנֶה — Another strong hint of opulent sacrifice or lavish cult in Isa 43:22-28 is v. 24aA. Even though קָנֶה has a very broad range of meaning in the OT, scholars agree that in this verse it means an aromatic reed, probably *calamus*.[158] Since this sort of plant 'grows primarily in northwestern and central India ... and was imported into

---

143 E.g., Koole, NRS, ESV, JPS, NKJ.

144 E.g., Delitzsch, EIN, CEP and BKR.

145 NLT.

146 Baltzer.

147 U. Rüterswörden, "רָוָה," *TDOT* 13.357.

148 The context of רוה in Dt. 29:18(19) is difficult to determine.

149 Rüterswörden, "רָוָה," 361.

150 Thus LXX avoids the anthropomorphism by rendering 24ab as οὐδὲ τὸ στέαρ τῶν θυσιῶν σου ἐπεθύμησα. For this explanation, see, e.g., Watts, *Isaiah*, 139. He, however, erroneously translates ἐπεθύμησα as 'angered'. As Goldingay points out, Targum 'reverentially makes the altar the object of the soaking, rather than YHWH in person,' Goldingay, "Isaiah 43," 181.

151 Watts.

152 Oswalt.

153 Booij, Blenkinsopp, TNK, NJB.

154 North, Goldingay.

155 Elliger.

156 NIV.

157 GNV.

158 See BDB 889.

Palestine,'[159] it had to be purchased בְּכֶסֶף. Lamberty further points out that Jer 6:20 understands קָנֶה as 'one of the most precious (imported) sacrificial offerings for Yahweh.'[160]

This word-study brought out the aspect of high demand in יגע and עבד, and the lavishness hinted by רוה and קָנֶה, implying a demanding and opulent cultic practice (or rather its absence).

Also the broader context (viz. the preceding verses of ch. 43) suggests that the issue in v. 22 is not the direction or the quality of קרא but its quantity. If YHWH is the only real God and saviour (vv. 8-13), if his power over the nations and nature is unlimited (vv. 2-7 and 14-20), if he not only created and formed Israel (vv. 1, 15, and 21) but promises and is able to take care of her in every situation (vv. 2-7 and 14-20) because she is precious in his sight and he loves her (v. 4), it would be the most natural thing for Israel in exile to 'cry her head off' in calling on YHWH.[161] The emphatic word order at the beginning of v. 22 very likely expresses the surprise over the contrasting reality described in vv. 22-24. V. 22 would then read as follows: 'Yet me [the almighty and loving God] you have not invoked, O Jacob, to the point that you would have wearied yourself for me, O Israel.'[162] The preceding two verses set up for this surprise by stating that YHWH is honoured for his works even by the wild animals (v. 20), and that to declare his praise was the very purpose for which YHWH has formed the people of Israel (v. 21).[163]

This notion is reflected even in v. 24b, where the introductory adverb אַךְ seems to function restrictively (*only*) rather than adversatively (*but*). In similar cases, where אַךְ introduces a clause that elaborates the meaning of the preceding negative clause, the restrictive function of this adverb is either the only possible, or makes a better sense than the adversative one.[164] Furthermore, DI uses אַךְ in only two

---

159 H. Lamberty-Zielinski, "קָנֶה," *TDOT* 13.68.

160 Lamberty, "קָנֶה," 68.

161 As Ps 50:15 encourages, וּקְרָאֵנִי בְּיוֹם צָרָה.

162 As Booij correctly points out, the consecutive clause (v. 22aB) obtains its modality of *irrealis* from the negation in the main clause (v. 22aA), meaning that Jacob/Israel actually has not wearied herself for YHWH, see Booij, "Negation," 396.

163 Koole observes this contrast, augmented also by the use of כבד in vv. 20 and 23, see Koole, *Isaiah III/1*, 339. As Melugin states, 'in the context of the present arrangement of units, v. 22ff. follow from v. 20-21,' Melugin, *Formation*, 117. Calvin also observes this connection, arguing that in v. 22 YHWH 'confirms by an indirect reproof what he said in the preceding verse, that it was not by any merits of his people that he was induced to act so kindly towards them,' Calvin, *Isaiah*, 345.

164 For illustration, see: Gen 34:14-15, 23; Exod 12:16; 1 Sam 20:39; 1 Kgs 22:43-44 (2 Chr 20:32-33); Jer 3:12-13; Ps 37:8; Job 14:21-22 (13:15 is questionable).

more places, 45:14 and 24, both with restrictive function. The disjunctive accent *r^evia^ʿ* (אַ֣ף) may intensify this function, bringing out the paradox: the *only* respects in which Jacob/Israel outdid herself was חַטָּאוֹת and עֲוֹנוֹת .

Such a reading of Isa 43:22-24, however, differs from the one proposed by the majority of interpreters in the following ways:

— As the discussion about the form showed, its nature is not accusatory, but descriptive.

— Its focus is consistent throughout the whole stanza: the fact that Jacob/Israel did not outdo herself in worshipping YHWH (v. 22) is further illustrated in vv. 23a and 24a.

— It is in harmony with vv. 23b, where YHWH states that he did not require demanding worship.

— It elegantly sets up the stage for the stanza's closing bicolon; the only activity towards YHWH, in which Jacob/Israel outdid herself, is described in v. 24b: הֶעֱבַדְתַּנִי בְּחַטֹּאותֶיךָ הוֹגַעְתַּנִי בַּעֲוֹנֹתֶיךָ

Structurally speaking, v. 22 as an opening bicolon sets up the idea of the whole stanza,[165] which is expanded via a tour in vv. 23-24a, and culminates in v. 24b – a closing bicolon. This reading appears to be the most natural and the most conflict-free.

5.5.2. Stanza III: Correlation of 26-27 and 28

Scholars' treatment of vv. 26-28 as a unity is often based on the assumption that its form is a trial speech, where v. 26 is an appeal to a trial, v. 27 an accusation, and v. 28 a verdict (condemnation, announcement of punishment).[166] Prompted by what appear to be technical terms for a judicial accusation, viz. הַזְכִּירֵנִי, נִשָּׁפְטָה, and סַפֵּר, they make the trial-speech form the starting point for their interpretation of the rest of the stanza. When it comes to structural analysis, this preconception inevitably results in understanding v. 28 as an outcome of v. 27. Whether translating both verbal expressions in v. 28 as *waw* consecutive plus preterite, or, as indicated by MT, a simple

---

165 As observed by Calvin, '*calling on* the name of God includes the whole of the worship of God, the chief part of which is "calling upon him;" and, therefore, following the ordinary manner of Scripture, he has put a part for the whole,' Calvin, *Isaiah*, 345.

166 See, e.g., Schoors, *I am God*, 193-197, Westermann, *Isaiah 40-66*, 133.

(conjunctive) *waw* plus imperfect, the function of the initial *waw* is to introduce a result clause: 'Therefore/So/That is why I (have) profaned ...'[167] or 'Therefore/So I will profane ...'.[168] This interpretation is certainly legitimate,[169] but not the only, and not necessarily the most plausible one.

The relationship between vv. 27 and 28 would change if the initial *waw* in v. 28 is understood as performing its most common, co-ordinative function: instead of reading v. 27 as a description of why and v. 28 of how the people have been or will be punished, these verses should rather be viewed as a list of reasons why Jacob/Israel is bound to fail the challenge in v. 26: סַפֵּר אַתָּה לְמַעַן תִּצְדָּק. Goldingay defends this reading (supported by LXX), arguing that the chiastic structure of vv. 27 and 28 speaks against understanding v. 28 as a conclusion or a result of what precedes, and that the prophet would have used more perceptible rhetorical devices if v. 28 was meant to be a grand finale of the passage. He concludes that if the expression וָאֲחַלֵּל 'is heard as a *w*-consecutive, it almost suggests more a further elaboration of Israel's predicament in its failure.'[170] As the studies of the progress in v. 27 and of the terms in v. 28 above confirm, Israel's 'ununterbrochenen Sündengeschichte'[171] with its from-bad-to-worse dynamic resulted in the damned present. It makes perfect sense to read vv. 27-28 the same way as vv. 22-24, viz. descriptively. In combination with v. 26, such a reading makes very clear to the people in exile that they have nothing to set forth in order to be justified, neither their present or past moral actions (vv. 24b and 27 respectively), nor their present cultic activities or cultic status (vv. 22-24a and 28 respectively).

5.5.3. Stanza II: Relation of 25 to Its Immediate Context

The theme of v. 25 is so different from what precedes in vv. 22-24 and from what follows in vv. 26-28 that to establish a structural link with either section is problematic, if not impossible. Westermann prefers to deal with this verse at the very end of his discussion of 43:22-28.[172] Merendino allows for DI authorship of v. 25, claiming that it 'enthält

---

167 NRS, TNK, KJV, JPS, NLT, NJB
168 NKJ, NIV, NAS, ESV
169 For result clauses constructed by means of a simple consecutive sequence, see Williams §525.
170 Goldingay and Payne, *Isaiah 40-55*, 1.316.
171 Expression from Elliger, *Deuterojesaja*, 384.
172 Westermann, *Isaiah 40-66*, 133.

einen gut deuterojesajanischen Gedanken,' but he believes that it has been composed and moved to its current position from other parts of DI, possibly from around 44:22 or 48:11, by a later editor. Merendino even offers a motive behind such "cut-and-paste" method: 'Der Interpolator wollte die harte Anklage der Verse 22-24.26-28 gegen Israel mildern und hat es getan durch Hinzufügung eines Heilswortes.'[173]

Notwithstanding the obscurity, there are those who try to establish the connection one way or another. Thus, e.g., Koole links v. 25 with the preceding section via v. 24b, arguing that cola of vv. 22-25 fell into two groups: the first vv. 22, 23b, and 24b, where 'יגע talks about the weariness associated with Israel's religion,' and the second vv. 23a, 24a, and 25 where 'Yahweh refers to himself by אָנֹכִי, לִי, לְכִי and לְמַעֲנִי.'[174] Since the members of each group repeatedly alternate, Koole believes that vv. 22-25 create one section that can be subdivided into vv. 22+23a, 23b+24a, and 24b+25. In spite of the attractive regularity, Koole's argument must be resisted. Alternating the members of the two suggested groups is mixing apples with oranges, for the function of the references to YHWH in vv. 23a and 24a is of a different kind from the ones in v. 25.[175]

If one wishes to establish a connection on a catch-word principle, then v. 25 would go more likely with what follows, for as many as three roots used in this verse are repeated in vv. 26-27: זכר, לְמַעַן, and פשע. In fact, Korpel and de Moor argue that v. 25 and v. 26 should be taken as one strophe on the basis of the repetition of the first two roots plus the occurrence of personal pronouns in both verses, referring to it as parallelism.[176] Catch-word principle, however, has a fundamentally different function from parallelism when it comes to structure. 'The transition from vs. 25 to 26 is a typical dt.-Isaian wordplay. The root זכר, used twice in the same context, has two concretely distinct meanings.'[177] The same can be said about the repetition of לְמַעַן here. Moreover, the claim that there is a thematic unity in vv. 25-28, viz. justification of Israel's punishment, is simply wrong.[178]

Treating v. 25 as a separate stanza seems to be the best option for the following reasons:

---

173 Merendino, *Der Erste*, 351.

174 Koole, *Isaiah III/1*, 340.

175 The links between vv. 22-24 and v. 25 that Koole suggests on pp. 347-48 are not structural and cannot be justified without buying into his interpretation of the text.

176 Korpel and de Moor, *Structure*, 198.

177 Schoors, *I am God*, 194.

178 *Contra* Korpel and de Moor, *Structure*, 202.

— It does not share any of the links that connect vv. 22-24 (as listed in 5.5.1). [179]

— Its theme is radically different from the one in vv. 26-28.

— It makes perfectly good sense on its own.

— 1QIsa^a and 1QIsa^b leave a narrow space open not only after v. 24, but also after v. 25. MT interprets the first as Setuma, while ignoring the second. Nevertheless, there is noteworthy evidence that v. 25 has been understood as a separate unit at least by one ancient tradition.

Apparently, there is a merit in Westermann's approach – reading v. 25 not in connection with, but in contrast to what precedes and follows. As already argued by Calvin, YHWH

contrasts his mercy with all other causes, as if he declared that he is not induced by anything else to pardon sins, but is satisfied with his mere goodness, and, consequently, that it is wrong to ascribe either to merits or to any sacrifices the redemption of which he is the Author by free grace.[180]

The translation of Isa 43:22-28 below enhances this reading.

5.6. Translation of Isa 43:22-28

22 Yet me you have not invoked, Jacob,
to the point that you would have wearied yourself for me, Israel.
23 You have not brought me your sheep for burnt offerings,
     or honored me with your sacrifices.
I have not enslaved you with offerings,
     or tyrannized you with frankincense.
24 You have not bought me sweet cane with money,
     or lavished on me the fat of your sacrifices.
Only, you have enslaved me with your sins;
you have tyrannized me with your iniquities.

---

179 Including the one of alternation of lineally and chiastically parallel bicolons, for the parallelism in v. 25 is only partial (contra Koole).

180 Calvin, Isaiah, 348-349. As Jensen observes, this contrast between Israel's sinfulness and YHWH's mercies is characteristic for DI. 'It is precisely where the recipients are incapable of helping themselves that grace is most clearly manifested,' Jensen, Ethical Dimensions, 154.

²⁵ I, I am He
   who blots out your transgressions for my own sake,
   and will not remember your sins.

²⁶ Remind me. Let us dispute with one another.
You recount so that you may be proved right.
²⁷ Your first ancestor sinned,
and your interpreters transgressed against me,
²⁸ and I have desecrated the princes of the sanctuary,
I have turned Jacob into an impurity,
                and Israel into a blasphemy.

5.7. Conclusion

The picture resulting from the above exegesis of Isa 43:22-28 is as
follows: Jacob/Israel's cultic activities are inadequate (vv. 22-24a) and
their cultic status is the opposite of holiness (v. 28). Moreover, their
righteousness cannot be derived from past or present; it is annulled by
sin from the very beginning (v. 27aA), throughout history (v. 27aB),
and to the very present-day (v. 24b). In short, neither the cult nor the
ethics of Israel could possibly contribute to the reversal of the situation
that resulted from her sin.   It is exclusively because of YHWH's
forgiveness and his holy status that the sin is abolished (v. 25) and
salvation is made possible (44:1-5).[181] In this soteriological disputation,
the omnipotence of YHWH is pictured against the impotence of Israel,
and the holiness of YHWH against the impurity of Jacob. Ezek 36:22 may
serve as a summary of this disputation: לֹא לְמַעַנְכֶם אֲנִי עֹשֶׂה ... כִּי
אִם־לְשֵׁם־קָדְשִׁי אֲשֶׁר חִלַּלְתֶּם
    This important exilic lesson about the limitations of cult and ethics
with regard to salvation is consistent with the Priestly teaching: sins
and transgressions lead into desecration and cause an impurity that can
be removed neither by rituals nor ethics, viz. moral impurity. In
Luther's words, Isa 43:22-28 'is nothing but a complete abolition of all
our resources.'[182] In this situation, things can be put aright with YHWH
only because of his grace and only for his own sake.

---

181 As Goldingay points out, '"for Yhwh's [name's] sake" … is the consideration that
    comes into play when there is no other to appeal to,' Goldingay and Payne, *Isaiah 40-
    55*, 1.313.
182 *LW* 17.98.

Chapter 6: Cult and Ethics
in Isaiah 58

6.1. Introduction

The themes of cult and ethics run throughout the whole of Isa 58. Hanson rightly calls this chapter 'a classic example of prophetic tradition in the Bible. Here the fidelity of the Third Isaiah circle to the central themes of justice and proper worship developed by Amos, Hosea, Isaiah, and Jeremiah comes to clear expression.'[1] Far less clear, however, is the relation between these themes – the subject of the present thesis. Again, the exegesis of the passage represents the mainstay of the investigation. Before turning to the text, two terms that are used throughout this chapter, namely allusion and eschatology, require a brief comment.

6.1.1. Allusion in TI

According to Sommer, 'a close examination of [chs. 40-66] shows Deutero-Isaiah to be one of the most allusive ancient Israelite authors.'[2] This observation holds true especially for chs. 56-66; it is probable that by the time of their composition (discussed in 6.2.1), most of what today is known as the Torah and the Prophets already obtained the status of 'Holy Scripture'.[3] According to Schmid, this status facilitated allusions:

---

1   Hanson, *Isaiah 40-66*, 204.
2   Benjamin D. Sommer, *A Prophet Reads Scripture: Allusion in Isaiah 40-66* (Contraversions: Jews and Other Differences; Stanford, CA: Stanford University Press, 1998) 3. He uses the label Deutero-Isaiah for chs. 40-66.
3   As Sommer points out, 'Deutero-Isaiah had scripture, but he did not have canon. He regarded some older texts as authoritative and sacred,' but he 'had no finite list of sacred works – new prophecies could occur, and hence new scripture could be composed,' Sommer, *Allusion*, 182. For the differentiation between Scripture and canon, see John Barton, *Oracles of God: Perceptions of Ancient Prophecy in Israel after the Exile* (London: Darton Longman and Todd, 1986).

Die sprachliche Fixierung und Tradierung solcher Maximen, die Allgemeingültigkeit beansprucht, entkleidet diese der Bindung an ihrem geschichtlichen Ort und ihrer Einmaligkeit. Die unmittelbar erlebten und verstandenen Zusammenhänge werden objektiviert und damit unge- schichtlich. Sie verlieren den direkten Bezug zur begegnenden Wirklichkeit und stehen in der Vorratskammer der Sprache bereit, in einer neuen geschichtlichen Situation Verwendung zu finden und dort Hilfe zu sein.[4]

Childs therefore correctly insists that the most fruitful method for determining the purpose of TI is to recognize the central role of allusion in this book.[5] Also Sommer speaks about the centrality of allusion in Isaiah 40-66; according to him, these chapters are a composition in which 'the use of older texts becomes a primary concern.'[6]

Before applying the method proposed by Childs, it is important to mention two of its main drawbacks. First, to determine an allusion is notoriously nebulous: even if the rate of linguistic similarities between two texts is satisfactory, problems such as dating, original source, or editorial additions still remain. As Schultz demonstrates, 'although the criteria for identitying allusions have become increasingly sophisticated, a troubling degree of subjectivity remains in employing them.'[7] Second, even more subjective is to determine the author's reason for making the allusion. Sommer suggests some general motives: by alluding to an already authoritative work, a new statement may bolster its own authority, and, at the same time, it 'keeps the older work alive and maintains their relevance.' Allusion can also 'distance the new work from the old, since it is precisely when one juxtaposes two works (as one is forced to do by allusion) that one notices their differences.' As far as Isa 40-66 is concerned, Sommer believes that the author 'alluded to earlier texts as he composed, not merely to update

---

4   Hans Heinrich Schmid, *Wesen und Geschichte der Weisheit: Eine Untersuchung zur Altorientalischen und Israelitischen Weisheitsliteratur* (BZAW 101; Berlin: A. Töpelmann, 1966) 79.

5   See Childs, *Isaiah*, 444-448. Child uses the term intertextuality here, but if, as he argues, its primary purpose in TI is 'in signaling continuity with a prior tradition,' the term allusion is preferable. As Sommer clarifies, 'intertextuality is concerned with the reader or with the text as a thing independent of its author, while influence and allusion are concerned with the author as well as the text and reader. Intertextuality is synchronic in its approach, influence or allusion diachronic or even historicist.' Since Isaiah 40-66 is 'very concretely rooted in a readily identifiable historical situation,' a diachronic approach 'will prove both usable and enriching,' Sommer, *Allusion*, 8-9.

6   Sommer, *Allusion*, 165.

7   Richard L. Schultz, *The Search for Quotation: Verbal Parallels in the Prophets* (JSOTSup 180; Sheffield: Sheffield Academic Press, 1999) 49. See there for further treatment of this subject.

the work of one figure or school, but to reinforce and revitalize a complex, varied Hebrew literary tradition that had experienced a crisis.'[8] While the above motives are plausible, the point about the crisis of the Hebrew literary tradition raises some doubts. Supposedly, this crisis in post-exilic times was caused by the failure of the former prophecies (especially those of DI) to be fulfilled. If this were the case, alluding to such prophecies would be counterproductive. It will be argued in the discussion below that people's frustration expressed in Isa 58 (see v. 3a) did not result from "unfulfilled prophecies" of DI, but from the absence of God's response to the people's present religious activities. Furthermore, the primary function of DI's descriptions of the future was not to make promises that would come true upon people's return from exile, but to demonstrate the sovereignty, omnipotence, and grace of YHWH. For this reason, DI referred to the future *as well as* to the past. As Hanson puts it, 'the message of Second Isaiah does not constitute a scientific prediction of future events; rather, it is a visionary description of God's plan for creation and of the part that faithful Israel was to play in that plan.'[9] One should allow for the possibility that the returnees understood DI's prophecies accordingly, and that their expectations based on his message were not totally unrealistic. As Barton points out, the time factor is not essential in this mode of reading a prophecy: 'Since interest in the future … is part of a desire to present God as perfectly in control of history which he directs according to his own plans and wisdom, it is almost a matter of indifference exactly when the predicted events are to come about.'[10] In any case, this problem illustrates that determining the prophet's reason for making an allusion depends on one's presuppositions about the prophetic literature.

These considerations should raise one's level of caution with regard to allusions and conclusions based on them. It needs to be remembered that any argument for an allusion and the reason behind it is cumulative and always subjective. In the words of Sommer, it 'is an art, not a science.'[11]

---

8   Sommer, *Allusion*, 18-19 and 131.
9   Hanson, *Isaiah 40-66*, 188.
10   Barton, *Oracles*, 224.
11   Sommer, *Allusion*, 35.

6.1.2. Eschatology in TI

Eschatology concerns 'the last things'. Klausner specifies that the word 'last' can be understood 'either absolutely as referring to the ultimate destiny of mankind in general or of each individual man, or relatively as referring to the end of a certain period in the history of mankind or of a nation that is followed by another, entirely different, historical period.'[12] While this specification is useful for distinguishing between the late and the early OT understanding of the concept, it does not work for the eschatology of TI. As Klausner himself recognizes,

> with Deutero-Isaiah there begins a more transcendent concept of eschatology; climactic events in history are viewed not so much as the beginning of a new historical era brought about by human means, but rather as a transformation of the world on a cosmic scale produced by God's extraordinary intervention in man's history.[13]

Isa 56-66 reflects this transitory state by referring to the relative as well as the absolute 'last things'. Heaton's definition seems to be the most appropriate for the exilic and early post-exilic eschatological material: 'Eschatology denotes that complex of teaching which arose from the prophetic conviction that Yahweh, the living God, was inaugurating a new action in history in relation to his people and to the consummation of his purpose.' As Heaton comments, the terms in this definition are wide enough to include the prophets' preaching of judgement as well as their promises of salvation.[14]

Eschatology in Isa 58 utilizes a number of pictures, metaphors, and expressions, most of which are familiar from the earlier prophetic texts. More importantly, Isa 58 relates eschatology to two other vital concepts in the religion of ancient Israel – cult and ethics. This connection comes naturally, for eschatology as understood by the OT is fundamentally relational; it is the product of the proper relationship between YHWH and his people. The essence of eschatology is described by YHWH's words in Exod 29:45 – וְשָׁכַנְתִּי בְּתוֹךְ בְּנֵי יִשְׂרָאֵל וְהָיִיתִי לָהֶם לֵאלֹהִים. The relationship between eschatology, cult, and ethics is explored throughout this chapter.

---

12   Joseph Gedaliah Klausner, "Eschatology," *Enc Jud* 6.860.
13   Klausner, "Eschatology," *Enc Jud* 6.870.
14   Eric William Heaton, *The Hebrew Kingdoms* (Oxford: Oxford University Press, 1968) 59.

6.2. Historical Background of Isa 58

6.2.1. Date of Isa 58

For the purposes of this chapter, the only advantage of a more precise dating than just the post-exilic period would be a possibility to establish a relative chronology between Isa 58-59 and the other passage that deals with the topic of fasting and ethics in the early post-exilic times, namely Zech 7-8. Zech 7:1 sets this text in early winter of 518, shortly after the rebuilding of the temple in Jerusalem has begun, and before it was dedicated in 515.[15] Unfortunately, there is no such date-reference in Isa 58. The religious practices, the social situation, and the expectations of the people mentioned in this chapter are the only possible indicators of its date of composition. Thus, e.g., Park argues that because the Sabbath is absent in Zechariah, it was not yet relevant in his time, but became prominent only during the time of Nehemiah, and, because it is of concern in Isa 58:13-14, Isa 58 originated in this period.[16] Besides arguing from silence, Park also overlooks the passages like Amos 8:4-8 or Ezek 20:12-24 where the observance of the Sabbath plays an important role.[17] In his attempt to date Isa 58, Watts believes that the social conditions in this text reflect the situation soon after the beginning of the rule of Artaxerxes, the third son of Xerxes, in 465, and prior to Ezra's appearance in 458.[18] Blenkinsopp, however, rightly comments that 'conditions in the early years of Persian rule could have been as bad or worse' than in the mid-fifth century B.C.E., 'given the drought, bad harvest, lack of employment, inflation, and social unrest (cf. Hag 1:5, 6, 10, 11; 2:16, 17; Zech 8:10).'[19] According to a number of scholars, vv. 1-4 presume the temple in operation, so they date the

---

15   515 as the year of the inauguration of the second temple is a present scholarly consensus, identifying the Persian king Darius mentioned in Ezra 6:1f with Darius Hystaspis (521-486). For a recent challenge to this consensus, see Lester L. Grabbe, *Ezra-Nehemiah* (Old Testament Readings; London: Routledge, 1998) 123-138. He identifies Darius from Ezra 6 with Darius II Ochus (424-405). Another, more recent challenge comes from Diana Vikander Edelman, *The Origins of the Second Temple: Persian Imperial Policy and the Rebuilding of Jerusalem* (Bible World; London: Equinox Press, 2005). She fuses the temple reconstruction with Nehemiah's wall building completed in 445.

16   See Park, *Gerechtigkeit Israels*, 248.

17   For sabbath observance in general, see below (6.3.2). For further discussion on the Sabbath in these texts, see Appendix 2.

18   Watts, *Isaiah*, 265-267.

19   Joseph Blenkinsopp, *Isaiah 56-66: A New Translation with Introduction and Commentary* (AB 19B; New York; London: Doubleday, 2003) 178.

composition of Isa 58 (or at least these verses) shortly after 515.[20] However, as Sommer rightly objects, none of TI's references to the temple (56:7, 60:7, 62:9, 65:11, 66:6) explicitly state that it has been rebuilt.[21] Furthermore, the cultic activities mentioned in ch. 58 do not necessitate the temple either.[22] Instead of the state of the temple, Sommer offers other clues such as 'the interest these chapters display in issues that concern other authors in that age: the inclusion of foreigners in the Judean community (Isa 56:1-7; cf. Ezra 9.1-4, Neh 9.2); the nature of the priesthood (Isa 61.5-6; cf. Ezekiel 44); the cleavage between different factions (Isa 57.19-21, 65.13; cf. Ezra 4.1-5).'[23] These clues, however, may point to any time after a group of Judeans moved from Babylonia to Judah and faced these kinds of issue.

In this situation, it seems best to go by a scholary consensus. Schramm provides a helpful overview of the various dates for Isa 58 as given by some of the most influential scholars: not long after 515 (Elliger), 5th century (Volz), post-exilic (Fohrer), contemporary with Haggai and Zechariah (Soggin), around 530 for vv. 1-12 and later, when composing the framework, for vv. 13-14 (Westermann), early post-exilic (Pauritsch), early post-exilic for vv. 1-12 and 475-425 for vv. 13-14 (Hanson).[24] With the exception of vv. 13-14, an early post-exilic date for Isa 58 emerges from this overview as a consensus of 20th century scholarship. This, of course, leaves the relative chronology between Isa 58 and Zech 7-8 open.

6.2.2. Authorship of Isa 58

The question about the authorship of Isa 58 closely relates to one's view of the composition of the book of Isaiah as a whole, and of chs. 40-66 in particular. For the purpose of this chapter, there is no need to add to or

---

20 Thus, e.g., Rainer Albertz, *A History of Israelite Religion in the Old Testament Period*, trans. John Stephen Bowden (London: SCM Press Ltd, 1994) 494 and 635. He suggests that Isa 58 has grown successively between 515 and 450.

21 Sommer, *Allusion*, 188.

22 An existence of a temporary sacred structure for use before the completion of the Temple is also a real possibility, see V. A. Hurowitz, "Temporary Temples," in *Kinattutu ša darâti: Raphael Kutscher memorial volume*, ed. Anson F. Rainey (Tel Aviv Occasional Publications 1; Tel Aviv: Emery and Claire Yass Publications in Archaeology, 1993).

23 Sommer, *Allusion*, 188.

24 Brooks Schramm, *The Opponents of Third Isaiah: Reconstructing the Cultic History of the Restoration* (JSOTSup 193; Sheffield: Sheffield Academic Press, 1995) 16-20.

enter into the discussion with some of the latest thorough studies of TI's composition.[25] While the importance of such studies is recognized throughout this chapter, a word of caution from Schramm puts some of their criteria into the right perspective:

> Arguments based on compatibility of subject matter, or lack thereof, are notoriously subjective. It is simply wrong for a modern interpreter to assume that an ancient Hebrew prophet could not have changed his style or even his message over the course of a career. Even what a modern person would view as blatant contradiction should not be regarded as automatic grounds for positing multiple authorship.[26]

If the author of Isa 58 was one of the returnees from Babylon, the dramatic events during the lifetime of his generation could account for the differences between DI and TI.[27] However, this theory is no less hypothetical then the ones of multiple authorship. Pragmatically speaking, when tracing a development of a particular theological idea within the lifetime of one generation, it makes little difference whether this process took place in a single mind or is a product of several people. Since the text itself does not yield any information about the author, it is more sound to speak not about a prophetic figure (as an individual historical personality), rather about 'a genuine prophecy that responds to the divine word, "Thus says Yahweh," an integral part of the larger prophetic book of Isaiah.'[28] The indistinctness of the date and the authorship of TI may well be intentional, performing a function similar to alluding – to tighten up the connection with the previous parts of the book of Isaiah.

With regard to the overall thesis, one additional word of caution about the author(s) of TI seems to be appropriate to counter some of the stereotypes about the prophets: advocating social justice for the weak ones of the society does not turn the prophet into a socialist revolutionary. In words of Williamson, 'the concerns for social justice and for cultic purity are certainly illuminated by sociological analysis, but that does not demand that they be necessarily taken as partisan,

---

25 See, e.g., Wolfgang Lau, *Schriftgelehrte Prophetie in Jes 56-66: Eine Untersuchung zu den literarischen Bezügen in den letzten elf Kapiteln des Jesajabuches* (BZAW 225; Berlin: Walter de Gruyter, 1994), P. A. Smith, *Rhetoric and Redaction in Trito-Isaiah: The Structure, Growth, and Authorship of Isaiah 56-66* (VTSup 62; Leiden: Brill, 1995).

26 Schramm, *Opponents*, 21.

27 This line of argument for a unity of the authorship of Isa 40-66 is pursued by Haran and Sommer, et al.

28 Childs, *Isaiah*, 443.

any more than in the case of Amos or Ezekiel.'[29] A closer look at the audience of Isa 58-59 brings some more light into this issue.

6.2.3. Audience of Isa 58

Strictly speaking, this oracle is not against the whole people of Israel. Park believes that the addressee is 'eine bestimmte Gruppe' with two main characteristics: based on vv. 2, 3a, 4b and 5, they are 'die formal Jhwh-Gläubigen', and, based on vv. 3b, 4a, 6, 7, 9b, and 13, they are 'die die sozial Schwächeren unterdrückt'.[30] The first characteristic presupposes a group of worshipers that believed in enhancing YHWH's יְשׁוּעָה and צְדָקָה by increasing cultic activities, irrespective of their own מִשְׁפָּט and צְדָקָה. Such cult-based soteriology could originate in priestly and temple-related circles, but, because of its attractiveness and simplicity, it could as well be a product of popular theology. The second characteristic assumes a delineation of the post-exilic community along social and economic lines. In spite of our limited knowledge of the social order in TI's time, it is safe to exclude from the criticism of this poem the weaker ones of the society, such as ill-treated labourers (עָצֵב with נגשׂ in v. 3), the oppressed (רְצוּצִים in v. 6), hungry, poor, homeless, and naked (עֲנִיִּים מְרוּדִים, רָעֵב, and עָרֹם in v. 7), and to assume that the criticism was addressed to those in whose power it was to improve the pitiful conditions of these groups.

Obviously, the political and religious leaders meet the profile. Albertz believes that 'the dispute was predominantly carried on at two levels: by a part of the aristocracy who were in solidarity with the poor against their colleagues who were not, and by groups of the lower class against their aristocratic oppressors, but also at times against their supporters.'[31] Preaching against this crowd would certainly require extra courage, as the command in v. 1a, esp. the phrase 'do not hold back', seems to imply.[32] Nevertheless, there is no reason to reduce the addressees of Isa 58-59 to aristocrats only. Park correctly concludes: 'Obwohl es sich nicht bestimmen läßt, wer ursprünglich zu wem gesprochen hat, zeigt der dritte Teil im ganzen, daß die prophetischen Gerichts- und Heilsansagen für das ganze Volk, das diese Worte in

---

29   Williamson, "Israel in Transition," 152.

30   Park, *Gerechtigkeit Israels*, 230-231.

31   Albertz, *Israelite Religion*, 2.500.

32   The expression אַל־תַּחְשֹׂךְ is also used in Isa 54:2 (fem.) for encouragement. For a similar command in a similar situation, see Jer 26:2.

seiner jeweiligen Gegenwart las und hörte, Gültigkeit hatten.'[33] As will be argued below (*contra* Hanson), Isa 58 does not offer any unambiguous evidence of a class-divided society (whether on economic or theological basis) and of a tension between these classes. Besides the address in v. 1, Schramm is correct that also the phrase כְּגוֹי אֲשֶׁר־צְדָקָה עָשָׂה in v. 2 'supports the contention that no specific group is singled out for criticism but rather the people as a whole.'[34]

6.3. Cultic Background of Isa 58

In one of his articles, Barton pays tribute to Wellhausen for 'discovering the Exile', namely its crucial role in forming the religion of Israelites. His apt summary of Wellhausen's contribution to OT scholarship provides a solid starting point for sketching the cultic background of the post-exilic Israelite community, so it is worth quoting in full:

> The experience of being exiled in a foreign land, without national institutions such as the monarchy and the Temple, had made the Israelites turn in on themselves and ask questions about their religious identity. The leading people among them had developed the blueprints for life in a restored community, where obedience to carefully devised rituals would replace the chaotic spontaneity which had encouraged the syncretistic tendencies now being punished by Yahweh. Israel could become a confessional, rather than a national community.[35]

It will be argued below that the unique opportunity for post-exilic Judah to get things right stimulated cultic and ethical zeal that found its ultimate expression in eschatology. In particular, it will be demonstrated how this *Sitz im Kult* elucidates the ethical and cultic issues addressed in Isa 58. First, however, a closer look at two cultic expressions that seem to come to prominence during and after the Exile is needed – fasting and the Sabbath.

6.3.1. Fasting

Herr rightly observes that many OT passages indicate the use of fasting 'as a means of winning divine forgiveness ..., implying that fasting is basically an act of penance, a ritual expression of remorse, submission,

---

33   Park, *Gerechtigkeit Israels*, 214.
34   Schramm, *Opponents*, 134.
35   Barton, "Wellhausen's *Prolegomena*," 328.

and supplication.'[36] Its close connection with Yom Kippur is, therefore, appropriate. However, unlike Yom Kippur, fasting itself has never been meant to have an expiatory function in the OT.[37] Its function was preparatory, symbolizing human status before God. Hermisson correctly states that the OT fasting 'ist aber nicht eigentlich ein Mittel mehr, mit dem man Jahwe beeinflussen, zwingen kann, sondern bringt die von ihm geforderte Haltung des Menschen zeichenhaft zum Ausdruck.'[38] As suggested by Jer 14:12a 'Although they fast, I do not hear their cry, and although they offer burnt offering and grain offering, I do not accept them,' fasting and sacrifices can have the same purpose – to evoke God's (favourable) attention. This seems to be the reason for fasting also in Isa 58: God would see people's fasting, notice their self-affliction (v. 3a) and grant their pious desires described in v. 2.

As Brongers points out, 'communal fasts were continually in danger of being conceived of by participants as an *opus operatum* and consequently were open to prophetic criticism.'[39] Preuss specifies that in fasting-critical passages like Isa 58 'the basic criticism is that one's demeanor toward God ('fasting') should be commensurate with one's demeanor toward one's fellow human beings, and that social action constitutes an expression of true fasting.'[40] Since this criticism occurs only in post-exilic texts (besides Isa 58, also Zech 7, and possibly Joel 2:12-14 and Jonah 3:5-10),[41] it can be suggested that the ethical dimension of fasting is an invention of the later prophets. Podella, among others, believes that 'die Notwendigkeit dieser Ergänzung der Fastenriten durch soziales Handeln ... hat ihren Grund in der Auseinandersetzung zwischen traditionell priesterlicher Kultauffassung und

---

36   Moshe David Herr, "Fasting," *Enc Jud* 6.1190.

37   As Preuss correctly points out, 'fasting is not attested in the OT as an atonement ritual,' H. D. Preuss, "צום," *TDOT* 12.298.

38   Hans-Jürgen Hermisson, *Sprache und Ritus im altisraelitischen Kult; zur "Spiritualisierung" der Kultbegriffe im Alten Testament* (WMANT 19; Neukirchen-Vluyn: Neukirchener Verlag des Erziehungsvereins, 1965) 78.

39   H. A. Brongers, "Fasting in Israel in Biblical and Post-Biblical Times," in *Instruction and Interpretation: Studies in Hebrew Language, Palestinian Archeology and Biblical Exegesis* (OTS; Leiden: E. J. Brill, 1977) 20.

40   Preuss, "צום," *TDOT* 12.300.

41   Hermisson is correct that 'Jer 14:12 gehört nicht in diesen Zusammenhang; daß Fasten hier veräußerlich und "dingliche fromme Leistung" (ThWB IV, S.929), daß das Hertz des Volkes nicht dabei sei, ... ist angesichts der Klage des Volkes in v 7-9 und 19-22 nur schwer zu behaupten,' Hermisson, *Sprache und Ritus*, 80. Joel is questionable because of its dating, and Jonah is not a criticism, but a description of true fasting. These texts are discussed in Appendix 2.

prophetischer Sozialkritik.'[42]   An analogous argument can be raised concerning the ethical dimension of the Sabbath observance, and is therefore addressed in detail partially in the following section, and partially in the functional analysis of Isa 58 below.

6.3.2. Sabbath

In the last century, studies of the religion of ancient Israel exhibited some fascination with the origins of the Sabbath. Arguments were based mostly on the etymology of the Hebrew term שַׁבָּת and on comparative philology.[43] De Vaux in his book on ancient Israel reacted to these attempts with suspicion; he not only questions the tracing of the Sabbath's origin to the Babylonians, the Canaanites, or the Qenites, but also the validity of the quest as such. He claims that whatever its origin, the Sabbath 'in Israel … took on a religious significance which it did not possess before.'[44] It seems pragmatic, therefore, to move away from the question about the origin of the Sabbath and focus instead on Sabbath's nature and character in Israel's religion.

6.3.2.1. Nature of Sabbath Observance

The fact that the Sabbath was celebrated even in Israel's early days is generally undisputed. Scholars, however, disagree about the nature of this festival in various periods of Israel's history.[45] Many follow Wellhausen's idea of its transformation from a pre-exilic festival of joy and pleasure to a post-exilic day of ascetic abstinence.[46] Thus de Vaux believed that the 'rigid prohibitions' to do business, to travel, to carry a load, etc., were built into Sabbath observance only after the return of the Jews from Babylon. In contrast, he pictured the pre-exilic Sabbath as

---

42   Thomas Podella, *Ṣôm-Fasten: Kollektive Trauer um den verborgenen Gott im Alten Testament* (Alter Orient und Altes Testament; Bd. 224; Neukirchen-Vluyn: Verlag Butzon & Bercker Kevelaer, 1989) 223.

43   See, e.g., E. Haag, "שָׁבַת," *TDOT* 13.387-397, esp. 388-389.

44   De Vaux, *Ancient Israel*, 479.

45   A major ongoing controversy in the discussion about pre-exilic versus post-exilic Sabbath observance concerns the proposal that it was monthly before the exile and weekly only after the exile. Since it does not affect the present argument, there is no need to enter this debate here. For a solid starting point and bibliography on this controversy, see Williamson, *Isaiah 1-27*, 94.

46   See Wellhausen, *Prolegomena*, 110.

a day of rest, a joyful feast on which people visited sanctuaries or went to consult a 'man of God', and, even though normal heavy work and commercial transactions were interrupted, short journeys were allowed.[47] The flaw in this theory is apparent from the passages that de Vaux quotes in support: the Sabbath is neither the subject nor the focus of 2 Kgs 4:23, Hos 2:13, Amos 8:5, and Isa 1:13, and therefore these texts cannot be contrasted with those that specifically deal with Sabbath observance, e.g., Jer 17:21-22 or Isa 58:13. In addition, the Exodus and Deuteronomy passages on work prohibition are too general to be used in an argument about the intensity of Sabbath regulations. There is simply no pre-exilic evidence that would favor the notion that the later texts introduced 'rigid prohibitions' into what used to be 'a joyful feast-day'[48] over the view that these later passages reflect and interpret the meaning of 'keeping the Sabbath day holy' in their particular *Sitze im Leben*. In fact, Ezek 20, in which the prophet laments over Israel's desecration of the Sabbath in the past, suggests that the following quote from Weinfeld is closer to mark: 'The stress laid upon the Sabbath in exilic and postexilic literature ... attests not to innovation but to the resurgence and strengthening of an ancient but sadly neglected observance.'[49]

6.3.2.2. Character of Sabbath Observance

Scholars often elaborate on the differences between the two Decalogue passages and their treatment of Sabbath observance. It seems that while the focus of Deut 5:13-15 is social and philanthropic, it is cultic and religious in Exod 20:8-11.[50] In spite of the different emphases, the character of the reasons for keeping the Sabbath and of its practical outcome is the same: the reason in Exodus is to recall God's mighty act of creation (20:11), and in Deuteronomy God's mighty act of deliveran-

---

47   De Vaux, *Ancient Israel*, 482.

48   *Contra* de Vaux, *Ancient Israel*, 482.

49   Weinfeld, *Law*, 30.

50   Scholars tend to explain this "discrepancy" in a historical-chronological way. Thus, for instance, Haag believes that the 'Dtn version of the Sabbath commandment served as the basis for the reinterpretation of the Sabbath commandment within the horizon of P in the version in Exodus (Ex. 23:12),' Haag, "שַׁבָּת," *TDOT* 13.393. On the other hand, Weinfeld believes that both D and P portray the Sabbath in accordance with their particular agenda: 'The author of P specifically selected the sacral reason and developed it in his own way, while Deuteronomy chose the social motivation and formulated it to suit his unique purposes, i.e. humanly,' Weinfeld, *Law*, 85.

ce (5:15), so both reasons have a cultic character. The practical outcome of Sabbath observance in both versions is the right to rest for all the people (and animals) in the land, regardless of their status and origin, so its character is ethical. According to Andreasen, contemporary scholars generally recognize that '[the Sabbath] very early held both social (perhaps humanitarian) and religious qualities.' He maintains that '[the] nexus of social and religious/cultic factors for the original Sabbath ... is based on the fact that the seventh day occurs in the ancient Near Eastern texts in connection with myth and cult, and it appears to have affected not only ritual but also the ordering of society.'[51] While the character of the Sabbath observance almost certainly developed throughout Israel's history, it is safe to talk about its cultic and social dimensions in the time of TI.[52]

The cultic character of the Sabbath is evident, and hardly requires substantiation.[53] The ethical motive for Sabbath observance, however, needs to be argued more thoroughly. It comes explicitly not only in Deut 5:14, but also in Exod 23:12 – 'on the seventh day you shall rest, so that your ox and your donkey may have relief, and your homeborn slave and the resident alien may be refreshed.' The rationale for this ethical dimension is found in Deut 5:15 – 'Remember that you were a slave in the land of Egypt, and the LORD your God brought you out from there with a mighty hand and an outstretched arm; therefore the

---

51 Niels-Erik Andreasen, "Recent Studies of the Old Testament Sabbath," *ZAW* 86 (1974) 453-469: 455-456.

52 This duality of the Sabbath's character may account for its position in the Decalogue. According to Lowery, 'the sabbath law occupies a pivotal position in both versions of the Decalogue [...] standing at the crux of theology and ethics. The verses before the sabbath law address Israel's relationship with God, and the laws that follow regulate social relationships within and between households. Sabbath grounds all those relationships in the identity of God as creator of the world and liberator of Israel.' R. H. Lowery, *Sabbath and Jubilee* (Understanding Biblical Themes; St. Louis, Mo.: Chalice Press, 2000) 106.

53 McKay argues that, because there is no description of 'communal sabbath religious rituals and practices for non-priestly Jews' in any of the surviving texts from the period up to 200 CE, non-priestly Jews had 'no religious duties peculiar to the sabbath,' Heather A. McKay, *Sabbath and Synagogue: The Question of Sabbath in Ancient Judaism* (Religions in the Graeco-Roman World, v. 122; Leiden: Brill, 1994) 247. The major flaw in her thesis is her understanding of worship. According to her, it consists of activities like sacrificing plants and animals, dancing, playing music, singing hymns or psalms, reading or reciting sacred texts, prayers and blessings' (p. 3), but does not include abstinence from certain activities during the Sabbath. The solemn rest on the Sabbath day, however, does have cultic character, for, as Exod 16:23 and other OT texts specify, it is observed "to the Lord" (ליהוה). For the cultic character of the Sabbatical rest, see also the exegesis of Isa 58:13 below.

LORD your God commanded you to keep the sabbath day.' The fact
that this reference to the Exodus is often used as a reason for social
justice (Deut 24:18-22; 10:19; Exod 23:9; Lev 19:34) further strengthens
the case for the ethical characteristic of the Sabbath.[54] Falk, therefore,
rightly insists that the Sabbath symbolizes and represents both law and
ethics, the two aspects of the faith of Israel.[55]

The connection between the Sabbath and ethics becomes even more
apparent when one does not think about the Hebrew term שַׁבָּת
quantitatively, as a day or a year, or a set of rules and regulations, but
sees it as a *religious concept* that describes the *quality* of a particular time
period or a certain activity. This view entails bringing into the
discussion all the religious festivals that include the terms שַׁבָּתוֹן ,שַׁבָּת,
or שַׁבַּת שַׁבָּתוֹן in their designation: the Day of Atonement (Lev 16:31;
23:32), New Year's day (Lev 23:24), the first and the eighth day of the
Feast of Booths (Lev 23:39), the Sabbath Year (Lev 25:4,5), and the
Sabbath itself (besides already mentioned passages, see also Lev 23:3;
Exod 16:23; 31:15; and 35:2).[56] The overlap of the ethical dimension of
these festivals is manifest. For example, Deuteronomy gives the same
rationale for observing the Sabbath Year in 15:15 as for keeping the
Sabbath in 5:15, namely YHWH's deliverance of Israel from Egypt's
slavery.[57] The Sabbath Year with its extension in the Year of Jubilee
puts a special emphasis on the social aspect of שַׁבָּת, demanding concern
for the hungry (Exod 23:11), remission of debts (Deut 15:1), setting the
slaves free (Deut 15:12), etc. Lowery persuasively argues that 'Sabbath
traditions continue the social-economic focus of sabbath year. The
sabbath day functions as a "little jubilee," a weekly celebration of the
principles expressed in sabbath-year and jubilee release,' and insists
therefore that 'sabbath day and sabbath year are thematically

---

54   '[In Deuteronomy,] God derives the Sabbath not from Creation, as in P, but from
Exodus.' Weinfeld, *Law*, 85. Based on this Exodus reference, de Vaux states that 'the
Sabbath is connected with the history of salvation,' de Vaux, *Ancient Israel*, 481. This
link is further developed by Haag, "שַׁבָּת," *TDOT* 13.393, and will become important
in the discussion of Isa 58:13-14.

55   See Falk, "Law and Ethics," passim.

56   Legitimacy of including these festivals in the discussion about the character of
Sabbath is supported also by Lev 25:2 where the Sabbath year is designated simply
as שַׁבָּת לַיהוָה, and by Exod 23:9-12 where the seventh year and the seventh day are
tied together into a coherent unit.

57   Park is correct that 'sowohl im Dekalog als auch in den ältesten Sozialgesetzgebun-
gen wird die Thematik der Nächstenliebe bzw. der sozialen Solidarisierung ... auf
die Zeit der ägyptischen Gefangenschaft Israels bzw. auf die Befreiungstat Jhwhs
bezogen,' Park, *Gerechtigkeit Israels*, 239.

connected and properly read through the same theological lens.'[58] The analysis of Isa 58 below will demonstrate how the ethical dimension of the Sabbath observance overlaps with the Day of Atonement.

At this point, it is helpful to realize that the development of the concept of Yom Kippur from the predominantly social (release of debts and declaration of freedom) to the principally soteriological (redemption and forgiveness of sins) is relatively late. Even though, as Weinfeld demonstrated from several Ugaritic texts, 'the connection between the earthly "release of debts" and the divine one seems to be very old,' the ethical character of the Day of Atonement would very likely still dominate in the time of TI. According to Weinfeld, 'the freedom proclaimed of the Day of Atonement (Lev. 25.10) underwent a process of spiritual metamorphosis during the second temple period, so that the proclamation of freedom brought about not only the physical liberation of slaves and of land, but also the liberation of the soul and its restoration to its pure source.'[59]

6.3.3. Role of Cult in Isa 58

As the detailed analysis of the text below will demonstrate, the emphasis on ethics in Isa 58 does not imply a repudiation of cult, just as, e.g., the emphasis on the temple in Haggai does not deny the role of ethics in eschatology.[60] For TI, cult plays an important role in defining the identity of the post-exilic society. Blenkinsopp is very likely correct that 'for the first time there existed a situation in which the issue of membership was no longer ascriptive and unproblematic. Membership therefore called for recognizable distinguishing characteristics.'[61] Cult

---

58 Lowery, *Sabbath*, 146 and 63. For additional support of the connection between the Sabbath, the Sabbath Year and the Year of Jubilee see Matitiahu Tsevat, "The Basic Meaning of the Biblical Sabbath," *ZAW* 84 (1972) 447-459.

59 Moshe Weinfeld, *Normative and Sectarian Judaism in the Second Temple Period* (Library of Second Temple Studies 54; London: T & T Clark, 2005) 227-229.

60 In words of Smith, 'the difference between Haggai and TI2 is one of emphasis and not of kind,' Smith, *Rhetoric*, 198.

61 Blenkinsopp, *Isaiah 56-66*, 181.

could provide such a platform,[62] functioning not centrifugally as
Hanson seems to imply,[63] but centripetally as suggested by Williamson:

> The inclusion of the diaspora as 'Israel' in Isa. 56.8 and of the cult
> community in 66.20 as 'the children of Israel' is suggestive of an inclusive
> rather than sectarian definition of the community. For such reasons it does
> not seem impossible that our passages still reflect the hopes that centred
> round the initial restoration of the cult.[64]

As v. 1 indicates, the intention of Isa 58-59 is not to broaden the
difference between 'physical' and 'true' Israel, but to enhance the
transformation of the former to the latter. An important part of this
process is to correct people's theological misconceptions. Isa 58 uses
two cultic practices, fasting and Sabbath observance, to illuminate how
cult and ethics are interrelated in Yahwism. Both Isa 58 and 59 respond
to the peoples' question in v. 3a about YHWH's lack of response. The
problem is neither in God's ability (59:1) nor in his willingness and
readiness to act (59:15b-20); it is neither in the object of peoples' pious
desires spelled out in v. 2,[65] nor in people's cultic expressions in v. 5 (as
the analysis below shows). 58:1a and especially 59:2 make explicitly
clear that the problem is people's פֶּשַׁע and חַטָּאת, more specifically the
absence of מִשְׁפָּט and צְדָקָה (58:2 and esp. 59:4, 9, and 14), caused by
people's selfish desires (58:3b and 13) and documented most visibly in
the ill-treatment of the weaker ones of the society (58:3b-4, 6-7, 9b-
10a).[66] Since 'the LORD of hosts is exalted in justice (בַּמִּשְׁפָּט), and the
Holy God shows himself holy (נִקְדָּשׁ) in righteousness (בִּצְדָקָה)' (Isa
5:16), any positive manifestation of his presence (קִרְבַת אֱלֹהִים) in the
midst of people whose pursuit of their own desires results in
perversion of מִשְׁפָּט and צְדָקָה is excluded. קִרְבַת אֱלֹהִים is impossible

---

62   Schramm maintains that, according to TI, 'only those who properly adhere to the
      cult of YHWH, as this cult is understood by the author, are to be considered "YHWH's
      servants", while those who engage in cultic acts like those described in 65.1-7, 11b,
      and 57.3-13 and so on are to be excluded,' Schramm, *Opponents*, 158-159.

63   According to Hanson, 'the hierocratic party' exercised control not only over their
      fellows whom they oppressed, but also over the cult, 'representing, it would seem,
      the normative cult,' giving rise to two opposing (religious) traditions represented in
      Isa 58. See Paul D. Hanson, *The Dawn of Apocalyptic* (Philadelphia: Fortress Press,
      1975) 110-111.

64   Williamson, "Israel in Transition," 150-151.

65   The possibility of their fulfilment is indicated in 58:8-9a, 10b-12 and 14.

66   Hermisson's question about this and similar "Kultpolemik" texts already includes
      the answer: 'Polemisieren die Propheten gegen den *Kult*, oder greifen sie nicht
      vielmehr den *Menschen* an, der den Kult isoliert hat und sich hier einen Raum für
      Jahwe in seinem Leben ausspart, während er sonst seine eigenen bösen Wege geht?'
      Hermisson, *Sprache und Ritus*, 84.

when רָחַק מִשְׁפָּט מִמֶּנּוּ (59:9) and תַּעֲמֹד צְדָקָה מֵרָחוֹק (59:14); in fact, these expressions should be understood as antonyms. As far as the cult (represented in Isa 58 by fasting and Sabbath) is concerned, to pursue one's own pleasure on God's holy day (58:13aB) seriously distorts the picture which the cultic worship of YHWH is to reflect; it misses one important dimension, namely the ethical character of YHWH. Such 'voice cannot be heard on high' (58:4b), for it would mean God's consecration of his distorted image.[67]

6.4. Literary Genre of Isa 58

There is no consensus among scholars about the genre of Isa 58. For instance, Koenen labels vv. 3-12 as *Diskussionswort*,[68] but Smith rightly objects that, in the light of vv. 1-2, this designation is far too weak.[69] Westermann reads Isa 58 as a speech of admonition (*Mahnrede*), because it is the form of the central part (vv. 5ff), to which the other parts are related.[70] But Lau objects that 'doch nicht Mahnung steht im Vordergrund, sondern prophetische Kritik am Fasten in Verbindung mit eschatologischen Forderungen, die in Heilszusagen einmünden.' He also declines to identify parts of 58 as prophetic torah, suggested for vv. 1-8 by Lescow,[71] or for vv. 6-7 by Elliger,[72] claiming that 'der Kult spielt für den Verfasser keine erkennbare Rolle.'[73] He, however, does not consider vv. 13-14, where cult gains in importance, to be an original part of Isa 58. In any case, it seems that no single designation does justice to the form of Isa 58. Lau acknowledges this mixture, reasoning that: 'es ist charakteristisch für einen eschatologischen Text, daß in ihm unterschiedliche Gattungselemente ineinanderfließen.'[74]

---

67   For more arguments along these lines, see Helen Schüngel-Straumann, *Gottesbild und Kultkritik vorexilischer Propheten* (Stuttgarter Bibelstudien 60; Stuttgart: KBW Verlag, 1972).

68   Klaus Koenen, *Ethik und Eschatologie im Tritojesajabuch: Eine Literarkritische und Redaktionsgeschichtliche Studie* (WMANT 62; Neukirchen-Vluyn: Neukirchener Verlag, 1990) 98.

69   Similarly Lau, *Schriftgelehrte Prophetie*, 240, n174.

70   Westermann, *Isaiah 40-66*, 333. He is followed by Koole, *Isaiah III/3*, 120.

71   Theodor Lescow, *Das Stufenschema: Untersuchungen zur Struktur alttestamentlicher Texte* (BZAW 211; Berlin: De Gruyter, 1992) 118f.

72   Karl Elliger, *Die Einheit des Tritojesaia, Jesaia 56-66* (BWANT 45; Stuttgart: W. Kohlhammer, 1928) 15.

73   Lau, *Schriftgelehrte Prophetie*, 240, n174.

74   Lau, *Schriftgelehrte Prophetie*, 240.

Hanson in his analysis of TI introduced an idea of salvation – judgement oracle. Although Isa 58 is not its prime example, Hanson believes that it 'adumbrates' this hybrid form, vv. 2-5 being the judgment section, and vv. 6ff the salvation section.[75] In support, scholars often point out possible connections of Isa 58:1 with Hos 8:1[76] and Mic 3:8b[77].'[78] Koenen, among others, also believes that 'der imp. sg. von קרא nimmt die Berufung Deuterojesajas auf (Jes 40,6), die Aufforderung אל תחשׁך geht auf Jes 54,2 zurück, und הרם קולך zitiert Jes 40,9, wo eben diese Aufforderung an die Freudenbotin Zions ergeht.'[79] While these echoes are probable, scholars tend to base on them a questionable conclusion that, as Smith puts it, 'the purpose of this combination of introductory formulae from DI and pre-exilic prophets is to underline that the announcement to be made is one of both judgment and salvation.'[80] Hanson has combined this form with his proposed dichotomy in the community: vv. 2-5 pronounce a judgement against the cultic observances of the hierocratic group, while vv. 6-12 are the words of salvation spoken to the visionaries.[81] The main fallacy of this designation is the claim that some part of Isa 58 resembles the form of a judgement oracle. In their discussion about the possible meaning of 1aB (כַּשׁוֹפָר הָרֵם קוֹלֶךָ) commentators often list different occasions for which שׁוֹפָר was used in ancient Israel, e.g., to announce a (holy) war, a cultic festival, or God's judgement. While an allusion to some of these occasions is likely (see 6.6.4), it is the *metaphorical* use of שׁוֹפָר that should be determinative in the search for the meaning of this phrase. The closest parallel, therefore, is Ezek 33:1-20, where the prophet's announcement of God's word to the people is compared to a sentinel's blowing שׁוֹפָר. This parallel is strengthened by the similarity of the announcements' contexts: people are asking about

---

75   Hanson, *Dawn*, 106-107.

76   'Set the trumpet (שׁוֹפָר) to your lips! One like a vulture is over the house of the LORD, because they have broken my covenant, and transgressed (פשׁע) my law.'

77   '… to declare (נגד) to Jacob his transgression (פֶּשׁע) and to Israel his sin (חַטָּאת).'

78   See, e.g., Westermann, *Isaiah 40-66*, 334. *Contra* the allusion to Hos 8:1, see Seizo Sekine, *Die Tritojesajanische Sammlung (Jes 56-66) Redaktionsgeschichtlich Untersucht* (BZAW 175; Berlin: De Gruyter, 1989) 122-123. Sommer believes that the whole Isa 58:1-11 depends on Mic 3:5-12, Sommer, *Allusion*, 76-78. Except for the above quoted similarity, the rest of his arguments are unpersuasive.

79   Koenen, *Ethik und Eschatologie*, 95.

80   Smith, *Rhetoric*, 105. Lau's reason for the allusions is more likely: 'Der Autor von Jes 58,1-12 stellt sich folglich in Anlehnung an DtJes als unmittelbar von Jahwe beauftragter Prophet dar.' He describes the form of this text as 'Scheltrede' where 'eschatologische Heilsansage' is admixed, Lau, *Schriftgelehrte Prophetie*, 240-241.

81   Hanson, *Dawn*, 106-107.

YHWH's ways (Isa 58:2 and Ezek 33:10), questioning the fairness of his dealing with them (Isa 58:3 and Ezek 33:17 and 20). The main problem is, again, people's פֶּשַׁע and חַטָּאת (Isa 58:1 and Ezek 33:10).   The purpose of Ezekiel's announcement is clearly defined – to warn (hiph. of זהר) the people about a potentially mortal danger (33:7f). The verb זהר in the sense 'to warn' is almost exclusively used in the OT in the way that was defined by Jethro in his advice to Moses in Exod 18:20 – 'Teach (וְהִזְהַרְתָּה) them the statutes and instructions and make known to them the way they are to go and the things they are to do.' This was the main role of Moses – the prophet *par excellence*, of Israel's spiritual leaders (according to 2 Chr 19:10), of Ezekiel (according to Ezek 3 and 33),[82] and very likely of the prophet in Isa 58 as well. Park correctly observes that 'die prophetische Verkündigung in Jes 58,1f. ist also keine Ankündigung des Gerichtes Gottes etwa in Form eines Krieges, sondern zielt auf das Heil durch die Hinwendung von oberflächlichen kultischen Handlungen zu einem Tun der sozialen Gerechtigkeit als Bedingung für das Heil.'[83]

Even if one includes ch. 59, the judgment in vv. 15b-20 is directed not against God's people, but only against his adversaries and enemies. Since these are mentioned in parallel to the coastlands, God's judgment in this passage seems to concern the foreigners only. However, as Schramm points out, 'when צריו and איביו are read in the light of 59.20, it becomes clear that these terms refer not to foreigners but to those within the restoration community who do not שׁבי פֶּשַׁע.'[84] For Zion, more specifically for 'those in Jacob who turn from transgressions' and for those who suffer from injustice, this is an oracle of salvation. In addition, even though it is not uncommon to use different forms in a single oracle, it would be very unusual to address two opposing groups in one speech without explicitly indicating it. Park, therefore, aptly repudiates the above proposal of Hanson: 'Obwohl die Bestimmung der Angeredeten im Tritojesajabuch wichtig wäre, ist es doch nicht möglich, sie je nach der Heils- und Gerichtsansage des Propheten zu bestimmen. Wichtig ist: Was der Text selbst nicht sagt, muß offen gelassen werden.'[85]

This discussion leads to the conclusion that if a designation of the genre of Isa 58 is necessary (and, because it does not appear to be

---

82   זהר II in these two chapters occurs 15 times out of it total 21 occurrences in the OT.

83   Park, *Gerechtigkeit Israels*, 236.

84   Schramm, *Opponents*, 141. Furthermore, Schramm states that 'Isa. 1.24b, 27-28a is closely related to 59.18-20 and offers justification for this interpretation.'

85   Park, *Gerechtigkeit Israels*, 213.

generic, it probably isn't), the best choice seems to be to opt for a general and wide ranging definition such as offered by Smith, who understands chs. 58-59 as a prophetic sermon that includes various forms, like an introduction in vv. 1-2 or a prophetic accusation in vv. 3b-5.[86]

6.5. Structural Analysis and Text-Critical Issues of Isa 58

The variety of opinions on the delimitation of colons and stanzas reflects the importance of the structural analysis of this chapter for its overall understanding. Again, the following discussion is not comprehensive, but focuses primarily on the elements related to the overall question about the relationship between cult and ethics in the book of Isaiah. The same methodological principles as in the structure and syntax study of Isa 1:10-17 and 43:22-28 apply.

---

86 Smith, *Rhetoric*, 102. Also Blenkinsopp states that Isa 58 'is much closer to the genre of sermon, than of prophetic oracle,' Blenkinsopp, *Isaiah 56-66*, 178. Similarly Schramm: 'The passage begins as if it were an oracle of judgment, but upon further reading it becomes clear that we are dealing with a "sermon" or a "speech of admonition", the purpose of which is to call the community to a change of behavior,' Schramm, *Opponents*, 133.

Strophe and Poetic Device	MT of Isaiah 58 (BHS)	Colon	St
Bicolon with semantic paral.	קְרָא בְגָרוֹן אַל־תַּחְשֹׂךְ	1aA	
	כַּשּׁוֹפָר הָרֵם קוֹלֶךָ	1aB	
Bicolon with partial paral.: V NP2 NP1 // NP2' NP1' (verb gap.) and tradit. word-pairs.	וְהַגֵּד לְעַמִּי פִּשְׁעָם	1bA	I
	וּלְבֵית יַעֲקֹב חַטֹּאתָם	1bB	
Three bicolons structured in a concentric chiasm (abc), each with semantic parallelism (in b partial, in c chiastic).	וְאוֹתִי יוֹם יוֹם יִדְרֹשׁוּן	2aA	
	וְדַעַת דְּרָכַי יֶחְפָּצוּן	2aB	
	כְּגוֹי אֲשֶׁר־צְדָקָה עָשָׂה	2bA	
	וּמִשְׁפַּט אֱלֹהָיו לֹא עָזָב	2bB	
	יִשְׁאָלוּנִי מִשְׁפְּטֵי־צֶדֶק	2cA	
	קִרְבַת אֱלֹהִים יֶחְפָּצוּן	2cB	
Bicolon with partial paral.: M V₁ V₂ // V₁' NP₁' V₂'.	לָמָּה צַּמְנוּ וְלֹא רָאִיתָ	3aA	II
	עִנִּינוּ נַפְשֵׁנוּ וְלֹא תֵדָע	3aB	
Bicolon with partial chiasm: M V NP₁ // NP₁' V'.	הֵן בְּיוֹם צֹמְכֶם תִּמְצְאוּ־חֵפֶץ	3bA	
	וְכָל־עַצְּבֵיכֶם תִּנְגֹּשׂוּ	3bB	
Bicol. with partial paral.: NP₁ V // NP₁' NP₂' (verb gapping).	הֵן לְרִיב וּמַצָּה תָּצוּמוּ	4aA	
	וּלְהַכּוֹת בְּאֶגְרֹף רֶשַׁע	4aB	
Closing monocolon.	לֹא־תָצוּמוּ כַיּוֹם לְהַשְׁמִיעַ בַּמָּרוֹם קוֹלְכֶם	4b	
Three bicolons structured in a concentric chiasm (abc), each with semantic parallelism (in a and c partial, in b chiastic).	הֲכָזֶה יִהְיֶה צוֹם אֶבְחָרֵהוּ	5aA	
	יוֹם עַנּוֹת אָדָם נַפְשׁוֹ	5aB	
	הֲלָכֹף כְּאַגְמֹן רֹאשׁוֹ	5bA	
	וְשַׂק וָאֵפֶר יַצִּיעַ	5bB	
	הֲלָזֶה תִּקְרָא־צוֹם	5cA	
	וְיוֹם רָצוֹן לַיהוָה	5cB	
Opening monocolon.	הֲלוֹא זֶה צוֹם אֶבְחָרֵהוּ	6a	
Bicolon with semantic and grammatical parallelism.	פַּתֵּחַ חַרְצֻבּוֹת רֶשַׁע	6bA	III
	הַתֵּר אֲגֻדּוֹת מוֹטָה	6bB	
Bicolon with chiastic parallelism: V NP₁ // V' NP₁'	וְשַׁלַּח רְצוּצִים חָפְשִׁים	6cA	
	וְכָל־מוֹטָה תְּנַתֵּקוּ	6cB	
Bicolon with partial chiastic parallelism: M V NP₁ NP₂ // NP₁' V' NP₂'	הֲלוֹא פָרֹס לָרָעֵב לַחְמֶךָ	7aA	
	וַעֲנִיִּים מְרוּדִים תָּבִיא בָיִת	7aB	
Bicolon with semantic parallelism	כִּי־תִרְאֶה עָרֹם וְכִסִּיתוֹ	7bA	
	וּמִבְּשָׂרְךָ לֹא תִתְעַלָּם	7bB	

Strophe and Poetic Device	MT of Isaiah 58 (BHS)	Colon	St
Bicolon with chiastic paral.: V NP₂ NP₁ // NP₁′ NP₂′ V′.	אָז יִבָּקַע כַּשַּׁחַר אוֹרֶךָ	8aA	
	וַאֲרֻכָתְךָ מְהֵרָה תִצְמָח	8aB	
Bicolon with partial chias.: V NP₂ NP₁ // NP₁′ V′.	וְהָלַךְ לְפָנֶיךָ צִדְקֶךָ	8bA	III
	כְּבוֹד יְהוָה יַאַסְפֶךָ	8bB	
Bicolon with semantic and grammatical parallelism.	אָז תִּקְרָא וַיהוָה יַעֲנֶה	9aA	
	תְּשַׁוַּע וְיֹאמַר הִנֵּנִי	9aB	
Bicolon with partial paral.: V M NP₁ // NP₁′ (verb gapping).	אִם־תָּסִיר מִתּוֹכְךָ מוֹטָה	9bA	
	שְׁלַח אֶצְבַּע וְדַבֶּר־אָוֶן	9bB	
Bicolon with chiastic paral.: V NP₂ NP₁ // NP₁′ NP₂′ V′.	וְתָפֵק לָרָעֵב נַפְשֶׁךָ	10aA	
	וְנֶפֶשׁ נַעֲנָה תַּשְׂבִּיעַ	10aB	
Bicolon with partial chiasm: V NP₂ NP₁ // NP₁′ NP₂′.	וְזָרַח בַּחֹשֶׁךְ אוֹרֶךָ	10bA	
	וַאֲפֵלָתְךָ כַּצָּהֳרָיִם	10bB	
Tricolon with partial paral.: V NP₁ M // V′ M′ NP₂′// V″ NP₂″	וְנָחֲךָ יְהוָה תָּמִיד	11aA	
	וְהִשְׂבִּיעַ בְּצַחְצָחוֹת נַפְשֶׁךָ	11aB	IV
	וְעַצְמֹתֶיךָ יַחֲלִיץ	11aC	
Tricolon with partial parallelism, verb gapping in bB and exposition in bC	וְהָיִיתָ כְּגַן רָוֶה	11bA	
	וּכְמוֹצָא מַיִם	11bB	
	אֲשֶׁר לֹא־יְכַזְּבוּ מֵימָיו	11bC	
Bicolon with partial chiasm: V M NP₁ // NP₁′ V′.	וּבָנוּ מִמְּךָ חָרְבוֹת עוֹלָם	12aA	
	מוֹסְדֵי דוֹר־וָדוֹר תְּקוֹמֵם	12aB	
Bicolon with partial paral.: V M NP₂ // NP₂′ (verb gapping).	וְקֹרָא לְךָ גֹּדֵר פֶּרֶץ	12bA	
	מְשֹׁבֵב נְתִיבוֹת לָשָׁבֶת	12bB	
Bicolons a and c, both with partial parallelism (verb gapping) plus monocolon b, structured in a concentric chiasm (abc).	אִם־תָּשִׁיב מִשַּׁבָּת רַגְלֶךָ	13aA	
	עֲשׂוֹת חֲפָצֶיךָ בְּיוֹם קָדְשִׁי	13aB	
	וְקָרָאתָ לַשַּׁבָּת עֹנֶג לִקְדוֹשׁ יְהוָה מְכֻבָּד	13b	V
	וְכִבַּדְתּוֹ מֵעֲשׂוֹת דְּרָכֶיךָ	13cA	
	מִמְּצוֹא חֶפְצְךָ וְדַבֵּר דָּבָר	13cB	
Monocolon plus bicolon with semantic and grammatical parallelism.	אָז תִּתְעַנַּג עַל־יְהוָה	14a	
	וְהִרְכַּבְתִּיךָ עַל־בָּמוֹתֵי אָרֶץ	14bA	
	וְהַאֲכַלְתִּיךָ נַחֲלַת יַעֲקֹב אָבִיךָ	14bB	
Closing monocolon.	כִּי פִּי יְהוָה דִּבֵּר	14c	

6.5.1. Isa 58:1

The first verse is clearly an introduction. The uncertainty is whether it introduces only ch. 58, or 59 as well. Koenen assigns v. 1 to a redactor, claiming that the prophet's task to announce to the people their rebellion (פֶּשַׁע) and sins (חַטָּאת) is not carried out in the rest of ch. 58, rather in 59.[87] Smith rightly objects, that such division is entirely artificial, because in ch. 58 'verses 3b-5 clearly attack the misconduct of the people', and 'while vv. 6-12 may not treat of the people's sins of commission, they certainly focus on their sins of omission.'[88] Moreover, v. 1 sets the perspective of how the rest of the chapter is to be understood and interpreted. Park seems to be correct that 'ohne V.1 vor allem der gesamte Sinn der gewollten Komposition von Jes 58 verloren geht.'[89] Obviously, a proper evaluation of the introductory role of v. 1 can come only after a thorough analysis of the whole chapter.

6.5.2. Isa 58:2-3a

Verse 2 raises a number of exegetical questions: 'Fragt das Volk nach Gestzesbelehrung oder nach Heil? Meint דעת דרכי יהוה in V. 2 die Kenntnis der Gebote oder der Zukunft, und ist קרבת אלהים als Annäherung an Gott oder als Nahen Gottes zu verstehen?'[90] The expression מִשְׁפְּטֵי־צֶדֶק is also ambiguous, allowing for either an ethical and ritual or eschatological construal. As for the syntax, the function of the initial ו and the preposition כ in 2b have been disputed. Again, these questions about v. 2 cannot be answered in isolation from the rest of the chapter, so the conclusions in this section will be more fully justified by the functional analysis below.

First, the overall tenor of the verse needs to be determined. Park reads it as YHWH's ironic denunciation of the people's hypocritical cultic activities. On the other side, Blenkinsopp maintains that this 'flattering reference to [people's] positive religious outlook' does not

---

87 'Die bedingten Heilsverheißungen von v5-12 können kaum für die in v1 angekündigte Scheltrede gehalten werden. Erst in Kap. 59 fallen wieder die Stichworte חטאת und פֶּשַׁע,' Koenen, *Ethik und Eschatologie*, 91.

88 Smith, *Rhetoric*, 104.

89 Park, *Gerechtigkeit Israels*, 214.

90 Park, *Gerechtigkeit Israels*, 199. The same questions are raised and addressed in Koenen, *Ethik und Eschatologie*, 92f.

seem to be ironic.[91] As further analysis confirms, the issue in Isa 58-59 is not the presence of cultic activities, but the absence of צדקה and מִשׁפָּט, as indicated also in this verse. The denunciation of cultic practices would then be rather out of place. The only irony here is that the nation that does not practice צֶדָקָה and has forsaken מִשׁפָּט of their God is asking him for מִשׁפְּטֵי־צֶדֶק.[92] The preposition כ in 2b should then be read as *irrealis*, relating both to the preceding v. 2a and to the following v. 2b. This double duty is supported by its central position in the chiastic structure of the verse (see the chart above).

The rest of the exegetical questions in v. 2 fit under one heading: Is the subject matter of the expressions in 2a and 2c ethics and ritual, or is it eschatology? Smith argues for 'a primarily ethical and ritual construal' of the statements in v. 2a and 2c. Based on the use of מִשׁפטי צדק in Ps 119 (vv. 7, 62, 106, and 164) and Deut 16:18, he believes that 'what is being referred to here is primarily priestly and legal instruction or decision making.' He also observes that the plural of the term דֶּרֶךְ usually has ethical content in DI and TI, and that 'the term קרבה is used otherwise only with reference to a human being drawn near to God (Ps. 73:28), although the verb קרב can refer to God's drawing near (cf. Isa 56:1; Lam 3:57) or to priests' drawing near to God (Ex. 40:32; Ez. 44:15).'[93] However, the arguments for an eschatological reading are more persuasive. First, contra Smith, קרבת אלהים in Ps 73:28 does not imply 'a human being drawing near to God', but is as ambiguous as in Isa 58:2 and should be translated accordingly – 'nearness of God'.[94] Second, Lau (among others) prefers to read קרבת אלהים as *genetiv. subjectivus*, arguing that the expression denotes 'den speziellen eschatologischen Horizont der Gemeinde.'[95] Third, the support for an eschatological reading also comes from the parallel with 56:1. As Park observes, besides צדקה, מִשׁפָּט, and עשה, this verse also uses the verb קרב, here as an 'eschatologischer Ausdruck.'[96] Koole further develops this parallel: after stating that the relative clause in 58:2bA (אֲשֶׁר־צֶדָקָה עָשָׂה) recalls 56:1, he concludes: 'The people believe

---

91 Blenkinsopp, *Isaiah 56-66*, 176. Childs also maintains that 'v.2a is not a description of false piety, but a proper response to God,' Childs, *Isaiah*, 477.

92 As observed by Polan, who supports this reading with the chiastic structure of the verse; see Gregory J. Polan, *In the Ways of Justice toward Salvation: A Rhetorical Analysis of Isaiah 56-59* (American University Studies. Series VII, Theology and Religion; vol. 13; Frankfurt am Main: Peter Lang, 1986) 194.

93 Smith, *Rhetoric*, 106.

94 For more discussion and connection of Isa 58-59 with Ps 73, see Appendix 2.

95 Lau, *Schriftgelehrte Prophetie*, 243.

96 Park, *Gerechtigkeit Israels*, 221.

that they meet the requirement of "doing righteousness" stated there and so can lay claim to the coming salvation.'[97] Fourth, even though Koenen, like Smith, observes that the expression (מִשְׁפְּטֵי־צֶדֶק)ה (pl.) 'begegnet im Alten Testament nur noch 4mal in Ps 119 und ist dort immer ethisch zu verstehen,' he nonetheless opts for the eschatological reading of v. 2, arguing 'daß die Bescheinigung, getreu den Gesetzen Gerechtigkeit zu üben, im Tritojesajabuch singulär wäre und daß es nur hier um eine Annäherung an Gott statt um das Kommen Gottes ginge.'[98] Finally, the eschatology in vv. 8-9a, 10b-12, and 14 stipulates the reading of all the expressions in vv. 2a and 2c with this horizon in mind, juxtaposing them with the ethical construal of the expressions in v. 2b. This juxtaposition is supported by the chiastic structure of the verse, and justifies the following conclusion from Koole:

> Just as the people themselves believe that they are acting righteously and are not neglecting God's justice, so they ask now not for God's 'laws' (which they apparently know already), but expect from God that he, too, will act righteously, that for his part he will likewise give his צְדָקָה as 'salvation' (56:1b), and that he will exercise his מִשְׁפָּטִים = 'judgements' in favour of the hard-pressed congregation.[99]

This play on the ethical and soteriological meanings of מִשְׁפָּט and צְדָקָה is a powerful rhetorical device that both exposes the nature of the problem and suggests its solution: people are longing for God's (soteriological) מִשְׁפָּט and צְדָקָה and, indeed, these are about to come (56:1, 59:15b-20). However, they do not seem to realize that for those whose behaviour does not reflect these characteristics (ethical מִשְׁפָּט and צְדָקָה), the upcoming glorious event will have catastrophic results. The solution is to שִׁמְרוּ מִשְׁפָּט וַעֲשׂוּ צְדָקָה (56:1), as exegetically developed in 58:6f.

The question in v. 3a is straightforward. Here, as well as in v. 5, צוֹם is used interchangeably with עִנָּה נֶפֶשׁ. Herr is correct that these two expressions are parallel, but not synonymous; the latter has a broader meaning, and 'includes fasting as part of a general regimen of abstinence.' According to him, in poetic passages like Isa 58:5, the root צוֹם has taken on the broader sense of עִנָּה נֶפֶשׁ.[100]

---

97 Koole, *Isaiah III/3*, 126. The relationship between Isa 58 and 56:1-8 is discussed below (6.8.2).

98 Koenen, *Ethik und Eschatologie*, 92.

99 Koole, *Isaiah III/3*, 127.

100 Herr, "Fasting," *Enc Jud* 6.1189.

6.5.3. Isa 58:3b-4

The initial וְ in 3bB seems to function consequentially, rather than epexegetically.[101] In other words, oppressing the workers (3bB) is not an illustration how the people pursue their desires (3bA), but the result of such pursuit. This reading makes better sense also in v. 4a: people surely did not fast in order to quarrel and fight (לְ of purpose),[102] but, because they pursued (their own) pleasure, they ended up quarreling and fighting (לְ of product or result) on a fast day.[103] This function of לְ here is confirmed by its use in the last colon of v. 4, which declares that such fasting will not *result in* the people's voice being heard (לְהַשְׁמִיעַ) on high.

The meaning of חֵפֶץ needs to be determined not only in connection with v. 3b, but also with v. 2, where the same root is used. Lau is correct that the use of the root חפץ in these verses is hardly accidental. 'Sie wurde im Kontrast zu ihrer Verwendung in V.2 gewählt. Daher kann die von den Kommentatoren durchweg vermutete Bedeutung "Beschäftigung" hier nicht befriedigen.'[104] Translating חֵפֶץ as 'pleasure', 'delight' or 'desire' is to be preferred,[105] as it brings out the contrast in vv. 2-3, the contrast between the theory and the practice of the people: in theory, they are inquiring after what pleases God, but in practice they are after their own pleasures. Besides v. 3bA, the only other place in BH where the combination of חֵפֶץ with מצא occurs is v. 13bC. The comparison shows that the main problem is not חֵפֶץ as such, but the occasion during which it is pursued: בְּיוֹם צֻמְכֶם (v. 3) and בְּיוֹם קָדְשִׁי (v. 13). צוֹם as well as שַׁבָּת are to be יוֹם רָצוֹן לַיהוָה (v. 5) and יְהוָה מְכֻבָּד עֹנֶג לִקְדוֹשׁ (v. 13); therefore, people are to do what YHWH chooses (v. 6f) and what pleases him (56:4). Pursuing other choices and pleasures frequently produces injustice and thereby desecration of cultic activities such as fasting (vv. 3f), the Sabbath (v. 13), or sacrifices (66:3-4).[106]

The expression עַצְּבֵיכֶם תִּנְגֹּשׂוּ in 3bB is ambiguous. The verb נגשׂ is connected with the oppression of the Israelites by Pharaoh's

---

101 See JM §117e. For epexegetical וְ, see *IBHS* 39.2.4.

102 *Contra* Koole, who believes that לְ with the nouns and the infinitive in v. 4a 'convey the intention of the current fasting and the preposition is used in an ironical sense,' Koole, *Isaiah III/3*, 132.

103 For the above uses of לְ, see Williams §277, 278, and 279.

104 Lau, *Schriftgelehrte Prophetie*, 244.

105 Thus, e.g., NJB or NAU. Also LXX understands חֵפֶץ this way, rendering it as θέλημα.

106 Notice the use of חפץ and בחר in 66:3-4.

taskmasters (נֹגְשֵׂי פַרְעֹה) in Egypt, and therefore a synonym of harsh treatment of a labourer. While, as in the case of 'pursuing one's own pleasure' in the previous line, such treatment may not be unlawful *per se*, it is explicitly forbidden during the Sabbatical year in Deut 15:2f.[107] In fact, it was very likely the connection with Deut 15 that prompted the emendation of the *hapax legomenon* עַצְּבֵיכֶם to עֹצְבֵיכֶם ('your debtors').[108] Koole, however, sufficiently demonstrated that such emendation is not necessary, and that 'it is simpler to interpret *עָצֵב or *עָצַב as "toiling", and נגש as "to spur on" (9:3 etc.), and to leave undecided whether somebody has got into this position as a result of debts or other circumstances.'[109]

Various emendations have been proposed also for the phrase וּלְהַכּוֹת בְּאֶגְרֹף רֶשַׁע (4aB). LXX renders רֶשַׁע as ταπεινόν ('humble', 'poor'), probably reading רָשׁ.[110] Koole rightly objects that this reading fails to do justice to v. 6,[111] the only other place in the book of Isaiah where the noun form רֶשַׁע occurs. Emending אֶגְרֹף to מִגְרָף (as, e.g., Westermann) is to replace one obscure expression with another. True, the only other occurrence of אֶגְרֹף in Exod 21:18 is inconclusive,[112] but if MT is granted, it offers a very good parallel to Isa 58:4aB – both places describe striking (hiphil of נכה) with a fist (בְּאֶגְרֹף) as a result of רִיב. MT of Isa 58:4aB should therefore be retained.

6.5.4. Isa 58:5

Several commentators observe that the verb יִהְיֶה in 5aA is metrically striking, and suggest its omission.[113] The facts that it does not have a corresponding part in 5c (see the parallel below) and that it does not appear in the almost identical v. 6a support the omission. According to

---

107 The connection of נגש with the Sabbatical year will become important when discussing the unity of Isa 58 in 6.6.4, because v. 3bB is an illustration of not keeping the sabbath principle on the fast day.

108 See BHS apparatus on Isa 58:3.

109 Koole, *Isaiah III/3*, 131. Similarly, Blenkinsopp considers this emendation unnecessary 'because *ngś* refers to oppression of various kinds, not just exacting payment for debts,' Blenkinsopp, *Isaiah 56-66*, 175.

110 Thus Joseph Ziegler, *Untersuchungen zur Septuaginta des Buches Isaias* (Alttestamentliche Abhandlungen, Bd. 12, Heft 3; Münster i. W.: Aschendorffschen Verlagsbuchhandlung, 1934) 129.

111 Koole, *Isaiah III/3*, 132.

112 The phrase באבן או באגרף is missing in the Samaritan Pentateuch.

113 See, e.g., Hanson, *Isaiah 40-66*, 101.

Koole, however, the verb יִהְיֶה 'says that what takes place is not a true fast.'[114] Syntactically speaking, הֲכָזֶה יִהְיֶה does not refer to the rest of 5aA, but to the list of cultic activities in 5aB-b, translating 5aA as: 'Should the fast that I choose be like this: ...?' Since this construction makes good sense,[115] and since omitting a word purely on aesthetical grounds is dubious, יִהְיֶה in v. 5a should be retained.

V. 5a parallels v. 5c:

הֲכָזֶה יִהְיֶה צוֹם אֶבְחָרֵהוּ יוֹם עַנּוֹת אָדָם נַפְשׁוֹ 5a

תִּקְרָא־צוֹם   וְיוֹם רָצוֹן לַיהוָה: הֲלָזֶה 5c

With a hint of irony, this parallel reveals people's misconception about fasting: they believe that all that it takes to *please YHWH* is to *afflict themselves*. There is no ground, however, to conclude that the author is scorning the various ritual expressions listed in this verse. Other places in the OT, like Ps 35:13 where similar forms of affliction are mentioned, treat them with dignity.

6.5.5. Isa 58:6

The choice of the rare vocabulary in this verse is interesting. As the discussion in Appendix 2 demonstrates, the use of חַרְצֹב here and in Ps 73:4 – the only other occurrence of this root in BH – is most likely not a coincidence. שׁלח and חָפְשִׁי in 6cA is an established word pair ('to let go free'),[116] mostly referring to a release of a Hebrew slave in the seventh year (Exod 21:2f, Deut 15:12f). The emphasis on מוֹטָה (twice in v. 6, once in v. 9) is also telling. This term occurs four more times in BH as a metaphor,[117] always with God as agent who breaks it (always שׁבר) to set his people free from their oppressors. Another infrequent verb נתר I is also connected with God's deliverance – Ps 146:7 says that 'the Lord sets prisoners free' (יְהוָה מַתִּיר אֲסוּרִים). No doubt the post-exilic

---

114 Koole, *Isaiah III/3*, 133.

115 For similar construction, see, e.g., 1 Sam 8:11f or Deut 18:3. Also the phrase in Isa 56:12b can be rendered this way: 'and tomorrow will be like this: great beyond measure.'

116 In BHS, חָפְשִׁי occurs 17 times, 12 times in connection with שׁלח.

117 In Lev 26:13, Ezek 30:18 and 34:27, and, as מוֹט, in Nah 1:13. In its literal sense 'yoke', מוֹטָה occurs in 1 Chr 15:15 and, as a sign, in Jer 27-28.

community was praying to God to perform these acts again on their behalf. The message of v. 6 is that unless the people imitate God in their behaviour towards their neighbour, treating each other as he has treated them in history and as they ask to be treated by him now, he will not listen to their plea.

6.5.6. Isa 58:7

The same message continues in v. 7. Ps 146:7 comes up again, where YHWH is the one who 'gives bread to the hungry' (נֹתֵן לֶחֶם לָרְעֵבִים), just as Israel is expected to do in v. 7aA. Because colon 7aB has one more accented syllable than the other lines in the verse, eliminations of either final בַּיִת or initial עֲנִיִּים have been suggested.[118] However, בַּיִת with the hiphil of בוא is an established pair, and the rare noun מְרוּד is always connected with עֳנִי (besides Isa 58:7, also in Lam 1:7 and 3:19). Both pairs add up in a meaningful statement, so MT should be retained. Polan draws attention to the God-like behaviour: just as YHWH brings strangers into his house in Isa 56:7, so should the people of Israel provide the shelter for the homeless.[119] This parallel continues in 7bA, where clothing the naked is demanded. As Koole observes, 'in this Deut. 10:18f. holds up God's own actions as an example for his people: He gives food and clothing to the orphan, widow, and stranger, and in doing so executes his "justice".'[120]

As for 7bB, the hithpael of עלם connects this line with Deut 22:1-4.[121] Here, as in Isa 58:7b, this rare form is preceded twice by the verb ראה (vv. 1 and 4), and always followed by the preposition מִן. The difference is that whereas in Isa 58:7bB the object is a human being (בָּשָׂר),[122] in Deut 22:1-4 it is any animate and inanimate possession that one's neighbour had lost. In the case of an unknown owner, the finder

---

118 For more details, see, e.g., Koole, *Isaiah III/3*, 138-139.

119 Polan, *Justice*, 34.

120 Koole, *Isaiah III/3*, 140.

121 Out of its total six occurrences in BH, the hithpael of עלם is found three times in Deut 22:1-4.

122 Dahood's suggestion to translate בָּשָׂר as 'meat', based on its (supposed) chiastic correspondence to לֶחֶם in 7aA, is unpersuasive; see Mitchell Dahood, "The Chiastic Breakup in Isaiah 58,7," *Biblica* 57 (1976) 105. Koole (among others) is probably correct that בָּשָׂר here 'can be taken in the broadest possible sense,' meaning 'all humanity', as in Isa 66:16f, Koole, *Isaiah III/3*, 140. The personal suffix, however, might restrict the meaning here to one's fellow countrymen, as indicated by what seems to be a doublet in LXX - τῶν οἰκείων τοῦ σπέρματός σου. See Seeligmann, *Septuagint*, 35.

is to bring the object into his house until the owner claims it – a procedure reminiscent of Isa 58:7aB. The message of Isa 58:7 is clear: while the command לֹא תוּכַל לְהִתְעַלֵּם ('you must not remain indifferent', Deut 22:3b TNK) concerns one's possession, it certainly applies to one's neighbour.[123] Furthermore, 'if people take no notice of each other, they need not complain that God "hides himself" from their supplications, Ps. 55:2 etc.'[124] Also, as Polan observes, the verb ראה in this verse may be a reaction to its use in v. 2: 'as [the people] complain that God does <u>not see</u> their fasting, they are told in response to keep their eyes open so as to see the needs of another individual and to care for that need.'[125]

6.5.7. Isa 58:8-9a

Scholars generally agree that v. 8b reuses Isa 52:12b.[126] The fact that instead of יהוה in 52:12 it is now people's צֶדֶק that leads them should not be seen as TI's reinterpretation of DI (e.g., to emphasize the benefits of people's righteous behaviour),[127] because it is parallel to כְּבוֹד יְהוָה,[128]

---

123 Blenkinsopp also clarifies the meaning of וּמִבְּשָׂרְךָ לֹא תִתְעַלָּם in Isa 58:7 by Deut 22:1-4 as 'pretending that these people are not there, persuading oneself that someone else will take care of them or just wishing they would go away,' Blenkinsopp, *Isaiah 56-66*, 180.

124 Koole, *Isaiah III/3*, 140. See also the hiphils of עלם, esp. in Isa 1:15 for YHWH hiding his eyes from the people's prayers.

125 Polan, *Justice*, 33.

126 Isa 58:8b   וְהָלַךְ לְפָנֶיךָ צִדְקֶךָ כְּבוֹד יְהוָה יַאַסְפֶךָ׃
     Isa 52:12b: כִּי־הֹלֵךְ לִפְנֵיכֶם יְהוָה וּמְאַסִּפְכֶם אֱלֹהֵי יִשְׂרָאֵל׃
     Because of this allusion, some scholars take v. 8b as a later addition. This is unlikely, for, as Park correctly observes, Israel's צֶדֶק and YHWH's כְּבוֹד 'haben eine außergewöhnliche theologische Bedeutung im Sinne der gesamten Komposition von Jes 58 mit den Themen Kultus, Gerechtigkeit und Eschatologie,' Park, *Gerechtigkeit Israels*, 223-224.

127 *Contra*, e.g., R. N. Whybray, *Isaiah 40-66* (NCBC; London: Oliphants, 1975) 216. He, among others, believes that צִדְקֶךָ here summarizes people's righteous behaviour as described in vv. 6-7.

128 As Polan observes, this parallel also clarifies the meaning of צדק in this verse: 'The parallel character of צדק and כבוד shows the sense of צדק to be salvific instead of moral as seen in 58:2,' Polan, *Justice*, 213. The replacement of אֱלֹהֵי יִשְׂרָאֵל from 52:12 by כְּבוֹד יְהוָה might be due to the so called 'kabod theology', as described by Tryggve N. D. Mettinger, *The Dethronement of Sabaoth: Studies in the Shem and Kabod Theologies* (Old Testament Series 18; Lund: CWK Gleerup, 1982).

and in v. 11aA it is again יְהוָה who guides his people.[129] In addition, Polan correctly maintains that the light breaking forth like the dawn (שַׁחַר) in v. 8a probably symbolizes YHWH's coming and his presence among his people.[130] Because these expressions refer more likely to YHWH than to the people, some translations and commentators render צִדְקֶךָ as 'your vindicator',[131] referring to the equation 'YHWH = our justice' in Jer 23:6 and 33:16. However, Koole rightly objects that such identification does not appear in TI, and suggests that צִדְקֶךָ here stands for the 'salvation' promised by God 'in the sense that God does "justice" to his people, as was petitioned in v. 2bB (מִשְׁפְּטֵי־צֶדֶק).'[132] The parallel with 52:12b is, therefore, complete, and, as Childs observes, the term צֶדֶק 'is employed again in its original prophetic sense (41:2; 45:8, 24).'[133]

The message of vv. 6-8 is not just about how to improve the people's life conditions, as, e.g., Prov 21:21, where the one who pursues צְדָקָה וָחֶסֶד will find חַיִּים צְדָקָה וְכָבוֹד. The expression כְּבוֹד יְהוָה often stands for God's presence in the decisive events of Israel's *Heilsgeschichte*. It plays a crucial role in Ezekiel's visions, and its return into the temple marks the beginning of the eschatological era (Ezek 43:5 and 44:4). Also DI connects the appearance of כְּבוֹד יְהוָה with the glorious age to come (Isa 40:5).[134] As the functional analysis below confirms, כְּבוֹד יְהוָה in v. 8 very likely refers to קִרְבַת אֱלֹהִים in v. 2. These two expressions semantically overlap,[135] describing the most significant characteristic of the eschatology – the presence of YHWH in the midst of his people. Gammie rightly argues that the expression כְּבוֹד יְהוָה belongs to that aspect of holiness that Otto labels as

---

129 A word of caution from Childs seems to be appropriate here: 'The general lack of exact verbal correspondence is only a sign of the role of memory still at work, and the divergence is not automatically to be pressed as an intentional reinterpretation at each point of difference,' Childs, *Isaiah*, 442.

130 Polan, *Justice*, 216. *HALOT* points out some of the uses of שַׁחַר referring to a divine name (see the references there), one of which is the personal name שְׁחַרְיָה in 1 Chr 8:26.

131 For translations, see, e.g., NRSV and TNK. For commentators, see, e.g., Young who argues that 'the *righteousness* of the people is their Lord Himself, Edward J. Young, *The Book of Isaiah: The English Text, with Introduction, Exposition, and Notes* (NICOT; Grand Rapids, MI: Eerdmans, 1965) 3.421.

132 Koole, *Isaiah III/3*, 142.

133 Childs, *Isaiah*, 479. צֶדֶק should be understood in this sense also in Isa 62:2, again parallel to כְּבוֹד.

134 For כְּבוֹד יְהוָה in connection with eschatology, see Weinfeld, "כָּבוֹד," *TDOT* 7.34-36.

135 TNK most often translates כְּבוֹד יְהוָה as 'the Presence of the Lord'.

'overpoweringness' or *maiestas*,[136] and Isa 58 reassures the people that if their behaviour is compatible with God's holiness, this *maiestas* will gather them in, being closely connected with them. [137]

V. 9a, with its promise of restored communication and relationship between YHWH and the people,[138] corresponds to the complaint of v. 3a.[139] Furthermore, as Blenkinsopp correctly observes, 'the assurance contingent on the performance of true fasting with which this second response ends (vv 8-9) reveals the true nature of the complaint,' namely eschatological. He also draws the parallel between vv. 8-10 and Isa 60:1, where the same eschatological language is to be found: 'Arise, shine; for your light (אוֹרֵךְ) has come, and the glory of the LORD (כְּבוֹד יְהוָה) has risen (זָרָח) upon you,' adding that 'in later Isaianic passages, and in Jewish end-time imagery in general, "light" stands for the consummation, the fulfillment of the people's aspirations.'[140]

6.5.8. Isa 58:9b-10a

Several emendations have been suggested in this text. When it comes to the ones in v. 9b as proposed, e.g., in BHS, one has to agree with Lau that these are 'überflüssig und nicht gerechtfertigt.'[141] More serious, however, is the puzzling meaning of v. 10aA, as documented by a great variety of translations.[142] The most elaborate discussion of this verse comes from Hurowitz.[143] First, he rejects the often proposed

---

136 Gammie, *Holiness*, 7.

137 The parallel of v. 8b with 52:12 prompts many scholars to read יַאַסְפֶךָ at the end of the verse as piel rather than MT's qal, and translate it as 'to be your rear guard' instead of 'to gather you (in)'. This suggestion, however, does not necessarily change the meaning of the colon, for piel of אסף can also be rendered 'to gather' in most of its instances, Isa 52:12 included. LXX renders this form with the participle of the verb ἐπισυνάγω ('to gather'). Lau's argument for translating אסף as "sammeln" is based on the observation that 'Sammlung' is an important theme in DI; see Lau, *Schriftgelehrte Prophetie*, 252.

138 קרא and piel of שׁוע is a word-pair (see Ps 18:7 and Jonah 2:3). According to Polan, קרא here 'is a synonym for prayer or beseeching the Lord,' Polan, *Justice*, 184. The same meaning of קרא is very likely also in 43:22.

139 'Der Prophet geht mit der Heilszusage V.9a nun direkt auf die in V.3a geäußerte Klage ein,' Lau, *Schriftgelehrte Prophetie*, 253.

140 Blenkinsopp, *Isaiah 56-66*, 180.

141 Lau, *Schriftgelehrte Prophetie*, 253.

142 For a good summary of various interpretations, see Koole, *Isaiah III/3*, 146-147.

143 V. A. Hurowitz, "A Forgotten Meaning of Nepeš in Isaiah LVIII 10," *VT* 47 (1997) 43-52.

emendation of נַפְשֶׁךָ to לַחְמְךָ,[144] based mainly on LXX: καὶ δῷς πεινῶντι τὸν ἄρτον ἐκ ψυχῆς σου. Hurowitz argues that, rather than indicative of a variant *Vorlage*, LXX is actually 'the first witness to the tradition of compound interpretation.' Then he draws attention to an Akkadian cognate of Hebrew נֶפֶשׁ, namely *napištu*, one of whose meanings is 'sustenance'. This 'forgotten meaning' of נֶפֶשׁ is, according to Hurowitz, highly likely also in Ps 106:15 and possible in Ps 78:18 and Hos 9:4.[145] If granted, Isa 58:10aA translates as 'if you extend your sustenance to the hungry.' Hurowitz's argument is attractive, because this rendering makes good sense. However, as Barr sufficiently demonstrated, the transference of the meanings between cognates of various (even related) languages is hazardous,[146] more so in the case of such frequent words as נֶפֶשׁ and *napištu*. Until a new evidence is brought up, sheer prudence requires Hurowitz's proposal to remain an isolated voice. Nevertheless, his argument against the emendation of נַפְשֶׁךָ in v. 10aA is solid, and, for now, it seems best to retain the ambiguity of this verse by rendering it as 'if you extend yourself to the hungry.'

The context of v. 10a supports the retaining also of the second נֶפֶשׁ in the verse. As an object of ענה, נֶפֶשׁ pairs up with צוֹם in vv. 3 and 5, where they both represent the concept of fasting. In the first protasis-apodosis (vv. 6-9a) the key word is צוֹם, and נֶפֶשׁ is absent, while in the second pair (vv. 9b-12) the key word is נֶפֶשׁ, and צוֹם is absent. It seems that the reinterpretation of the concept of fasting continues in vv. 9b-12 without mentioning צוֹם, but with נֶפֶשׁ alluding to it.[147] This allusion is especially apparent in 10aB which reverses the usual idea of 'afflicting one's soul' (piel of ענה with נֶפֶשׁ as direct object as in vv. 3 and 5, and seven other times in BH) by fasting to satisfying 'the soul of an afflicted one' (נֶפֶשׁ with niphal participle of ענה). Fasting is therefore redirected and reversed – from starving oneself to feeding one's neighbour.[148] It

---

144 See, e.g., BHS apparatus.

145 Also the phrase וְאָכַלְתָּ עֲנָבִים כְּנַפְשְׁךָ שָׂבְעֶךָ in Deut 23:25 would make a good sense when translated with this meaning: 'you may eat grapes as your sustenance, (namely as) your fill.' Another possibility is Deut 24:6.

146 See James Barr, *Comparative Philology and the Text of the Old Testament* (Oxford: Clarendon Press, 1968).

147 The absence of צוֹם after 9a has often been an argument for taking vv. 9b-12 as a later addition, see, e.g., Whybray, *Isaiah 40-66*, 212. Oswalt correctly states that 'although fasting is not mentioned specifically, it is clearly in view, as v. 10a shows,' Oswalt, *Isaiah 40-66*, 505.

148 As many scholars pointed out, נֶפֶשׁ in 10aB likely means 'throat', and its repetition from the previous line produces a pun.

seems that, in order to make his point, the author plays on the various meanings of נֶפֶשׁ. Its central position in the chiastic structure of this bicolon (ABC / C'B'A') also speaks for its retention and of its importance in this text.[149]

With the exception of Ezek 27:33 and this verse, the agent of satisfying (hiphil of שׂבע, 16 times total) is always God. The prophet's appeal to satisfy the needs of the afflicted therefore urges the people to engage themselves in a God-like activity (as in the previous protasis).

6.5.9. Isa 58:10b-11

As in the previous apodosis, the author uses familiar images to describe the eschatological future: נחה 'often refers to God's guidance during the Exodus,'[150] God satisfying his people's needs and reversing their life conditions is a frequent picture in Psalms,[151] 'flourishing' bones occur also in the eschatological context of Isa 66:14, and the expression וְהָיִיתָ כְּגַן רָוֶה is found in Jer 31:12, also in an eschatological context.[152]

6.5.10. Isa 58:12

The similarity between 58:12 and 61:3c-4 is striking. If recent theories about the composition of TI, proposed, e.g., by Lau or Smith, are correct, 61:3c-4 served as *Vorlage* for 58:12.[153] Besides the unifying theme of restoration, the shared or similar vocabulary and phrases betray a strong dependence of one text on the other:

---

149 For details on the structure of this verse, see Polan, *Justice,* 218.

150 Koole, *Isaiah III/3,* 148.

151 See, e.g., the similarities between vv. 11-12 and Ps 107:36-37. The expression כַּצׇּהֳרַיִם in v. 10b is found elsewhere only in Ps 37:4.

152 This allusion is strengthened by the fact that Jer 31:12 also talks about people's נֶפֶשׁ, and that רָוֶה (adjectival form of רוה) occurs only once more in BH – Deut 29:18.

153 They both argue that Isa 56-66 contains several layers of tradition. Sommer, however, takes issue with Lau, objecting to his *Tradentenkreise*: 'The alleged differences between the groups rest on types of thematic interest present in certain texts; thus Lau's divisions amount to a map of major themes in these chapters rather than the source-critical finding that he believes them to be. At times his divisions require carving up coherent texts into different levels of composition; that this style of analysing prophetic texts is quite common does not make it any less speculative or unlikely,' Sommer, *Allusion,* 220.

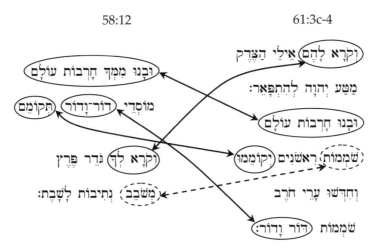

58:12   61:3c-4

This parallel throws light on several obscurities in 58:12. First, the points that can be deduced from the similarities:

— The almost identical phrase וּבָנוּ חָרְבוֹת עוֹלָם in 61:4a may explain the grammatically odd construction in 58:12aA: 'Grammatisch korrekt muß also וְנִבְנוּ gelesen werden, doch es ist nicht auszuschließen, daß die Vorlage den Autor dermaßen beeinflußt hat, daß er sich zu grammatisch ungeschickten und sogar falschen Konstruktionen hinreißen ließ.'[154]

— The same mechanism very likely accounts for the singular וְקֹרָא in 58:12bA instead of expected וְקֹרְאוּ as in 1QIsa[a], *die Vorlage* being Isa 61:3cA. The concept of giving a new name through the prepositional phrase קרא plus לְ is characteristic of TI.[155] Polan observes that 'the particular manner in which the verb קרא is used with the inseparable preposition לְ is a way of expressing a blessing endowed by God to his people in the literary context of 56-66.'[156]

— Lau believes that the subject of וּבָנוּ in 58:12 is 'die eschatologische Heilsgemeinde, die zuvor und im folgenden in der 2.m.Sg. angesprochen ist.'[157] Park uses the parallel with 61:4 to identify this 'eschatologische Heilsgemeinde' more closely. He

154 Lau, *Schriftgelehrte Prophetie*, 256. This mechanism deserves more attention in BH exegesis.

155 Besides these verses, it also occurs in 60:14b, 62:2b, 4b, and 12.

156 Polan, *Justice*, 222.

157 Lau, *Schriftgelehrte Prophetie*, 255.

believes that 'they' in 61:4 is closely connected with the people in the previous vv. 1-3, referring to the oppressed (עֲנָוִים), brokenhearted (נִשְׁבְּרֵי־לֵב), captives (שְׁבוּיִם), prisoners (אֲסוּרִים), and those who mourn for Zion (אֲבֵלֵי צִיּוֹן).[158] The connection with Isa 58 is appealing: Isa 58 is also concerned with the weak ones of the society, and the mourning in 61:3 is reminiscent of fasting in Isa 58. 'Deshalb ist das Subjekt der Wiederaufbau-arbeit diese Heilsgemeinde, die soziale Gerechtigkeit prakti-ziert.'[159]

— The additional expression שֹׁמְמוֹת רִאשֹׁנִים in 61:4 helps to clarify that the expressions חָרְבוֹת עוֹלָם and מוֹסְדֵי דוֹר־וָדוֹר refer to the past, not the future.

Second, the differences between Isa 58:12 and 61:4 are even more significant, because they help to clarify whether the restoration in 58:12 is literal (rebuilding Jerusalem) or metaphoric (rebuilding the people of God):

— The only difference between the two initial phrases of Isa 58:12 and 61:4 is the additional מִמְּךָ in 58:12aA, referring very likely to the audience of this oracle as defined above. The previous verse compares those who obey the prophet's admonition to an everlasting spring of water. If the meaning of the root of חָרְבוֹת in v. 12aA (חרב – 'be dry, dried up') comes to the fore, the two ideas nicely connect. מִמְּךָ would then be translated by the usual 'from you', מִן being the one of source.[160] In addition, texts like Jer 12:16 show that בנה can be used in the metaphorical sense of 'to build up' or 'to (re)establish' the people. 58:12aA, therefore, could be understood as a meta-phorical remake of 61:4aA.

— The noun מוֹסָד (or מוּסָד or מוֹסָדָה) occurs predominantly in a construct with אֶרֶץ and other material entities. However, it is also used metaphorically in Isa 28:16-17, parallel to a cornerstone that is being laid in Zion with מִשְׁפָּט as the line and צְדָקָה as the plummet. This use would fit well in Isa 58:12,[161] and explain the author's choice over the contrasting expression שֹׁמְמוֹת in his *Vorlage*, Is 61:4aB and especially bB.

---

158 Park, *Gerechtigkeit Israels*, 272.

159 Park, *Gerechtigkeit Israels*, 272. The connection between Isa 58 and 61 is discussed in 6.8.3.

160 For the מִן of source, see Williams §322. This connection is elaborated by Koole, *Isaiah III/3*, 151-152.

161 *HALOT* also suggests the metaphorical use of מוֹסָד in Isa 58:12 (#4899).

Most significant for the literal or metaphorical understanding of 58:12 is the meaning of the two names in 12b. The names in the parallel 61:3c are undoubtedly metaphors, but, since the expressions in 58:12b allow for both interpretations, they must be examined first on their own grounds.

Besides Isa 58:12, the words of which the first name גֹּדֵר פֶּרֶץ consists occur next or alongside each other six more times in BH, *always* as a metaphor. With people as subject, this combination can represent a result of antisocial behaviour of an individual (Ecc 10:8) or of a nation (Ezek 13:5 and 22:30). In Amos 9:11, God says that one day he will raise up 'the booth of David that is fallen, and repair its breaches (וְגָדַרְתִּי אֶת־פִּרְצֵיהֶן), and raise up (אָקִים) its ruins, and rebuild it (וּבְנִיתִיהָ) as in the days of old'. The similarities with Isa 58:12 are obvious. Lau believes that the author of Isa 58:12 has borrowed the picture of YHWH as a repairer of breaches from Amos and applied it to his audience with a new purpose in mind – 'nicht die frühere Daviddynastie wird wiederhergestellt, sondern der frühre soziale Wohlstand.'[162] Another possible source to which Isa 58:12 (and 11) may be alluding is Isa 5. There, because of the absence of מִשְׁפָּט and צְדָקָה (v. 7b), God has decided to break down the wall (פָּרֹץ גְּדֵרוֹ) of his vineyard (v. 5) and to deprive it of rain (v. 6). Leaving the metaphor, the houses of Israel and Judah will be uninhabited (אֵין יוֹשֵׁב, v. 9) and the people will be dying of hunger and be parched (צִחֵה) with thirst (v. 13). Isa 58:11-12 is a reversal of this picture: because of the presence of social justice, God will satisfy people's needs even in parched places (צַחְצָחוֹת),[163] and they will become like a garden with never-failing supply of water (v. 11). Their places will be inhabitable (לָשֶׁבֶת) and they will be called גֹּדֵר פֶּרֶץ (v. 12).[164]

As far as the name מְשֹׁבֵב נְתִיבוֹת לָשֶׁבֶת is concerned, Park follows Polan in arguing for a metaphorical understanding by connecting it to 59:8, where it is said about the people that they do not know the way of

---

162 Lau, *Schriftgelehrte Prophetie*, 257. Apparently, he reads the expression in both texts metaphorically.

163 Linking צַחְצָחוֹת with another *hapax legomenon* צִחֵה supports the translation 'parched places' as well as explaining its use in v. 11. For translating it as "Glänzendes" in the sense of delicacies ("Leckerbissen"), see Klaus Koenen, "Textkritische Anmerkungen zu schwierigen Stellen im Tritojesajabuch," *Biblica* 69 (1988) 564-573.

164 Williamson observes a similar reversal of Isa 5:8-10 (and 6:11-13) in 49:14-21. He also notices the possible connection between Isa 5 and 58, but does not regard it as particularly strong, since it does not attest 'the full range of verbal links,' Williamson, *Book Called Isaiah*, 55. It could be argued, however, that the range of the above links between Isa 5 and 58 is comparable with the one observed by Williamson between Isa 5 and 49.

peace (דֶּרֶךְ שָׁלוֹם), there is no justice (מִשְׁפָּט) in their paths, they made
their roads (נְתִיבוֹתֵיהֶם) crooked and no one who walks in them knows
peace (שָׁלוֹם). Park is very likely correct that the preference for the
relatively rare expression נְתִיבָה over other possible terms[165] indicates
the antithetical connection with 58:12, namely, 'in der Namensnennung
in 58:12bß steht (מְשֹׁבֵב נְתִיבוֹת לָשָׁבֶת) "der Wiederhersteller der Straße
zum Wohnen" im Gegensatz zu denen, die in 59,8 ohne Recht ihre
Straße (נְתִיבוֹתֵיהֶם) krumm machen und keinen Frieden kennen.'[166]
Interestingly, the noun נְתִיבָה occurs only in Hebrew poetry and is
almost always used metaphorically. Park also points to Isa 32:17-18,
where the peaceful and safe dwelling of the people is the result of
צְדָקָה. Polan adds another interesting parallel: there is an expression in
Job 24:13b that also combines the plural of נְתִיבָה with the verb יֹשׁב –
יָשְׁבוּ בִּנְתִיבֹתָיו. Here, as in 59:8, the noun נְתִיבָה 'is in parallel with דרכיו
and refers to a way of life opposed to God's ways.' Considering also the
fact that the noun דֶּרֶךְ in TI almost always expresses a *modus operandi*
(as, e.g., in 58:2 and 13, or in 59:8), Polan concludes that נְתִיבוֹת in
58:12b 'can be interpreted in a metaphorical manner referring to a way
of life that is put into practice.'[167] This understanding coincides very
well with the following verse, where the proper way of living is
addressed again, this time focusing on the Sabbath. The repetition of
two out of the three roots of v. 12bB in the opening colon of v. 13 gives
a strong hint to read v. 13 epexegetically, supporting thus the
metaphorical reading of the name in v. 12bB. Finally, an additional
support comes from the Targum. Its paraphrastic interpretation is
unambiguous in metaphorical understanding of Isa 58:12b: 'and they
shall call thee, The restorer of the right way, The converter of the
wicked to the law.'[168]

6.5.11. Isa 58:13

In its attempt to make better sense of 13aA, BHS proposes emending
מִשַּׁבָּת to בַּשַּׁבָּת. This form, however, does not occur in any of the
Hebrew manuscripts, and the only version that supports it is *Vetus
Latina*. Brongers retains MT, arguing that 'an anderen vergleichbaren

---

165 Park suggests דֶּרֶךְ or מְסִלָּה as alternatives. However, the use of אֹרַח is more likely,
    as in very similar Prov 2:15 אֲשֶׁר אָרְחֹתֵיהֶם עִקְּשִׁים וּנְלוֹזִים בְּמַעְגְּלוֹתָם

166 Park, *Gerechtigkeit Israels,* 274.

167 Polan, *Justice,* 223-224 and 32.

168 John Frederick Stenning, *The Targum of Isaiah* (Oxford: Clarendon Press, 1949) 194.

Stellen wird statt שׁוּב hi, מנע (Prov 1 15), סוּר hi (Prov 4 27) oder כלא (Ps 119 101) verwendet, und zwar immer mit der Präposition מִן.'[169] 1QIsaᵃ also supports MT by supplying מִן in the second part of the colon (מעשׂות instead of MT's עֲשׂוֹת).[170]   If the 'metaphorical mode' of the previous verses continues in this colon (see the discussion below), than Koole's understanding v. 13aA is noteworthy: 'the movement is spatially conceived, there is talk of dry places, a garden, and walls, and this is matched by the idea of the Sabbath as a holy space which one's feet should not touch.'[171] Also Delitzsch reads v. 13aA metaphorically and spatially, stating that it is equivalent to 'if thou do not tread upon [Sabbath's] holy ground with a foot occupied with its everyday work.'[172]

The structure of the bicolon 13a as well as of the whole verse contributes to the interpretation of 13aA. In the parallel colon aB, יוֹם קָדְשׁי corresponds to שַׁבָּת, and עֲשׂוֹת חֲפָצֶיךָ to תָּשִׁיב רַגְלֶךָ. It is possible to read aB epexegetically, explaining the metaphor in aA. Thus Delitzsch: 'עֲשׂוֹת which follows is not elliptical ..., but an explanatory permutative of the object "thy foot:" "turn away thy foot," viz. from attending to thy business (a defective plural) on my holy day.'[173] This reading is encouraged by the chiastic structure of the whole verse, where the bicolon a corresponds to the bicolon c, colon b being the centre. The shared terminology supports this structure, and, at the same time, connects the colons:

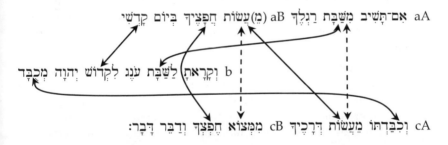

---

169 H. A. Brongers, "Einige Bemerkungen zu Jes 58:13-14," *ZAW* 87 (1975) 212-216.

170 Even though the form מעשׂות nicely corresponds with משׁבת and occurs also in the last part of the verse (and in Isa 56:2 – a similar text), the supplying of מן is not necessary, because, as GK §199hh points out, 'in poetic parallelism the governing power of a preposition is sometimes extended to the corresponding substantive of the second member.'

171 Koole, *Isaiah III/3*, 155.

172 Delitzsch, *Prophecies of Isaiah*, 2.393-394.

173 Delitzsch, *Prophecies of Isaiah*, 2.394. For another example of using the hiphil of שׁוּב with רֶגֶל as a metaphor for the way of living, see Ps 119:59.

The expression תָּשִׁיב רַגְלֶךָ in aA corresponds to another unusual phrase עֲשׂוֹת דְּרָכֶיךָ in cA. Brongers correctly points out that the closest parallel to this phrase can be found in Jdg 17:8 – לַעֲשׂוֹת דַּרְכּוֹ. Based on the comparison, he believes that this expression 'handelt sich um Reisen, besonders um Geschäftsreisen.'[174] While Brongers's observation is essentially correct, the restriction of this expression to 'Geschäftsreisen' is not justified and seems to be just a result of his "business interpretation" of vv. 13-14. In this case, the second part of the bicolon c is of significant help, for it can function epexegetically just as in the bicolon a. Regardless of the exact meaning of the obscure expression דַּבֵּר דָּבָר,[175] this reading makes חפץ the key word of the a-c parallel. חפץ plays an important part in two other closely related TI texts, namely 56:1-8 and 66:1-4,[176] making the same point – the people are not to pursue their own חֵפֶץ, rather the things in which YHWH חָפֵץ, such as חֶסֶד מִשְׁפָּט וּצְדָקָה בָּאָרֶץ (Jer 9:23) or דַּעַת אֱלֹהִים (Hos 6:6). To these texts, the author of Isa 58:13 adds: Especially on the Sabbath!

6.5.12. Isa 58:14

The similarities between v. 14b and Deut 32:13a are undeniable. The phrase 'riding upon the heights of the earth' occurs only here, and, according to Westermann, it is in both cases 'purely metaphorical.'[177] Also the parallel v. 14bB is a metaphor. To pinpoint the meaning of these metaphors comes close to destroying them, but their parallelism and a closer look at the particular expressions allow for some demarcation:[178]

— The object of the relatively frequent prepositional phrase רכב על is almost always a vehicle, either an animal (cherub included), a chariot, or a cloud.[179] Obviously, 'riding upon the heights of the land' can only be understood metaphorically. Since the metaphorical language seems to be characteristic of

---

174 Brongers, "Jes 58:13-14."
175 After a detailed discussion of this phrase, Koole concludes that 'it probably relates to trade', translating it as 'speaking a word (about it)', Koole, *Isaiah III/3*, 158.
176 For more detail comparison of these passages with Isa 58, see 6.8.2 and 6.8.4 respectively.
177 Westermann, *Isaiah 40-66*, 342.
178 Suggestions such as the one of Westermann, that v. bA means 'high over all depressions and obstacles,' ignore the parallelism.
179 The exceptions are Ps 45:5 and 2 Kgs 13:16. In Lev 15:9 the object is a saddle – a derivation from a vehicle.

the previous apodoses as well, there is no reason to mitigate the metaphor here by translating רכב על as 'to bring up' (as LXX, ἀναβιβάζω ἐπὶ), 'set atop' (as NRS in Deut 32:13), 'set astride' (as TNK in Isa 58:14), or 'put/place on' (as NAU in 2 Kgs 13:16).

— The correlation of בָּמֳתֵי אָרֶץ and נַחֲלַת יַעֲקֹב clarifies that both expressions relate to the Promised Land, not 'the earth' in general, as אֶרֶץ in this verse is often translated.[180]

— Because of the connection between mountains and fertility, and LXX's rendering of בָּמֳתֵי אָרֶץ as τὰ ἀγαθὰ τῆς γῆς, Brongers argues 'daß sich der Inhalt der Zusage auf den Besitz der landwirtschaftlich besten Gebiete bezieht.'[181] While he may be correct, the more important reason for using this particular expression here may be to create a link with not only Deut 32:13, but also with the other two texts that mention it, namely Amos 4:13 and Mic 1:3, where YHWH, in his victorious intervention, is דֹרֵךְ עַל־בָּמֳתֵי אָרֶץ. Koole connects these pictures and concludes regarding Isa 58:14b that 'the true Victor is Yahweh, who saves his people and allows them to share in his victory by fulfilling the promise of the land, Deut. 32:13.'[182]

Even without precisely deciphered metaphors, it is obvious that v. 14b describes an eschatological era, in which the relationship between YHWH and his people is at its best, materializing itself in the Promised Land.

Because of the connection of Isa 58:14 with Deut 32:13, Smith suggests that the phrase כִּי פִּי יְהוָה דִּבֵּר in this verse 'does not … function structurally to bring the poem in 58:1-14 to a conclusion, but rather points to the reuse of an earlier text, a divine word, which is going to be fulfilled.'[183] Even though determining the precise function

---

180 See, e.g., KJV, NRSV, NAB, NEB, or TNK. As far as the identification of נַחֲלַת יַעֲקֹב with the land is concerned, Fishbane argues that the transformation from 'the people as YHWH's inheritance' in Deut 32:9 to 'the land as the inheritance of the people' in Isa 58:14 'fully accords with the pervasive post-exilic concern with return to the land, with the added factor that true Sabbath observance is the key to sustained tenure there,' Michael A. Fishbane, *Biblical Interpretation in Ancient Israel* (Oxford, New York: Clarendon Press; Oxford University Press, 1985) 478-479.

181 Brongers, "Jes 58:13-14."

182 Koole, *Isaiah III/3*, 160.

183 Smith, *Rhetoric*, 114. The same point is made and argued in more detail by Fishbane, *Interpretation*, 477-479.

of this and similar phrases in the prophetic oracles seems unlikely,[184] 'it
is difficult to escape the conclusion that this rarely used phrase
functioned among some tradents as a means of supplementing and/or
coordinating divine oracles.'[185]   Therefore, reading the final phrase פִּי
כִּי דִּבֶּר יְהוָה as the last words of the quote in v. 14 (as in, e.g., NRSV or
NJB) rather than the closure of the whole discourse (as in, e.g., NIV or
NAS) is to be preferred.

6.6. Functional Analysis of Isa 58

Park, opposing the majority opinion about the unity of Isa 58, claims
that 'die innere Struktur des Textes Jes 58 bietet ihrem Verständnis
nach als Einheit keine Schwierigkeiten, da kein einziger Vers durch die
Annahme einer redaktionellen Bearbeitung aus dem gesamten Text
herausgetrennt zu werden braucht,' and concludes that 'in der jetzigen
Endgestalt von Jes 58 gibt es nichts, daß dazu zwingt, einen inneren
Bruch anzunehmen.'[186] This section tests the validity of his statement.
While briefly examining some links between strophes and stanzas,
special attention is paid to the most controversial issue in the functional
analysis of Isa 58 – the relationship between vv. 1-12 and vv. 13-14.

6.6.1. Isa 58:1-3a

The question about the relationship of v. 2 with the preceding strophe
boils down to the question about the function of the initial וֹ in 2aA: is it
adversative, explicative, concessive, or a later addition?[187] Based on the
structure and syntax analyses above, it seems that vv. 2-3a are best
understood as a description of the situation to clarify the prophet's task

---

184 Koole does not give any suppor for stating that the formula כִּי פִּי יְהוָה דִּבֶּר (and its
     variations) never functions as a quoting reference, see Koole, *Isaiah III/3*, 161.
185 Samuel A. Meier, *Speaking of Speaking: Marking Direct Discourse in the Hebrew Bible*
     (VTSup 46; Leiden: Brill, 1992) 158.
186 Park, *Gerechtigkeit Israels*, 204 and 207.
187 For the list of options and their promoters, see, e.g., Koenen, *Ethik und Eschatologie*,
     92. The idea of a later addition is supported by the omission of this conjunction in
     1QIsa[a] and 1QIsa[b] (reflected in LXX and V) and promoted by Hans Kosmala, "Form
     and Structure of Isaiah 58," *Annual of the Swedish Theological Institute* 5 (1967) 69-81:
     72.

in v. 1.[188] The expression וְאוֹתִי occurs also in the preceding chapter (57:11),[189] where it puts emphasis on YHWH as the one whom people do not remember, do not think of, and do not fear, but worship other gods. However, the nature of the people's פֶּשַׁע and חַטָּאת in ch. 58 is not idolatry; וְאוֹתִי here clarifies that the problem is not about people's relationship with God as expressed in cult, but, as the following verses show, about their relationship with their neighbour as expressed in behaviour. It seems, therefore, that the initial ו in this case performs an explicative function, and v. 2aA should then be translated 'To be sure, Me they seek daily,' as in TNK.[190]

Concerning the relation of v. 3a to v. 2, Smith suggests that v. 2 'provides a general overview of the people and their current forms of activity, while the fasting referred to in v. 3a is a specific example of their attempts to put into practice what they understand to be Yahweh's wishes.'[191] Consequently, if the fasting in Isa 58 exemplifies the positive religious activities of v. 2,[192] it cannot be viewed as negative.[193] The complaint in v. 3a is based on the belief described in passages like Deut 4:7-8 'For what other great nation has a god so near to it as the LORD our God is whenever we call to him? And what other

---

188 Koole expresses a similar opinion. He believes that 'the line [2aA] should be seen as an explanation of the task in v. 1,' Koole, *Isaiah III/3*, 125.

189 Interestingly, Isa 57:11 and 58:2 are the only two places in BHS where the full form וְאוֹתִי occurs.

190 Modified word order for emphasis. TNK has 'To be sure, they seek Me daily.'

191 Smith, *Rhetoric*, 107. Also Lau and Koole understand v. 3a as an illustration of v. 2: 'This complaint concretely conveys what the previous line has said about the absence of God's "righteous decisions" and his "approach", and the interrogative particle links up directly with the verbs "to ask" and "to desire" used there,' Koole, *Isaiah III/3*, 128.

192 Childs claims that the expression מִשְׁפְּטֵי־צֶדֶק should be construed negatively as 'legal decisions directed against others on [the petitioner's] behalf.' He then carries this negative connotation over to קִרְבַת אלהים, taking it as an example of how the people 'rejoice in their own religious agenda,' Childs, *Isaiah*, 477. Such reading, however, would be at odds not only with the previous part of the verse (supported by chiasm), but also with the rest of the OT, where activities described by these terms are encouraged and viewed positively. For the chiastic structure of v. 2, see Polan, *Justice*, 192-194.

193 One can only speculate why the author singled out fasting, when, as in the former prophetic texts on a similar topic, a more appropriate example of people's attempts would be sacrifice. Blenkinsopp is certainly correct that 'the most important and paradigmatic form of "approach to God" (*qirbat 'ĕlohîm*) was through sacrifice, by "bringing near" (*hiqrîb*) a victim,' Blenkinsopp, *Isaiah 56-66*, 177. However, one must resist the temptation to draw conclusions from this oddity about, e.g., the date of the passage or the growing importance of fasting and the Sabbath over sacrifices in the post-exilic period.

great nation has statutes and ordinances as just as this entire law that I am setting before you today?' These verses illuminate the connection between v. 3a and the previous verse – the connection between God's nearness, calling on him, and his statutes and ordinances.

<h3 style="text-align:center">6.6.2. Isa 58:3b-7</h3>

Because vv. 3b-4 address social misbehavior during the time of fasting and v. 5 describes the formalism of fasting, many scholars treat them as two separate units, assigning vv. 3b-4 to a redactor.[194] Koenen, however, observes two important connections: 'V3b-4 und 5-12 werden durch ihr starkes soziales Interesse zusammengehalten, und v9a bezieht sich mit seiner Erhörungsverheißung auf v4b.'[195] True, the text would read more smoothly without vv. 3b-4, but Sekine calls for a more open-minded approach: 'Man sollte darin eher die lebendige Schreibart des Autors, der nicht immer eine genaue logische Gedankenführung beachtet, erkennen und darf nicht jede logisch ein bißchen fremdartige Stelle glätten.' Applying this approach to the discussed verses, he concludes: 'Da es keine weiteren Indizien für eine redaktionelle Bearbeitung in V. 3-5 gibt, müssen wir bei der Interpretation bleiben, daß V. 3b-4 und V. 5 zwei verschieden Arten des Verfalls der Fastens beschreiben.'[196]

While correct in defending the originality of vv. 3b-4, Sekine's understanding of the unit may appear to support the popular conclusion that v. 5 is God's repudiation of formalism.[197] Sekine, however, clarifies: 'Aber „ein Fasten, wie ich (=Jahwe) es haben will" (V. 6a), das in V.6b-7.9b-10a geschildert wird, hat nicht „Formalismus", sodern nur „asoziales Vergehen" kritisch im Auge.'[198] In other words, v. 5 must not be read in isolation from either the previous or the following verses.[199] YHWH's question in 5aA, 'Should the fast that I

194 See, e.g., Karl Pauritsch, *Die neue Gemeinde: Gott sammelt Ausgestossene und Arme (Jesaia 56-66). Die Botschaft des Tritojesaia-Buches literar-, form-, gattungskritisch und redaktionsgeschichtlich untersucht* (Analecta biblica 47; Rome: Biblical Institute Press, 1971) 74f, Westermann, *Isaiah 40-66*, 333, Whybray, *Isaiah 40-66*, 212.

195 Koenen, *Ethik und Eschatologie*, 97.

196 Sekine, *Tritojesajanische Sammlung*, 125.

197 Thus, e.g., Koole believes that 'v.5 criticizes the ritual itself,' Koole, *Isaiah III/3*, 116. See also Pauritsch, *Die neue Gemeinde*, 74.

198 Sekine, *Tritojesajanische Sammlung*, 125.

199 Contra Lau, who believes that 'der Autor in V.5 auch die äußerlichen Rites des Fastens verwirft' and that 'Man kann diese Argumentation nicht durch einen

choose be like this: ... ?' is answered in vv. 6-7. Shramm correctly states that 'verses 5-7 approach the question of fasting in typical prophetic hyperbolic fashion by juxtaposing acts of social justice with the common rituals of fasting,' just as in Isa 1:10-17.[200] Also the sarcasm of 5bA (the comparison of bowing one's head to a bulrush) and the overall negative tone implied by the questions may be relative, expressed in dialectic negation.[201] The link between vv. 5 and 6-7 is strengthened also by 6a that copies 5aA and asks: 'Is not this the fast that I choose: ...?' Within its context, v. 5 simply states that fasting is more than *just* ritual – it also has its ethical dimension. The rest of the chapter confirms that 'in diesen Versen wird das Fasten also nicht grundsätzlich verworfen, sondern vielmehr darauf hingewiesen, daß das Verhalten des Menschen zu Gott nicht von seinem Verhalten zu den Mitmenschen getrennt werden kann.'[202]

6.6.3. Protasis-Apodosis Pairs in Isa 58:6-14

Isa 58:6-14 consists of three protasis-apodosis pairs: vv. 6-7 and 8-9a,[203] vv. 9b-10a and 10b-12, and vv. 13 and 14. This rather unusual structure led many scholars to treat some parts (esp. the second and the third pair) as secondary and/or to rearrange their sequence.[204] Here again, the above quote from Sekine about the 'Gedankenführung' expressed in 'die lebendige Schreibart des Autors' suffices to repudiate most of the objections. The changes of person and number within this text more

---

konstruierten Gegensatz zwischen V.3b.4 und V.5ff. entschärfen,' Lau, *Schriftgelehrte Prophetie*, 244.

200 Schramm, *Opponents*, 135.

201 Booij defines dialectic negation as a rhetorical feature that 'aims at emphasizing the essential and bringing it out in fuller relief,' Booij, "Negation," 400.

202 Hermisson, *Sprache und Ritus*, 83.

203 The protasis of vv. 8-9a are vv. 6-7, not just 7b. Koole distinguishes between temporal and logical use of אז, stating that 'because vv. 6-7 are not formally a conditional protasis, the temporal meaning ('later') of the particle comes more to the fore,' Koole, *Isaiah III/3*, 141. This designation, however, is inconsistent with the next two protasis-apodosis pairs, where both of the protases are introduced by the conditional אם. The nature of the relationship between protases and apodoses in Isa 58 is a matter of theology rather than grammar.

204 For a list of proposals, see Park, *Gerechtigkeit Israels*, 224-225.

likely indicate allusions, echoes, use of established expressions, etc., than the work of a redactor.[205]

There is no reason to treat vv. 9b-12 as secondary on the basis of their content, for, as Koenen observes, 'die Verse weisen zum Vorhergehenden keinerlei Spannungen auf und können deswegen zur Grundschicht gezählt werden.'[206] Smith identifies a thematic link between vv. 6-14 and the rest of the chapter: 'The author responds to the question raised by the people by instructing them in a positive manner concerning the kind of behaviour which will win God's favour and attention, and which will hasten the era of salvation and enable them to participate in it.'[207] With the help of Koole, it is possible to argue that vv. 9b-10a correspond to vv. 3b-4 and 6-7 as follows: v. 9bA sums up vv. 3bB and 6, v. 9bB sums up v. 4a, and v. 10a sums up v. 7.[208] Park even notices a rhetorical device that connects the various parts of Isa 58, showing the development from fasting to ethics and from ethics to salvation:

$$\text{עִנִּינוּ נַפְשֵׁנוּ} \text{ (v.3)} — \text{נֶפֶשׁ נַעֲנָה תַּשְׂבִּיעַ} \text{ (v. 10)} — \text{נַפְשֶׁךָ} \text{ ... הִשְׂבִּיעַ} \text{ (v. 11).}[209]$$

Polan comments on the literary function of this link that 'the repetition of the words in reversed order highlights the change that is taking place.'[210] In addition, he observes that the use of the roots חפץ and ענג in ch. 58 serves to heighten two important movements: vv. 2-12 'stress a direction away from self and toward one's neighbour,' and vv. 13-14 'continues the orientation away from self, but now culminating in the Lord.'[211] It can be said that the dynamic of people's life in the new era is described by the amalgamation of these two vectors. To argue this position, however, an elaborate argument is needed to defend the place of vv. 13-14 in the original text.

---

205 Needless to say, to harmonize person and number in a text would be an easy fix for any redactor. For a solid attempt to explain the person/number changes in Isa 58, see Park, *Gerechtigkeit Israels*, 209-214.

206 Koenen, *Ethik und Eschatologie*, 97.

207 Smith, *Rhetoric*, 111. Similarly, Oswalt argues that if vv. 13-14 are the conclusion of Isa 58, then the fact that they 'address Sabbath keeping, not fasting, shows that fasting is not the real issue of the chapter, but rather what pleases God (cf. vv. 1-2),' Oswalt, *Isaiah 40-66*, 502.

208 See Koole, *Isaiah III/3*, 118-121.

209 See Park, *Gerechtigkeit Israels*, 267.

210 Polan, *Justice*, 220-221.

211 Polan, *Justice*, 229.

6.6.4. Isa 58:13-14

For many commentators, the main subject of Isa 58 is fasting, more specifically its formal observance versus the practice of social justice. Consequently, they often treat those passages of the chapter that deal with a different subject as unoriginal parts of the poem. Thus, e.g., Hoppe believes that since vv. 1-12 'deal with the theme of fasting and justice' and vv. 13-14 'present the ideal of Sabbath observance,' the latter must be a secondary addition.[212] Those who opt for only one, more general subject of Isa 58, such as proper behaviour during religious festivals, run into difficulty in reconciling the ways in which each section handles this subject. The following quote from Emmerson aptly describes the frustration:

> The concluding section (vv. 13-14), although consistent with the preceding verses in structure as a conditional promise, in tone as an exhortation, and in subject matter as concerned with a religious institution, in this instance the sabbath, nevertheless differs remarkably in its attitude. There is here no radical attempt to reinterpret traditional forms of sabbath observance but a reaffirmation of customary practice with no apparent acknowledgement of any social dimension.[213]

In addition, what seems to be consistent to Emmerson, namely the form and the structure, is questioned by other scholars. Westermann points out the difference in the form: 'Verses 3f. are a forthright allegation ..., but v. 13 is mere admonition.'[214] Kosmala finds the structure of vv. 13-14 suspicious. He admits that '[its] composition has a symmetrical form; in the disposition of the contents, however, i.e., in its structure, the poem is not symmetrically built.' This, according to Kosmala, shows its 'inferior artistic quality' and 'does not reach the artistic beauty' of the preceding part of Isa 58.[215] On top of the above arguments, the major gap that precedes vv. 13-14 in 1QIsaᵃ is often interpreted as a definite sign of separation between the two parts of Isa 58.

---

212 Leslie J. Hoppe, "Isaiah 58:1-12, Fasting and Idolatry," *BTB* 13, no. 2 (1983) 44-47.

213 Grace I. Emmerson, *Isaiah 56-66* (OTG; Sheffield: JSOT Press, 1992) 26-27. Similarly, Koenen states that according to him, 'mahnen beide Texte zum rechten Verhalten an bestimmten Tagen,' but, in contrast to vv. 5-12, in vv. 13-14 'wird hier nicht aktive Nächstenliebe, sondern Ruhe gefordert,' Koenen, *Ethik und Eschatologie,* 88 and n164. Lau speaks about 'zweifellos krassen Übergang zu der Sabbatthematik,' Lau, *Schriftgelehrte Prophetie,* 257.

214 Westermann, *Isaiah 40-66,* 341.

215 Kosmala, "Isaiah 58," 79. He, nevertheless, considers Isa 58:13-14 to be an original poem, without additions or insertions.

How then can Muilenburg claim that without vv. 13-14 the 'poem remains a torso,'[216] and Crenshaw even call v. 14 'the climactic crown of the whole poem'?[217] First, the objections against the formal differences carry little weight and can easily be repudiated. The gap and the new line after v. 12 in 1QIsa[a] do not have to indicate the separation between the two parts. As Park observes, 'solche Freizeilen finden sich jedoch mehrmals in 1QJes[a], und trotzdem stehen die betroffenen Textteile in einen verständlichen Zusammenhang miteinander.'[218] Kosmala's comparison of the two structures in Isa 58 is highly subjective, especially after his "reproduction" of the first part.[219] In light of the fact that we just do not know how Hebrew poetry works, judging the artistic quality of an ancient Hebrew poem by the criteria of a twentieth century scholar seems rather presumptuous. As far as the use of the two different forms is concerned, there is no reason why any poet should confine himself to only one form per poem. Moreover, the difference in forms is disruptive only when one looks at vv. 3f and vv. 13f separately. Sekine, however, rightly objects to such methodology; according to him, 'dürfte es sinnvoller sein, von einem Verhältnis zueinander als von "Abstand" zu reden;' and, in the case of Isa 58, 'allein sollte sich die Aussage besser auf V. 3-5 und auf V. 5b beziehen.'[220]

The use of rhetorical analysis for or against the unity of Isa 58 is also highly questionable. Scholars generally recognize the occurrence of keywords, catchwords, and other rhetorical devices in a text, but the way they interpret this evidence often differs significantly. For example, Koenen believes that the term קרא has the same function in both v. 12 and v. 13, namely 'Namensgebung'. Based on observations about how 'Namensgebung' operates in what he calls 'der Grundschicht' of Isa 56-66 (including Isa 58:12), Koenen claims that the instance in Isa 58:13 'steht ... jedoch im Unterschied zu den Namensgebungen der Grundschicht erstens nicht im Kontext einer Verheißung, sondern einer Forderung, und zweitens gilt der Name hier

---

216 James Muilenburg, "The Book of Isaiah, Chapters 40-66," in *The Interpreter's Bible* (New York: Abingdon Press, 1956) 677.

217 James L. Crenshaw, "W^eDŌRĒK 'AL-BĀMŌTÊ 'ĀRETS," *CBQ* 34 (1972) 39-53: 50.

218 Park, *Gerechtigkeit Israels,* 227. For one example, he refers to the major gap in 1QIsa[a] 41 between vv. 26 and 27, a text that is obviously a unity. (There is a misprint in Park's reference – 42 instead of 41.) In addition, he points out the absence of a division mark in 1QIsa[a] 66 between vv. 22 and 23, where the latter addresses a new subject, namely the Sabbath.

219 See Kosmala, "Isaiah 58," 73-79.

220 Sekine, *Tritojesajanische Sammlung,* 129.

nicht Israel oder dem Zion, sondern dem Sabbath.'[221] This to him is one of the signs that vv. 13-14 come from a redactor. On the other hand, for Polan the verbal root קרא 'establishes links between the different strophes' of Isa 58.[222] He observes that this root 'is evenly distributed throughout the literary unit (58:1a, 5c, 9a, 12b, 13b),' and, apart from 58:9a where it probably refers to prayer, it performs the function 'of "acknowledging" on four different levels: the people's sins, the proper observance of a fast, a new name, and the description of the Sabbath.'[223] Koenen similarly interprets 'die Stichwortverbindungen' at the end of v. 12 and the beginning of v. 13:

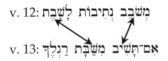

v. 12: מְשֹׁבֵב נְתִיבוֹת לָשָׁבֶת

v. 13: אִם־תָּשִׁיב מִשַּׁבָּת רַגְלֶךָ

He states that 'zum einen findet sich in beiden Stichen die Wurzel שׁוב, zum anderen bilden die Wörter לשבת und משבת ein Wortspiel.' According to Koenen, this is 'für den Redaktor typische Verknüpfungstechnik,' and he suggests that 'es ist sogar möglich, daß לשבת den Redaktor erst auf die Idee brachte, den ihm wichtigen Gedanken der Sabbatheiligung nachzutragen.'[224] Again, Polan argues that the way שׁוב functions in vv. 12 and 13 is characteristic of the larger unit Isa 56-59, namely it 'reflects the choice one makes in following one's own will toward sin (57:17; 58:13) or walking in the ways of God (58:12; 59:20).'[225] As far as the wordplay is concerned, Torrey regarded punning and homonymy a characteristic phenomenon of Isa 40-66.[226] Even though Driver did not agree with all Torrey's examples, he endorsed his overall thesis and added some new instances of wordplay in Isa 40-66.[227] Later on, Payne raised a word of caution, criticizing this thesis on several grounds. He persuasively showed that many examples from Torrey or Driver are highly subjective and

---

221 Koenen, *Ethik und Eschatologie*, 89.

222 Polan, *Justice*, 190.

223 Polan, *Justice*, 184.

224 Koenen, *Ethik und Eschatologie*, 89.

225 Polan, *Justice*, 33.

226 Charles Cutler Torrey, *The Second Isaiah: A New Interpretation* (New York,: C. Scribner's Sons, 1928) 199-202.

227 G. R. Driver, "Is. xl-lxvi, Linguistic and Textual Problems," *JTS* 36 (1935) 396-406: 406. Neither Torrey nor Driver seems to distinguish between homonymy and homography or paronomasia.

questionable.[228] Nevertheless, all these studies agree that punning in the book of Isaiah is not unusual. Because of its frequency, a word-play cannot be taken as a sign either of original authorship or of redaction. One last example of an argument based on rhetorical analysis: several scholars recognize that the noun חֵפֶץ occurs as an object of the verb מצא only twice, namely in Isa 58:3 and 13. While, e.g., Smith and Barré interpret this fact as one of the links that unites vv. 13-14 with the rest of the chapter,[229] Koenen takes it as another 'für den Redaktor typische Verknüpfungstechnik.'[230]

As has just been illustrated, the results of rhetorical analysis can be used to support even opposing arguments, and should not therefore be decisive for the unity of Isa 58. Moreover, Smith is correct that 'if the substance and content of [vv. 13-14] cannot be reconciled with the preceding material then no amount of rhetorical features can save them from exclusion from the original poem.'[231] This statement can be extended to the arguments above concerning form, structure, and other textual features.[232] Certain attempts at reconciliation of this kind come from scholars who believe that vv. 13-14 address an issue that is different from, yet in some relation to the issues in vv. 1-12. For example, Koole sees this relation as antithetical: 'the Sabbath becomes the counterpart of the fast-day' for the following reasons: 'the practice of fasting involves all kinds of social oppression, but the Sabbath gives rest to all,' 'fasting seems to be necessarily accompanied by a somber ritual …, but the Sabbath is a "delight" …,' fast-days 'are chosen randomly' and 'are no more than human institution', but 'the Sabbath is a holy day instituted by God.'[233] Another attempt to justify vv. 13-14

228 D. F. Payne, "Characteristic Word-Play in "Second Isaiah": A Reappraisal," *JSS* 12 (1967) 207-229.

229 Smith, *Rhetoric,* 113. Michael L. Barré, "Fasting in Isaiah 58:1-12: A Reexamination," *BTB* 15, no. 3 (1985) 94-97.

230 Koenen, *Ethik und Eschatologie,* 113-114.

231 Smith, *Rhetoric,* 113.

232 A unique attempt to explain the existence of vv. 13-14 in Isa 58 comes from Sherwood, who believes that 'redaction compounds the punning, disjunctive elements already at work in the text,' Yvonne Sherwood, "'Darke Texts Needs Notes': On Prophetic Prophecy, John Donne and the Baroque," *JSOT* 27 (2002) 47-74: 55, n27. The major problem with this suggestion is that Sherwood, among many others, presupposes that vv. 1-12 in Isa 58 are 'a radical reinterpretation of what fasting means' and vv. 13-14 describe 'a thoroughly traditional attitude towards the sabbath', and that compounding these passages created 'considerable conceptual discomfort' even for the original reader. The discussion below counters this very presupposition.

233 Koole, *Isaiah III/3,* 118 and 156.

as an original part of Isa 58 comes from G. Smith. He believes that the Sabbath was the only institution not affected by the 'wholesale destruction of religious forms, which took place at the overthrow of Jerusalem,' because its subsistence did not depend on the Temple and the Altar. Consequently, 'the prophet, then, enforces the Sabbath simply on account of its religious and Godward aspect.'[234] Fairly common is the taking of vv. 13-14 as complementary to the rest of the chapter, adding a cultic dimension to the ethical one. Thus, according to Sekine, vv. 6f and 9b-10a 'stellen nämlich die ideale Beziehung zu Menschen dar, und V. 13 ... die ideale Beziehung zu Gott.'[235]

As interesting as these suggestions are, they neither eliminate nor contradict the theory about a secondary addition, because they understand both parts of Isa 58 as self-contained units. If that is accepted, the following quote from Blenkinsopp would still hold true: 'There is, at any rate, no longer a concern for the humanitarian or philanthropic aspect of the Sabbath rest, comparable to the accusation of exploiting the fast days in 3b-4, and in agreement with the Deuteronomic formulation of the Sabbath command (Deut 5:12-15).'[236] To argue the opposite takes more than just showing, e.g., that there is no conflict between the social concerns of vv. 1-12 and the cultic interest in vv. 13-14. Childs' claim that the true Sabbath observance 'is fully congruent with the stipulation for the obedient response of feeding the hungry and caring for the poor'[237] is certainly correct, but does not explain why fasting, social justice, and the Sabbath appear next to each other in Isa 58. Instead of just advocating a mere compatibility of vv. 1-12 and vv. 13-14, the goal of the following discussion is to show that vv. 13-14 are an integral part of Isa 58, and that no reconciliation with the preceding verses was necessary for an ancient reader.

A promising attempt comes from Smith, who claims that 'the demand for Sabbath observance may have had a social impetus at its roots, since (according to Deut. 5:12-15) the Sabbath was intended as a day of rest from work.'[238] Barré offers one explicit link in support of this point: 'keeping the Sabbath meant granting at least temporary release from the "yoke," a concern voiced in v. 6.'[239] However, the most

---

234 George Adam Smith, *The Book of Isaiah*, new and rev. ed. (London: Hodder & Stoughton, 1927) 454.
235 Sekine, *Tritojesajanische Sammlung*, 130. Similarly Polan, *Justice*, 229.
236 Blenkinsopp, *Isaiah 56-66*, 181.
237 Childs, *Isaiah*, 481.
238 Smith, *Rhetoric*, 113.
239 Barré, "Fasting," 96.

elaborate and persuasive argument for the unity of Isa 58 comes from
Park. The reference to שׁוֹפָר in v. 1 takes him to Lev 23 and 25, where
the trumpet blast announces the Day of Atonement, the Sabbath Year,
and the Year of Jubilee. He rightly observes that

> Nach Lev 25 sind Lärmblasetag, Versöhnungstag, und Sabbatjahr bzw.
> Jobeljahr in besonderer Weise miteinander verbunden. Diese Verbindung
> zeigt die Abhängigkeit der Versöhnung der Menschen von seinem
> Verhalten zu sienen Mitmenschen. Auffällig häufig kommt die Sabbat-
> bzw. Ruhethematik in Lev 23 und 25 vor und steht dort an zentraler
> Stelle.[240]

This quotation reaffirms what the above discussion about the Sabbath
characteristics has shown, namely that one should think of the sabbath
concept as represented not only by the Sabbath day, but also by the
Sabbath year, the Year of Jubilee, and the Day of Atonement.[241] Once
these festivals are taken into consideration, the connections between Isa
58:13-14 and the rest of the chapter are manifold.

For instance, Park shows how the idea of freeing the oppressed,
breaking every yoke, and helping those without food, clothes, or
shelter in Isa 58:6, 7, and 10 closely corresponds with the requirements
of the Sabbath year and the Year of Jubilee observance in Lev 25.[242] It is
noteworthy that the Hebrew word for yoke (מוֹטָה) that comes up three
times in Isa 58 (v. 6 twice and v. 9) is used outside the Prophets only
once, namely Lev 26:13. This verse and its nearby parallel 25:55 list the
underlying principle for observing God's statutes and commandments
in general and the Sabbath year and the Year of Jubilee in particular: 'I
am the LORD your God who brought you out of the land of Egypt, to
be their slaves no more; I have broken the bars of your מוֹטָה and made
you walk erect' (26:13), and 'For to me the people of Israel are servants;
they are my servants whom I brought out from the land of Egypt: I am
the LORD your God' (25:55). As mentioned earlier, the Decalogue
passage in Deut 5 gives the same rationale for observing the Sabbath.
Another link between Isa 58:1-12 and the concept of שַׁבָּת is found in v.
6: the Hebrew adjective חָפְשִׁי ('set free', 'free') is a technical term in the
Sabbath year regulations. Out of its total 17 occurrences in the OT, חָפְשִׁי

---

240 Park, *Gerechtigkeit Israels*, 237-238.

241 For the discussion of this proposal, see 6.3.2.2 above.

242 'Darüber hinaus liegt der Hauptgrund einer solchen Anlehnung von Jes 58 und diese
     tradition ... vor allem darin, daß der Freilassung der mit Unrecht Gefesselten (V.6.9b)
     und des ethischen Verhaltens gegenüber den Armen (V.7.10a) in Jes 58 genau auf die
     wirtschaftliche und soziale Institution des priesterlichen Sabbatjahres (שׁנת שׁבתון
     Lev 25,2-7) und Jobeljahres (שׁנת היובל Lev 25,8-55) bezieht,' Park, *Gerechtigkeit Israels*,
     239.

is found ten times explicitly connected to the Sabbath year. Also the verb נגשׂ ('to oppress', 'to force to work') in v. 3 is a technical term in Deut 15:1-3 for one aspect of the Sabbath year, namely the remission of debts. The logic that connects all the above terms is the same behind Isa 58 as behind the Sabbath year or the Year of Jubilee: 'Throughout the ancient world, debt, taxes, forced labor, debt slavery, and national subjugation were described metaphorically as wearing a yoke or carrying a burden. To be liberated from these burdens was to "break or loosen the yoke" and shake it free from your shoulders.'[243]

Fishbane's exegesis of Isa 58:1-12 as haggadic establishes an important link between this text and the Pentateuchal law. He believes that vv. 1-12 are 'an *aggadic* exposition of a legal *traditum*,' namely the Day of Atonement. His supporting argument is worth quoting in full:

> [In Isa 58:1-12,] there is, in fact, an unmistakable external reference to the language used by the prophet: specifically, Isaiah makes explicit use of terms found in Lev. 16 and 23:24-32 – two biblical texts which deal with fasting and cultic-ascetic practices. In these documents it is recorded that a trumpet blast was sounded on the Day of Atonement (Lev. 23:24) and the people were required to afflict themselves (וְעִנִּיתֶם אֶת־נַפְשֹׁתֵיכֶם, 16:31 and 23:27, 32; cf. 16:29, 23:28) – so as to be purified of their sins (16:30). Moreover, during this day Aaron officially confessed all the people's sins and transgressions (כָּל־פִּשְׁעֵיהֶם לְכָל־חַטֹּאתָם, 16:21).[244]

As is often the case with a cumulative argument, its individual parts can be questioned. One can object that, besides proclaiming Yom Kippur, the sound of שׁוֹפָר was used to announce various other things, such as danger, war, etc. Also the expression 'to afflict oneself' (piel of ענה with נֶפֶשׁ as direct object) is not exclusive to the Day of Atonement, as documented by Num 30:14 and Ps 35:13. [245] Finally, the occurrence of פֶּשַׁע and חַטָּאת in both texts is not decisive, for this pair is fairly frequent in the OT.[246] However, the fact that all the three expressions are characteristic of the Day of Atonement, and that they occur together elsewhere only in Isa 58 makes Fishbane's case very strong.[247]

In addition, at least two more links between Isa 58 and Yom Kippur can be established. The first one has to do with enabling unholy people

---

243 Lowery, *Sabbath*, 49.

244 Fishbane, *Interpretation*, 305-306.

245 Apart from these two references, this phrase occurs five times in connection with the Day of Atonement (Lev 16:29, 31; 23:27, 32; Num 29:7) and twice in Isa 58 (vv. 3 and 5).

246 It occurs twice in Lev 16 and twenty-one times elsewhere.

247 Park in his discussion of Lev 23 and 25 also observes that 'die bisher genannten Themen – den Schofar zu blassen, keinerlei Arbeit zu tun, sich selbst zu demütigen und die Sabbatthematik – finden sich in Jes 58,' Park, *Gerechtigkeit Israels*, 238.

to draw near to the holy God on the Day of Atonement. The
introduction to Lev 16 (vv. 1-2) is significant:

> The LORD spoke to Moses after the death of the two sons of Aaron, when
> they drew near before the LORD (בְּקָרְבָתָם לִפְנֵי־יְהוָה) and died. The
> LORD said to Moses: Tell your brother Aaron not to come just at any time
> into the sanctuary inside the curtain before the mercy seat that is upon the
> ark, or he will die.

Detailed instructions for sacrifices and purification follow in order to
delineate what is necessary when a High Priest, as a representative of
the whole people, is to draw near before the holy God. The parallel
with Isa 58 is tangible: here the people 'delight to draw near to God
(קִרְבַת אֱלֹהִים)' (v. 2), and the role of the prophet is to change this
approaching from being ineffective (v. 3a and 4b), even offensive to
God (v. 5), into being efficacious (vv. 8-9a, 10b-12, 14) and pleasing to
him (v. 6a). The prophet carries out this task in the two interwoven
stages: announcing to people their פֶּשַׁע and חַטָּאת, and giving them the
instructions for purification.[248] As shown above, he elaborates on the
Sabbath year, the Year of Jubilee, and the Day of Atonement, in order to
bring out the ethical dimension of what is essentially a cultic issue. In
the words of Lowery, 'when Israel exercises jubilee self-restraint for the
sake of the poor and the well-being of the land, they purify and prepare
themselves. In these acts of mercy and justice, Israel encounters God.'[249]

The second additional link is the command to observe שַׁבָּת. Both
chapters in Leviticus demand not only that the people would afflict
themselves (וְעִנִּיתֶם אֶת־נַפְשֹׁתֵיכֶם), but also that they would keep
שַׁבַּת שַׁבָּתוֹן – a sabbath of complete rest (Lev 16:31 and 23:32). Fishbane
misses the connection with Isa 58 because he agrees with Kosmala that
vv. 13-14 are a later addition. Surprisingly, it is Kosmala who
(somewhat ambiguously) makes the link between Yom Kippur and Isa
58:13-14; he states that because the Sabbath observance in v. 13 is
characterized by the expressions עֲשׂוֹת חֲפָצֶיךָ and מִמְּצוֹא חֶפְצְךָ, it
echoes 'the only other day on which "no work at all" was to be done,'
namely Yom Kippur.[250] Herbert also allows for the influence of the Yom
Kippur text in Lev. 16 on Isa 58: 'the association of "sabbath" with self-

---

248 To fully appreciate the scope and the interwovenness of these two stages, one needs
     to include ch. 59 as well. For the connection between 58 and 59, see 6.8.1 below.

249 Lowery, *Sabbath*, 72.

250 Kosmala, "Isaiah 58," 80. Of course, Kosmala uses this connection as a trigger for
     another editorial activity: 'It is therefore not surprising that the editor of Is. 58 saw
     that something is missing in the context of the discourse on the fast; the injunction
     for the Sabbath was, therefore, inserted in verse 3b.'

mortification in Lev. 16:31 may account for the inclusion of verses 13-14.'[251]

These two connections further strengthen Fishbane's theory that 'the Pentateuchal legal materials dealing with the rules and regulations of the Day of Atonement ... serve as the linguistic and ideological matrix for their inversion and reapplication in Isaiah's discourse.'[252] He follows with the word of caution not to understand Isa 58:1-12 as antinomian. This warning, however, is unnecessary; if one includes the Sabbath regulations of v. 13, Isa 58 is fully compatible with the ideological matrix provided by the Pentateuchal law. In fact, Fishbane's conclusion with regard to fasting in Isa 58:1-12 that 'what the prophet ultimately seeks to effect is a social-spiritual extension of an authoritative religious practice'[253] should be extended to the Sabbath as well.

One more link is worth mentioning. The above discussion showed a close correspondence between the protases in Isa 58 (vv. 6-7, 9b-10a, 13) and the Sabbath, the Day of Atonement, the Sabbath year and the Year of Jubilee regulations in Lev 16, 23 and 25. Analogically, there is also a strong parallel between the apodoses of Isa 58 (vv. 8-9a, 10b-12, and 14)[254] and Lev 26:3-9: both passages warrant an abundance of food and prosperity (Isa 58:8a, 10b, 11b, 14b[255] and Lev 26:4-5, 9-10), peace and security (Isa 58:8b, 12, 14b[256] and Lev 26:6-8), and an intimate relationship with YHWH (Isa 58:8b, 9, 11a, 14a and Lev 26:11-12).

To sum up the above discussion, if Isa 58:1-12 is read through the lens of the Sabbath, the Sabbatical year, the Year of Jubilee, and the Day of Atonement regulations in Leviticus, the sabbath concept turns out to be all-encompassing in Isa 58, and vv. 13-14 then come naturally as the chapter's grand finale.

---

251 Arthur Sumner Herbert, *The Book of the Prophet Isaiah, Chapters 40-66* (Cambridge Bible Commentary; Cambridge: Cambridge University Press, 1975) 144.

252 Fishbane, *Interpretation*, 305.

253 Fishbane, *Interpretation*, 305.

254 There is an interesting link between the apodoses in v. 14 and v. 11: while the phrase וְהִרְכַּבְתִּיךָ עַל־בָּמֳתֵי אָרֶץ almost certainly reflects Deut 32:13, the expression וְנָחֲךָ יְהוָה is very likely based on the preceding verse 12 of the Deuteronomy poem.

255 For the possibility that בָּמֳתֵי אָרֶץ refers to the fruitfulness of the land, see the LXX rendering τὰ ἀγαθὰ τῆς γῆς and Brongers, "Jes 58:13-14."

256 According to Crenshaw the metaphors in v. 14 'imply undisturbed possession of the land,' Crenshaw, "WᵉDOREK 'AL-BAMOTE 'ARETZ," 50-51. Brongers also allows for a security/military interpretation of this text – see Brongers, "Jes 58:13-14," 215. See the above discussion in 6.5.12.

6.7. Translation of Isa 58

[1] Shout out, do not hold back!
Lift up your voice like a trumpet!
Announce to my people their rebellion,
to the house of Jacob their sins.

[2] To be sure, me they seek daily,
desiring to know my plans,
as if they were a nation that practised righteousness
        and did not forsake the ordinance of their God;
they wish for my salvific judgments,
they desire the nearness of God.
[3] "Why do we fast, but you do not see?
Why afflict ourselves, but you do not notice?"
Look, on your fast day, you pursue your own desire,
        and so spur on all who toil for you.
[4] Look, your fasting results in quarrelling, fighting
        and striking with a wicked fist.
Fasting as you do today will not result in your voice being heard on
high.

[5] Should the fast that I choose be like this:
        a day to afflict oneself,
        to bow down the head like a bulrush,
        and to lie in sackcloth and ashes?
Will you call this a fast,
        a day acceptable to the LORD?
[6] Is not this the fast that I choose:
        to loose the bonds of injustice,
        to undo the thongs of the yoke,
        to let the oppressed go free,
        and to break every yoke?
[7] Is it not to share your bread with the hungry,
        and bring the homeless poor into your house;
        when you see the naked, to clothe him,
        and not to hide yourself from your own kin?

[8] Then your light shall break forth like the dawn,
    and your healing shall spring up quickly;
    your salvation shall go before you,
    the glory of the LORD shall gather you in.
[9] Then you shall call, and the LORD will answer;
you shall cry for help, and he will say, Here I am.

If you remove the yoke from among you,
    the pointing of the finger, the speaking of evil,
[10] if you extend yourself to the hungry
    and satisfy the needs of the afflicted,
then your light shall rise in the darkness
    and your gloom be like the noonday.
[11]   and the LORD will guide you continually,
    and satisfy your needs in parched places,
    and make your bones strong;
    and you shall be like a watered garden,
        like a spring of water,
            whose waters never fail.
[12] From you the ancient ruins shall be rebuilt,
you shall reestablish the foundations of old;
you shall be called 'Breach-mender',[257]
    'Restorer of the [right] ways for living'.

[13] If you avert your foot from [desecrating] the sabbath,
    from going after your own desires on my holy day;
if you call the sabbath a delight and the holy day of the LORD
honorable;
if you honor it [by refraining] from carrying on your own ways,
    from pursuing your own desire and dealings;
[14] then you shall take delight in the LORD,
    and I will make you ride upon the heights of the Land;
    I will feed you with the heritage of your ancestor Jacob,

for the mouth of the LORD has spoken!

---

257 Expression borrowed from NJB.

6.8. Isa 58 and Related Passages in TI

The main purpose of demonstrating the unity of Isa 58 was to lay a
foundation for answering the question as formulated by Park: 'In
welchem Zusammenhang stehen unsere Themen Kultus, soziale
Gerechtigkeit, Halten des Sabbats und Eschatologie nun hier in Jes 58
besonders für das Gottesvolk Israel?'[258] If Isa 58 is assessed
independently of the rest of TI, one could simply conclude that 'im text
selbst sind die Forderungen nach sozialer Gerechtigkeit und nach dem
Halten des Sabbats Bedingungen für das Heil.'[259] However, all the
themes of Isa 58 are addressed in other parts of TI as well. Besides
58:13, the Sabbath is mentioned also at the beginning and at the end of
TI (56:2-6, and 66:23) – a prominent placement that shows the
significance of the Sabbath concept in the book. Another important
theme, justice, opens the book (56:1), and occurs in almost every
chapter of TI, most notably in 59. Finally, the most outstanding theme,
eschatology, is expressed in various forms and descriptions throughout
the whole TI. To get a more complete picture how these themes
function in TI, it is beneficial to compare Isa 58 with those passages that
juxtapose at least two of them. Such texts are found in Isa 59, 56, 61,
and 66.

6.8.1. Isa 58 and 59

While the unity of Isa 58 and 59 is still far from being generally
accepted, recent scholarship recognizes more and more connections
between these two chapters.[260] Smith offers probably the most
comprehensive list of features shared by 58 and 59.[261] For the purposes
of this chapter, the most important lexical one is that 'the roots צדק and
שפט function throughout the poem as keywords expressing one of the
principal themes of the poem, the relationship between the people's
social and communal wrongdoing and the delay of God's salvation (cf.
56:1).'[262] As for the structural unity, Smith suggests that vv. 58:1b and

---

258 Park, *Gerechtigkeit Israels*, 208.
259 Park, *Gerechtigkeit Israels*, 205.
260 For instance, Blenkinsopp observes: 'In contrast to what precedes and follows, chs.
     58-59 have a consistency of subject mater, approach, and tone that sets them apart as
     a distinct section,' Blenkinsopp, *Isaiah 56-66*, 176.
261 See Smith, *Rhetoric*, 99-101.
262 Smith, *Rhetoric*, 101.

59:20 create an envelope which summarizes the purpose of the unit: to announce to the people of Jacob their transgressions so that YHWH can come as Redeemer for those who repent. Several themes that run through both chapters serve this purpose; while for Koenen it is 'das Problem der Heilsverzögerung' that closely connects Isa 58 and 59,[263] for Park the connection is 'durch das einheitliche Thema von Recht und Gerechtigkeit für die Unterschicht und die Unterdrücken.'[264] At the same time, Park follows Smith and others who agree that 'Jes 59,1f. zeigt eine konkrete theologische Antwort auf die Frage, die in 58,3 gestellt wurde.'[265]

Ch. 59 not only reinforces the message of ch. 58, but significantly develops it. Vv. 9-15a describe how people understood, or rather were supposed to understand, the prophet's message: because their transgressions before YHWH are many (v. 12a), he takes no notice of their fasting. Cult disappears altogether from the picture, and the theme of מִשְׁפָּט וּצְדָקָה returns to the fore. Another important development is found in vv. 15b-20, namely an assurance that 'Yahweh is not oblivious to the situation among the people, but will certainly intervene and manifest himself to them.'[266] These verses rebut the impression of ch. 58 that the realization of YHWH's מִשְׁפָּטִי־צֶדֶק depends on people's מִשְׁפָּט וּצְדָקָה. The opposite is the case – the lack of אֱמֶת and מִשְׁפָּט (v. 15) and someone who would intervene (מַפְגִּיעַ, v. 16) prompts YHWH to take decisive action. Equipped with his own צְדָקָה and יְשׁוּעָה, but also with נָקָם and קִנְאָה, he is coming to establish מִשְׁפָּט on the earth. This intervention means different things to different entities: redemption to Zion (v. 20), and rendering requital to the rest of the earth (vv. 18-19) so it would fear YHWH.[267] The message so far is not different from DI. However, the delineation of the entities is not only geographical, but also spiritual: YHWH comes with wrath and requital to his adversaries and enemies, but as Redeemer to those in Jacob who turn from transgressions. The parallelism in v. 20 means either reduction or redefinition of what the term Zion represents: it says either that only those from Zion who repent will be redeemed, or that

---

263 Koenen, *Ethik und Eschatologie*, 101.

264 Park, *Gerechtigkeit Israels*, 251.

265 Park, *Gerechtigkeit Israels*, 250.

266 Smith, *Rhetoric*, 123.

267 Two notes about the obscure v. 18: First, the expression גְּמוּל שַׁלֵּם לְ is not necessarily negative, as Prov 19:17 testifies. It rather means 'rendering requital', as the phrase כְּעַל גְּמֻלוֹת כְּעַל יְשַׁלֵּם implies. Second, אִיִּים is a merismus for all the earth, as מִמַּעֲרָב and מִמִּזְרַח־שֶׁמֶשׁ in the following verse confirm.

the new, redeemed Zion consists of those in Jacob who repent.[268] Either way, ch. 58 shows that the prophet's (and YHWH's) aspiration is to amalgamate the physical and the spiritual Zion, so *all* in Jacob would be redeemed.

This brief discussion suggests that chs. 58 and 59 complement and complete each other, resulting in a coherent message.

6.8.2. Isa 58 and 56:1-8

The parallel between Isa 58 and Isa 56:1-8 prompted Smith to suggest that the author of the poem 58:1-59:20 responds to the people's complaint against God in 58:3a by 'reinterpreting the preaching of TI (60:1-63:6) in the light of the criteria set out in 56:1-8.'[269] Even though the interdependence of these passages is open to question, the fact is that ethics, cult and eschatology are inseparably interwoven and convey the same (soteriological) idea in chs. 58 and 56:

— In the introductory verses of ch. 56, namely vv. 1-2,[270] the exhortation to proper ethical conduct (keeping מִשְׁפָּט, doing צְדָקָה and refraining from doing all evil) and cultic conduct (keeping שַׁבָּת from profaning it) is stimulated by YHWH's forthcoming יְשׁוּעָה and צְדָקָה.[271] This connection is exegetically developed in the rest of the passage. Even though the form of ch. 58 is rather different, the relations between these key concepts are essentially the same.

---

268 A possible parallel of such a redefined Zion can be found in Isa 1:27, where, as Williamson believes, Zion 'stands as a more or less abstract concept for the ideal people of God,' Williamson, *Isaiah 1-27*, 155. It may even be suggested that it is to this kind of Zion that Isa 60:1f speaks. E.g., Oswalt believes that this material 'is addressed to the faithful in Israel,' Oswalt, *Isaiah 40-66*, 537. In that case, the supposition that Isa 58 turns the unconditional promises of Isa 60 into conditional would be false. Then, in the present setting, 60:1f would read as a description of the consequences that follow from 58-59 for Zion that consist of שָׁבֵי פֶשַׁע בְּיַעֲקֹב (59:20). The limitations of the present thesis does not allow for the proper evaluation of this proposal.

269 Smith, *Rhetoric*, 101.

270 For supporting arguments to read vv. 1-2 as an introduction, see, e.g., Smith, *Rhetoric*, 50f.

271 Schramm correctly argues that 'the conjunction כִּי that begins the second half of v. 1 is not to be understood in a conditional but rather in a causative sense. The community is commanded to keep justice and practice righteousness because (i.e., in light of the fact that) קְרוּבָה יְשׁוּעָתִי לָבוֹא וְצִדְקָתִי לְהִגָּלוֹת,' Schramm, *Opponents*, 119.

— Cult, ethics and eschatology appear together again in 56:4-5. The expression וּבָחֲרוּ בַּאֲשֶׁר חָפָצְתִּי in v. 4 almost certainly refers to ethics rather than cult: YHWH delights (חפץ) in steadfast love, justice, and righteousness (Jer 9:23 and Mic 7:18), and the things that please (חפץ) him are obedience and compliance, steadfast love and knowledge of him, rather than sacrifices and offerings (1 Sam 15:22 and Hos 6:6). In Isa 58:3 and 13, people are warned not to follow their own חֵפֶץ, for, according to 66:4, to choose what does not please YHWH is evil. As for the cult, according to Park, 'insbesondere wird auch in Jes 56, wie in Jes 58,13f., die Sabbatobservanz zu einer zentralen Bedingung für die Teilhabe am Heil gemacht.'[272]

— Vv. 6-7 are a variation on the same theme. While the expression בִּבְרִיתִי מַחֲזִיקִים ('the ones who hold fast to my covenant', exclusive to vv. 4 and 6) includes both ethics and cult, the overall emphasis of this passage is on cult. For the purposes of the main thesis, it is significant that one of the eschatological realities in v. 7 is YHWH's acceptance (לְרָצוֹן) of burnt offerings (עֹלָה) and sacrifices (זֶבַח) from all who meet the cultic and ethical criteria of v. 6 – a reversal of Jer 6:20b, where YHWH claims: 'Your burnt offerings (עֹלָה) are not acceptable (לֹא לְרָצוֹן), nor are your sacrifices (זֶבַח) pleasing to me.' In addition, Schramm believes that Isa 56:7 'is evidently to be seen as a reversal of the prophecy of Isa. 1.15.'[273]

— Smith is correct that 'as 56:1 plays on the ethical and soterio-logical uses of צדקה, so 58:1-59:20 plays on the ethical and soteriological significance of משפט and צדקה in order to underline the relationship between ethics and salvation.'[274] Polan is even more specific:

> The two uses of צדקה in 56:1a,1b serve as a guide for understanding the twofold use of the word in 56:1-59:20: the call to practice righteousness in 56:1 displays both the exercise of righteousness (57:1) and its lack (57:12; 58,2; 59:4,9,14); the announcement of God's approaching deliverance in 56:1b is explained in the imagery of both the new exodus of 58:8 and the Divine Warrior (59:16,17).[275]

---

272 Park, *Gerechtigkeit Israels*, 221.
273 Schramm, *Opponents*, 117 n3.
274 Smith, *Rhetoric*, 102.
275 Polan, *Justice*, 31.

— As in Isa 58, specific words and phrases in 56:1-8 reveal a close connection with the legal material in the Pentateuch, especially the Sabbath passage in Exod 31:12-17.[276] In both chapters, the text revolves around the sabbath concept.[277]

— Proper ethical and cultic conduct results in both passages in the realization of eschatology, confirmed by a new name (56:5 and 58:12).

6.8.3. Isa 58 and 61

Koenen believes that the instructions in Isa 58:1 contradict the instructions in Isa 61:1-4: 'Hier ergeht der Befehl, dem Volk seine Sünde zu verkünden (קרא), dort schickt Jahwe jemanden zu den Trauernden, um ihnen die Heilsbotschaft zu verkünden (קרא).'[278] However, as Park rightly observes, Isa 58:3-12 and 59:1-15a (the text that Koenen considers to be a unity, 'Grundschicht des Tritojesajas'), address both themes: the sins of the people *as well as* their salvation. As shown by the analysis of vv. 13-14 above, ch. 58 and 61:1-4 'im Sinne des Interesses für die sozial Schwächere mit dem Jobel- und Sabbatjahr verknüpft ist.'[279]

Instead of contradiction, it is therefore more fitting to talk with Smith and Lau about reinterpretation of Isa 61 in 58. Lau compares the phrase יוֹם רָצוֹן לַיהוָה in 58:5cb with 61:2aA, believing that

> der Autor von Jes 58* zitiert wörtlich die Wendung aus TrJes 61,2, was die Erwähnung von לַיהוָה in der Jahwerede erklärt. Er ersetzt dabei das ihm wegen seiner eschatologischen Erwartung einer schnellen Wandlung der Verhältnisse wahrscheinlich unliebsame "Jahr" durch יוֹם und macht damit unzweifelhaft deutlich, daß er die Wendung auf den "Tag Jahwes" bezogen wissen will.

---

276 As persuasively demonstrated by Roy D. Wells, "'Isaiah' as an Exponent of Torah: Isaiah 56:1-8," in *New Visions of Isaiah*, ed. Roy F. Melugin and Marvin A. Sweeney (JSOTSup 214; Sheffield Academic Press, 1996) 140-155. For the same conclusion, see also Sommer, *Allusion*, 150.

277 Fishbane believes that TI 'echoes the contemporary ideology of the axial position of the Sabbath – an ideology which ... saw in the desecration of the Sabbath the principal reason for Judea's destruction , and, correspondingly, believed its reconsecration to be vital,' Fishbane, *Interpretation*, 479.

278 Koenen, *Ethik und Eschatologie*, 95.

279 Park, *Gerechtigkeit Israels*, 215.

When comparing the eschatological messages of the two chapters and taking into consideration one more related text, namely Isa 49:8f, Lau sees another and more important difference. According to him, in Isa 58

> der (allerdings auch nur scheinbar) ambivalente Charakter der Vorlage wird in Anlehnung an Jes 49,8 in Heilsansage abgeändert, vgl. V.8ff. Mit dieser Heilsansage, die auch in Jes 49,8 eine Erhörung der Gebete der Gemeinde mit einschließt, warden – im Unterschied zu Jes 49,9, wo Jahwe lediglich zur Flucht auffordert – konkrete Barmherzigkeitsforderungen und darüber hinaus sozialethische Vorhaben verknüpft.

Lau concludes that 'während in den Vorlagen schon durch die Verkündigung veränderte Verhältnisse entstehen, wird in Jes 58 alles vom Handeln der Gemeinde und Jahwes erwartet.'[280] However, if texts with similar vocabulary and themes convey different messages, one cannot simply assume that they reflect different views. In this case, the difference is not of eschatological outlook, but merely of focus: Isa 49:8bf describes the glorious purpose for which YHWH saved his people בְּעֵת רָצוֹן, Isa 61 describes the characteristics of שְׁנַת רָצוֹן לַיהוָה that fully coincide with the purpose in ch. 49, and Isa 58 teaches the people in the words of 61 and 49 what יוֹם רָצוֹן לַיהוָה is really about, so they can participate in that glorious era.[281] All three texts are in harmony, representing the same view of eschatology.

6.8.4. Isa 58 and 66:1-4

The text in Isa 66:1-4 is often interpreted as a denunciation of temple and sacrifices.[282] This reading is encouraged by, e.g., NRSV which assumes כ comparationis in v. 3: 'Whoever slaughters an ox is like one who kills a human being, …' However, as already observed by Delitzsch, if this was the meaning of the passage, the prophet would not only contradict himself (compare, e.g., 66:6 and 20f, 56:4-7, and 60:7 and 13), but also other prophets, 'such as Ezekiel and Zechariah, and the spirit of the Old Testament generally, in which the statement, that whoever slaughters a sacrificial animal in the new Jerusalem will be as bad as murderer, has no parallel, and is in fact absolutely impossible.'[283]

---

280 Lau, *Schriftgelehrte Prophetie*, 246.
281 As Park correctly comments on Isa 58: 'Zwar ist die Aufforderung, Gerechtigkeit zu üben eine Bedingung für die Teilhabe am Heil, aber das heißt nicht, daß solches menschliche Tun eine Voraussetzung für das eschatologische Kommen Jhwhs ist,' Park, *Gerechtigkeit Israels*, 267.
282 For an extensive list of scholars who adhere this view, see Koole, *Isaiah III/3*, 477.
283 Delitzsch, *Prophecies of Isaiah*, 2.494.

NRSV takes its hint from 1QIsaᵃ, which adds the comparative particle before the second part of the first colon in v. 3aA (כמכה איש), or from LXX using a particle of comparison ὡς for the rest of the pairs of participles, or from V that uses *quasi qui* for each of the pairs in v. 3. As compelling as this evidence seems, it cannot be used cumulatively. While V is consistent in its understanding of the pairs of participles as comparatives, the fact that 1QIsaᵃ places כ *comparationis* between the first pair only is rather striking. Furthermore, LXX renders this first pair altogether differently: it specifies the agent of the action as ὁ ἄνομος, meaning the lawless person violating primarily *moral* standards.[284] This specification turns the focus from the temple and sacrifices to the character or attitudes of persons involved: on one side, there are the humble and contrite in spirit who tremble at God's word (v. 2b), on the other those who have chosen their own ways and in their abominations take delight, those who did what was evil in God's sight and chose what did not please him (vv. 3b and 4b). Based on the parallel with 1 Kgs 8:27f, Blenkinsopp correctly comments that 'support of the temple is consistent with disavowal of certain attitudes to temple worship or with rejection of its current functionaries.'[285] It may be concluded that, just as Isa 1:11-15, v. 3a describes those who mix legitimate rituals with illegitimate behaviour, thus turning the former into abominations. [286] This understanding of the text would then be fully in accord with the spirit of the Old Testament: 'When one will not listen to the law, even one's prayers are an abomination' (Prov 28:9), while the sacrifices of those who choose the things that please God will be accepted on his altar (Isa 56:4 and 7).[287]

An objection can be raised that, unlike the other passages above, Isa 66:3 does not refer to ethics, but only to cultic malpractices. Thus, e.g., Westermann believes that while the first member of each pair in v. 3a concerns 'the regular sacrifices to Yahweh', the second describes the practice of 'loathsome animal cults', such as sacrificing humans, dogs,

---

284 See the definition of ἄνομος in BDAG 685.

285 Joseph Blenkinsopp, "A Jewish Sect of the Persian Period," *CBQ* 52 (1990) 5-20: 9.

286 This reading is syntactically justified by the suggestion of Rofé to understand the first part of each expression in v. 3a as subject and the second as predicate and object, e.g., 'those who are slaughtering an ox are striking a man,' etc. See A. Rofé, "Isaiah 66.1-4: Judean Sects in the Persian Period as Viewed by Trito-Isaiah," in *Biblical and Related Studies Presented to Samuel Iwry*, ed. Ann Kort and Scott Morschauser (Winona Lake, IN: Eisenbrauns, 1985) 208-209.

287 Notice the identical vocabulary:

56:4 וּבָחֲרוּ בַּאֲשֶׁר חָפָצְתִּי

66:4 וּבַאֲשֶׁר לֹא־חָפַצְתִּי בָּחָרוּ

or swine.[288]   However, Rofé rightly insists that interpreting the expression מַכֵּה־אִישׁ in v. 3aA as a reference to human sacrifices is without support.[289] Just as used and developed in 58:4, the hiphil of the verb נכה predominantly means 'to strike, smite', referring to acts of physical violence, even to the point of death. Moreover, because of the surrounding participles in v. 3a (שׁוֹחֵט, זוֹבֵחַ, and עֹרֵף), מַכֵּה here very likely refers to striking with a fatal outcome, meaning 'to kill'.[290] In fact, the exact phrase מַכֵּה אִישׁ is used in the Law concerning murder in Exod 21:12.   While the rest of the participle pairs in v. 3a may be a polemic against syncretism,[291] v. 3aA criticizes mixing YHWH's cult with ethical misconduct, probably manslaughter.[292] Dim seems to be correct that the most important thing in Isa 66:1-4 is 'a humble obedience to YHWH's word, manifested in his word and preferences (vv. 2b & 4), an obedience that would then flow into temple building (vv. 1-2a) and sacrifices (v. 3ab). It is then that authentic worship would inspire right living.'[293] Again, the theology of this passage concurs with the one of Isa 58.

6.9. Conclusion

As the survey above shows, the interconnectedness of the themes as well as the message that results from Isa 58 is not essentially different

---

288 Westermann, *Isaiah 40-66*, 414.

289 Rofé, "Isaiah 66," 211.

290 Contra Rofé, who sees no support for rendering the hiphil of נכה here as 'murder'. While it is rendered as 'striking' in the majority of its occurrences, texts like Isa 37:36-38 demonstrate that the hiphil of נכה can also stand for 'killing'.

291 Just as in the case of מַכֵּה־אִישׁ, it is far from certain that the other second members of each pair in v. 3 refer to cultic malpractices: there is no support in the OT of equating 'breaking dog's neck' (עֹרֵף כֶּלֶב) with the sacrifice of dogs, דַּם־חֲזִיר may require an emendation (see BHS apparatus) that would move the focus from illegitimate sacrifices to unclean food (חֹמֵד־חֲזִיר, 'one who enjoys a swine'), and the meaning of מַזְכִּיר אָוֶן is obscure, not excluding the ethical interpretation of this phrase. For more details, see, e.g., Emmanuel Uchenna Dim, *The Eschatological Implications of Isa. 65 and 66 as the Conclusion of the Book of Isaiah* (Bible in History 3; Bern, Oxford: Peter Lang, 2005) esp. 128-140.

292 Koole also comes to this conclusion. He even suggests that the second participle pair in 3aA about breaking a dog's neck may also refer to ethical misconduct, and that the words about the people choosing their own ways in v. 3bA are to be understood as 'the everyday wicked and unjust attitude to life,' referring back to v. 3aA. For more details, see Koole, *Isaiah III/3*, 477-480.

293 Dim, *Eschatological Implications*, 139.

from, let alone in contradiction to, the similar passages in TI.[294] Even the frequent opinion that this chapter has turned some of the previously unconditional promises into conditional ones is put to rest when the apodoses in Isa 58 are viewed as the (logical) consequences of their protases.[295] Williamson's claim that to speak about a promise in Isa 58:14 'seems almost to be a misnomer' because 'it is simply a case of stating that the conclusion will follow from the premise,'[296] can be extended to all the apodoses in Isa 58.

As far as cult and ethics are concerned, the prophet in Isa 58 emphasizes the apparently neglected ethical dimension of fasting and the Sabbath. This he does not do at the expense of, but alongside their cultic dimension. Williamson aptly summarizes the need for such a message:

> Just as ceremony can easily degenerate into a purely personal and self-satisfying activity of the ghetto, so the practice of ethics can become an independent goal in itself, divorced from its biblical roots in a proper relationship with God. Neither is correct, according to this chapter. Rather, the point is to establish both on a proper footing.[297]

Metaphorically speaking, ethics and cult in Isa 58 are two sides of the same coin. The ethics side lists the coin's value, reading משפט וצדקה. The cultic side gives the coin its validity and (being a true Hebrew coin) instead of image, it simply reads ליהוה. Isaiah 59 makes clear that this coin cannot buy salvation; God saves for his own sake. The people, however, can obtain a very precious commodity for it – communion with YHWH, eschatology realized.

---

294 Lau correctly comments that in Isa 58, 'der Autor verknüpft unterschiedliche Heilstraditionen zu einem eschatologischen Konglomerat, so daß in der Auseinandersetzung mit dem Fasten der Gemeinde weder der Bezug auf den "neuen Exodus" DtJes' noch auf den Epiphaniegedanken TrJes' überraschen muß,' Lau, *Schriftgelehrte Prophetie*, 253.

295 See the note about Isa 60:1f above.

296 H. G. M. Williamson, "Promises, Promises! Some Exegetical Reflections on Isaiah 58," *Word and World* 19 (1999) 153-160: 159. The following general statement of Gammie is certainly true about the apodoses of Isa 58: 'The biblical focus is never on abstract causality but rather on divine intentionality in response to and in the light of human deeds,' Gammie, *Holiness*, 94.

297 Williamson, "Promises," 158.

Conclusion

As discussed in Chapter 1 (esp. 1.4.1), the fact that the pre-exilic and post-exilic prophets spoke very differently about the cult of ancient Israel resulted in various theories and stereotypes about the role of cult and ethics in the Prophets. Scholars have used examples like the mentioning of the Sabbath in the context of Isa 1:10-17 in comparison to Isa 58 to contrast the antagonistic treatment of cult in the prophets of the monarchy with its positive handling in the prophets of the Second Temple period. Based on the findings of Chapters 4-6, this brief conclusion suggests an answer to why the role of cult and ethics seems to differ in each part of the book of Isaiah, and proposes further applications of the present thesis.

First, the close examination of Isa 1:10-17, 43:22-28 and 58 has revealed that these prophetic oracles very likely assumed the same conception of rituals, impurity, holiness, and cult in general. These (unspoken) assumptions were as follows:

— The main purpose of certain rituals is to attract and maintain YHWH's presence among the people.

— Because YHWH is holy, his presence requires purity.

— There is an impurity that no ritual can remove, caused by such grievous misbehaviour as idolatry, murder, or adultery.

— This 'moral impurity' defiles not only the sinner, but also the land and the Temple. Unless blotted away by YHWH (forgiveness), it results in separation from YHWH, death, and expulsion from the land (exile). It is, therefore, the very opposite of the rituals above, reversing what they produce.

— If these cultic concepts are mixed, moral impurity turns the rituals into an abomination.

— The only thing people can do for cult to become effective is to eliminate every source of moral impurity and hope for YHWH's forgiveness.

Second, the role of cult and ethics in the examined passages differs with regard to the desired outcome not in spite of but because of the same cultic assumptions. Its fluctuation just demonstrates 'the fact that the mission of the prophet is dependent on the conditions of time and space.'[1] As discussed in 4.2, 5.2, and 6.2, these conditions were radically different in each case, especially when it comes to cult:

— In Isa 1:10-17, the people live in their land and worship in the Temple. However, their behaviour keeps polluting them, the land, and the Temple with moral impurity to the point that it becomes intolerable for YHWH and he is about to stop forgiving them (the dawn of doom). Because of this impurity, the rituals designed to attract and maintain YHWH's presence are counter-productive. The only way the people can possibly prevent, or at least delay the doom is to practise ethics so as not to increase this impurity. These seem to be the reasons for the negative role of cult and the positive role of ethics in Isa 1:10-17.

— In Isa 43:22-28, the people are in exile and the Temple is in ruins. YHWH is about to forgive their sins and deliver his people from the oppression (the dawn of deliverance). When the people's cultic status and ethical behaviour are considered, it becomes obvious that nothing that the people are or do can contribute to their rescue. YHWH's acting solely for his own sake turns out to be the only solution and good news for Israel. In Isa 43:22-28 account of deliverance, cult and ethics play a neutral role.

— In Isa 58, the purified people are back in the purified land, rebuilding their religious and social life. The conditions of time and space are right for YHWH to live in the midst of his people for ever (the dawn of eschatology). YHWH's presence remains the act of grace, for it was he who granted these conditions and chose to abide among these people in this land. However, his presence also creates conditions for the people and the land: the only way to live with the Holy One is to remain pure, for holiness and impurity do not mix. This "God-with-us" element accounts for the positive role of ethics as well as of cult in Isa 58.

Thus the role of cult throughout the book of Isaiah alternates between negative, neutral, and positive, depending on certain conditions of the people and the land. These conditions were essentially cultic, just like

---

1   Jensen, *Ethical Dimensions*, 159. According to him, the reason for such a different place of cult in the post-exilic oracles was that 'those who had returned from exile needed a focus and an identity, and in urging the rebuilding the Temple, Haggai and Zechariah were helping to make sure that focus would be religious and in the line of the traditional faith.'

the perspective from which the authors of the prophetic oracles evaluated them (*sub specie sanctitatis Dei*). The underlying assumptions of this perspective seem to be the ones listed above.

Finally, as shown in Part I, these assumptions result from cultic conceptions of (im)purity, holiness, or the land that are compatible with their definition in Priestly literature. Although cultic in nature, their value can be severely affected by the immoral behaviour of the people. To reduce the detriment caused by modern (western) categories when applied to the religion of ancient Israel, it would be more appropriate to view this interdependence as the ethical dimension of cult. The present thesis explored and confirmed the existence of this dimension in the book of Isaiah. On its own, cult seems to play a positive role throughout the book, gaining in importance in the context of eschatology.[2] When the focus is on its ethical dimension, the book of Isaiah appears to be no different from the other prophetic literature and the rest of the OT in which, as Koole maintains, 'the cult has every right to exist, provided that it goes with the right ethos. Hence [Isa] 1:11-15 is followed by vv. 16ff., Amos 5:21-23 by v. 24, Mic. 6:6f. by v. 8 and [...] Zech. 7:1-7 by vv. 8ff.; cf. also Ps. 51:19 with v. 21.'[3] Just as in the analysed Isaianic texts, the ethical dimension of cult transpires in these and other cult-critical passages, enabling us to understand them from cultic perspective. By comparing Isa 58 with selected non-Isaianic OT texts, Appendix 2 only briefly illustrates how this understanding of a cult-critical passage fits into the general picture of cult in the OT, augmenting its ethical dimension. A thorough study of this kind, however, would require a separate monograph.

---

2   See, e.g., 19:19; 27:13; 56:7; 60:7; 66:20.
3   Koole, *Isaiah III/3*, 135-136.

Appendix 1: Isa 1:10-17 and Priestly Literature

The purpose of this appendix is to observe possible literary and linguistic relations between Isa 1:10-17 and the two priestly schools, P and H. Two columns of the chart below list some of the characteristics of P and H detected by Knohl in *The Sanctuary of Silence* and by Milgrom in his commentary on Leviticus, in the chart referred to as K and M respectively, followed by page references. Since, according to Knohl, the style of P radically changes after the revelation of the name of YHWH to Moses in Exod 7, only the characteristics of P after this event are considered. Furthermore, only those characteristics are listed whose presence, or at least some resemblance, can be attested in Isa 1:10-17. Each characteristic of P has its H counterpart listed in the same line, followed by an indication '-' if unattested or '✓' and examples if attested in Isa 1:10-17. Arguments in defence of a particular understanding of these examples can be found throughout Chapter 4. Additional discussion of some of the more questionable relations between Isa 1:10-17 and the Priestly literature follows the chart.

#	Characteristic of P	Isa 1: 10-17	Characteristic of H	Isa 1:10-17
1	אלהים is never juxtaposed to יהוה and never used as name for God (K 124-125)	-	אלהים used in posses. construct. or as a noun after a depend. word (K 168-169)	✓ v. 10: דְּבַר־יְהֹוָה, תּוֹרַת אֱלֹהֵינוּ
2	Absence of the first person in God's speech, impersonal descript. of God's activities (K 125)	-	Personalized accounts of speech and action of God (K 169-170; M 1326)	✓ לָמָּה־לִּי, אֵינֶנִּי שֹׁמֵעַ and others
3	Avoidance and suppression of anthropomorphisms for God (K 128-137)	-	Bodily parts of God, his human-like actions, states, and emotions (K 170-171)	✓ נַפְשִׁי, עֵינַי,פָּנַי, נִלְאֵיתִי and others

4	Avoidance of mentioning the relationship of posses. between God and the Tabernacle (K 130)	-	Establishing the relation of possession between God and the Tabernacle (K 70, 108)	√ traces in חֲצֵרִי and לִרְאוֹת פָּנַי
5	Avoidance of direct connection between YHWH and food (K 30)	-	No hesitancy to connect YHWH with food and eating (K 30)	√ שָׂבַעְתִּי
6	Cultic system lacks motives and justifications (K 106-107, 141)	-	Contain moralizing passages and ideological justificat. (K 107; M 38)	√ vv. 13c, 15c, and 16-17
7	All commandments relate exclusively to the ritual-cultic sphere (K 138-139, 173, 225-230 versus M 21-26, 42, 2440-2446)	-	Combination of the cultic laws with the observance of moral behaviour and justice (K 175-180, 193, 225-230; M 1400-1404)	√expressed negatively in vv. 13c and 15c, positively in vv. 16-17
8	If used, chiastic structure is always simple and straightforward (M 39)	-	Complex chiastic symmetry, e.g., binary opposition (M 39-42, 1319-1323)	√ vv. 11 and 16-17
9	שַׁבָּת not designated as מוֹעֵד in original P (M 19-21)	-	שַׁבָּת designated as מוֹעֵד (M 19-21, 27, 1955-57)	√ v. 13bα parallel to 14aα
10	Characteristic cultic terminology, rigid distinction (M 35-42; K 106-110)	√ vv. 11-15	Cultic termin. of P plus new terms, flex. use (M 35-42, 1325-32; K 106-10, 178-9)	√ vv. 11-15, בקשׁ ,תּוֹעֵבָה, עָתוּד
11	Holiness limited, static, and not explicitly connected with ethics (M 48-49, 1397-1400; K 197)	-	Holiness extended, dynamic, with ethical dimension (M 48-49, 1397-1400; K 180f, 198)	√purificat. connected with ethics in vv. 16-17

Some of the points in the chart require a more detailed discussion:

Ad 3, 4, and 5: Knohl regards these characteristics as a part of P's agenda to prevent religious syncretism. More specifically, the avoidance of anthropomorphisms prevents anthropomorphic imagery of God, the avoidance of mentioning the relationship between God and the Tabernacle averts the anthropomorphic association of God's residence, and the avoidance of direct connection between YHWH and food suppresses the idea that sacrifices are God's food. In his discussion of P's anti-anthropomorphism Knohl concludes: 'It seems that the opposition to the anthropomorphic coloring of the acts of atonement, as described in non-Priestly sources, is at the heart of PT's [Priestly Torah] system.'[1]

Ad 9: Milgrom observes that H, contrary to P, labeled שַׁבָּת as מוֹעֵד (see Lev 23:2-3). He places this innovation of H in the time of exile when, due to the detachment from the Temple, the other מוֹעֲדִים were inoperative.[2] Milgrom also points out that what impelled H with regard to שַׁבָּת did not apply to חֹדֶשׁ, judged from its absence in Lev. 23 when compared to the P list in Num. 28. It is important to add that these observations are valid only if Knohl/Milgrom's theory of H editorial work on P is accepted also in Num 28-29, namely that the superscript and the subscript of these two chapters are H's addition. If granted, Isa 1:13-14 would also qualify as one of such instances, for שַׁבָּת in 13b is replaced by מוֹעֵד in 14a, whereas חֹדֶשׁ is just repeated and therefore not מוֹעֵד.[3] An attractive way to explain this seemingly clumsy repetition of חֹדֶשׁ would be to assign v. 14a to what Milgrom designates as an H redactor (HR) from the time of exile.[4] As Milgrom observes, such redundancy is a characteristic technique in H: 'The remarkable thing about the structure [of H] is that it accounts for every single word. The alleged redundancies, which have been the despair of critics (see the commentaries), make perfect sense once it is realized that they fulfil an aesthetic purpose.'[5] It is possible that sometimes they fulfil a theological purpose as well.

Ad 10: Milgrom and Knohl demonstrated how H is purposefully built on P in order to indicate not only the differences but also the

---

1   Knohl, *Sanctuary*, 136.

2   See Milgrom, *Leviticus 1-16*, 27.

3   Milgrom quotes this passage as an evidence for the opposite, viz. שַׁבָּת is not מוֹעֵד. He, however, does not consider the relation of these two verses within the structure – see 4.5.2.4.

4   See also David Noel Freedman, *The Unity of the Hebrew Bible* (Ann Arbor: University of Michigan Press, 1991) 6-12.

5   Milgrom, *Leviticus 1-16*, 42.

continuity of this new priestly school with its heritage.[6] It is therefore
understandable that P and H share a lot of terminology, such as the
cultic terms that also occur in Isa 1:11-15. Some terms used in
connection with the cult by H, however, are absent from P,[7] תּוֹעֵבָה
being one of them.[8] Beside the supposed correlation of the date, the
setting of this term in Isa 1:13 is also similar – connected to cult, in what
resembles the form of Priestly Torah.[9] However, the occurrence of
תּוֹעֵבָה in this verse can also be explained by the influence of the
Wisdom literature on Isaiah, where this word is frequently found (e.g.
twenty-one times in Proverbs). Moreover, Prov 28:9 uses תּוֹעֵבָה along
with תְּפִלָּה and תּוֹרָה (identical words as in Isa 1:13, 14, and 10) to
describe what seems to be the same idea as in Isa 1:10-17: 'When one
will not listen to the law, even one's prayers are an abomination.'
Nevertheless, since the dating as well as the direction of possible
influence of Proverbs on Isaiah is questionable, and since the two
arguments are, in the light of our discussion, not mutually exclusive, it
is of some value to mention even this "weakest link".

Listing בקֹשׁ and עַתּוּד as the other two examples is justified only if
we accept Knohl's rather extensive definition of the H corpus.[10] Even if
granted, since בקֹשׁ in H does not occur in a context similar to Isa 1:12, it
is an argument from silence. The context of עַתּוּד in Num 7 is similar to
Isa 1:13, but, even though some editorial work of H can possibly be
traced in this chapter,[11] there seems to be no good reason why עַתּוּד
should be a part of H's editorial agenda.

Ad 11: Milgrom and Knohl agree that while P's doctrine of holiness
is static and limited to the sanctuary, priests and Nazirites, H's concept
of holiness is dynamic and extended to the land and to all who reside
in it (all Israel and even the resident alien). The dynamic nature of
holiness in H is due to its ethical dimension. H talks about a process of
sanctification, using the term מְקַדֵּשׁ,[12] applicable to both the laity and
the priesthood. Conversely, since impurity and holiness are antonyms,

6   See, e.g., Knohl, *Sanctuary*, 168, Milgrom, *Leviticus 17-22*, 1352-1355.
7   For their (incomplete) list and discussion, see Knohl, *Sanctuary*, 106-110, Milgrom, *Leviticus 1-16*, 35-42.
8   As observed by Milgrom, *Leviticus 17-22*, 1569. Wildberger also puts this word in cultic category, based on its occurrence in a declaratory formula in Deuteronomy, Leviticus, and Ezekiel, see Wildberger, *Jesaja*, 36.
9   See the discussion on the form of this passage in 4.3.
10   For the Knohl's list of the H corpus passages see Knohl, *Sanctuary*, 104-106.
11   For example vv. 22-29a, as argued in Milgrom, *Leviticus 17-22*, 1339.
12   This participial construction occurs only in H and in the book of Ezekiel. Exod 31:13 is regarded by both Milgrom and Knohl as H.

pollution in H also has a non-ritualistic dimension.[13] As shown in 2.5, Isaiah seems to share H's concept of holiness, so in 1:10-17 he challenges all the people (v. 10) to participate in the process of sanctification (vv. 16-17, starting with רַחֲצוּ הִזַּכּוּ). These commands of purification are not followed by guidelines for bringing a sacrifice,[14] but by a call to change the people's lifestyle (חִדְלוּ הָרֵעַ לִמְדוּ הֵיטֵב) and ethical behaviour (v. 17). As argued throughout Chapter 4, Isaiah's appeal does not speak against sacrifices. Moreover, it seems to support the idea presented in H, namely that the holiness of the people is also reliant upon their ethical behaviour. Miller, when discussing H's view of holiness, also makes this connection with the prophets:

> To the extent that the community was to be holy because the Lord was holy (Lev. 19:2), no area of life and no time or space was relegated to the common or profane, at least implicitly. Such an understanding seems to lie behind the prophetic emphasis on holiness as a requirement of the people that should be reflected as much in social life as in cultic ritual.[15]

If Knohl/Milgrom's dating of P and H is correct, the text of Isa 1:10-17 could epitomize a prophetic initiative to bring about the shift of emphasis from P's focus on rituals to H's focus on the ethical dimension of cult.[16] Obviously, the above observations do not amount to a proof, and their force can only be applied cumulatively, along with a detail analysis of the theological and ideological grounds of Isa 1:10-17 based on the exegesis of this text (see Chapter 4). Nevertheless, the results of the above test support the thesis that Isaiah 1:10-17 reflects the characteristic features of what according to Knohl and Milgrom was its contemporary theological development, viz. the shift from P to H.

---

13 See Milgrom, *Leviticus 1-16*, 46-49.

14 As it is characteristic in P, where 'the sacrificial system is intimately connected with the impurity system,' Milgrom, *Leviticus 1-16*, 49.

15 Miller, *Religion*, 144.

16 Miller arrives at the similar conclusion: 'Isaiah preached in a context where only one of these spheres [viz. cult and ethical] was perceived to be a matter of holiness – whether ideologically or only in practice – and his preaching was a corrective away from the emphasis reflected in the Priestly literature and toward the Holiness Code's insistence on the moral sphere as the locus of holy living,' Miller, *Religion*, 158.

Appendix 2: Isa 58-59 and Non-Isaianic OT Texts

As a result of recent Isaianic scholarship, links between a TI passage and texts in the other parts of the book of Isaiah are almost expected. In the case of ch. 58, Schottroff maintains that the most important influence comes from DI: 'Vor allem aber sind es Worte, Wendungen und Bilder, die ... in Kapitel 40-55 des Jesajabuches gebraucht, die von dem in Jes. 58 redenden Propheten aufgegriffen und variiert werden.'[1] He illustrates this by comparing 58:8b with 52:12 (see 6.5.7), and concludes that the author of 58:1-12 is 'ein Prophet, der tief in den Traditionen der ihm voraufgehenden Prophetie verwurzelt ist und an ihnen seine Anschauungen, seine Ausdrucksweise und vor allem auch seine Hoffnungen gebildet hat.'[2] Similarly, Koenen believes that the reason why the author of Isa 58-59 alludes in v. 1 to Isa 40:6 and 9, 54:2, (and to Hos 1:8 and Mic 3:8) is 'mit den Zitaten von v1 will der Verfasser zeigen, in welche Tradition er die Verkündigung von Jes 58,3-59,15a einreiht.'[3] The interconnectedness of Isa 58 and the rest of the book is discussed throughout the present thesis (esp. 6.8). This appendix compares Isa 58-59 with some of those OT texts that are outside of the book of Isaiah and juxtapose (at least partially) the themes addressed by this passage, namely cult, ethics, and eschatology. The purpose is to point out the similar treatment of these themes in the selected passages.

1. Isa 58-59 and Zech 7-8

Isa 58 and Zech 7 display a number of similarities. Blenkinsopp even inclines to believe that Zech 7:4-14 'served as a model for both Isa 58:3b-4 and 58:5-9a.'[4] Duhm compares the question in Isa 58:3a to the one about fasting in Zech 7:3b in relation to the people's eschatological expectations, and generalizes them as follows: 'Warum kommt die

---

1   Willy Schottroff, "'Unrechtmäßige Fesseln Auftun, Jochstricke Lösen' Jesaja 58,1-12, Ein Textbeispiel zum Tema 'Bibel und Ökonomie'," *BI* 5 (1997) 263-278: 266.

2   Schottroff, "Jesaja 58,1-12," 266.

3   Koenen, *Ethik und Eschatologie*, 95.

4   Blenkinsopp, *Isaiah 56-66*, 178.

eschatologische Wendung noch immer nicht und müssen wir noch immer fasten?'⁵ However, even though fasting comes to the fore in both of the questions, they are essentially different: while Isa 58:3a asks why God does not respond to fasting, Zech 7:3b asks whether fasting is relevant under the new circumstances. The similarities between the two passages come mainly with the answers of the prophets, who use these questions for the same purpose – to point out the importance of the ethical dimension of cult in the light of the upcoming eschatological era. Both prophets diagnosed a similar problem behind the different questions: as in Isa 58:3b, Zechariah's main objection to peoples fasting was that they observed it (and other religious festivals) for selfish reasons (Zech 7:5-6).⁶ Also the solution is similar: just as in Zech 7:9-10, the goal in Isa 58 is to turn people's focus from themselves (vv. 3b-5) to their neighbor (vv. 6-7, 9a-10a) and start to behave ethically.

Zechariah believes that the same problem as well as the same solution with regard to the cultic activities was addressed by pre-exilic prophets (7:7). Even though his exhortation to social justice is most reminiscent of Jer 7:5-6,⁷ Isa 1:10-17 can be included as well. The cult in Zech 7 is represented by fasting, in Isa 1 by sacrifices, religious gatherings and prayer, and in Jer 7 by sacrifices and the temple. All three agree that people's reliance on any form of cult without ethics, especially without social justice, resulted or will result in the destruction of the temple and Jerusalem and in exile. Delivered during the time of the temple rebuilding, Zechariah's lesson had a special vigor: just as Jeremiah used the destruction of the former sanctuary in Shiloh to obliterate the false sense of security and trust in Solomon's temple, Zechariah used the destruction of Solomon's temple as a warning not to repeat the mistakes of the past. That, according to him, was the main reason for the commemoration of the national disasters; if people focus on practising ethics, the purpose of fasting is accomplished.

Zech 8 contains all the characteristic concepts of prophetic eschatology: restoration of Zion and Jerusalem (v. 3), return of the

---

5   Bernhard Duhm, *Das Buch Jesaia*, 4-th ed. (Göttinger Handkommentar zum Alten Testament. 3. Abt., Prophetischen Bücher; Bd. 1; Göttingen: Vandenhoeck & Ruprecht, 1922) 436.

6   Park concludes that 'der Grund der Fastenkritik in Jes 58 liegt auch darin, daß das Fasten gerade nicht für Jhwh, sondern vielmehr für das Volk selbst betrieben wird,' Park, *Gerechtigkeit Israels*, 243.

7   Zech 7:10a is almost identical with Jer 7:6a (same terms, reversed order):

Zech 7:10a   וְאַלְמָנָה וְיָתוֹם גֵּר וְעָנִי אַל־תַּעֲשֹׁקוּ

Jer 7:6a   גֵּר יָתוֹם וְאַלְמָנָה לֹא תַעֲשֹׁקוּ

people (v. 7), repopulation of Jerusalem (vv. 4-5, 8), repossession of the land and its products (v. 12), good and long living (vv. 4-5, 19), nations seeking YHWH in Jerusalem (vv. 20-23), reversal of fasting into celebration (v. 19) and of a curse into a blessing (v. 13), and, above all, re-establishment of YHWH's presence in the midst of his people (v. 3) so they will be his people and he will be their God בֶּאֱמֶת וּבִצְדָקָה (v. 8). There is one additional concept: Israel's ethical behaviour is not a precondition but a result of this glorious age. Park, after demonstrating the close connection between Zech 7, 8, and 1, makes this point clear:

> In diesem Zusammenhang geht es um sociale Gerechtigkeit aber nicht als menschliche Verpflichtung für das kommende Heil Gottes, also nicht als Voraussetzung, sondern in der nahenden Heilszeit als eine dafür passende gesellschaftliche Ordnung. Nach dem Bericht von Sach 1,12-17 und 8,1-15 obliegen Gericht und Heil für Jerusalem/Zion ganz allein Jhwh. Der Mensch ist nur zur Gerechtigkeit verpflichtet besonders beim Gerichtsprozeß (8,16-17, vgl. 7,9; Jes 59,3f). [...] Das Heil Gottes hängt vom menschlichen Verhalten nicht ab. [...] Das Heilshandeln/die Heilsansage Gottes ist begründet einzig in seinem Willen mit großen Eifer (קִנְאָה) (8,2f. vgl. V.14b).[8]

As Lau observes, this eschatological picture seems to contradict Isa 58: 'Während in Sach 8 eine bedingungslose Heilsansage folgt, wird in Jes 58 das eschatologische Heil mit dem eschatologischen Tun verknüpft.'[9] However, as already noted above, Isa 58-59 does not urge people to act justly so that the eschatological age may come, but, because it is coming, that they may take part in it. Just as when comparing this passage with Isa 61 (see 6.8.3), the difference between Isa 58-59 and Zech 7-8 is not of eschatological outlook, but of focus.

2. Isa 58 and Ezek 18 and 20

The sabbath concept plays an important part in exilic Ezek 20.[10] It is a covenantal sign between YHWH and his people (vv. 12 and 20), and its desecration (חלל I) alongside the disobedience of YHWH's decrees and the rejection of his laws caused, according to Ezek 20, two great

---

8   Park, *Gerechtigkeit Israels*, 245-246.
9   Lau, *Schriftgelehrte Prophetie*, 245.
10 Since Ezek 20 consistently uses the plural form שַׁבְּתוֹתַי (vv. 12, 13, 16, 20, 21, 24), Block is very likely correct that 'included would also be the special holy days on which all work ceased, as well as the sabbatical years and the year of Jubilee' Daniel Isaac Block, *The Book of Ezekiel, Chapters 1-24* (NICOT; Grand Rapids, MI; Cambridge: W.B. Eerdmans, 1997) 632.

tragedies in Israel's *Heilsgeschichte* – desert wandering and Babylonian exile (vv. 13 and 21f respectively).[11] Vv. 27f give the impression that this desecration and rebellion consisted purely of people's cultic misconduct – idolatry as commonly understood.[12] However, keeping (שָׁמַר), following (הָלַךְ), and executing (עָשָׂה) YHWH's statutes (חֻקּוֹת) and ordinances (מִשְׁפָּטִים), or rejection (מָאַס) of them in vv. 11, 13, 16, 19, 21, and 24 certainly point to the Holiness code (Lev 18:4, 5, 26; 19:37; 20:22; 25:18; 26:15, 43) where the predominant context is ethical behaviour.[13] The same expressions are characteristic also of Ezek 18 (vv. 9, 17, 19, and 21), summarizing some cultic but mostly ethical issues, again reminiscent of H:

> If he does not eat upon the mountains or lift up his eyes to the idols of the house of Israel, does not defile his neighbor's wife or approach a woman during her menstrual period, does not oppress anyone, but restores to the debtor his pledge, commits no robbery, gives his bread to the hungry and covers the naked with a garment, does not take advance or accrued interest, withholds his hand from iniquity, executes true justice between contending parties, ... (vv. 6-8, similarly in vv. 10-13 and 14-17).

The above things are summarized by another characteristic word-pair of Ezek 18 – מִשְׁפָּט וּצְדָקָה (vv. 5 and 27, in vv. 19 and 21 combined with חֻקּוֹת). Weinfeld persuasively demonstrated that this expression functions as a hendiadys for the concept of social justice in the OT.[14] As Gammie concludes, in 18:5-18 'Ezekiel also sets forth the outlines for a moral theology that may justifiably be called a theology of the ethical requirements of holiness.'[15]

---

11 The idea of profaning (חלל) sabbaths occurs besides Ezekiel only in Exod 31:14, Neh 13:17-18, and Isa 56:2 and 6. Nehemiah also refers to it as the reason behind the exile and as the lesson that by now should have been learned by 'the nobles of Judah'.

12 For an attempt to define idolatry also as a distortion of social justice, see Hoppe, "Isaiah 58."

13 Notice the similarity between Ezek 20:11 and Lev 18:5, especially the identical last colon:

Ezek 20:11 וָאֶתֵּן לָהֶם אֶת־חֻקּוֹתַי וְאֶת־מִשְׁפָּטַי הוֹדַעְתִּי אוֹתָם אֲשֶׁר יַעֲשֶׂה אוֹתָם הָאָדָם וָחַי בָּהֶם

Lev 18:5a וּשְׁמַרְתֶּם אֶת־חֻקֹּתַי וְאֶת־מִשְׁפָּטַי אֲשֶׁר יַעֲשֶׂה אֹתָם הָאָדָם וָחַי בָּהֶם

Zimmerli believes that this 'reference to the character of the commandments which make life possible ... must certainly derive from the laws of admission to the sanctuary' Walther Zimmerli, *Ezekiel: A Commentary on the Book of the Prophet Ezekiel* (Hermeneia; Philadelphia: Fortress Press, 1979) 410. Besides purity, a great portion of these laws concerns ethical behaviour (compare Ps 15).

14 Moshe Weinfeld, "Justice and Righteousness - The Expression and its Meaning," in *Justice and Righteousness: Biblical Themes and their Influence*, ed. Yair Hoffman and Henning Reventlow (JSOTSup 137; Sheffield: JSOT Press, 1992).

15 Gammie, *Holiness*, 50. One of his supportive arguments is the number of similarities of this text with the stipulations in Ps 15 for those who would ascend on the *holy* hill.

The legitimacy of interpreting the observance or refusal of the statutes and ordinances in Ezek 20 with the help of Ezek 18 is supported by the similarity of both the form and the content of their main arguments. As Zimmerli correctly observes, 'the parallel casuistic outlining of three phases of history with the exodus events [20:5-9, 10-17, and 18-26] … recalls the casuistic series of three generations in Ezek 18.'[16] Even more striking, however, is the similarity between the contents of the two structures: the topic is the just and merciful reaction of YHWH to the unjust and perverted action of Israel, as explicitly stated in 18:25f.   Both illustrations are built on the comparisons between former and present generations. The point in ch. 18 is that YHWH holds every generation responsible for its own action. Thus a son of a wicked father would save his life when he turns away from his father's or from his own wickedness (vv. 14-17 and 21-22). However, as the illustration in ch. 20 shows, this case remained hypothetical throughout Israel's history; in spite of YHWH's instructions and salvific acts, the people 'like father like son' kept rejecting YHWH's statutes and ordinances and were profaning his sabbaths from the very beginning of Israel in Egypt till Ezekiel's days (vv. 18-21, 30, 36).[17] The links between Ezek 18 and 20 allow for a synchronic reading of these two chapters. Such reading justifies Gosse's proposal that the association between 'to keep justice' and 'to keep the Sabbath' in Ezek 18 and 20 is reminiscent of Isa 56:1-8.[18] In addition to Gosse's mostly rhetorical arguments, this parallel is reinforced by the similarity of both texts' climaxes: in Ezek 20:40-41 as well as in Isa 56:7-8, YHWH accepts (רָצוֹן, רצה and even דרש) the people as well as their sacrifices, offerings and gifts on his holy mountain (הַר־קָדְשִׁי).

---

16   Zimmerli, *Ezekiel*, 406. Because such casuistic structure can be found several times in Ezekiel (3:17ff, 14:12ff, 33:1ff), Zimmerli justifiably calls this 'a distinctive feature of Ezekiel's composition.'

17   Fishbane believes that 'Ezekiel has used the pentateuchal topos of apostasy in the desert in order to *explain* Israel's exile in Babylon as a punishment deflected from the original perpetrators and transferred to a late generation' Fishbane, *Interpretation*, 366.   If correct, chs. 20 and 18 would be irreconcilable (as Fishbane himself recognizes), for the latter emphatically rebuts the concept of vicarious punishment. However, Ezekiel in ch. 20 makes clear that his generation suffers because it is guilty of the same sins as their ancestors (vv. 27f) and therefore bound to undergo the same judgement (vv. 36-38). The basis for Fisbane's argument, namely that Ezek 20:33 is an haggadic exegesis of Exod 32:30f, is doubtful. For an attempt to reconcile what Block believes to be the tension between Ezekiel's historical determinism as presented in ch. 20 and the individualistic ethics of ch. 18, see Block, *Ezekiel 1-24*, 630.

18   Bernard Gosse, "Sabbath, Identity and Universalism Go Together after the Return from Exile," *JSOT* 29 (2005) 359-370.

Analogically, Ezek 18 and 20 corresponds well with Isa 58. In both passages, the people desire to consult (דרש) YHWH (Ezek 20:1f and Isa 58:2), but he refuses to communicate (Ezek 20:3, 31 and Isa 58:3). Consequently, the people question YHWH's character (Ezek 18:2, 19, 25, 29 and Isa 58:3). YHWH (through Ezekiel and Isaiah) censures their theology by referring to the Holiness Code to remind them what it takes to approach him, the Holy One (Ezek 18:6-9, 10-13, 14-17; 20:7, 11-12, 18-20; Isa 58:6f and the related passages in Leviticus).[19] Cultic purification is not enough, and can even be counterproductive if not accompanied by social justice.[20] On the other hand, the combination of ethics and cult through keeping, following, and executing YHWH's statutes and ordinances guarantees the fulfillment of the people's eschatological dreams: they will live (Ezek 18:9, 17, 19, 22, 27, 28, 32; 20:11, 21; Isa 58:8) in abundance (Isa 58:11-12, 14) in the promised land (Ezek 20:6, 40, 42; Isa 58:12) and in relationship with their God (Ezek 20:40f; Isa 58:8, 9, 11, 14).[21]

3. Isa 58 and Amos 8:4-8

Amos 8:4-6 describes the misconduct of Israel's merchants: they rigorously observe new moon and sabbath festivals, but they deal dishonestly and mercilessly with their customers during the work days. As in Isa 58, the cultic and the ethical dimension of sabbath concept are present. Wolff notices the connection: 'The injunction against marketing appears to belong to the older regulations concerning sabbath rest; the context in Amos 8:4 and 6 suggests that the social concern of protecting slaves played a part in it.'[22] Based on the difference between v. 6 and what seems to be its template in Amos 2:6, Jeremias believes that '8:6 is no longer concerned with the problem of

---

19 Because of the similarity of the expressions about feeding the hungry clothing the naked, Lau rightly believes that 'der Verfasser von Jes 58* hier auf die Beschreibung des Gerechten in Ez 18 Bezug nimmt,' Lau, *Schriftgelehrte Prophetie*, 248. This parallel might account for additional בגד in Isa 58:7 of 1QIsaᵃ, as influenced by Ezek 18:7.

20 The similarity of the ethical language between Ezek 18:7 and Isa 58:6-7 is noteworthy.

21 Lau also notices the connection: 'In Ez 18,9 wird dem gerecht Handelnden zugesagt, "das er das Leben behalten sole" (חָיֹה יִחְיֶה), d. h. er soll dem Gericht Jahwes entkommen ... In Jes 58,8ff. hingegen wird dem gerecht Handelnden eschatologyschen Heilsfülle zugesagt, der Gerichtsaspekt klingt nur noch aus weiter Ferne an und ist vergangenen Zeiten zugeordnet (vgl. V. 12),' Lau, *Schriftgelehrte Prophetie*, 249.

22 Hans Walter Wolff et al., *Joel and Amos: A Commentary on the Books of the Prophets Joel and Amos* (Hermeneia; Philadelphia: Fortress Press, 1977) 327.

debt slavery in the technical sense; this is rather a case of figurative meaning.'[23] In any case, a certain degree of generalizing is required to fully appreciate the point of this passage. 'The normative presupposition of the indictment is not so much any single instance or list of commandments in Israel's legal tradition, as the total tendency and intention of the covenant law to protect and maintain the disadvantaged members of society.'[24] In the words of Lowery, the privileged wealthy completely misunderstood the significance of sabbath relief, for 'sabbath is a day of rest, but more fundamentally, it is a call to economic justice.'[25] The appeal for connecting the sabbath observance with ethical behaviour is reminiscent of and in accord with Isa 58.

4. Isa 58-59 and Joel 2

Facing the great and terrible יוֹם־יְהוָה (v. 11), Joel in ch. 2 urges the people to return to YHWH with all their heart, fasting, weeping, and mourning (v. 12). The criticism of cult is subtle, consisting of one sentence in v. 13a: 'Rend your hearts and not your clothing.' Hermisson rightly comments that 'die Absicht dieses Satzes ist ja gar nicht, den Hörern diesen Ritus zu verwehren. Seine Betonung liegt vielmehr ganz in der ersten Hälfte … und er bedarf der Antithese, um das Bildwort zu vervollständigen.' In this verse, Joel simply teaches the people that 'die Bußriten sind nur dann sinnvoll, wenn der Mensch mit seinem "Herzen" beteiligt ist.' Hermisson concludes: 'Das kultische Handeln wird eben mit diesem Wort nicht ausgeschlossen, sondern im Blick auf den Handelnden selbst interpretiert. Dabei ist der Blick auf das Herz des Menschen umfassender als ein bloßer Vergleich zwischen kultischem und sittlichem Handeln.'[26]

Even though Joel calls people to a true repentance, the question מִי יוֹדֵעַ יָשׁוּב וְנִחָם in v. 14 indicates that its positive outcome is not automatically guaranteed. Joel seems to be aware that, in spite of people's genuine repentance, YHWH's response may be וְלֹא נִחַמְתִּי וְלֹא אָשׁוּב (Jer 4:28). In Jer 14:1-15:9, the people not only fasted (v. 12) and mourned (אבל, v. 2), brought sacrifices and offerings (v. 12), and

23 Jörg Jeremias, *The Book of Amos: A Commentary* (OTL; Louisville: Westminster John Knox Press, 1998) 148.
24 James Luther Mays, *Amos: A Commentary* (OTL; London: SCM, 1969) 143.
25 Lowery, *Sabbath*, 115.
26 Hermisson, *Sprache und Ritus*, 81.

displayed their humiliation in all kinds of cultic ways (vv. 2-4), but also recognized their sins with true remorse (vv. 7, 20) and plead for God's forgiveness (vv. 8-9, 21-22). Yet the response is that YHWH will punish their sins (vv. 10, 16) even if Moses and Samuel interceded for them (15:1), for he was 'weary of relenting' (נִלְאֵיתִי הִנָּחֵם, 15:6). Positive outcome of a true repentance is described in 2 Kgs 22. In this text, king Josiah humbled himself, wept, rent his clothes (vv. 11 and 19), and, just as Joel enjoins the people, his heart 'was penitent' (רכך, v. 19, NRSV). Because of this, YHWH spared him the upcoming disaster (vv. 19-20).

As Joel 2:18f describes, it is not people's repentance, but YHWH's jealousy for his land and his compassion (חמל) upon his people that inaugurates the eschatological era: the land greatly prospers (vv. 21-22), the people live in abundance and security (vv. 19-20, 23-26), and the relationship between them and their God is restored (vv. 26-27) because YHWH is בְּקֶרֶב יִשְׂרָאֵל (v. 27). Again, the themes of cult, ethics, and eschatology are connected in the same way in Joel 2 as in Isa 58-59.

5. Isa 58-59 and Jonah 3

In Jonah 3, the repentance in Nineveh includes cult (represented by fasting, sackcloth, and prayer) as well as ethics: וַיָּשֻׁבוּ אִישׁ מִדַּרְכּוֹ הָרָעָה וּמִן־הֶחָמָס אֲשֶׁר בְּכַפֵּיהֶם (v. 8b),[27] and is followed by the same expression of hope in the effectiveness of this repentance as in Joel: מִי־יוֹדֵעַ יָשׁוּב וְנִחַם הָאֱלֹהִים (v. 9a).[28] The probability that this text is relatively young should not lead to the conclusion that the idea of practising ethics along with cult is a late development. Hermisson comments on this text that 'wenn hier menschliches Tun im sozialen und im kultischen Bereich zueinandergehören, so entspricht das dem alten Verständnis.'[29]

There are several linguistic links and points of contrast between this text and Isa 58-59, especially with regard to fasting:

— While self-afflicting, sackcloth, and ashes are present in both, only the Jonah text mentions turning away from evil ways and violence. Isa 58, on the other hand, mentions oppression, quarrelling, fighting, and striking with a wicked fist during the fast (vv. 3b-4).

---

27 The first part of this call to repentance (וַיָּשֻׁבוּ אִישׁ מִדַּרְכּוֹ הָרָעָה) is characteristic of Jeremiah, see Jer 18:11; 25:5; 26:3; 35:15; 36:3 and 7.

28 A very similar question with the same expectation is found also 2 Sam 12:22.

29 Hermisson, *Sprache und Ritus*, 84.

— In Isa 59:6, it is said about the people that there is חָמָס בְּכַפֵּיהֶם;
   in Jonah 3:8, people are to turn away מִן־הֶחָמָס אֲשֶׁר בְּכַפֵּיהֶם.

— In Isa 59:6, people try to cover themselves (hithpael of כסה)
   with 'spider's web', the works of their iniquities; in Jonah 3:8,
   people cover themselves (hithpael of כסה) with sackcloth – the
   sign of repentance.

— The results are different as well: in Isa 58:3, according to the
   people, God does not see (ראה) their fasting, nor notices (ידע)
   their self-affliction; in Jonah 3:10, God saw (ראה) what the
   people of Nineveh did, and renounced (niphal of נחם) the
   punishment.

According to Jonah 3:10, God's "change of mind" was prompted by the
people's change of behaviour: כִּי־שָׁבוּ מִדַּרְכָּם הָרָעָה.[30] However, as
Jonah recognizes, it ultimately was YHWH's attributes listed in 4:2 that
averted the disaster; true fast is meaningful only because YHWH is
אֵל־חַנּוּן וְרַחוּם אֶרֶךְ אַפַּיִם וְרַב־חֶסֶד וְנִחָם עַל־הָרָעָה. The understanding of
the role of cult and ethics with regard to salvation in Jonah 3 is in
accord with Isa 58-59.

6. Isa 58-59 and Mal 2:17-3:18

The themes of Isa 58-59 reappear in what is likely the later text of Mal
2:17-3:18.   This text conveys the same message: while the people
complain about YHWH's passivity on their behalf (2:17; 3:14-15),
Malachi ensures them of YHWH's forthcoming epiphany that is
independent of their behaviour (3:1). This 'day when YHWH acts'
(3:17a) will not only mark the beginning of the eschatological era for
those who return to YHWH and serve him (3:7, 17b), but also מִשְׁפָּט
against those who do not fear him and practice injustice (3:5, 7-9), and
the division between צַדִּיק and רָשָׁע becomes final (3:18). Then the
offerings of Judah and Jerusalem will be pleasing to YHWH, because the
people will practice the cult בִּצְדָקָה (3:3-4). Consequently, the material
blessings will realize as well (3:10-12).

---

30   Jonah 3:10, just like 3:8, refers to Jer 18:7f (notice esp. the same vocabulary in v. 8).

7. Isa 58-59 and Ps 73

Since the date of Ps 73 is far from certain,[31] this section only observes some of the similarities between this text and Isa 58-59. First, there are several strong semantical and rhetorical links:

— The noun חַרְצֻב occurs only in Ps 73:4 and Isa 58:6.

— עֹשֶׁק as object of דבר occurs only in Ps 73:8 and Isa 59:13.

— If MT of Ps 73:28 is accepted,[32] the expression קִרְבַת אֱלֹהִים occurs only here and in Isa 58:2.

— The picture of covering oneself with violence as with a garment is found only in Ps 73:6, Isa 59:6 and possibly Mal 2:16.

— The complaint of the psalmist about unnoticed or unrewarded godliness in Ps 73:13 is reminiscent of Isa 58:3a. Also, both Ps 73:11 and Isa 58:3a are concerned with theodicy and dispute God's omniscience.

— Just as Isa 59:20 redefined the term Zion, Ps 73:1 redefines the term Israel – instead of the physical offspring of Jacob, it now consists of those who are pure in heart (לְבָרֵי לֵבָב).[33]

Second, there is an important thematic link, namely that קִרְבַת אֱלֹהִים does not allow for co-existence of רֶשַׁע and שָׁלוֹם. This message is the agenda of both Ps 37 and Isa 58-59. Even though the combination of רֶשַׁע and שָׁלוֹם is not found in Isa 58-59 explicitly, it is certainly implicit in 59:8, where 'they' refers to the wicked ones as described in vv. 3-8. Furthermore, the last line before Isa 58-59 – אֵין שָׁלוֹם ... לָרְשָׁעִים (Isa 57:21) – could well serve as a sub-title to this unit. Besides Ps 73:3 and Isa 57:21, the combination of רֶשַׁע and שָׁלוֹם occurs only once more in BH, namely in Isa 48:22. Interestingly, it is in all three instances followed by a complaint about the uselessness of what seems to be a

---

31 Day dates Ps 73 into the post-exilic period. His argument is mainly based on the assumption that 73:24 speaks about the afterlife, and that this belief 'was slow in emerging in ancient Israel and developed in the post-exilic period, so any references to this in the Psalms must therefore date from that time,' John Day, "How many Pre-exilic Psalms are there?," in *In Search of Pre-Exilic Israel: Proceedings of the Oxford Old Testament Seminar*, ed. John Day (JSOTSup 406; London: T & T Clark International, 2004) 242.

32 BHS suggests various emendations in the apparatus. However, the textual evidence supports MT.

33 The suggestion of BHS (preferred by NRSV) to emend לְיִשְׂרָאֵל for לְיָשָׁר אֵל is not based on any textual evidence. For a positive description of בַּר־לֵבָב, see Ps 24.

proper behaviour[34] and some form of the repudiation of this complaint. Large portion of Ps 73 and Isa 58-59 describes the acts of רְשָׁעִים, and both texts (esp. Ps 73:18-20 and Isa 59:8) make clear that שָׁלוֹם רְשָׁעִים in Ps 73:3 is in fact an oxymoron. The message of both Ps 73 and Isa 58-59 is clear: if people desire קִרְבַת אֱלֹהִים and שָׁלוֹם, they must do away with רֶשַׁע.

Concluding Remark

A good number of other OT texts could be added here. Of course, a proper analysis of this sort would require a separate monograph. The brief comments and observations above hopefully show that such a quest would be both meaningful and worthwhile.

---

34 Ps 73:13 – 'All in vain I have kept my heart clean and washed my hands in innocence.'
Isa 49:4 – 'I have labored in vain, I have spent my strength for nothing and vanity.'
Isa 58:3 – 'Why do we fast, but you do not see? Why humble ourselves, but you do not notice?'

Bibliography

Ackroyd, Peter R. Exile and Restoration: A Study of Hebrew Thought of the Sixth Century B.C., OTL; London: SCM, 1968.

Aejmelaeus, Anneli. "Function and Interpretation of כי in Biblical Hebrew." JBL 105 (1986): 193-209.

Albertz, Rainer. A History of Israelite Religion in the Old Testament Period. Translated by John Stephen Bowden; London: SCM Press Ltd, 1994.

Anderson, Gary A. Sacrifices and Offerings in Ancient Israel: Studies in their Social and Political Importance, Harvard Semitic Monographs 41; Atlanta, GA: Scholars Press, 1987.

Andreasen, Niels-Erik. "Recent Studies of the Old Testament Sabbath." ZAW 86 (1974): 453-469.

Baltzer, Klaus. Deutero-Isaiah: A Commentary on Isaiah 40-55, Hermeneia; Minneapolis, MN: Fortress Press, 2001.

Barr, James. The Semantics of Biblical Language; London: Oxford University Press, 1961.

—, Comparative Philology and the Text of the Old Testament; Oxford: Clarendon Press, 1968.

Barré, Michael L. "Fasting in Isaiah 58:1-12: A Reexamination." BTB 15, no. 3 (1985): 94-97.

Barthélemy, Dominique. Critique textuelle de l'Ancien Testament, 2: Isaïe, Jérémie, Lamentations, Rapport final du Comité pour l'analyse textuelle de l'Ancien Testament hébreu, Orbis biblicus et orientalis 50/2; Fribourg, Göttingen: Editions universitaires, Vandenhoeck & Ruprecht, 1986.

Barton, John. Oracles of God: Perceptions of Ancient Prophecy in Israel after the Exile; London: Darton Longman and Todd, 1986.

—, "Wellhausen's Prolegomena to the History of Israel: Influences and Effects." In Text & Experience: Towards a Cultural Exegesis of the Bible, edited by Daniel L. Smith-Christopher, 316-329. Sheffield: Sheffield Academic Press, 1995.

—, Understanding Old Testament Ethics: Approaches and Explorations; Louisville, KY; London: Westminster John Knox Press, 2003.

—, "The Prophets and the Cult." In Temple and Worship in Biblical Israel, edited by John Day, 111-122. London: T & T Clark International, 2005.

Barton, John, and Julia Bowden. The Original Story: God, Israel and the World; London: Darton Longman and Todd, 2004.

Begrich, Joachim. "Das priestliche Heilsorakel." ZAW 52 (1934): 81-92.

—, "Die priesterliche Tora." In Werden und Wesen des Alten Testaments : Vorträge gehalten auf der Internationalen Tagung Alttestamentlicher

Forscher zu Göttingen vom 4.-10. September 1935, edited by Johannes Hempel, Friedrich Stummer and Paul Volz, 63-88. Berlin: A. Töpelmann, 1936.

—, Studien zu Deuterojesaja, BWANT 4e; Stuttgart: Kohlhammer, 1938.

Ben Zvi, Ehud. "The Prophetic Book: A Key Form of Prophetic Literature." In The Changing Face of Form Criticism for the Twenty-First Century, edited by Marvin A. Sweeney and Ehud Ben Zvi, 276-297. Grand Rapids, MI; Cambridge, U.K.: W.B. Eerdmans, 2003.

Blank, S. H. "The Curse, Blasphemy, the Spell and the Oath." HUCA 23 (1950/51): 73-95.

Blenkinsopp, Joseph. "A Jewish Sect of the Persian Period." CBQ 52 (1990): 5-20.

—, "An Assessment of the Alleged Pre-Exilic Date of the Priestly Material in the Pentateuch." ZAW 108 (1996): 495-518.

—, Isaiah 1-39: A New Translation with Introduction and Commentary, AB 19; New York: Doubleday, 2000.

—, "Cityscape to Landscape: The 'Back to Nature' Theme in Isaiah 1-35." In 'Every City Shall be Forsaken': Urbanism and Prophecy in Ancient Israel and the Near East, edited by Robert D. Haak and Lester L. Grabbe, 35-44. Sheffield: Sheffield Academic Press, 2001.

—, Isaiah 40-55: A New Translation with Introduction and Commentary, AB 19A; New York; London: Doubleday, 2002.

—, Isaiah 56-66: A New Translation with Introduction and Commentary, AB 19B; New York; London: Doubleday, 2003.

Block, Daniel Isaac. The Book of Ezekiel, Chapters 1-24, NICOT; Grand Rapids, MI; Cambridge: W.B. Eerdmans, 1997.

Booij, T. "Negation in Isaiah 43:22-24." ZAW 92 (1982): 390-400.

Bourdillon, M. F. C., and Meyer Fortes, eds. Sacrifice. London: Academic Press for the Royal Anthropological Institute of Great Britain and Ireland, 1980.

Braaten, Laurie J. "Earth Community in Hosea 2." In The Earth Story in the Psalms and the Prophets, edited by Norman C. Habel, 185-203. Sheffield: Sheffield Academic, 2001.

Brongers, H. A. "Einige Bemerkungen zu Jes 58:13-14." ZAW 87 (1975): 212-216.

—, "Fasting in Israel in Biblical and Post-Biblical Times." In Instruction and Interpretation: Studies in Hebrew Language, Palestinian Archeology and Biblical Exegesis, 1-21. Leiden: E. J. Brill, 1977.

Brueggemann, Walter. Isaiah. 2 vols, Westminster Bible Companion; Louisville, KY: Westminster John Knox Press, 1998.

Budde, Karl. Die Bücher Samuel. Vol. 8, Kurzer Hand-Commentar zum Alten Testament; Tübingen: J.C.B. Mohr, 1902.

Calvin, John. Commentary on the Book of the Prophet Isaiah. Translated by William Pringle. Vol. 3, Calvin's Commentaries; Grand Rapids, MI: Baker Book House, 1998.

Campbell, Antony F. 1 Samuel, FOTL 7; Grand Rapids, MI; Cambridge: W.B. Eerdmans, 2003.

—, "Form Criticism's Future." In The Changing Face of Form Criticism for the Twenty-First Century, edited by Marvin A. Sweeney and Ehud Ben Zvi, 15-31. Grand Rapids, MI; Cambridge, U.K.: W.B. Eerdmans, 2003.

Carroll, Robert P. "Prophecy and Society." In The World of Ancient Israel: Sociological, Anthropological and Political Perspectives, edited by R. E. Clements, 203-225. Cambridge: Cambridge University Press, 1989.

—, "The Myth of the Empty Land." Semeia 59 (1992): 79-93.

Childs, Brevard S. Memory and Tradition in Israel, SBT 37; London: SCM Press, 1962.

—, Isaiah, OTL; Louisville, KY; London: Westminster John Knox Press, 2001.

Clements, R. E. God and Temple; Oxford: Blackwell, 1965.

Clines, David J. A. Job 1-20, WBC 17; Dallas, TX: Word Books, 1989.

Cogan, Mordechai. Imperialism and Religion: Assyria, Judah, and Israel in the Eighth and Seventh Centuries B.C.E, SBLMS 19; Missoula, MT: Scholars Press, 1974.

Cogan, Mordechai, and Hayim Tadmor. II Kings: A New Translation with Introduction and Commentary, AB 11; New York: Doubleday, 1988.

Collins, Terence. Line-forms in Hebrew Poetry: A Grammatical Approach to the Stylistic Study of the Hebrew Prophets, Studia Pohl. Series Maior 7; Rome: Biblical Institute Press, 1978.

Cothey, Antony. "Ethics and Holiness in the Theology of Leviticus." JSOT 30 (2005): 131-151.

Courtman, Nigel B. "Sacrifice in the Psalms." In Sacrifice in the Bible, edited by Roger T. Beckwith and Martin J. Selman, 41-58. Carlisle, UK; Grand Rapids, MI: Paternoster Press, Baker Book House, 1995.

Crenshaw, James L. "WᵉDŌRĒK 'AL-BĀMŌTÊ 'ĀRETṢ." CBQ 34 (1972): 39-53.

Dahood, Mitchell. "The Chiastic Breakup in Isaiah 58,7." Biblica 57 (1976): 105.

Davies, Andrew. Double Standards in Isaiah: Re-Evaluating Prophetic Ethics and Divine Justice, Biblical Interpretation Series 46; Leiden: Brill, 2000.

Davies, W. D. The Gospel and the Land: Early Christianity and Jewish Territorial Doctrine; Berkeley; London: University of California Press, 1974.

Day, John. "How many Pre-exilic Psalms are there?" In In Search of Pre-Exilic Israel: Proceedings of the Oxford Old Testament Seminar, edited by John Day, 225-250. London: T & T Clark International, 2004.

De Vaux, Roland. Ancient Israel: Its Life and Institutions. Translated by John McHugh; London: Darton Longman and Todd, 1961.

Delitzsch, Franz. Biblical Commentary on the Prophecies of Isaiah, Clark's Foreign Theol. Libr. 4th ser. vol. 14, 15; Edinb., 1867.

Dim, Emmanuel Uchenna. The Eschatological Implications of Isa. 65 and 66 as the Conclusion of the Book of Isaiah, Bible in History 3; Bern, Oxford: Peter Lang, 2005.

Douglas, Mary. Natural Symbols: Explorations in Cosmology; London: Barrie & Rockliff Cresset Press, 1970.

—, "Holy Joy: Rereading Leviticus: The Anthropologist and the Believer." Conservative Judaism 46, no. 3 (1994): 3-14.

—, Leviticus as Literature; Oxford: Oxford University Press, 2000.

—, Purity and Danger: An Analysis of Concept of Pollution and Taboo, Routledge classics; London: Routledge, 2002 (1966).

Driver, G. R. "Is. xl-lxvi, Linguistic and Textual Problems." JTS 36 (1935): 396-406.

Driver, S. R. A Treatise on the Use of the Tenses in Hebrew and Some Other
    Syntactical Questions. 2d ed, Clarendon Press Series; Oxford: Clarendon
    Press, 1881.
—, An Introduction to the Literature of the Old Testament, International
    Theological Library; Edinburgh: Clark, 1891.
—, A Critical and Exegetical Commentary on Deuteronomy. 3rd ed, ICC;
    Edinburgh: T. & T. Clark, 1902.
Duhm, Bernhard. Das Buch Jesaia. 4-th ed, Göttinger Handkommentar zum
    Alten Testament. 3. Abt., Prophetischen Bücher; Bd. 1; Göttingen:
    Vandenhoeck & Ruprecht, 1922.

Edelman, Diana Vikander. The Origins of the Second Temple: Persian Imperial
    Policy and the Rebuilding of Jerusalem, Bible World; London: Equinox
    Press, 2005.
Elliger, Karl. Die Einheit des Tritojesaia, Jesaia 56-66, BWANT 45; Stuttgart: W.
    Kohlhammer, 1928.
—, Deuterojesaja, BKAT 11; Neukirchen-Vluyn: Neukirchener-Verlag, 1978.
Emmerson, Grace I. Isaiah 56-66, OTG; Sheffield: JSOT Press, 1992.

Falk, Ze'ev W. "Law and Ethics in the Hebrew Bible." In Justice and
    Righteousness: Biblical Themes and Their Influence, edited by Yair
    Hoffman and Henning Reventlow, 82-90. Sheffield: JSOT Press, 1992.
Fishbane, Michael A. Biblical Interpretation in Ancient Israel; Oxford, New
    York: Clarendon Press; Oxford University Press, 1985.
Follingstad, Carl Martin. Deictic Viewpoint in Biblical Hebrew Text: A
    Syntagmatic and Paradigmatic Analysis of the Particle yk (kī); Dallas, TX:
    SIL International, 2001.
Freedman, David Noel. The Unity of the Hebrew Bible; Ann Arbor: University
    of Michigan Press, 1991.
Fullerton, K. "The Rhythmical Analysis of Is. 1:10-20." JBL 38 (1919): 53-63.

Gammie, John G. Holiness in Israel, Overtures to Biblical Theology;
    Minneapolis: Fortress Press, 1989.
Geller, Stephen A. "A Poetic Analysis of Isaiah 40:1-2." The Harvard
    Theological Review 77, no. 3/4 (1984): 413-420.
Goldingay, John. "Isaiah 43, 22-28." ZAW 110 (1998): 173-191.
—, Old Testament Theology, vol. 1: Israel's Gospel; Downers Grove, IL:
    InterVarsity Press, 2003.
—, The Message of Isaiah 40-55: A Literary-Theological Commentary; London:
    T & T Clark, 2005.
Goldingay, John, and David F. Payne. A Critical and Exegetical Commentary
    on Isaiah 40-55. 2 vols, ICC; London; New York: T&T Clark, 2006.
Gordon, R. P. 1 & 2 Samuel: A Commentary; Exeter: Paternoster, 1986.
Gosse, Bernard. "Sabbath, Identity and Universalism Go Together after the
    Return from Exile." JSOT 29 (2005): 359-370.
Grabbe, Lester L. Ezra-Nehemiah, Old Testament Readings; London:
    Routledge, 1998.

Gray, George Buchanan. A Critical and Exegetical Commentary on the Book of Isaiah I-XXVII, ICC; Edinburgh: T&T Clark, 1912.

Green, Barbara. How Are the Mighty Fallen?: A Dialogical Study of King Saul in 1 Samuel, JSOTSup 365; London: Sheffield Academic Press, 2003.

Green, William B. "The Ethics of the Old Testament." Princeton Theological Review 27 (1929): 153-193.

Greenstein, Edward L. "One More Step on the Staircase." UF 9 (1977): 77-86.

Gunkel, Hermann, and Joachim Begrich. Introduction to Psalms: The Genres of the Religious Lyric of Israel, Mercer Library of Biblical Studies; Macon, GA: Mercer University Press, 1998.

Habel, Norman C. The Land is Mine: Six Biblical Land Ideologies, Overtures to Biblical Theology; Minneapolis: Fortress Press, 1995.

Hänel, Johannes. Die Religion der Heiligkeit; Gütersloh: C. Bertelsmann, 1931.

Hanson, Paul D. The Dawn of Apocalyptic; Philadelphia: Fortress Press, 1975.

—, Isaiah 40-66, Interpretation; Louisville, KY: John Knox Press, 1995.

Hayes, John Haralson, and Stuart A. Irvine. Isaiah, the Eighth Century Prophet: His Times & His Preaching; Nashville: Abingdon Press, 1987.

Heaton, Eric William. The Hebrew Kingdoms; Oxford: Oxford University Press, 1968.

Hendel, Ronald S. "Prophets, Priests, and the Efficacy of Ritual." In Pomegranates and Golden Bells: Studies in Biblical, Jewish and Near Eastern Ritual, Law, and Literature in Honor of Jacob Milgrom, edited by David P. Wright, David Noel Freedman and Avi Hurvitz, 185-198. Winona Lake, IN: Eisenbrauns, 1995.

Herbert, Arthur Sumner. The Book of the Prophet Isaiah, Chapters 40-66, Cambridge Bible Commentary; Cambridge: Cambridge University Press, 1975.

Hermisson, Hans-Jürgen. Sprache und Ritus im altisraelitischen Kult; zur "Spiritualisierung" der Kultbegriffe im Alten Testament, WMANT 19; Neukirchen-Vluyn: Neukirchener Verlag des Erziehungsvereins, 1965.

Heschel, Abraham Joshua. The Prophets; New York: Harper & Row, 1962.

Hibbard, James Todd. Intertextuality in Isaiah 24-27: The Reuse and Evocation of Earlier Texts and Traditions, FAT 16; Tübingen: Mohr Siebeck, 2006.

Holladay, John S. "The Kingdoms of Israel and Judah: Political and Economic Centralization in the Iron IIA-B (ca. 1000-750 BCE)." In The Archaeology of Society in the Holy Land, edited by Thomas Evan Levy, 368-398. London: Leicester University Press, 1995.

Holladay, William Lee. Jeremiah 1: A Commentary on the Book of the Prophet Jeremiah, Chapters 1-25, Hermeneia; Philadelphia: Fortress Press, 1986.

Hoppe, Leslie J. "Isaiah 58:1-12, Fasting and Idolatry." BTB 13, no. 2 (1983): 44-47.

Houston, Walter J. "Toward an Integrated Reading of the Deitary Laws of Leviticus." In The Book of Leviticus: Composition and Reception, edited by Rolf Rendtorff, Robert A. Kugler and Sarah Smith Bartel, 142-161. Leiden: Brill, 2003.

—, "Was there a Social Crisis in the Eighth Century?" In In Search of Pre-Exilic
    Israel: Proceedings of the Oxford Old Testament Seminar, edited by John
    Day, 130-149. London: T & T Clark International, 2004.
Hubert, Henri, and Marcel Mauss. Sacrifice: Its Nature and Function; Chicago:
    University of Chicago Press, 1964.
Hurowitz, V. A. "Temporary Temples." In Kinattutu ša darâti: Raphael
    Kutscher memorial volume, edited by Anson F. Rainey, 37-50. Tel Aviv:
    Emery and Claire Yass Publications in Archaeology, 1993.
—, "A Forgotten Meaning of Nepeš in Isaiah LVIII 10." VT 47 (1997): 43-52.

Jacob, Edmond. Theology of the Old Testament; London: Hodder & Stoughton,
    1958.
Janzen, David. The Social Meanings of Sacrifice in the Hebrew Bible: A Study of
    Four Writings, BZAW 344; Berlin: Walter de Gruyter, 2004.
Jensen, Joseph. The Use of tôrâ by Isaiah: His Debate with the Wisdom
    Tradition, CBQ monograph series 3; Washington, D.C.: Catholic Biblical
    Association of America, 1973.
—, Isaiah 1-39, Old Testament Message, vol. 8; Wilmington: Michael Glazier,
    1984.
—, Ethical Dimensions of the Prophets; Collegeville, MN: Liturgical Press,
    2006.
Jeremias, Jörg. The Book of Amos: A Commentary, OTL; Louisville:
    Westminster John Knox Press, 1998.
Johnson, Dan G. From Chaos to Restoration: An Integrative Reading of Isaiah
    24-27, JSOTSup 61; Sheffield: JSOT Press, 1988.
Jones, Gwilym H. 1 and 2 Kings, NCBC; Grand Rapids, MI, London: Eerdmans,
    Marshall Morgan & Scott, 1984.
Jones, O. R. The Concept of Holiness; London: Allen and Unwin, 1961.

Kaiser, Otto. Isaiah 1-12: A Commentary. Translated by John Bowden. 2nd ed,
    OTL; London: SCM, 1983.
Kelle, Brad E. Hosea 2: Metaphor and Rhetoric in Historical Perspective,
    Academia Biblica 20; Leiden, Boston: Brill, 2005.
Khan, Geoffrey. Studies in Semitic Syntax, London Oriental Series 38; Oxford:
    Oxford University Press, 1988.
Klawans, Jonathan. Impurity and Sin in Ancient Judaism; New York, Oxford:
    Oxford University Press, 2000.
—, Purity, Sacrifice, and the Temple: Symbolism and Supersessionism in the
    Study of Ancient Judaism; Oxford; New York: Oxford University Press,
    2006.
Klein, Ralph W. 1 Samuel, WBC 10; Waco, TX: Word Books, 1983.
Klostermann, August. Der Pentateuch, Beiträge zu seinem Verständnis und
    seiner Enstehungsgeschichte; Leipzig, 1893.
Knight, Douglas A. Rediscovering the Traditions of Israel: The Development of
    the Traditio-Historical Research of the Old Testament, with Special
    Consideration of Scandinavian Contributions. Rev. ed, SBL Dissertation
    Series 9; Missoula, MT: Society of Biblical Literature: distributed by
    Scholars Press, 1975.

Knohl, Israel. The Sanctuary of Silence: The Priestly Torah and the Holiness School; Philadelphia: Fortress Press, 1995.

Koenen, Klaus. "Textkritische Anmerkungen zu schwierigen Stellen im Tritojesajabuch." Biblica 69 (1988): 564-573.

—, Ethik und Eschatologie im Tritojesajabuch: Eine Literarkritische und Redaktionsgeschichtliche Studie, WMANT 62; Neukirchen-Vluyn: Neukirchener Verlag, 1990.

Koole, Jan Leunis. Isaiah III/1. Translated by Anthony P. Runia, HCOT; Kampen: Kok Pharos, 1997.

—, Isaiah III/3. Translated by Anthony P. Runia. Vol. 3, HCOT; Leuven: Peeters, 2001.

Korpel, Marjo C. A., and Johannes C. de Moor. The Structure of Classical Hebrew Poetry: Isaiah 40-55, OTS 41; Leiden: Brill, 1998.

Kosmala, Hans. "Form and Structure of Isaiah 58." Annual of the Swedish Theological Institute 5 (1967): 69-81.

Kraus, Hans-Joachim. Worship in Israel: A Cultic History of the Old Testament. Translated by Geoffrey Buswell; Oxford: Blackwell, 1966.

Kugel, James L. The Idea of Biblical Poetry: Parallelism and Its History; New Haven; London: Yale University Press, 1981.

Kutsch, Ernst. "Die Wurzel rc[im Hebräischen." VT 2 (1952): 57-69.

Lau, Wolfgang. Schriftgelehrte Prophetie in Jes 56-66: Eine Untersuchung zu den literarischen Bezügen in den letzten elf Kapiteln des Jesajabuches, BZAW 225; Berlin: Walter de Gruyter, 1994.

Leene, Hendrik. "Isaiah 27:7-9 as a Bridge between Vineyard and City." In Studies in Isaiah 24-27, edited by Hendrik Jan Bosman and Harm van Grol, 199-225. Leiden: Brill, 2000.

Lescow, Theodor. Das Stufenschema: Untersuchungen zur Struktur alttestamentlicher Texte, BZAW 211; Berlin: De Gruyter, 1992.

Levenson, Jon Douglas. Creation and the Persistence of Evil: The Jewish Drama of Divine Omnipotence; San Francisco, London: Harper & Row, 1988.

—, The Hebrew Bible, the Old Testament, and Historical Criticism: Jews and Christians in Biblical Studies; Louisville, KY: Westminster/John Knox Press, 1993.

Levine, Baruch A. Leviticus; Philadelphia: Jewish Publication Society, 1989.

Liss, Hanna. "The Imaginary Sanctuary: The Priestly Code as an Example of Fictional Literature in the Hebrew Bible." In Judah and the Judeans in the Persian Period, edited by Oded Lipschitz and Manfred Oeming, 663-689. Winona Lake, IN: Eisenbrauns, 2006.

Long, V. Philips. The Reign and Rejection of King Saul: A Case for Literary and Theological Coherence; Atlanta, GA: Scholars Press, 1989.

Lowery, Richard H. The Reforming Kings: Cult and Society in First Temple Judah, JSOTSup120; Sheffield: JSOT Press, 1991.

—, Sabbath and Jubilee, Understanding Biblical Themes; St. Louis, Mo.: Chalice Press, 2000.

Lundbom, Jack R. Jeremiah 1-20: A New Translation with Introduction and Commentary, AB 21A; New York, London: Doubleday, 1999.

Martens, E. A. God's design: A Focus on Old Testament Theology. 2nd ed;
Grand Rapids, MI, Leicester: Baker Book House, Apollos, 1994.

Marx, Alfred. "The Theology of the Sacrifice according to Leviticus 1-7." In The
Book of Leviticus: Composition and Reception, edited by Rolf Rendtorff,
Robert A. Kugler and Sarah Smith Bartel, 103-120. Leiden: Brill, 2003.

Mays, James Luther. Amos: A Commentary, OTL; London: SCM, 1969.

McCarter, P. Kyle. I Samuel: A New Translation; Garden City, N.Y.:
Doubleday, 1980.

McCarthy, Dennis J. "Notes on the Love of God in Deuteronomy and the
Father-Son Relationship between Yahweh and Israel." CBQ 27 (1965): 144-
147.

McKay, Heather A. Sabbath and Synagogue: The Question of Sabbath in
Ancient Judaism, Religions in the Graeco-Roman World, v. 122; Leiden:
Brill, 1994.

McKay, J. W. Religion in Judah under the Assyrians 732-609 BC, SBT 26;
London: SCM, 1973.

Meier, Samuel A. Speaking of Speaking: Marking Direct Discourse in the
Hebrew Bible, VTSup 46; Leiden: Brill, 1992.

Melugin, Roy F. "Deutero-Isaiah and Form Criticism." VT 21 (1971): 326-337.

—, The Formation of Isaiah 40-55, BZAW 141; Berlin: De Gruyter, 1976.

—, "Figurative Speech and the Reading of Isaiah 1 as Scripture." In New
Visions of Isaiah, edited by Roy F. Melugin and Marvin A. Sweeney, 282-
305. Sheffield: Sheffield Academic Press, 1996.

Merendino, Rosario Pius. Der Erste und der Letzte: Eine Untersuchung von Jes
40-48, VTSup 31; Leiden: Brill, 1981.

Mettinger, Tryggve N. D. The Dethronement of Sabaoth: Studies in the Shem
and Kabod Theologies, Old Testament Series 18; Lund: CWK Gleerup,
1982.

Milgrom, Jacob. "Concerning Jeremiah's Repudiation of Sacrifice." ZAW 89
(1977): 273-275.

—, Studies in Cultic Theology and Terminology. Edited by Jacob Neusner,
SJLA 36; Leiden: Brill, 1983.

—, Leviticus 1-16: A New Translation with Introduction and Commentary, AB
3; New York, London: Doubleday, 1991.

—, "Does H advocate the Centralization of Worship?" JSOT 88 (2000): 59-76.

—, Leviticus 17-22: A New Translation with Introduction and Commentary,
AB 3A; New York: Doubleday, 2000.

—, Leviticus 23-27: A New Translation with Introduction and Commentary,
AB 3B; New York, London: Doubleday, 2001.

Miller, Patrick D. The Religion of Ancient Israel; Louisville, KY: Westminster
John Knox Press, 2000.

Mowinckel, Sigmund. He That Cometh; Oxford: Blackwell, 1956.

Muilenburg, James. "The Book of Isaiah, Chapters 40-66." In The Interpreter's
Bible, 381-773. New York: Abingdon Press, 1956.

Nicholson, Ernest W. The Pentateuch in the Twentieth Century: The Legacy of
Julius Wellhausen; Oxford: Clarendon, 1998.

Niditch, Susan. "The Composition of Isaiah 1." Biblica 61 (1980): 509-529.

Nielsen, Kjeld. Incense in Ancient Israel, VTSup 38; Leiden: Brill, 1986.

Nissinen, Martti. "City as Lofty as Heaven: Arbela and other Cities in Neo-Assyrian Prophecy." In 'Every City Shall be Forsaken': Urbanism and Prophecy in Ancient Israel and the Near East, edited by Robert D. Haak and Lester L. Grabbe, 172-209. Sheffield: Sheffield Academic Press, 2001.

North, Christopher R. The Second Isaiah: Introduction, Translation and Commentary to Chapters XL-LV; Oxford: Clarendon Press, 1964.

Noth, Martin. Exodus: A Commentary. Translated by John Stephen Bowden, OTL; London: SCM, 1962.

Orlinsky, Harry Meyer, and Norman Henry Snaith. Studies on the Second Part of the Book of Isaiah, VTSup 14; Leiden: Brill, 1967.

Oswalt, John. The Book of Isaiah, Chapters 1-39, NICOT; Grand Rapids, MI: Eerdmans, 1986.

—, The Book of Isaiah, Chapters 40-66, NICOT; Grand Rapids, MI; Cambridge: Eerdmans, 1998.

Otto, Rudolf. The Idea of the Holy: An Inquiry into the Non-rational Factor in the Idea of the Divine and Its Relation to the Rational. Translated by John W. Harvey. 2nd ed; London: Oxford University Press, 1950.

Park, Kyung-Chul. Die Gerechtigkeit Israels und das Heil der Völker: Kultus, Tempel, Eschatologie und Gerechtigkeit in der Endgestalt des Jesajabuches (Jes 56, 1-8; 58, 1-14; 65, 17-66, 24), Beiträge zur Erforschung des Alten Testaments und des Anitken Judentums, Band 52; Frankfurt: Peter Lang, 2003.

Pauritsch, Karl. Die neue Gemeinde: Gott sammelt Ausgestossene und Arme (Jesaia 56-66). Die Botschaft des Tritojesaia-Buches literar-, form-, gattungskritisch und redaktionsgeschichtlich untersucht, Analecta biblica 47; Rome: Biblical Institute Press, 1971.

Payne, D. F. "Characteristic Word-Play in "Second Isaiah": A Reappraisal." JSS 12 (1967): 207-229.

Podella, Thomas. Şôm-Fasten: Kollektive Trauer um den verborgenen Gott im Alten Testament, Alter Orient und Altes Testament; Bd. 224; Neukirchen-Vluyn: Verlag Butzon & Bercker Kevelaer, 1989.

Polan, Gregory J. In the Ways of Justice toward Salvation: A Rhetorical Analysis of Isaiah 56-59, American University Studies. Series VII, Theology and Religion; vol. 13; Frankfurt am Main: Peter Lang, 1986.

Polaski, Donald C. Authorizing an End: The Isaiah Apocalypse and Intertextuality. Vol. 50, Biblical Interpretation Series; Leiden: Brill, 2001.

Premnath, D. N. "Latifundialization and Isaiah 5.8-10." JSOT 40 (1988): 49-60.

Quinn-Miscall, Peter D. 1 Samuel: A Literary Reading, Indiana Studies in Biblical Literature; Bloomington, IN: Indiana University Press, 1986.

Rad, Gerhard von. Old Testament Theology. Translated by David Muir Gibson Stalker; New York: Harper & Row, 1965.

—, "The Promised Land and Yahweh's Land in the Hexateuch." In The Problem of the Hexateuch and Other Essays, 79-93. Edinburgh; London: Oliver & Boyd, 1966.

Raphael, Melissa. Rudolf Otto and the Concept of Holiness; Oxford: Clarendon Press, 1997.

Ringgren, Helmer. The Prophetical Conception of Holiness, Uppsala Universitets Årsskrift 12; Uppsala: A.-B. Lindquist, 1948.

Roberts, J. J. M. "Isaiah in Old Testament Theology." Intrepretation 36 (1982): 130-143.

Rodd, Cyril S. Glimpses of a Strange Land: Studies in Old Testament Ethics; Edinburgh: T.&T. Clark, 2001.

Rofé, A. "Isaiah 66.1-4: Judean Sects in the Persian Period as Viewed by Trito-Isaiah." In Biblical and Related Studies Presented to Samuel Iwry, edited by Ann Kort and Scott Morschauser, 205-217. Winona Lake, IN: Eisenbrauns, 1985.

Rosenbaum, Michael. Word-Order Variation in Isaiah 40-55: A Functional Perspective, SSN 35; Assen: Van Gorcum, 1997.

Rowley, Harold Henry. The Faith of Israel: Aspects of Old Testament Thought; London: SCM, 1956.

—, Worship in Ancient Israel: Its Forms and Meaning; London: S.P.C.K., 1967.

Schmid, Hans Heinrich. Wesen und Geschichte der Weisheit: Eine Untersuchung zur Altorientalischen und Israelitischen Weisheitsliteratur, BZAW 101; Berlin: A. Töpelmann, 1966.

Schoors, A. I am God your Saviour: A Form-Critical Study of the Main Genres in Is. xl-lv, VTSup 24; Leiden: Brill, 1973.

—, "The Particle yk." In Remembering All the Way: A Collection of Old Testament Studies Published on the Occasion of the Fortieth Anniversary of the Oudtestamentisch Werkgezelschap in Nederland, edited by A. S. van der Woude, 240-276. Leiden: Brill, 1981.

Schottroff, Willy. "'Unrechtmäßige Fesseln Auftun, Jochstricke Lösen' Jesaja 58,1-12, Ein Textbeispiel zum Tema 'Bibel und Ökonomie'." BI 5 (1997): 263-278.

Schramm, Brooks. The Opponents of Third Isaiah: Reconstructing the Cultic History of the Restoration, JSOTSup 193; Sheffield: Sheffield Academic Press, 1995.

Schultz, Richard L. The Search for Quotation: Verbal Parallels in the Prophets, JSOTSup 180; Sheffield: Sheffield Academic Press, 1999.

Schüngel-Straumann, Helen. Gottesbild und Kultkritik vorexilischer Propheten, Stuttgarter Bibelstudien 60; Stuttgart: KBW Verlag, 1972.

Schwartz, Baruch J. "The Bearing of Sin in the Priestly Literature." In Pomegranates and Golden Bells: Studies in Biblical, Jewish and Near Eastern Ritual, Law, and Literature in Honor of Jacob Milgrom, edited by David P. Wright, David Noel Freedman and Avi Hurvitz, 3-21. Winona Lake, IN: Eisenbrauns, 1995.

Seebass, Horst. "Tradition und Interpretation bei Jehu ben Chanani und Ahia von Silo." VT 25 (1975): 175-190.

Seeligmann, Isac Leo. The Septuagint Version of Isaiah: A Discussion of Its Problems; Leiden: E. J. Brill, 1948.

Sekine, Seizo. Die Tritojesajanische Sammlung (Jes 56-66) Redaktionsgeschichtlich Untersucht, BZAW 175; Berlin: De Gruyter, 1989.

Sherwood, Yvonne. "'Darke Texts Needs Notes': On Prophetic Prophecy, John Donne and the Baroque." JSOT 27 (2002): 47-74.

Simpson, J. A., and E. S. C. Weiner. The Oxford English Dictionary. 2nd ed; Oxford: Clarendon Press, 1989.

Smart, James D. History and Theology in Second Isaiah: A Commentary on Isaiah 35, 40-66; London: Epworth, 1967.

Smith, George Adam. The Book of Isaiah. new and rev. ed; London: Hodder & Stoughton, 1927.

Smith, P. A. Rhetoric and Redaction in Trito-Isaiah: The Structure, Growth, and Authorship of Isaiah 56-66, VTSup 62; Leiden: Brill, 1995.

Snaith, Norman Henry. "Sacrifices in the Old Testament." VT 7 (1957): 308-317.

Sommer, Benjamin D. A Prophet Reads Scripture: Allusion in Isaiah 40-66, Contraversions: Jews and Other Differences; Stanford, CA: Stanford University Press, 1998.

Spieckermann, Hermann. Juda unter Assur in der Sargonidenzeit, Forschungen zur Religion und Literatur des Alten und Neuen Testaments 129; Göttingen: Vandenhoeck & Ruprecht, 1982.

Spreafico, Ambrogio. "Nahum i 10 and Isaiah i 12-13: Double-Duty Modifier." VT 48 (1998): 104-110.

Steck, Odil Hannes. Bereitete Heimkehr: Jesaja 35 als redaktionelle Brücke zwischen dem Ersten und dem Zweiten Jesaja, Stuttgarter Bibelstudien 121; Stuttgart: Verlag Katholisches Bibelwerk, 1985.

Stenning, John Frederick. The Targum of Isaiah; Oxford: Clarendon Press, 1949.

Stern, Ephraim. "Religion in Palestine in the Assyrian and Persian Periods." In The Crisis of Israelite Religion: Transformation of Religious Tradition in Exilic and Post-Exilic Times, edited by Bob Becking and Marjo C. A. Korpel, 245-255. Leiden: Brill, 1999.

Sweeney, Marvin A. Isaiah 1-4 and the Post-Exilic Understanding of the Isaianic Tradition, BZAW 171; Berlin; New York: De Gruyter, 1988.

—, "Textual Citations in Isaiah 24-27: Toward an Understanding of the Redactional Function of Chapters 24-27 in the Book of Isaiah." JBL 107 (1988): 39-52.

—, Isaiah 1-39: With an Introduction to Prophetic Literature, FOTL 16; Grand Rapids, MI: Eerdmans, 1996.

—, Form and Intertextuality in Prophetic and Apocalyptic Literature, FAT 45; Tübingen: Mohr Siebeck, 2005.

Thompson, J. A. The Book of Jeremiah, NICOT; Grand Rapids: Eerdmans, 1980.

Torrey, Charles Cutler. The Second Isaiah: A New Interpretation; New York,: C. Scribner's Sons, 1928.

Tsevat, Matitiahu. "The Basic Meaning of the Biblical Sabbath." ZAW 84 (1972): 447-459.

Vargon, Shmuel. "The Historical Background and Significance of Isa 1, 10-17." In Studies in Historical Geography and Biblical Historiography: Presented to Zecharia Kallai, edited by Gershon Galil and Moshe Weinfeld. Leiden: Brill, 2000.

Vriezen, Theodore C. "Einige Notizen zur Übersetzung des Bindewortes kī." In Von Ugarit nach Qumran: Beiträge zur alttestamentlichen und altorientalischen Forschung, edited by Johannes Hempel and Leonhard Rost, 266-273. Berlin: A. Töpelmann, 1958.

—, "Essentials of the Theology of Isaiah." In Israel's Prophetic Heritage: Essays in Honor of James Muilenburg, edited by Bernhard W. Anderson and Walter J. Harrelson, 128-146. London: SCM, 1962.

Waldow, Hans Eberhard von. Der traditionsgeschichtliche Hintergrund der prophetischen Gerichtsreden, BZAW 85; Berlin: A. Töpelmann, 1963.

—, "Israel and Her Land: Some Theological Considerations." In A Light unto My Path: Old Testament Studies in Honor of Jacob M. Myers, edited by Carey A. Moore, 493-508. Philadelphia: Temple University Press, 1974.

Watson, Wilfred G. E. Classical Hebrew Poetry: A Guide to Its Techniques, JSOTSup 26; Sheffield: JSOT Press, 1984.

Watters, William R. Formula Criticism and the Poetry of the Old Testament, BZAW 138; Berlin: De Gruyter, 1976.

Watts, John D. W. Isaiah 34-66, WBC 25; Waco, TX: Word Books, 1987.

Weinfeld, Moshe. "Ancient Near Eastern Patterns in Prophetic Literature." VT 27 (1977): 178-195.

—, "Justice and Righteousness - The Expression and its Meaning." In Justice and Righteousness: Biblical Themes and their Influence, edited by Yair Hoffman and Henning Reventlow, 228-246. Sheffield: JSOT Press, 1992.

—, The Place of the Law in the Religion of Ancient Israel, VTSup 100; Leiden: Brill, 2004.

—, Normative and Sectarian Judaism in the Second Temple Period, Library of Second Temple Studies 54; London: T & T Clark, 2005.

Wellhausen, Julius. Prolegomena zur Geschichte Israels. 5 ed; Berlin: G. Reimer, 1899.

Wells, Roy D. "'Isaiah' as an Exponent of Torah: Isaiah 56:1-8." In New Visions of Isaiah, edited by Roy F. Melugin and Marvin A. Sweeney, 140-155: Sheffield Academic Press, 1996.

Westermann, Claus. Basic Forms of Prophetic Speech; London: Lutterworth Press, 1967.

—, Isaiah 40-66: A Commentary, OTL; Philadelphia, PA: The Westminster Press, 1969.

Whitehouse, Owen C. "Holiness: Semitic." In Encyclopædia of Religion and Ethics, edited by James Hastings, John A. Selbie and Louis H. Gray, 751-759. Edinburgh: T. & T. Clark, 1913.

Whybray, R. N. Isaiah 40-66, NCBC; London: Oliphants, 1975.

Wildberger, Hans. Jesaja, BKAT 10; Neukirchen-Vluyn: Neukirchener Verlag des Erziehungsvereins, 1965.

Williamson, H. G. M. 1 and 2 Chronicles, NCBC; Grand Rapids, London: Eerdmans, Marshall Morgan & Scott, 1982.

—, "The Concept of Israel in Transition." In The World of Ancient Israel:
     Sociological, Anthropological and Political Perspectives, edited by R. E.
     Clements, 141-161. Cambridge: Cambridge University Press, 1989.
—, "Isaiah 1.11 and the Septuagint of Isaiah." In Understanding Poets and
     Prophets: Essays in Honour of George Wishart Anderson, edited by A.
     Graeme Auld, 401-412. Sheffield: JSOT Press, 1993.
—, The Book Called Isaiah: Deutero-Isaiah's Role in Composition and
     Redaction; Oxford: Clarendon Press, 1994.
—, "Promises, Promises! Some Exegetical Reflections on Isaiah 58." Word and
     World 19 (1999): 153-160.
—, "Isaiah and the Holy One of Israel." In Biblical Hebrew, Biblical Texts:
     Essays in Memory of Michael P. Weitzman, edited by Ada Rapoport-Albert
     and Gillian Greenberg, 22-38. Sheffield: Sheffield Academic Press, 2001.
—, "Biblical Criticism and Hermeneutics in Isaiah 1:10-17." In
     Vergegenwärtigung des Alten Testaments: Beiträge zur Biblischen
     Hermeneutik; Festschrift für Rudolf Smend zum 70. Geburtstag, edited by
     Christoph Bultmann, Rudolf Smend, Walter Dietrich and Christoph Levin,
     82 - 96. Göttingen: Vandenhoeck & Ruprecht, 2002.
—, "Review: Paulson Pulikottil, Transmission of Biblical Texts in Qumran: The
     Case of the Large Isaiah Scroll 1QIsa[a]." JTS 54 (2003): 641-646.
—, A Critical and Exegetical Commentary on Isaiah 1-27. Vol. 1, ICC; London,
     New York: T & T Clark, 2006.
Wolff, Hans Walter, S. Dean McBride, Waldemar Janzen, and Charles Albert
     Muenchow. Joel and Amos: A Commentary on the Books of the Prophets
     Joel and Amos, Hermeneia; Philadelphia: Fortress Press, 1977.
Wright, David P. "Observations on the Ethical Foundations of the Biblical
     Dietary Laws: A Response to Jacob Milgrom." In Religion and Law:
     Biblical-Judaic and Islamic Perspectives, edited by Edwin Brown Firmage,
     Bernard G. Weiss and John W. Welch, 193-198. Winona Lake: Eisenbrauns,
     1990.

Young, Edward J. The Book of Isaiah: The English Text, with Introduction,
     Exposition, and Notes, NICOT; Grand Rapids, MI: Eerdmans, 1965.

Ziegler, Joseph. Untersuchungen zur Septuaginta des Buches Isaias,
     Alttestamentliche Abhandlungen, Bd. 12, Heft 3; Münster i. W.:
     Aschendorffschen Verlagsbuchhandlung, 1934.
Zimmerli, Walther. Ezekiel: A Commentary on the Book of the Prophet Ezekiel,
     Hermeneia; Philadelphia: Fortress Press, 1979.
—, "The 'Land' in the Pre-Exilic and early Post-Exilic Prophets." In
     Understanding the Word: Essays in Honor of Bernhard W. Anderson,
     edited by James T. Butler, Edgar W. Conrad and Ben C. Ollenburger, 247-
     262. Sheffield: JSOT Press, 1985.

Index of Authors